Roman Historiography

Blackwell Introductions to the Classical World

This series will provide concise introductions to classical culture in the broadest sense. Written by the most distinguished scholars in the field, these books survey key authors, periods and topics for students and scholars alike.

Published

Greek Tragedy
Nancy Sorkin Rabinowitz

Roman Satire
Daniel Hooley

Ancient History
Charles W. Hedrick, Jr.

Homer, second edition
Barry B. Powell

Classical Literature
Richard Rutherford

Ancient Rhetoric and Oratory
Thomas Habinek

Ancient Epic
Katherine Callen King

Catullus
Julia Haig Gaisser

Virgil
R. Alden Smith

Ovid
Katharina Volk

Roman Historiography
Andreas Mehl, translated by Hans-Friedrich Mueller

Roman Historiography

*An Introduction to its Basic
Aspects and Development*

Andreas Mehl, translated by
Hans-Friedrich Mueller

WILEY Blackwell

This paperback edition first published 2014
English translation © 2014 Hans-Friedrich Mueller
Originally published in German under the title Römische Geschichtsschreibung, by Andreas
Mehl: © 2001 W. Kohlhammer GmbH, Stuttgart.

Edition history: 2001 W. Kohlhammer GmbH, Stuttgart (1e in German, 2001); Blackwell
Publishers Ltd (1e in English, hardback, 2011)

Registered Office
John Wiley & Sons Ltd, The Atrium, Southern Gate, Chichester, West Sussex, PO19 8SQ,
UK

Editorial Offices
350 Main Street, Malden, MA 02148-5020, USA
9600 Garsington Road, Oxford, OX4 2DQ, UK
The Atrium, Southern Gate, Chichester, West Sussex, PO19 8SQ, UK

For details of our global editorial offices, for customer services, and for information about
how to apply for permission to reuse the copyright material in this book please see our
website at www.wiley.com/wiley-blackwell.

The right of Andreas Mehl and Hans-Friedrich Mueller to be identified as the author of this
work has been asserted in accordance with the UK Copyright, Designs and Patents Act 1988.

Library of Congress Cataloging-in-Publication Data

Mehl, Andreas.
 [Romische Geschichtsschreibung. English]
 Roman historiography : an introduction to its basic aspects and development / Andreas
Mehl ; translated by Hans-Friedrich Mueller.
  p. cm. – (Blackwell introductions to the classical world ; 11)
 "Originally published in German under the title Romische Geschichtsschreibung ... c2001,
W. Kohlhammer, Stuttgart"–T.p. verso.
  Includes bibliographical references and index.
 ISBN 978-1-4051-2183-5 (hardback) ISBN 978-1-118-78513-3 (paperback)
 1. Rome–Historiography. 2. Historiography–Rome–History. 3. Historians–Rome–
History. 4. Rome–History–Sources. 5. Literature and society–Rome–History. 6. Latin
literature–History and criticism. I. Title.
 DG205.M44 2011
 937.0072–dc22

                                                                    2010047219

A catalogue record for this book is available from the British Library.

Cover image: Roman forum. Photo © Eva Rapoport / Dreamstime.com
Cover design by Workhaus

Set in 10.5/13pt by Toppan Best-set Premedia Limited
Printed in Malaysia by Ho Printing (M) Sdn Bhd

1   2014

Table of Contents

Translator's Preface

Andreas Mehl's title, *Roman Historiography: An Introduction to its Basic Aspects and Development*, is deceptively modest. Rooting his erudite and readable discussion in the context of its Greek antecedents, Mehl traces ancient historical writing about Rome from its beginnings (clan history, *Annales*) to its ends in both West (Orosius) and East (Procopius). What is astonishing is not that Mehl manages to discuss by name almost every historical writer of even fragmentary significance (or less) or even that he looks at their works in terms of essential themes (e.g. genre, teleology, the idea of Rome, exemplary moral conduct; he summarizes all this in Chapter 8). Rather, two features stand out: scrupulous attention to political context and to religious developments. These twin lenses allow us to observe the evolution (and interpenetration) of classically religious and Christian historiography – with novel insights. One example: many scholars dismiss Zosimus (fifth/sixth century AD) as derivative. Mehl, on the other hand, discovers a brilliant counterpart to Polybius (second century BC). Why? Both authors offered original interpretations of Roman history on the basis of religion. Bibliography, a catalogue of authors and editions, and an index lend added utility. Mehl's book should constitute required reading for serious students of Roman history and ancient religion, Christian or classical.

Scholars of Roman historiography, on the other hand, at least in the English-speaking world, may feel some disorientation when first they take this volume in hand. Much will seem familiar. Our scholarship too deals with truth, fiction, exemplarity, genre, narrative, rhetorical tropes. But Mehl's approach is not as literary. Politics, law, religion, Roman institutions, are integrated into the very texture of his argument. Mehl rescues more historical truth from ancient historiography than we have grown accustomed to expect from the more recent historiographical emphasis in English-language scholarship on ancient rhetoric. This scholarship, although it is certainly a factor in Mehl's survey, does not stand at its center. Mehl engages rather the German-language scholarship of Albrecht Dihle and Dieter Timpe, to name just two examples, with an immediate intensity scholarship in English generally reserves for such luminaries as A. J. Woodman or T. P. Wiseman. And, for this reason too, Mehl in English should appeal. This translation provides a snapshot of continental scholarship's approach to Roman historiography in a language more readily accessible to English-speaking scholars and students alike than the book's original academic German (a language no longer as widely or easily understood among us – to our loss).

A word of confession is in order. On Andreas Mehl's behalf and with his encouragement, I first proposed this translation in 2002. Al Bertrand, then editor of a rapidly growing catalogue in Classics, readily agreed, and asked me to translate. Serving as translator was not my original plan, nor was it in my proposal, but I believed in the book's importance, and (perhaps too) quickly agreed. Personal vicissitudes (pedestrian though they were) intervened, and work did not proceed smoothly, but the patience of Wiley-Blackwell, and the equally patient, but insistent, prods of subsequent editors, Haze Humbert and Galen Smith, kept my work on its slow and increasingly steady track to completion. I owe all three editors an enormous debt of gratitude, and offer here my public and sincerest thanks. When I completed a draft in March 2010, things began to proceed rapidly. Despite a busy term at his university, speaking engagements, and numerous editorial deadlines for his current projects, Andreas Mehl read through the entire translation, and offered detailed corrections. I thank him for his patience, good humor, and cheerful diligence under pressure. An anonymous reviewer also read the entire draft, correcting matters of both substance and style. To him too I offer my many and grateful thanks. Only for errors and infelicities that remain do I insist on full credit.

Hans-Friedrich Mueller
September 9, 2010
Union College, Schenectady, New York

Introduction: The Importance of Ancient Historiography and the Purpose of this Book

Although the subject of this book, ancient historiography and its practitioners, is a traditional one in the study of ancient history and classical philology, it requires some justification, or at least an explanation. General knowledge of, and new insights into, Greek and Roman culture has increased greatly since the nineteenth century, thanks in large measure to archeological discoveries and excavations as well as to insights provided by material culture and representational art. In this same period, literary documents – inscriptions, papyri, and coins – have not only increased the knowledge of scholars tremendously, but have also drawn the favorable attention of the general public especially when, in their reconstructions of the past, scholars have been able to combine archeological sources with their interpretations. This development shows no signs of abating, and has in fact only increased since the nineteenth and twentieth centuries. This results not only from the attention and scrutiny elicited by various discoveries, i.e., the *objects* of historical investigation, but also to an even greater extent from a fundamental change in the perception of the public, that is, the *subject* who investigates. Outside the realm of professional scholarship (but also to some extent here too), people have turned their attention away from works of literature. These works, because artistically complex and intellectually dense, can be interpreted only with difficulty. As a result, many have turned to the (only apparently) simpler and more authentic world offered by visual representations as well as short and often formulaic administrative and technical texts, in the expectation that here, finally, we will easily discover the pure and simple truth about the ancient world.

Roman Historiography: An Introduction to its Basic Aspects and Development,
First Edition. Andreas Mehl.
© 2014 Hans-Friedrich Mueller. Published 2014 by Blackwell Publishing Ltd.

The increase in knowledge from archeological, inscriptional, and other documentary sources may seem to diminish the importance of the historiographical traditions and literary texts of the Greeks and Romans, but this is hardly the case: non-literary documents, physical objects, and artworks may indeed provide detailed information, but only in regard to specific points. Now, as ever, our knowledge concerning ancient political history as a chronological sequence of circumstances rests almost entirely on Greek and Roman literature, primarily historiographical. Only in the broader context provided by this extensive continuum have we been able to make the specific advances in the knowledge that we have derived from the alternative sources just enumerated, and we may in fact appreciate their full historical value only when we anchor them in the wider web of history. If we also attempt to understand the past as it was experienced by the Greeks and Romans themselves (that is, according to their own understanding and critical awareness of their past in relation to their present – in short, their worldview as reflected in their past), we must do more than examine isolated facts from documents, material culture, and artworks – no matter how detailed or precise. If we seek their lived experience, we must turn to the reflections they record in their history. We find this rather specialized sort of meditation exclusively in literature, and above all in Greek and Roman historical writing. We find therefore two decisive reasons why anyone interested in the history of classical antiquity must continue to study, and learn to understand, ancient historiography as well as relevant authors and works.

There are considerable methodological differences between the study of ancient historiography and the modern practice of ancient history. As a result, we do not understand ancient methods as a matter of course. We must learn them, and, as far as Roman historiography is concerned, the present work offers some assistance. It has been conceived for students of the classics and ancient history in particular, but also for students of history more generally. It has also taken into consideration instructors in these areas. Beyond these specific groups, a wider circle of readers with interests in literature and history may find a useful introduction in these pages. For this reason, I have written the book in as generally accessible a fashion as possible. Chapters have been arranged chronologically. Subdivisions within chapters are partly chronological and partly devoted to questions of genre. This arrangement allows us to treat major developments in historiographical practice as well as individual authors and their works. In the analysis and critique of individual works, we direct our primary focus on content, form, and purpose as well as connections to other historiographical works and dependencies on them. We do this within the contexts of genre as well as language and style, and we also consider textual transmission (the history of the manuscripts on which our readings depend).

Some literary genres closely related to ancient historiography will receive occasional attention, such as early Roman historical epic in connection with our examination of Rome's first generation of historical writers (see below, Ch. 3.3, pp. 60ff.); antiquarian writing (see below, Ch. 4.6, pp. 96f.); chronography (see below, Ch. 4.1, pp. 69ff.; Ch. 5.2.4, pp. 119ff.; Ch. 7.3.2, pp. 223ff.); and *exempla*-literature (see below, Ch. 6.6, pp. 197f.). Although biography was a completely separate literary genre according to the ancient conception of biography and as a matter of course to the ancient authors themselves, we will treat it in detail here, inasmuch as ancient biography, for the modern student of ancient history, stands as a source whose value is often equivalent to ancient historical narratives (see below, Ch. 4.4, pp. 81ff.; Ch. 6.3, pp. 165ff.; Ch. 6.4, pp. 178ff.). From the age of Augustus, we shall also include Greek authors and their works to the extent that Roman history was their theme (*passim* from Ch. 5.2, pp. 110ff.; compare Ch. 1.2, pp. 12f. with note 4, p. 256). Christianity will be understood and consciously treated as an ancient phenomenon. For this reason, this account will consider the development of historiography within the special context of Christianity as well as its development between classical religion and Christianity. This requires a thorough summary of early Christian conceptions of history in general as well as those specifically concerning Roman history, together with the theological basis for these ideas (see below, Ch. 6.3.3, pp. 171ff.; Ch. 6.5.2, pp. 191f.; Ch. 7, pp. 199ff.). With the Christian Roman empire, one arrives at the epoch of the Germanic migrations and their impact on the Mediterranean. And with their historians, we find ourselves on the path to the Middle Ages, but an occasional glance in their direction is useful for the light these authors throw on the altered political situation of late antiquity with its concomitant shifts in outlook and "worldviews."

Readers will find in Chapter 8 a summary of various principles that informed Greek and Roman historical thinking. These results rest on the analyses of the preceding chapters. On the other hand, the arguments of Chapter 1 concerning the subject matter, origins, and characteristics of Roman historiography constitute the fundamental basis for comprehension of subsequent generalizations as well as the treatments of individual authors and works in Chapters 2 through 7. To facilitate the connections of general conclusions and arguments with information about individual authors and works, Chapter 1 offers numerous cross-references in advance, as it were, to details in subsequent chapters. The Roman historians we cite in this work are the relatively few among them whom we recognize as influential or about whom we have substantial knowledge. In the centrally important Chapters 2 through 7, effort has also been made to ensure that important aspects of historiographical issues under discussion will be manifest in the structure of these chapters themselves. Titles and subtitles have been designed as a chronological as well as historiographical map. The introductory paragraphs to these chapters provide orientation to contemporary political conditions and to the general characteristics of historiographical developments in the period under discussion as well as basic information about, and critical assessments of, the authors and works treated. More important ancient historians and biographers find a place by name as well in the subtitles and subdivisions of these chapters. All authors and works treated in this work may be found with references to the relevant pages in the "Index of Ancient Authors and Works (pp. 287ff.)."

The book has been conceived as a comprehensive basic introduction. Students who pursue a relevant discipline should find that this book will enable and facilitate further independent work. To this end, this work presents diverse modern views on critical issues and provides a select bibliography, which, of course, represents but a tiny fraction of international scholarship currently on abundant offer. Citation to secondary literature in the main text of this work as well as in footnotes has been limited to controversial points and verbatim quotations. Sections 2 through 7 in the Bibliography correspond to Chapters 2 through 7. The first section of the Bibliography has been divided into four subsections: (§1.1): ancient historical works, biographical works, and historical epics, together with commentaries and translations for respective authors and works; (§1.2): individual editions and, more crucially, collections of fragmentary works; (§1.3): recent standard reference works on the history of Greek and Roman literature and historiography; and (§1.4): other secondary works not devoted to individual authors or works, but to ancient, especially Roman, historiography and biography or their literary, social, and intellectual contexts.

Modern secondary literature is cited by the author's last name and with a number in square brackets [...] that refers to the section of the Bibliography where the full reference may be found. In those cases where further identifying details will be necessary, a keyword from the title will be provided immediately after the Bibliography's section number. Citations lacking a reference to a specific section of the Bibliography are always citations to editions of collected fragments either of historical works or of historical epics. These editions have all been grouped in section 1.2 of the Bibliography. Because their number is so large, only general reference can be made here to the detailed reviews of secondary literature pertaining to epochs, authors, and works of Roman historical writing that may be found in the internationally collaborative collection *Aufstieg und Niedergang der römischen Welt* ("Rise and Decline of the Roman World" = *ANRW*), which had been published in Berlin and New York since 1972, but has beeen abandoned before reaching its conclusion. The Bibliography does nevertheless contain references to some individual contributions to *ANRW*.

If readers engage more closely on their own with the subject matter of this book, they will of necessity turn to modern editions of ancient works, commentaries, and translations according to the needs of their independent pursuits. A selective guide to the most important of these publications may be found in section 1.1 of the Bibliography. Ancient historical works in Greek and Latin have been transmitted to us in an altogether incomplete and fragmentary state. Scholars have exerted every effort to reduce especially large gaps in the tradition through the collection (mostly with commentary) of fragmentary works or lost works documented in other ancient works (generally the works of other, later ancient authors). These editions of fragments help us to assign the proper place of individual historians in the development of ancient historiography as well as to appreciate individual achievement or, on the other hand, evaluate dependency on and deviation from predecessors. These qualities are admittedly difficult to measure, inasmuch as ancient historians did not systematically cite their sources. Working with texts that have come down to us in fragmentary condition requires a certain technical expertise as well as some practical experience.

We may refer here once again to the editions collected in section 1.2 of the Bibliography on pp. 270ff. The guide provided here to the peculiar requirements of working with fragments should also assist readers in following the discussions that this book devotes to the subject.

Those Roman historians who wrote in Greek have been collected in the Greek collection of Jacoby et al., *Die Fragmente der griechischen Historiker* ("The Fragments of the Greek Historians"), which we cite as *FGrH*. These Greek authors of Roman history have likewise been collected in the Roman, i.e., mostly Latin, collection of Peter, *Historicorum Romanorum Reliquiae* ("The Remains of the Roman Historians"), which we cite as **HRR**. Early Roman historical writers up to Lucius Scribonius Libo and autobiographers up to Lucius Cornelius Sulla are, regardless of the language of their works, now likewise printed in the three volumes of Chassignet, *L'Annalistique Romaine* ("Roman Annalistic Writing"), which we cite as **AR**. For historical writers up to Titus Pomponius Atticus, we also use the two-volume edition of Beck and Walter, *Die frühen römischen Historiker* ("The Early Roman Historians"), which we cite as **FRH**. For the fragments of Cato's *Origines*, we cite not *AR*, but Chassignet's separate edition devoted to this work, which we cite as **CC**. Surviving fragments of the works of later Roman historians (i.e., from the end of the Republican period, from the imperial period, and from late antiquity) can at present generally be found only in **HRR** (the exception would be individual historians whose fragments have been collected in separate editions). For some years, the scholarly community has eagerly awaited the new edition with English translation of **HRR** that has been announced by Timothy J. Cornell, Christopher J. Smith, and Edward Bispham, but this edition has not yet appeared. To the extent then that it is possible, these fragmentary collections will be cited in parallel.

The monumental work of the **FGrH** unfortunately still remains incomplete. For this reason, we must partially – although not for the very first Roman historians who wrote in Greek – make use especially of the older collection of Müller, his *Fragmenta Historicorum Graecorum* ("Fragments of the Greek Historians"), which we cite as **FHG**. Because, however, it provides the fragments more comprehensively and with better commentary, the **FGrH** is decidedly better than the **FHG**. The **FGrH** consists of volumes of various types. The *text* volumes provide ancient evidence for particular authors (each designated with a unique ordinal number) and their works (*Testimonia* = **T.** with consecutive enumeration of individual works) as well as verbatim quotations and paraphrases of content from their works which have not survived as such (these are the fragments = **F.** with consecutive enumeration). There are also volumes of *commentary* (the first volumes were composed in German, later volumes in English) as well as volumes containing notes to the volumes of commentary. The capital and lower case letters that appear on the spines of the volumes fail to provide a systematic means for their identification, and are thus best ignored by the user.

The two-volume collection of **HRR** is in need of supplements and revision, but, as we note above, has not yet been replaced. In this work, *Roman* numerals are used for the pages on which we find the modern account of, or commentary on, each particular author and his work. *Arabic* numerals are used for the pages that reproduce the consecutively numbered testimony ("witnesses" to the original text) and fragments. Differently from the practice of *FGrH*, the authors in *HRR* are not consecutively enumerated. The second volume, which begins with Marcus Tullius Cicero, starts its pagination afresh with Roman as well as with Arabic numerals. We must therefore include the volume number (I or II) with the citation. When we first take up a relevant author, we must thus also provide two citations: first with Roman numerals for those pages where we find the account of the author and then with Arabic numerals for the pages where we find the author's fragments. *AR* is arranged like *HRR*, and citations to it will be made analogously.[1] The authors in *FRH* are, as in *FGrH*, consecutively numbered. For this reason, to the extent that it is necessary, authors will be cited according to their *author numbers* in *FGrH* and *FRH*, but according to their *page numbers* in *HRR* and *AR*, or in both cases the name of the ancient author in question will be provided. One must keep in mind that as a consequence of the uncertain chronology in the sequence of these authors and their works, discrepancies will arise between the various collections of fragments as well as with this work.

Since the publication of *FGrH*, Part Four, IV A, Fascicle 1 (nos. 1000ff.), in 1998, the editors have begun including English *translations* of the fragments of the texts they reproduce. *AR* includes French translations, and *FRH* includes German translations of the fragments of the texts (in addition to extensive explanatory notes and commentary). For those fragments presented without translation, one must search for a translation under the author and work from which the fragment in question derives. The information necessary for identifying the source for a fragment will be provided by the collection of fragments in the form of a citation. The collection will, however, employ standard abbreviations for ancient authors and their works. To decipher these abbreviations, one must turn to standard lexicons of Greek and Latin which provide lists of abbreviations. Examples include the *Greek–English Lexicon* compiled by H. G. Liddell and R. Scott, revised and augmented throughout by H. S. Jones, with the assistance of R. McKenzie et al., Oxford, 1940 (ninth edition), *With a Revised Supplement* by P. G. W. Glare and A. A. Thompson, Oxford, 1996, and the *Oxford Latin Dictionary*, edited by P. G. W. Glare, Oxford, 1968–1982. Information about ancient authors who wrote in Greek or Latin and their works as well as about anonymously composed or preserved works in Greek or Latin, including bibliographical references to editions of the text, translations, bilingual editions, and commentaries can be found in numerous lexicons devoted to the ancient world and to ancient authors or ancient literature. Some examples of these lexicons may be found on pp. 264ff. in the guide to section 1.1 of the Bibliography.

I thank my colleagues for the help they have rendered: Hans Beck and Uwe Walter for providing an advance copy of the first volume of their edition of early Roman historians [Bibl. §1.2]; Burkhard Meissner; Isolde Stark; and most especially Dieter Timpe for reading the manuscript and for the suggestions for improvement that ensued, which proved very helpful indeed.

Addendum to this edition: When Hans-Friedrich Mueller took up the idea of translating my *Römische Geschichtsschreibung* into English, I was very naive about the translation of such a book, and I thus found his proposal pleasing without considering the difficulties and even risks of such an enterprise. Indeed, as I have learnt since, the peculiarities of the traditional academic German language would have rendered a translation of my book into Latin much easier than into English. Nonetheless, I am convinced that Hans-Friedrich Mueller has been successful with his translation. I see three reasons for his success: he is a classicist, his parents are American and German, and he worked hard, taking an enormous amount of time for his work of translation. I thank him for his extraordinary engagement, I add my thanks to Al Bertrand, Haze Humbert, and Galen Smith of Wiley-Blackwell, knowing quite well their patience, and to the helpful anonymous reviewer of Hans-Friedrich Mueller's translation – and I hope that my book is worthy of the efforts of all these persons.

1

Ancient Literature and Roman Historiography

For Greeks and Romans, historical narratives were hardly the products of scholarly inquiry in the modern sense. They were rather works of literature,[1] and for this reason an essential (though not decisive) approach to an understanding of ancient historiography lies in the history of ancient literature. It is standard practice today to investigate and interpret ancient literature for basic political, social, and intellectual contexts and developments. The object of this more than merely introductory chapter is to examine ancient, especially Roman, historiography as literature and to draw the lessons necessary for its proper understanding in the context of our own historiographical expectations. We seek here to establish what can and should be understood as *Roman* historiography as well as in what way this literary tradition was connected to Rome.

1.1 Roman Literature and its Relation to Greek Literature

For the development of Roman literature's formal qualities and peculiar subject matter, a variety of circumstances are of fundamental importance. Roman literature becomes accessible for us in the year 240 BC with the first performance (known to us) of a drama composed in the Latin language. A few decades earlier, Rome had unified the Italian peninsula by force of arms, even if not yet legally and administratively. A short time later, Rome was involved for the first time beyond Italy in a struggle over Sicily, and, likewise for the first time, with Carthage, which had long

Roman Historiography: An Introduction to its Basic Aspects and Development,
First Edition. Andreas Mehl.
© 2014 Hans-Friedrich Mueller. Published 2014 by Blackwell Publishing Ltd.

been the primary maritime power in the western Mediterranean (the First Punic War: 264–241 BC). Acute awareness of their own success as well as of criticisms leveled against them by those suffering from or threatened with Roman expansion led Roman writers from the time of the Second Punic War (218–201 BC) to make self-justifying representations of themselves as a people the central focus of their developing literature. The genres of epic and historiography played a special role in these efforts (see below, Ch. 1.2 p. 12; Ch. 3, p. 41; Ch. 3.1.1, pp. 43ff.; Ch. 3.3 pp. 60f.).

Roman literature – like the visual arts and with the same general consequences – originated and unfolded (or, to put it more precisely, was methodically fashioned) from the third to first centuries BC in continuous and intensive contact with *Greek* culture. Such contact was made possible, of course, by the expansion of Roman power, which brought with it the extension of Roman diplomacy and Roman armies and Roman fleets into Greek territories, and eventually the establishment of Roman administration from Southern Italy to Asia Minor and Syria. This process necessitated repeated and rather lengthy stays of Romans in Greece and the Greek cities on the western coast of Asia Minor and also extended visits of Greeks to Rome. In its beginnings and in its first two centuries, Roman literature was contemporaneous with the third great cultural epoch in Greek history: the Hellenistic era. Romans became intimately acquainted with this culture directly and immediately through *live* contact. Knowledge concerning cultural epochs preceding this age, on the other hand, the archaic and classical periods, could be acquired only indirectly through *cultural* contact. For this reason, archaic and classical Greek culture long exerted a weaker influence on the Romans than did contemporary, and ubiquitous, Hellenistic literature and art. The general influences of this period as well as its peculiar generic preferences permeated Roman literature much more quickly, and, as a result, the sequence of generic developments in Roman literature differs from its model and we find a variety of Greek phases simultaneously present in the mix. We do not find a neat sequence of archaic, classical, and Hellenistic, but instead Hellenistic, then archaic and classical, or all three at the same time.[2] For this reason, Romans could in their reception of Greek literature simultaneously pursue modern, classical, and archaic versions. In general, this continuous contact between Romans and Greeks induced Romans not only to assimilate, but even more to compete with, Greek literature and art. In the process Roman literature naturally lost its own distinctive features. Only much later after the acquisition of Greek and as a consequence of long and complex interactions with Greek literature could Roman writers once again fashion a literature of truly Roman stamp.

Many aspects of Greek culture came to Rome directly through the services of Greek-speaking slaves and personal tutors in the households of the wealthy and the political elite. Still, we must not forget that the first authors who wrote in Latin in Rome had come from southern Italy and therefore derived from areas in close proximity to Greek cities. Greek culture came to Rome from a variety of regions in the Italian peninsula and through various intermediaries, including Etruscans in particular, but also Italians linguistically related to Latin-speaking Romans, foremost among whom were Oscans. These cultural intermediaries had each adapted and appropriated Greek culture in their own way. Romans consequently sometimes imbibed their Greek not in the original, so to speak, but in an altered form.

The manner in which the Romans came to literary activity very much set the parameters for how they wished to shape it: they turned above all to concrete models and to readily available practices and theories (for rhetoric, see below, Ch. 1.3.1 pp. 18ff.). Their literary practices remained Greek for about three centuries, but, at later stages in the development of Roman literature (at least from the late Augustan period), their literary practices had become Roman and Latin in all essentials. This particular factor in the development of their literature required Romans to study models closely, quote them, and imitate them (this included making variations on originals), rather than invent original creations. The achievement of Roman literature lies in the intentional and experimental fashion in which authors joined elements derived from various periods in the history of the development of Greek literature into new combinations, together with features derived from contemporary practices. An eclectic attitude permitted literary practice to base itself on the principle of selection, and this is readily comprehensible, given the manifold varieties "on offer" in such a long literary tradition. The resulting syntheses, however, often subjected these appropriated and recombined elements to substantial modifications, especially when, as was not infrequently the case, they were drawn from assorted literary genres. Through such means Romans created a new and original literature both in sum total and in detail. And on this basis a Roman author self-consciously measured himself against predecessors and models, especially those whose works appeared similar to his own in genre or in purpose, but which, in comparison to his own, would appear less fully developed. Through such comparisons the Roman author was able to win the recognition he desired.

1.2 Roman Historiography and the City of Rome

We generally include under the rubric "Roman Literature" (of which our topic of Roman historiography constitutes a part) all Latin writings from antiquity, both pagan and Christian. In the Roman empire, however, two great literary languages were employed: Greek and Latin. We have just related (above in Ch. 1.1, p. 9) the impact that Greek literature had on Latin prose and poetry, especially in that period when Rome directly and indirectly spread its political power in Greece and the Hellenistic East, thereby incurring criticism of Roman policies. The effect of this situation on the development of early Roman historical writing was that its practitioners wrote their works in Greek for an essentially Greek-oriented audience. For this reason alone, we must discard the common notion that *Roman historiography*, as a branch of Roman literature, may be limited to the study of historical works in Latin.

We must also consider to what extent it may be meaningful, or perhaps even necessary, to include later historical works composed in Greek under the rubric of "Roman historiography." In the Roman empire, along with other non-Italians, Greeks too (among whom we may include those who had adopted Greek culture) actively served emperor and empire at the highest levels of society and government. They belonged consequently to the two highest social classes: the senatorial and equestrian orders. Other Greeks relevant here may not have entered into state service or service of the emperor, but belonged to the political classes of their own cities where, as office holders, they came into close contact with provincial Roman governors and their administrative staffs. Many Greeks who could afford it also spent extended periods in the city of Rome and won friends and patrons among Roman senators and equestrians. In this way, complex factors and circumstances (that could become traditions in their own right within individual families) introduced Greek writers to Roman ways of thinking about state and society: Rome was the natural center from which to rule the Roman empire and Rome's empire was conceived of as an equally natural unity.

Most historical writers of the imperial period, whether "Greek" or "Roman," came from circles that were defined as senatorial or equestrian according to their specific political and administrative functions or from local political elites in provincial cities. And their readers too, at least those to whom their works mattered, derived from these same social classes. There developed moreover in republican Rome for both Latins and Greeks a formulaic basis upon which to build historical composition:

past events were narrated according to the annual consulship, republican Rome's highest political office. For each consular year external (foreign) and internal (domestic) events would be narrated separately. In other words, although the chronological principle was primary, it could be modified and refined according to thematic considerations. Unlike the practice of Greek historiographical tradition, this *annalistic* principle (*annus* = year in Latin) characterized historians' narratives even of pre-historic Rome,[3] and was eventually adopted by such Greek authors as *Cassius Dio* (see below, especially Ch. 2.2, pp. 37ff.; Ch. 3.1.1, pp. 43f., Ch. 6.1.4, p. 153). Even if the number of those bilingually adept in Greek and Latin is estimated to be rather low, and did not include all senators and equestrians, it is nevertheless reasonable on the basis of the facts presented here, to include Greek authors of the imperial period on an equal footing in a history of Roman historiography and to this extent to follow Dihle's model [Bibl. §1.3].[4] When we include Greek authors we concentrate most reasonably on those who wrote *Roman* history. This approach is hardly arbitrary; indeed, the impossibility of confining Roman historiography to *one* language compels us to attempt another definition according to content.

In the literary traditions of the *Greeks*, historiography was closely connected with *ethnography*, and for this reason did not deal exclusively with Greek history. It encompassed the history of other peoples, and not only near neighbors, as is natural in political history, but rather peoples who lived at great distances. This may have happened mostly in connection with events of the Greek past, but from time to time also as an object in itself. The Greeks had also never united even a majority into a single state. For this reason, Greek historiography was unable to narrate the past of a great political entity, "Greece," or to describe the events leading to such a development. Instead, historians had to narrate the stories of individual states or make the conflicts between them their theme. Nor could an internal Greek world be juxtaposed against a non-Greek external world. The situation of Greek authors changed fundamentally, however, when they adopted the basic subject matter of *Roman* historiography.

The historical writings of *Roman* authors dealt from beginning to end almost exclusively with the history of Rome and the consequent expansion of the Roman empire. As one may surmise from this observation, the topic of "Rome" was transformed materially and conceptually from a city-state to the central power within an empire and thus to empire itself. Whatever was "foreign" therefore figured primarily not only as opponents or allies of Rome, but also conceptually in Roman thinking as the backdrop for Roman expansion and annexation. As soon as an area became part of the Roman empire politically, administratively, or culturally, its history became a part of the larger history of the Roman empire. Those peoples never subjected to Roman rule, as, for example, the "free" Germans, the empire of the Parthians and later the Sassanids, whose territories were never annexed by Rome, retained a place in Roman history as real or potential enemies, but, aside from such ethnological and cultural reflections as Tacitus' *Germania* (see below, Ch. 6.1.3, p. 137), they did not become objects of historical inquiry in their own right. This point must consequently be stressed, because very few works of Roman historiography failed to place Rome at the center, and instead focused on "the other." This is the case, however, only superficially: a more accurate examination soon reveals that those territories conquered and organized into an empire by Rome constitute the true point of departure even for these historical narratives, if not in theme, then in the assumed perspective of the contemporary reader (compare especially below, Ch. 5.2.3, pp. 116f., on Pompeius Trogus).

The historiography of the Roman empire (even if not from the pen of authors from Rome) kept its focus squarely on Rome as the site of government and administration. The quantity and concentration of historical representations decrease continuously as one moves from center to periphery. These proportions changed in the course of time when later emperors began to reside and rule outside Rome and Italy, and finally in the fourth century when other cities, most prominently Constantinople, became home to emperors and government, depriving Rome of these functions. Rome nevertheless played a special symbolic role in the preservation of the empire: an ideology that styled the city of Rome "Head of the World" (*caput mundi*) provided compensation for the loss of real political significance. For this reason it is not surprising that *Ammianus Marcellinus* not only wrote his Roman history in the city of Rome itself towards the end of the fourth century AD, but also in the parts of his historical narrative that survive devoted inordinate attention to the city far in excess of its contemporary political role (see below, Ch. 7.2, pp. 213f.). *Orosius* too made the city of Rome a pillar in his doctrine of the succession of empires when recounting the political history of this world as part of his universal history of Christian salvation (see below, Ch. 7.3.3, pp. 230ff.).

The central object of Roman history shifted over time. In the Republican period, we find the activities of leading Roman oligarchs as a group, in practice primarily those who belonged to the Senate as well as various outstanding personalities. In the imperial period, we find the reign of the emperor in the context of family and advisors (see below, Ch. 3.1.1, p. 47; Ch. 4.5.1, pp. 88ff.; Ch. 6, pp. 123f.; Ch. 7, pp. 201f.). Monarchical government thus reinforced a trend toward historical biography as well as historiography that verged on biography (see below, Ch. 6, pp. 123f.). Subjects other than the ones mentioned here receded into the background. In part they belong perhaps more properly to marginal areas of historiography or, as in the case of the history of Alexander the Great, they became (not coincidentally during the imperial period) objects of renewed interest to a Roman historiography concentrated on monarchs (see below Ch. 6.4.1, pp. 178ff.). We may for this reason indeed characterize Roman historical writing in the widest sense as the *history of Rome,* its leading men and its monarchical rulers in the context of territories governed by Romans or bordering on Roman territories.

Roman historiography defined according to these material and geographical principles had both *classically religious* (or "*pagan,*" the derogatory term invented by their adversaries) and *Christian* phases. Neither the ancient world in general nor the Roman empire in particular simply disappeared upon conversion to Christianity. We cannot ignore the substantial changes to political, cultural, and social life that were direct consequences of Christianization, but in all areas of life many remained consciously committed (and stubbornly so, we might say from a modern point of view) to older, traditionally religious ways: radical denial of ancient tradition, although necessary according to Christian doctrine, actually remained the exception. For this reason, much that was very old was usually preserved amid the new. This observation is valid also for the literature of Christian late antiquity. Literary activity was extraordinarily lively from the fourth through sixth centuries AD. Proportionately much more has been preserved of Christian productions than from the previous and much longer ages of literature purely or predominantly classical in their religious orientation. Historiographical works of late antiquity have also survived to our age. Insofar as they treat or touch on more ancient epochs of Roman history, they rely of necessity on pre-Christian sources. Oftentimes they adopt the judgments of these sources to the extent that their points of view may be reconciled with Christian moral principles or they interpret them in a Christian sense. On balance, Christian historiography can explicitly serve Christian positions in necessarily and decidedly "anti-pagan" fashion or, on the other hand, simply continue traditionally religious historiography, but under cover of an inconspicuous Christian style (see below, Ch. 7, pp. 200f.; Ch. 7.7.3, pp. 217f.).

The best place for writing historical works that had "Rome" as the main theme was the city of Rome itself and its environs. Here an author found the *Tabularium* (archives) of the Senate and later the archives of the emperors. Here too were private libraries as well as public ones (after the transition to the Principate), and it was here that one found at any time the most abundant and reliable sources for recent events. Nowhere else could one encounter such a wealth and variety of possible sources for information about the past events, in which Rome, the city and the state, had been involved. Readers for accounts of Roman history could naturally be found most easily in the city of Rome. Social history illuminates too the extraordinary significance of the city of Rome as a site both for the composition and for the reception of Roman history: the typical author as well as the typical reader of such works was a Roman senator or equestrian (see above, p. 12). He was himself active as a magistrate or pro-magistrate or perhaps employed in the civil or imperial administration in any number of various capacities. As such, he performed additional duties in Rome itself and its vicinity, and in the not infrequent intervals between official duties he found himself (by reason of social ties and origins) with his own kind in and near Rome. Continual exchange of opinions and information took place between authors of works on Roman history and potential as well as actual readers. Historical writing was in antiquity above all literature, and, as such, followed the rules of rhetoric (see below, Ch. 1.3.1, pp. 18ff.). For this reason, it was beneficial for the historian that, as its political importance increased, the city of Rome became central (and for a time in the Latin-speaking world absolutely central) for authors, orators, and teachers of oratory. Rome offered circles for the discussion of works in progress of every literary genre. Potential literary patrons were also concentrated in the capital. Granted, this was decidedly more important for poets, who were not in general members of the ruling class, than it was for historians who belonged to the senatorial and equestrian orders. Even in late antiquity (as we just noted above), the ideology of Rome, which Christians too had made their own, could occasion an extended stay in the city by an historian of the late fourth century (see below, Ch. 7.2, p. 208).

We must, on the other hand, circumscribe to some extent the city of Rome's significance as the site for composition and consumption of works of Roman historiography. Elsewhere too, above all in areas of Greek cultural influence and, in fact, especially there, where people found themselves in the crossfire of Roman campaigns of conquest and annexation, one took an interest (sometimes ill-omened) in Roman history.

Conscious of this, the first Romans made a point of writing in Greek, not Latin (see above, p. 12; below, Ch. 3, pp. 41ff.). The earliest traditions about Rome (which were utilized by Romans only much later) derived not from Roman, but from (Western) Greek pens, especially in Sicily and southern Italy, but elsewhere too in areas of Greek cultural influence. An unintended consequence of Romanization (insofar as it included adoption of the Latin language) was the growth of regional literary activity in Latin during the imperial period. We may note, for example, the rich cultural center of western North Africa and Carthage that, beginning in the second century AD, yielded a rich harvest of both traditionally religious and Christian literature and was served by important native schools of oratory and law. Because ancient historiography rested only in restricted circumstances and often not at all on the historian's own examination of primary sources, but instead generally turned to previous historical works (see below, Ch. 1.3.2, pp. 27f.), it was consequently possible to write about Rome and its empire in any location long-served by excellent libraries (as, for example, Alexandria in Egypt or Pergamum on the West Coast of Asia Minor). We should not conclude on this basis, however, that either historical works from the "provinces" (or, for that matter, works in other genres) were necessarily produced in isolation from each other. There was, on the contrary, regular and active contact between all genres and over long distances. People exchanged opinions through letters. They loaned, borrowed, and copied manuscripts. Those who were both wealthy and educated could use the entire Mediterranean as one large cultural space, and they could of course include the city of Rome or avoid it.

1.3 The Claims of Artistry and Truth in Ancient, especially Roman, Historiography

The Greeks assigned Clio, one of the nine Muses, to historiography. The Romans took the same view and continued to do so in late antiquity. According to ancient conceptions, the Muses wish to bring people *joy*, or, more simply and purely, to entertain, but also to *teach*. In these goals, which the ancient world ascribed to the Muses, we see mirrored nothing less than its conception of a cultivated life. Ancients saw the combination of pleasure *and* instruction as existentially important. Not only poets, but also historians (though hardly all of the latter) wanted to fulfill both aims, and often at the same time. Historians, depending on their object of inquiry, sometimes found the twin goals of "pleasure/entertainment" and "instruction" contradictory or mutually exclusive. In such instances, Clio revealed herself as a rather peculiar Muse.

1.3.1 Literary artistry and moral preoccupations in ancient historiography

"Muse" (actually *mousiké techne*) signified "artistry" or "artistic skill." The term refers to how one handled the means of a particular skill. Means consisted either of language (with all its characteristics) or the world of sounds or both at once.[5] Complete mastery (or mastery as nearly complete as possible) of the respective means, but also the capacity to play with them, brought forth a "work of art(istry)." Truth (insofar as one wishes to employ this expression here) or validity rests for this reason on the accurate and sure application of formal rules (for their own sake) upon specific subject matter. This explains the high value placed on formal aspects of literary works in antiquity. In particular, the three categories that determined a "work of artistry" stood in clearly defined relation to one another, so that a given formal genre belonged to a specific object of inquiry or content, and to both of these were available a set menu of modes of expression, and in literature this involved, of course, command of the necessary linguistic level with corresponding adjustment of stylistic characteristics. Generic and formal boundaries could be transgressed, genres and forms could, for example, be mixed, and this resulted in new combinations of formal categories along with contents and objects of inquiry, though it was of course both possible and necessary to find a path within formally defined fields, subject areas, and genres without offending established rules (see above, Ch. 1.1, p. 11). On the other hand, artistic and stylistic conventions had for the most part been established in the near or distant past, had been handed down from generation to generation, and were thus traditional in every sense of the word (including etymologically). Traditions, however, were at all times causes for the development of new forces. Sometimes traditions served as occasions for rebellions against themselves, but above all, especially where they were considered sacrosanct, they were frequently liable to slight revisions that led over time to long-lasting and major transformations.

In general, two or even more genres could be closely associated. The ancients reckoned that the more recent genre of historiography represented *epic* in prose. For this reason, historians had the duty to describe "great" events and persons, the deeds and destinies of heroes, kings and leading statesmen, taking care not to forget the associated actions of gods, and, with such content in mind, to cultivate an elevated style (which included darkly vague pronouncements as well). Given the close association between epic and historiography, it seems no accident then that the beginnings of Roman historiography and the first two Latin epics with Roman historical content were not only contemporaneous but also shared essentially the same subject matter: the most recent events of the Roman past. Nor does it seem coincidence that much later, in the Principate of Augustus, Roman historical self-portraiture once more produced almost contemporaneously two works that again derive from these two genres and that would become canonical: Vergil's epic, the *Aeneid* (which, of course, treats in the main not historical, but mythical, material) and Livy's *History of Rome from its Beginnings* (see below, Ch. 3.3, pp. 60ff.; Ch. 5.1, p. 100).

But Roman history was *drama* too, and very closely associated with tragedy:[6] for this reason, one finds in ancient, and especially Roman, historical narratives sequences of events and plots that have been composed in accordance with dramatic rules concerning climax, *peripeteia* (reversal of fortune), and catastrophe (the so-called episodic style in drama; compare below, Ch. 6.1.3, p. 150). An historical work encompassing many generations and diverse scenes of action could not be conceived, however, as drama without some complication, inasmuch as the unities of place and person and the construction of a central conflict were simply not possible, especially in light of usual Roman historiographical practice: annalistic presentation required the conscientious description of each event's location and resulted too in the splintering of series of connected events that stretched over a number of years. This made it practically impossible to bring the material together dramatically, unless the writer were willing to depart at least partially from an annalistic scheme (see above, Ch. 1.2, p. 13; below, Ch. 6.1.3, p. 145). One genre of historical writing, however, did permit an easier formulation as drama: the *historical monograph*. A clearly outlined plot and a narrowly circumscribed number of (main) actors, whose success or failure manifests itself in the action, make possible the composition of the whole as a drama (see below, Ch. 3.2.2, pp. 58f.; Ch. 4.5.1, pp. 86f., 90, and 93).

The linguistic and compositional elements of Greek, and thus Roman, literary works had to follow the rules of *rhetoric*. These rules had emerged in the fifth century BC, had been intensively developed in the fourth century, and had, ever since, been continuously promulgated and refined through a variety of theoretical approaches as well as through the practice of public speaking. The application of rhetoric was, according to the occasion and purpose, supposed to convince, to persuade, and to move the emotions or induce wonder or amazement. One effective example is the sudden reversal (*peripeteia*; Aristotle *Rhetoric* 1371.b.10, *Poetics* 1.1452.a.22–29), mostly from good to bad: the sudden overthrow or turning point became a customary and favorite rhetorical means for Roman historians from the time of Lucius Calpurnius Piso to explain the logic of a sequence of events or set of circumstances (see especially Ch. 3.2.2, pp. 56f.; Ch. 4.5.1, pp. 91f.). Commonplaces (Greek: *topoi*) were especially effective weapons in the arsenal of rhetoric. Commonplaces were designed to convince (*psychagogia*), and their universally plausible truths and seeming-truths would be illustrated concretely in particular cases (Latin: *exempla*) that generally counted as authentic or were represented as such by orators or writers. And, if one searched for illustrative examples, history was an almost inexhaustible treasure house. For this reason, rhetorical education included an historical component that modern readers would hardly expect to find in this area, and to such a comprehensive extent that, again, modern students would be astounded by its breadth. Historiography was for this very reason the subject of fundamental rhetorical discussions (Quintilian *Institutio Oratoria* ["Education of an Orator"] Book 10, especially 10.1.31–34). The transmission of history through instruction in rhetoric was thus the only sort of "historical study" undertaken by citizens, officials, and prospective literary writers, and – from a modern perspective – this was not unproblematic. This practice offered history exclusively in a form that carved it into individual stories, each of which supported some concretely instructive (and most often moralizing) purpose. History thus provided not the stuff of storytelling, but rather of argument. Moderns will find this appealing. But history as example was also applied directly to the present and near future, as if there were no qualitative difference between once upon a time and now. This, on the other hand, will appear questionable to us, because we observe here in embryo the dehistoricizing of history (see below, Ch. 6.6, pp. 197f.; Ch. 8, pp. 244f.). History as example to be followed or avoided is an idea, however, that offers a key to understanding ancient, especially Roman, historical thought.

The cultural influence of the Greeks on Romans and inhabitants of Italy was so powerful that their ruling class not only learned the Greek language, but also studied Greek literature and oratory as well as the rules that governed them, and they themselves learned to make use of these arts (see above, Ch. 1.1, pp. 9ff.). In the intensive phase of Hellenization in the second century BC, the study of rhetoric at Rome was thus at first tied to the use of the Greek language, even though Romans, thanks to their republican form of government, enjoyed a culture of public speaking. Instruction in Latin rhetoric – which made use of Greek precepts in an analogous fashion – was undertaken in Rome only in the first century BC after overcoming some resistance in conservative senatorial circles. A specialized literature then quickly developed, and reached its first, perhaps even decisive, high point in some of Cicero's works. Until the end of the ancient world, the subject matter of rhetorical training represented for the upper classes "the epitome of culture" (von Albrecht [Bibl. §1.3], p. 9), and, after overcoming some resistance, it would once again find its way into the aesthetics of Christian literature and its production. The application of rhetorical knowledge and ability in the composition of historical works was thus in Rome – and this was no less true among Greeks – a given, a matter of course. Readers expected it.

Historical literature could shine with a rhetorical glow especially when main characters stated their views or announced their intentions. This is one of the two decisive reasons why ancient historians – the Romans no less than the Greeks – placed special value on the insertion of speeches and/or letters into the action of their narratives. The aesthetic need for such "illuminations" (Lat. *lumina*) led of course to the introduction of speeches and letters that had actually been preserved, whether in writing or by tradition, but these were of necessity artistically recast according to the prevailing literary rules and thus, we might add, given a tendentious spin. And this practice led quite naturally to placing another kind of speech and letter in place of those speeches and letters that had actually been delivered, but not preserved: free composition of a speech or letter that would with more or less historical plausibility fit the historical context. This content would fit the context more or less in accordance with the literary ability of the author to weave appropriate historical garb for his insertions. Even as intellectually sober an historian as Thucydides failed to refrain from the insertion of speeches he had heard about only at third hand and which he had composed to fit various moments of decision (*History of the Peloponnesian War* 1.22). Not only in Athens, a genuine democracy characterized by a popular assembly, but also in communities with other kinds of constitutions as well as in small ethnic states or also, for example, in the Spartan-led Peloponnesian League, all decisions were made through a lengthy process of debate before larger or smaller public audiences. This constitutes the second decisive reason for the reproduction of speeches in historical narratives first among the Greeks and later the Romans – and even Thucydides frequently did the same thing.

The needs of rhetorical instruction as well as general interest in "purple passages" had the further consequence that some works of ancient literature, but especially historiographical ones, were not preserved in whole, but only in excerpts, specifically those parts in which one could observe especially impressive application of the rules of rhetoric, to wit: speeches and letters. For this very reason, we possess today almost exclusively just such passages from the *Histories* of Sallust (see below, Ch. 4.5.1, p. 90). On the other hand, there did exist some ancient writers of history, who censured their colleagues for their reproduction of speeches, and themselves avoided the practice. The reason for this was, however, not the problematic nature of the (defective) historicity of such speeches, but instead an aesthetic assessment of their worth: if one fit the speech to the historical speaker and context, as rules of rhetoric naturally demanded, then such a speech would disturb, if not destroy, the linguistic and stylistic unities that a work of literature – and thus of historiography – strove for. Historians of this tendency remained in fact the exception (see Ch. 1.3.2, p. 29). The practice of reproducing speeches which were never really fully preserved – or worse: their frequent wholesale invention was for ancient writers of history an unquestioned principle of composition. For modern historians of ancient history, this practice has become an utterly insoluble problem, unless, that is, one is willing to make a radical break, and to exclude all reproductions of speeches and letters from consideration as sources for ancient history on the grounds that they are ahistorical.

Although the Romans were confronted with highly developed rhetorical practices in Greek historiography and although they learned the details of rhetorical theory in the course of their instruction in Greek language and literature, nevertheless, there was, according to an assessment of *Cicero*, no Roman historiography that met high literary standards until well into the first century BC. Cicero saw the reason for this in the lack of a satisfactory *language* or *diction* for this kind of literature, that is, no thoroughly typical style that was generally obligatory for the genre (see below Ch. 4.3, p. 80). Only after Cicero's death did *Sallust* finally forge such a style, and only then much later was it adopted and then with certain modifications by *Tacitus* (see below, Ch. 4.5.1, p. 85 and 90; Ch. 6.1.3, p. 149). The singular conditions (described above) for the genesis of Roman literature can here be viewed clearly. Sallust essentially looked back on two models of very different origin and orientation: on the one hand, he looked to a literary model, the "classically" Greek Thucydides; on the other hand, in terms of diction and moral expectations, he looked to the "archaic" Roman *Cato* (see below Ch. 4.5.1, p. 90). Roman historiography in Latin developed more slowly as a literary genre than did other forms of Latin prose, but also much more slowly than Latin poetry. Latin prose, in fact, reached a first pinnacle in the age (as well as in the person) of Cicero, and Latin poetry was even then undergoing extensive transformation, and would soon, in the Augustan age, reach its zenith above all in Vergil and Horace. Roman historiography, by way of comparison, reached its culmination either in the works of the first century AD (which, because lost, we cannot assess) or perhaps later still in the two great works of Tacitus in the early second century AD (see below, Ch. 6, p. 126; Ch. 6.1.3, pp. 136 and 150f.).

We may draw two conclusions from the fact that ancient literature wished in general not only to entertain, but also in particular to teach: first, such instruction was not at all scientific (in the modern sense) with regard to its approach to fundamentals, secondly, because historiography aimed at instruction, not as a science, but as a literary genre or as a "Muse," it did so unsystematically, aiming rather, on the one hand, at the dissemination of generally conceived ethical values, and, on the other, at the simple gathering of information from previously published sources in diverse disciplines. The latter could in historiographical works either be inserted on some pretext occasioned by the text itself or simply appended in the midst of an ongoing chronological narrative as a so-called *excursus* (or digression). This was especially true for geographical topics, but also topics involving topography, ethnography, cultural history, and religion. Because of the conditions under which ancient historiography developed, *geography* was the most important of the disciplines associated with history (compare Lendle [Bibl. §1.3] pp. 6f. and 10ff. and Meister [Bibl. §1.3] pp. 15ff. and 19ff.). This remained the case through late antiquity, and, as a result, we frequently find that the same authors write both history *and* geography or that an historian introduces his work with a lengthy and detailed geographical description (compare, on the one hand, the geographer Strabo and, in his *Natural History*, Pliny; below, Ch. 5.2.1, p. 113; Ch. 6.1.2, p. 135, and, on the other hand, Orosius, below Ch. 7.3.3, p. 231). Although diverse areas of inquiry strove in the course of time to make separate disciplines of their subjects, their contents never became secret knowledge, and thus remained the property of the general culture, open to appropriation through self-study by any educated person with literary inclinations. Digressions into specialized areas of study could therefore bestow upon historical writers a coveted reputation for wide-reading and erudition. For this reason, such digressions became a fixed feature of ancient historiography (see below Ch. 4.3, p. 80). This practice reached its peak in the work of the Roman historian *Ammianus Marcellinus* (see below, Ch. 7.2, p. 210). Only exceptionally, however, do we find the integration of geography as a causal factor when it would be relevant to an historical and chronological report. Here we may cite Caesar's *Commentaries on the Gallic War* (see below Ch. 4.2.2, p. 74).

Like poets, historians served as *moral* authorities among Greeks and Romans – or so at least they claimed over and over again. The historian pointed out good and bad conduct amid the individual examples served up by the past, and was thereby able to instantiate conduct (Latin: *mores*), and render it concrete. Historiography therefore included a great deal of description and evaluation of individual actions as well as a person's failure to act. Another substantial moral factor for Roman, as opposed to Greek, historiography included, of course, the original situation under which historical writing developed at Rome, a time when Rome was engaged in great wars subject to critical scrutiny abroad. Roman historians sought above all to justify morally the reasons for, if not to demonstrate the actual necessity of, entering the wars that left Rome the dominant power in the western Mediterranean. Morality went hand in hand with the political work of justification (see above, Ch. 1.1, p. 9, below Ch. 3.1.1, pp. 43ff.). After Rome consolidated its power in the Mediterranean and beyond, other general moral values became more prominent, replacing earlier concerns for self-justification. In Roman eyes, the establishment of Roman hegemony ushered in a mutually interdependent duality of freedom and political order that had come into existence through Rome, and whose guarantor would likewise continue to be Rome, thus providing a fundamental justification for the development and existence of the Roman empire, as it would also eventually under Christian auspices as well (see below, Ch. 5.1, p. 109; Ch. 5.2, pp. 110ff.; Ch. 6.2.2, pp. 162ff.; Ch. 7.3.3, pp. 233f.). The conduct of statesmen and the elite classes of society in conjunction with the prosperous or evil condition of Rome and its empire was likewise evaluated by Roman historians on a purely moral basis (see below, Ch. 4.5.1, pp. 88ff.; Ch. 5.1, pp. 106ff.; Ch. 6.1.3, pp. 146f.; Ch. 7.2, pp. 213f.). It was therefore the Roman historian's self-evident task (self-evident because it was not critically examined or doubted) to convey both individual and collective moral codes through past actions and conduct set in the context of a practical and above all politically oriented system of values.

Moral thinking among Romans was easily merged with *legal* categories. These tend principally to formalization. And it is in this very activity that the Romans have been recognized as the masters and teachers of the European legal tradition from antiquity to modern jurisprudence. In contrast to the more pragmatically oriented Greeks, the causes of the wars waged, and almost always won, by Rome, corresponded to moral

principles as well as legal norms. On the legal side, the theory was encap-
sulated in the doctrine of "just war" (*bellum iustum*), and it was the
unavoidable duty of the authors of Roman history to demonstrate how
closely Romans and their state agents acted in accordance with its principles. In such justifications we can observe the manifestation of the
Romans' fundamentally legalistic outlook no less in their historiography
than we do in their jurisprudence. But this is not the end of the story.
If the Romans won wars, it was, they were convinced, because they
enjoyed better relations with the gods than did their opponents. The
relationship between human beings and gods was no different from that
among human beings themselves or between two states. The relationship
was at once moral and formally legal in character, and it was just this sort
of relationship that the Romans understood under the term *religio*. One
needed to take into account, of course, that the gods were much more
powerful than human beings and that within the context of the ongoing
mutual obligations of human beings and gods, it was especially important
for the individual or groups of people or (in particular) the state to recognize the will of the gods and to make the fulfillment of divine will the
fundamental basis of one's own, the group's, or the state's conduct. It
was consequently incumbent on Roman historians to account for the
indisputable successes of Roman arms and politics of the past by dem-
onstrating that their Roman ancestors were far better in fulfilling the will
of the gods than were all non-Romans of the time.

At first all this functioned smoothly, but, with the first signs of Roman
misrule in subject territories, or, at the latest, at the beginning of the
Romans' civil war in 133 BC, visible contradictions arose, that could be
used to argue against the Romans and their professed values (see below,
Ch. 4, pp. 63ff.). On the other hand, one could explain manifest problems in the course of Roman development as the result of lapses from
their own maxims of conduct, the keeping of which had brought such
success and prosperity to earlier generations. This is precisely Sallust's
line of reasoning (see below, Ch. 4.5.1, pp. 88ff.). Although this did
not sit as well with Rome's skeptical (to the point of hostile) attitude
toward innovation, one could also, on the other hand, recommend obe-
dience to new moral values. And, in the final analysis, one could always
plead helplessness and shock, while offering up the "the anger of the
gods:" Tacitus used this anger to explain the vicious assaults of Roman
emperors on the ruling class, which he saw as the last preserve of ancestral
liberty (Tacitus, *Annals* 16.16). The Christianization of larger popula-
tions in the third century AD entailed another and no less explosive
conflict of moral values that inevitably arose with the establishment of

Christianity in the fourth century as Rome's state religion: the new, all-inclusive doctrine demanded the adoption of its moral values by society and state. The intensity of this struggle was blunted by the fact that Christianity, as the state religion, tended to stress the equivalence or similarities of its ethical values to ancient moral values, and to argue that Christianity, in fact, provided a better realization of them than did the previous "heathen" establishment (see above, Ch. 1.2, pp. 14f.; Ch. 7, pp. 201f.). In general, we find clearly reflected in Roman historiography (much more clearly, in fact, than in the Greek historiography) both the social consensus, as well as the dissonant views, concerning the meaning, indeed the existence, of the society's fundamental values and their religious foundation. These values very early formed the basis for the view the senatorial class held of itself, they became traditional within Roman historiography among its first practitioners, and they were handed down from generation to generation with little or no change for an astonishingly long time.

1.3.2 "History is what actually happened" – ancient historiography and the modern science of history

Moral self-justification is indeed a special characteristic of Roman historiography as well as of its artistic aspirations, whereas morally instructive intent, and, from time to time, open partisanship characterize ancient historiography in general. Nevertheless, ancient historiography also included features that modern historians of ancient history recognize as constituent elements of their own more scientific practices. Chief among these was a *claim to truth* that rested on the investigation of facts, thus raising the expectation that the narrator was reliably able to recognize and describe past actions and situations as well as historical actors with conflicting points of view. This immediately imposes the necessity of linking and explaining past events logically in terms of material and motivation, and, in particular, requires an ability to reconstruct intent, causality, and consequences. According to our modern conceptions and understanding, we would characterize this as empirical research, because the historian, on the basis of past testimony concerning either its own time or an even earlier period, whether intentionally provided and preserved or not, examines the material critically for the purpose of extracting new insights, and thus practices *Quellenforschung* (the critical investigation of sources) as well as literary criticism.

The ancient conception of historical truth rested on two foundations. Firstly, the Greeks had already conceived of history as events that had actually taken place and as the recounting of actual events, and they distinguished this from the general truths that could be conveyed through the fictions of literary composition. By at least the beginning of the first century BC, the rhetorical doctrines of the Romans made a threefold distinction: *historia* was what had actually happened, an *argumentum* was a literary invention that corresponded to reality (this, according to ancient conceptions, could include something along the lines of an historical drama), and a *fabula* was a literary creation with no claims to reality.[7] The truth of history accordingly differs from the truth of literature, but does not stand diametrically opposed to it (see below, Ch. 3.3, p. 62). Young Romans of good families learned such distinctions during their literary and rhetorical training, as did those too, who would later decide to write history. For this reason, historiography's claims to truth were rooted in literary and rhetorical practice, and they were consequently recognized as a special characteristic of a literary genre distinct from the genre of poetry.

Secondly, *Thucydides* had in the fifth century BC established among the Greeks some methodological principles for investigating past events and their interconnections that remain valid to this day. Later, in the second century BC, *Polybius* had worked out this methodology in numerous details. For this reason, these two historians stand decidedly closer to the modern scientific practice of history than they do to the customary rhetorical and literary theory of their own day with its gradations of truthfulness. The postulates of both historians most likely remained unremarked and largely ignored even among the Greeks for this very reason. Roman historical writers, of course, read Thucydides' work from the middle of the first century BC, but they did so exclusively for its artistry and rhetoric. Turning to Polybius, we find an historical work whose very subject was of central importance to Rome's historians: Rome's rise to world power between the outbreak of the Second Punic War in 218 BC, the end of the Third Macedonian War in 168 BC, and the Third Punic War in 146 BC. The existence of Polybius' seemingly indispensable and detailed narrative led, however, to no discernible adoption of his historical methods: one merely needs to compare the Polybian original to Livy's adaptation, which lacks his model's methodology (see below, Ch. 5.1, pp. 104f.). It makes little sense, therefore, to accuse Roman historians of defective investigation and critical assessment of their sources, techniques they could easily have improved through Thucydides or Polybius.[8] Rather, we must content ourselves with the conclusion that the historical methodologies of Thucydides and Polybius resonated with neither Romans *nor* Greeks, as we, for our part, might

have expected as a matter of course. It is here precisely that we observe
the enormous difference between our modern conception of the science
of history and the ancient world's unambiguous majority view of historiography. This helps explain, for example, why the Roman historian
Sempronius Asellio, who shared important principles with Polybius,
enjoyed almost no influence whatsoever (see below, Ch. 3.2.2, pp. 59f.),
why *Sallust* imitated Thucydides only on linguistic and stylistic levels (see
below, Ch. 4.5.1, p. 90), and why *Livy*, who wrote a generation after
Sallust, found a Greek model not in Thucydides, but in the previous
generation and in an author whose historical work(s) Thucydides explicitly criticized: Herodotus (see below, Ch. 5.1, pp. 104f.).

As the very *absence* of a commonly used term for "source" in today's
sense would suggest, consistent and systematic investigation of sources
was for ancient historical writers not an expectation, but an exception.
Above all, from a modern point of view accustomed to systematic source
criticism, it always appears arbitrary where and how a Greek or Roman
historiographer obtained his materials, and likewise, whether he shared
any details of provenance with his readers or named the basis for his
information (source) in any given instance. For the ancient historical
writer, exemplary works mattered far more as models of style and moral
content than they did for their perceived objectivity. In general, when
dealing with the remote past, he simply (from our perspective) took an
older narrative, and rewrote it according to his own stylistic conceptions,
read perhaps one or at most a few parallel narratives, glancing now and
again in one or the other, and taking this or that to incorporate into his
own version. In this way his retelling, through the incorporation of
various older versions in the same context, could take on the characteristics of a pastiche. The narrator of earlier times rarely made use of
original sources or more general documents (see below, especially
Ch. 5.1, p. 104). The most recent events of the past, or what we now
call contemporary history, enjoyed great popularity in antiquity, especially among the Romans, and, quantitatively, it received the most
attention in those historical works that attempted to narrate history from
early times to the present. From the second century BC, a ready source
for accounts of contemporary history lay in commentaries, memoirs,
and autobiographies composed by politicians (see below, Ch. 4.2, pp.
69ff.). With their assistance, one could immediately write historical works,
on basis of which others would soon compose their own histories of
recent events (see below, Ch. 4.3, pp. 77ff.). In works of contemporary
history, the investigation of documents naturally took on greater significance than it did for more distant times, and in regard to one's own

experiences and recollections of them, one could check them through interrogation of contemporary witnesses, a practice that Thucydides had himself engaged in, and raised to a first principle. These means, however, were required only of the author who was the first to write about some event in the recent past, and even he was under no obligation to do this consistently or systematically.

Still, it has been argued: "all traces of the work that he [the Roman historian Tacitus] obviously did in archives and libraries in order to check with great conscientiousness his determination of the facts were erased through the completely transformed literary presentation" (Dihle [Bibl. §1.3], pp. 231ff.). Indeed, the rules prescribed a literary and rhetorical form that required in particular the linguistic and stylistic unity of a work. For historical narratives this required the linguistic reworking of all sources incorporated into one's own work, and correspondingly prohibited verbatim excerpts from the original, unless the quotation somehow fit the stylistic requirements of one's own text; nor was it, strictly speaking, permissible even to name the source for content that had been reworked. According to a strict interpretation of the rules (as we may determine from the condemnation that the historian Pompeius Trogus heaped on his colleagues Sallust and Livy), it was forbidden to provide verbatim quotations in historiographical works even of speeches (Trogus at Justin 38.3.11; see above, Ch. 1.3.1, pp. 21f.; cf. below, Ch. 7.1, pp. 204f., on Zosimus). The premise to Dihle's indirectly formulated conclusion is therefore correct. What we may question, of course, is a logic that beyond very little evidence or none at all posits a great deal: it is possible, but not necessary. We have no secure methodology that would allow us, on the basis of a few citations, to reckon on Tacitus' exhaustive search for, and diligent use of, original source material in an historical narrative as stylistically unified as his *Annals*. On the other hand, modern source criticism has indeed reached the same conclusions, but using methods that preclude making reverse inferences along the lines of Dihle.

For this reason the general (and rather negative) conclusions we have drawn here from a modern perspective remain valid. Nevertheless, we must proceed from the assumption that a Roman (or Greek) historian could have conceived an obligation for truth that met today's standards, including related historical methods. It is just this duty, and its concomitant maxims, that one ancient work studiously demonstrates and simultaneously evades. In fact, we find more doubtful material in it than in any other historical narrative that survives from the ancient world: dubious even in regard to its author (or authors), the late antique *Historia Augusta* deploys citations from "sources" precisely when it invents, and the narrative oscillates in very sophisticated fashion between historical reality and fiction – of course, the work itself proclaims this very procedure as a characteristic feature of historiography (*Historia Augusta, Aurelian* 2.1–1; cf. esp. 1.2ff.)! In this way, the author (or authors) of this peculiar biographical historical narrative confound the seemingly well-known tripartite division, which we introduced above: *historia–argumentum–fabula* ("history"–"argument"–"fable"), just as in another place in the same work (*Historia Augusta, Probus* 2.6–7) the demand for truthfulness in historiography is formulated only so that it may be contradicted by the citation of mendacious and fraudulent authors (see below, Ch. 6.3.3, pp. 175ff.). This clever and insouciant game with the fundamental principles of historical investigation (as we would formulate them today) demonstrates quite clearly their non-binding status in antiquity.

Within the narrow limits we have outlined, we must also examine the efforts of ancient historians in *source criticism*. Once again, a gulf opens between the worlds of *Thucydides* or *Polybius* and the remaining throng of historians, and it is fitting here to refer to the achievements of a *Livy* (which were modest from a modern point of view; see below, Ch. 5.1, pp. 104f.). Modern philological and historical research has concluded that ancient historians evaluated source material more by feel than methodologically strict and intellectually rigorous criteria. Behind this conclusion stands the concrete fact that the average ancient writer of history would consider narratives of the past trustworthy, and thus take smaller or larger bits from them, especially when these narratives corresponded to his own ideology or political position and personal frame of reference. This frame would be established for Roman authors primarily and most frequently through social class and the similar political duties shared by earlier and later authors. When in this way authors found sympathetic agreement with predecessors in repeated succession, regular chains of identical narrative and similarly identical interpretation resulted. To this general practice over many generations we may attribute the demonstrable uniformity of the historical tradition respecting the Roman emperors. We may observe this especially in the almost never altered classifications of each emperor under the rubrics of "good" or "bad," classifications retained even through the cultural transformation from classical religion to Christianity. The tradition permitted deviations by later authors in their presentations only in points of relatively minor detail (see below, Ch. 6, p. 126; Ch. 7, p. 201).

Such series of representations and interpretations generated according to the conditions we have just outlined lead to the conclusion that the trustworthiness of a late author's account and evaluation rest not on independent sources and witnesses, but instead on one author, namely, the one who stood at the beginning of the series, the one who, frequently enough, is no longer immediately perceptible. Despite these negative assessments and conclusions from our modern perspective, we should nevertheless keep in mind that, like the modern historian of ancient history who came after him, the ancient historiographer already faced a sometimes hopeless struggle with a defective and often rather contradictory tradition, when he wished to write about a past more distant than his own, and could thus easily be inclined to loose handling of the tradition's available fragments (in the case of speeches and letters, compare above, Ch. 1.3.1, p. 21; for modern methods of handling the fragmentary historiographical tradition, see above, Introduction, pp. 5ff.).

We must finally consider in the face of all this what an *ancient historiographer* was, and, more importantly, what he was not. In general, we can say that historical research and the composition of historical works did not serve as a vocation suitable for earning a living, nor was this an occupation that one learned systematically through some prescribed course of training. One could study (in the rhetorical schools) the linguistic, literary, and moral aspects of historiography (see above, Ch. 1.3.1, p. 19ff.). One tended rather to become an historiographer by chance, through the vicissitudes of one's own life. We find active politicians who were ambitious to shape the opinions of their contemporaries and successors. We find perhaps even more frequently former politicians, either excluded by advanced age or rendered ineffective through domestic or foreign controversies, but also politicians driven into exile. We find too the independently wealthy, for whom the writing of history served as a substitute for an unrealized political career (for whatever reasons). On the other hand, we also find wealthy antiquarians interested above all in "antiquities" of a cultural and religious sort. They devoted themselves to otherwise unusually detailed researches that generally (though not always) kept clear of politics – a decided disadvantage from the modern point of view (see below Ch. 4.6, pp. 96f.). The Greek and Roman historiographer generally belonged in all events to a family and to the class that did not have to live by its own labor and that actively participated in local and national politics. As a result, we find, positively, the historiographer's (pre-) acquaintance with his material and, negatively, the prejudices and one-sidedness of his social and family circles.

Aside from such exceptions as Livy (see below, Ch. 5.1, pp. 100f.), the Roman historian was until well into the imperial period a *senator* (see above, Ch. 1.2, pp. 12f.): historiography was, in the first place, the only kind of writing befitting a senator and it retained this exceptional position, especially vis-à-vis poetry, which senators began to practice only in the course of the first century BC, but which, however, never became a normal literary activity in senatorial circles. In the time of the Republic, one of the values a senator presupposed as universally binding was the political predominance of his social class in the Roman state, which was institutionalized in the Senate. As a consequence of this posture, the senatorial historiographer of the imperial period manifested palpable misgivings toward the imperial regime, inasmuch as the Senate, as an institution, had de facto lost any real possibility of reaching its own decisions independently of the imperial will, and the individual senator had, as a magistrate, been restricted to administrative and judicial functions. He did not, however, question the imperial system itself (see below, Ch. 6, pp. 121f.; Ch. 6.1, pp. 127f.). The second class (or order) of Roman citizens, the equestrian, trod mainly in the footsteps of the senators: equestrians too wrote Roman history, or perhaps Roman biography, and thereby either adopted the views of senatorial historiography or at least transmitted its perspectives (see below, Ch. 6.1.2, pp. 134f.; Ch. 6.3.1, pp. 168f.). If a free man who was the dependent of an important family through his ancestry and according to law (i.e., he was a client), wrote Roman history, his work was hardly independent of the traditions and political biases of his patron's family and clan. Still, however much a Roman historiographer pursued personal or political aims, he could not do so too openly, because, as an historian, he was nevertheless obligated, even if not very effectively, to practice the greatest possible objectivity. This was defined rather simply: the historian needed only to provide assurances that he wrote with regard for neither his own interests nor those of any associated groups, and that he had received no personal advantage from any of the historical personages described in his work (see below, Ch. 4.5.1, p. 86; Ch., 6, pp. 124f.; Ch. 6.1.3, pp. 139f.; also Ch. 4.3, pp. 79f.). Alas, this conception of objectivity found little support in the historiographer's materials and hardly any in his methods.

2

The Formation and Establishment of Tradition in the Ruling Class of the Early and Middle Roman Republic

Those who wish to acquaint themselves as well as others with earlier events, circumstances, and personages, and who wish to master the past intellectually and ideologically, have many options beyond historiography and the scientific practice of history. Many of these *non-historiographical forms* of passing along traditions, such as eulogies at funerals or ballads of wars and their heroes, are older than any and all historiography, and the contents of such commemorations were remembered at Rome after the rise of historiography, and were consequently incorporated by historiography as well. To this extent we may reckon these kinds of historical lore as precursors to historiography. They can, of course, also continue to be practiced alongside historiography: either separately or – something much more likely from the start – together, and interchangeably, with it. In both cases they are not, or are no longer, precursors to historiography. The retention and recollection of the past can, both by its subjects and in its objects, be represented by, and remain restricted to, a small circle of people, a family, a clan. In purely oral traditions, as more recent research of oral cultures has demonstrated, such practices may reach back only a few generations, successively consigning prior pasts to oblivion. Fundamentally, the lore of the past and the fact of its preservation do not necessarily lead to continuous and systematic conception and representation of broader connections among persons, themes, places, and times, which, because of their inevitable fullness of detail and manifold logical associations, can only be accomplished in writing. Consequently, although the formation and preservation of tradition does not necessarily

Roman Historiography: An Introduction to its Basic Aspects and Development,
First Edition. Andreas Mehl.

lead to the development of written recollections or to historiography and epic, it can lead in such a direction. And, at Rome, this is just what happened.

Alongside the influence of Greek literature and the Romans' engagement with it (which we sketched earlier; see above, Ch. 1.1, pp. 9ff.), definitively non-historiographical and very much traditionally Roman methods of preserving and memorializing the past had a decisive impact on the inception and further development of Roman historiography as well as on the Romans' general approach to the past. Some of these characteristics have naturally induced modern investigators to discredit the value of the historical information and its general reliability, if not dismiss it altogether.

2.1 Family Histories and Clan Traditions

In undemocratic circumstances, the ruling dynasty – or rather the ruling group of leading clans, families, or otherwise variously defined members – will according to its needs fashion an image of its own time for the next generation, and provide too a value system for its evaluation. The corresponding formation of tradition in Rome for purposes of preserving past lore as well as educating posterity in its interpretation belonged at first to a few clans, the patricians, and later, after the reconciliation of the orders in the fourth century BC, to the new senatorial elite that arose from patrician and some plebeian families, the nobility. The leading clans of republican Rome constructed, preserved, and transmitted their respective traditions above all through the following means: at banquets in homes one sang – as in many other aristocratically formed cultures – songs to the ancestors of the host. At the funeral for a member of the nobility, whether the deceased was a man or a woman, a close relative would deliver a speech in the market for both the deceased and his ancestors. The speaker recalled for his audience the society's prevailing standards, and would then measure and celebrate the deeds and conduct of the deceased according to them. The funeral cortège included individuals who wore wax masks of the deceased's long-dead male ancestors, and who were outfitted with senatorial, or even triumphal, garb along with the insignia of the highest office the ancestor had attained. These waxen portrait masks were normally stored together with descriptive inscriptions (or *tituli*) in the atrium of the house where on festival days, if not at all times, they would be on display for family members, the family's slaves, the patron's dependent clients, other visitors, and invited guests. Most of our knowledge about this derives from the detailed report of a Greek of the second century BC who was well acquainted with Rome, and very much admired it and its ruling elite (Polybius *Histories* 6.53–54). Graves – whether they housed the bodies or the ashes of the deceased – were likewise supplied with inscriptions, which perhaps resembled, or even recapitulated word for word, the contents of the inscriptions associated with the portrait masks. These inscriptions briefly listed without chronological details the essentials of the individual's life and achievements and with special reference to his participation in politics, that is, offices held and accomplishments achieved while in office. Depending on the arrangement of the grave site, these inscriptions were either generally visible to all passers-by or accessible only to family members. Depictions of triumphal processions – the victorious general in the garb of Jupiter or the dress of early Roman kings, vanquished enemies in chains, conquered territories (depicted through geographical peculiarities and brief explanatory descriptions), and raw plunder – could evoke intense and future remembrance among actual participants as well as among citizens and other spectators.

In all these matters, one self-interested group judged the past according to its own interests and the views it held about its place in society, which it characterized over and over again among its own members as well as among people more generally as a capacity for leadership and the highest political offices. This directly contributed to the continued exclusion of clans that did not already belong. We can see that the same thing happened politically and constitutionally when we view the representation of these groups in the lists of senators and in the Senate's claims to, as well as actual long-term role in, the leadership of the state. The closed nature of the nobility must be put in the context of the intense competition among its members, both as individuals as well as extended families and clans, for the status associated with the highest local and national offices. The competition within the ruling class that was, according to the Roman constitution, projected outside that circle onto the Roman people as a whole, consequently stamped the political behavior of the nobility and, as a result, on their formation of historical tradition. At the beginning of Rome's lore concerning its own past stood not the history of a community, but instead many divergent histories, varying in details both unimportant and significant, which individual families and clans had molded and passed down. To the extent that simple citizens and freedmen concerned themselves with the historical tradition at all, each would have accommodated himself in accordance with his status as a client to the historical version of his patron's clan or family. Only to a limited extent may we consider the chronicle-like listings of the chief priest an all-Roman corrective to these family traditions (see below, Ch. 2.2, pp. 37ff.).

An ideologically coherent interpretation of Rome's past could never-theless be melded from the republican period's family traditions in combination with the uniform guiding principles that the nobility shared as a group. Each present generation had only to adhere to the treasured past as embodied in the "customs of the ancestors" (*mos maiorum*). It was the central task of the first Roman historians to interpret the past accordingly (see below, Ch. 3.1–2, pp. 43ff.). Of course, the character of family memoirs curtailed possibilities for subsequent syntheses: to synchronize details, at least those provided by the *tituli*, especially given the failure to provide dates, must have proved difficult, if not impossible. Senatorial indifference to the mass of the citizen body of necessity led to a role for them in collective memories that was even more diminished than it had been in fact. The authentic and singular deeds and achieve-ments of one person belonging to a given clan could be transferred to another person, who belonged to a different family group. Such manipu-lation was rendered relatively simple by the Roman constitution which required double and multiple magistrates for the same annual offices. Cicero reports that exaggerations, and even inventions, concerning both persons and deeds were a standard method for families to augment their prestige (*Brutus* 62). Today we reckon that this practice was especially common for the early history of Rome until about 300 BC.

When, however, we examine the materials actually used for recalling the past, we must modify and restrict the validity of both modern and ancient criticism. The practice of setting up inscriptions posthumously was and remains problematic – we need only mention the example of inscriptions from the tomb of the Scipios (*Corpus Inscriptionum Latinarum* I.2 nos. 6ff.) – still, as soon as past events were recorded in writing, the narrow bounds of purely oral traditions could easily be burst, authentic transmission could reach much further back, and the many occasions for remembrances must have served to preserve their subject matter. Past events associated with one clan or family were hardly nar-rated within the circle of that family or clan alone, but found rather, as a result of marriage alliances and adoptions between leading families, necessarily also an audience in the members of those other families, as well as third parties, and, more importantly, the general public. "Checks" could thus arise among competing or "neutral" clans and families as well as the general citizenry itself. It would have been astonishing, at least in cases of extremely imbalanced presentations of family traditions, if some constraints had not been applied. This would have acted to prevent the invention and dissemination of inaccurate information derived from family lore. Despite, therefore, all these persistent hesitations concerning the reliability of family traditions either for their own or for Roman history, we should not categorically reject their value.

2.2 The *Annales Maximi* and the *Almanacs* of Publius Mucius Scaevola

Alongside the oral, pictorial, and written traditions of leading clans, Rome's citizenry possessed the written records of their community. The *pontifex maximus*, chief priest of Rome's priestly colleges, and, as such, also responsible for the public calendar, made, as part of his duties, very brief notes concerning events affecting the community. These notes were accordingly termed *Annales* ("notes on the year," that is, *Almanacs* or *Yearbooks*) and in reference to their author designated *Annales Maximi* (also *Tabulae pontificum maximorum* or *Tabulae annales*, HRR I, III / 3, AR I, XXIII / 1). The historical reliability of these notices remains, however, a controversial topic. Doubts arise from the chief priest's social sphere, from the form and subject matter of his notices, and from their transmission originally as inscriptions and later in book form.

In the city-states of classical antiquity, most priesthoods were honorary posts for outstanding citizens (male and sometimes female). In Rome the various state priesthoods carried varying degrees of social prestige and were bestowed on especially prominent senators. The position of *pontifex maximus* was generally reserved for someone who had reached the highest annual political office in the state, the consulate. The value-system of leading families could influence the performance of these men's duties as priests, whose activities were essential for the community's religious as well as civic life. Such influence could extend to the notices of events recorded by the *pontifex maximus*, especially in the selection of incidents and in the citation or omission of the individual actors involved in them.

An ancient critic, the elder Cato (second quarter of the second century BC; see below, Ch. 3.2.1, p. 52), was, as a writer of history, irritated at what he found in the epigraphic annals of the priests: monotonous series and repetitive lists of bizarre astronomical phenomena, disasters, and shortages in such essentials as grain (*HRR* Cato F. 77 = CC / *FRH* 4.1 = Schönberger F. 77). According to the thinking of Roman religion, such events and disasters signaled a disruption of the peace (or truce) between gods and human beings (*pax deorum*). Inasmuch as such occurrences required the community (as embodied in its highest organ, the Senate) to take steps to appease the gods through the offices of its priests, the chief priest will have been obligated to record the nature of each atonement as well as the date of its performance. The notices of the *pontifex maximus* thus primarily, if not exclusively, contained occurrences that had required ritual expiation. The entry of these notices on whitewashed wooden tablets, however, put strict limits on the physical durability of such records or perhaps necessitated re-copying inscriptions that were becoming illegible onto new wooden tablets.

During and after the period of the Gracchi's comprehensive social and political reform efforts, circa 130–115 BC, the incumbent *pontifex maximus, Publius Mucius Scaevola*, consul in 133, published in eighty book-scrolls the *Annales Maximi*, which had previously only existed as inscriptions. Even the fourth such scroll still related events that purportedly took place well *before* the foundation of Rome (*Origo gentis Romanae* 17.5). Scaevola's *Annales* must therefore have reproduced the pre-history of Rome in extremely great detail. This would have been the "history" of an illiterate age, in which, moreover, there could have been no Roman priesthoods, inasmuch as it was before the foundation of Rome. For this twofold reason, priestly annals from a time antedating Rome are an impossibility. If we accept this verdict, and consider the enormous magnitude of Scaevola's *Annales*, it follows that in the course of their publication the priestly annals had been significantly expanded with other historical traditions more or less well-documented.[1] Indeed, authors writing after Scaevola's publication of the *Annales Maximi* paint a picture of materials far richer than those described by the elder Cato, who died in 149 BC (cf. especially Cicero *De oratore* 2.51–53; Servius Auctus *Commentary on Vergil's Aeneid* 1.373). Because a comfortably useful, unbroken narrative was available in an edition created by, and stamped with the approval of, a *pontifex maximus*, and certainly also because the inscriptions of the white tablets and their lists of events had likely been discontinued as a result, no such inscriptions of the *Annales Maximi* were available for events after about 115 BC. This date consequently represents an important dividing line in the literary history of Roman historiography. Authors who took up historical writing after this date – and thus the majority of Roman historians who chronicled the period *before* 115 BC – likely read only Scaevola's edition, mistakenly considering it identical in content to the annual inscriptions of earlier chief priests.

We may draw the following conclusions and in doing so we concur with the majority of scholars (against Mommsen [Bibl. §1.4] I pp. 463ff., characterized as an older point of view, see especially Timpe [Bibl. §2: Mündlichkeit] pp. 268ff.; who also opposes von Albrecht [Bibl. §1.3] pp. 298f.): the priestly almanacs, i.e., their inscriptions, contained, as Cato tells us (see above, p. 37), almost exclusively sacral materials. What additional matters may possibly from time to time have found their way into them should not (*pace* Petzold [Bibl. §2]) be expanded through speculation. Precisely this sacred character and the restrictions resulting from it would have significantly reduced the freedom of priestly authors to shape the material as well as any opportunities to manipulate it. We must not, however, think of the materials derived from sources associated with priestly almanacs as historically harmless. On the contrary, as we have just indicated, notices with such a pedigree should be considered historically suspect, inasmuch as the majority of their references to Rome's long early history may be traced back to the publication of Scaevola's ahistorical book. We must always remain aware of the insuperable discrepancy between those works on the early history of Rome published before and after Scaevola. With one exception, authors before Scaevola, especially Fabius Pictor, treated early Roman history summarily because sufficient materials were lacking (see below, Ch. 3.1.1, pp. 44f.; Ch. 3.2.2, p. 57). We may contrast this with the Roman historiographers of later generations who with the help of Scaevola's work were able to present this same history in luxurious and vivid detail. This subsequently canonical mode of narrating early Roman history has led to our well-founded suspicion of it as invention.

In contrast to the ancient opinion of his work, Scaevola's almanacs do not belong under the rubric of "historical documentation." They are rather in form a chronicle-like literary narrative of mostly political and military Roman history, and, as such, must be reckoned not a "primary," but instead a "secondary," source. Many incidents depicted are demonstrably the result of a literary and fictional methodology, and we cannot reckon as historical source material, for example, the doubling of actual (and by this we mean unique) historical events or fancifully imaginative reconstructions based on the barest of factual notices. Scaevola could and did draw his materials from diverse genres and sources: a small portion from the inscriptions of the priestly annals, but mostly from the traditions of leading families or clans (see above, Ch. 2.1, pp. 34ff.), from the official and private notices of office holders (*Commentarii*: see below Ch. 4.2, pp. 69ff.), from the state's sacred calendars (*Fasti*), which for their part already pre-supposed historical traditions of another sort, and from historiographical works. In the case of the latter, Scaevola was by no means compelled to rely exclusively on Greek works. He could make use of the products of Roman historiography as well, which by his day had been in existence for at least eighty years (see below, Ch. 3, pp. 41ff.). To supplement the generally wretched records of early Roman history, Scaevola could always resort to Gnaeus Gellius, in whose work Roman historiography had for the first time been writ large (see below, Ch. 3.2.2, p. 57).

The relationship between Roman historiography and Scaevola's work has therefore a twofold character. On the one hand, Roman historiography before Scaevola, that is, early, so-called annalistic writing, had provided ready materials for his work. On the other hand, although he was not the first to write his history as "annals" (i.e., according to the yearly tenure of annual offices in continuous ongoing sequence), he was decidedly the first to conceptualize Rome's history from its beginning to the middle of the second century and into the revolutionary period, as an unbroken continuum of strictly sequential annual reports (*historia continua* or *perpetua*) and the first to furnish each and every year with events. In this way – although indirectly – he made possible works like Livy's. We may thus derive the persistence of applying annalistic principles to Rome's early history and its earliest ages not so much from the inscriptions of priestly almanacs as from their transformation and enormous expansion by Scaevola.

3

Early Roman Historiography: Self-Justification and Memory in earlier Annalistic Writing[1]

The ruling class of Rome was interested primarily in family traditions and secondarily in community remembrance. For these interests, they lacked nothing historiographically necessary. It was rather Rome's role in foreign affairs, i.e. Roman expansion, and, more than anything else, Rome's conduct before and during the Second Punic War against Hannibal and Carthage, that created an objective need – or at least led members of Rome's senatorial class to feel the need – for a self-justification that they could present to the wider literary and culturally Hellenistic world. And this they sought to do through the composition of history. As Chapters 1 and 2 describe in greater detail, a goodly number of materials lay ready to hand at the commencement of Roman historiography: (1) a *lingua franca* (here Greek) well equipped with literary and rhetorical resources; (2) a topic as well as a general thesis; (3) the most important sources; and (4) in connection with one of these sources, a source indispensable for the treatment of longer time spans: the *Annales Maximi*, which were initially available as inscriptions and later in the form of edited books, and which presented Roman historiography in the form of *yearbooks* (*annals*, hence the modern collective term of "annalistic history" or "annalistic writing").

Despite the external factors that occasioned the development of Roman historiography, its first practitioners did not derive their value-system from alien sources, especially not from the philosophically based ethics of the Greeks. As Romans, they instead applied the values of the senatorial aristocracy. Their traditional guiding principles concerning right and

Roman Historiography: An Introduction to its Basic Aspects and Development,
First Edition. Andreas Mehl.
© 2014 Hans-Friedrich Mueller. Published 2014 by Blackwell Publishing Ltd.

wrong conduct, individually as well as collectively, had been established long before anyone engaged in historiography. These values served as an ideal basis for works of Roman historiography whose authors themselves derived, of course, from the senatorial class. Once it had been established, the ruling elite deemed their code of conduct unalterable, and, inasmuch as most later Roman historians belonged to this class, this ancient, ever-identical code of conduct (*mos maiorum*) remained the measure of historiographical value through the centuries, despite profound changes in actual conditions. To this extent, the earliest Roman historiography became the model for all later Roman historiography. An initial methodology has seldom determined the shape of subsequent efforts so thoroughly as it did in this instance.

Holding fast to values established once and for all as an unchanging measure of past and present conduct made it easy for early annalists to weave together and blend the events and situations of the most diverse times from earliest times to the present, all judged according to a solid code of conduct. From a modern point of view, the dangers resulting from such a practice include doublets in the presentation of historical incidents and anachronisms in their presentation and evaluation. On the other hand, subtle analysis of the narrative content concerning an incident from *one* historical time period can sometimes reveal embedded content from another period; these can then be separated, thereby winning further historical insights. When the narratives of earlier historiographers are taken up by their successors with little or no change, we can sometimes even detect one set of past events mirrored in another. Livy's use of relatively late annalistic works stemming from well after the beginning of the civil wars (i.e., after 133 BC) for his narrative of early Roman history, especially the conflict of the orders (fifth–fourth centuries BC), therefore permits us to glimpse how contemporaries of the Gracchi and the following decades of civil war viewed these earlier events (see below, Ch. 4.1, pp. 66ff.; Ch. 5.1, p. 104).

Of course, the importance of the larger Greek world at the beginning of Roman historiography's development meant that its influence was more than just linguistic and literary. It influenced content too. A particular interest of Greek historiography was the description of the foundation (*ktisis*) and early history of cities, nations, and peoples. For this reason, as soon as they discovered Italy, along with Rome, as potential objects of inquiry somewhere around the middle of the second half of the fifth century BC, Greek historians immediately reported on the origins of this city called Rome (Antiochus of Syracuse *FGrH* 555 F. 6; Hellanicus of Lesbos *FGrH* 4 F. 84). Later Greek authors did so as well. Closing the list before the beginning of Roman historiography, *Diocles* of Peparethus wrote an account of his own about the foundation of Rome, which was then used by the first Roman historian *Fabius Pictor* (*FGrH* 820 T. 2a–b; *FGrH* 809 F. 4a = *HRR* I Fabius F. 5a = *AR* I Fabius F. 7 = *FRH* 1 F. 7a). The history of the foundation of Rome was thus a story that the Greeks told often, varied over time, and transformed. It was in this way that the later canonical version of Rome's foundation came to have Romulus found Rome some hundreds of years after Aeneas' arrival on the coast of Latium. This literary product of *Greek* authors was adopted by Roman historiography, and became part and parcel of Rome's general cultural inheritance (see below, Ch. 3.1.1, pp. 44f.).

3.1 Early Annalistic Writing (I)

Early Roman historiographers first followed the example set by the genre's orginator, *Quintus Fabius Pictor*. Together with their model, modern scholars treat this group as the representatives of early annalistic writing. This is not to say that among these historiographers changes and innovations were unknown. In this respect, *Marcus Porcius Cato* deserves special mention, and we will for this reason treat early annalistic writing under two subheadings, one beginning with Fabius Pictor and the other with Cato.[2] We shall leave aside altogether authors and works about whom and about which we know very little (for, however, Gaius Acilius, compare below, Ch. 4.1, p. 66).

3.1.1 Quintus Fabius Pictor

Quintus Fabius Pictor (*FGrH* 809; *HRR* I LXIX / 5; *AR* I LIV / 16; *FRH* 1), the first Roman historiographer, was a patrician and belonged to one of the most prominent noble families of his day. He was, for example, related to Quintus Fabius Maximus Verrucosus, who held many political and priestly offices, was several times elected consul before and during the Second Punic War, and was made dictator in 217 BC. Because his strategy was to harass without engaging the enemy, Fabius Maximus earned the additional name of "Cunctator" ("delayer"). In the final years of the war, in opposition to the plan of Publius Cornelius Scipio, he wanted to reach a military decision in Italy rather than bring the fight to North Africa. Domestically, his politics supported patricians at the expense of the plebeian nobility. Fabius Pictor, by way of comparison, was already before the Second Punic War a soldier in Rome's battles with the Gauls in northern Italy and also perhaps at the beginning of the war against Hannibal, but he apparently never held a military command. After the devastating Roman defeat at Cannae in 216 BC, he was a member of the senatorial commission sent to the oracle at Delphi. It was probably in the final years of the Second Punic War or perhaps shortly afterwards when he composed his *Romaïká* ("Roman matters"), i.e., a Roman history written in Greek. The work ranged from Rome's – mythical (according to our modern perspective) – origins to recent events of his own day, and was supposed to present a general picture of the political and cultural development of Rome, thereby offering a corrective to the unfavorable Greek accounts then current. As far as we can tell from surviving fragments and the use Polybius made of the work in the late second century BC, the *Romaïká* were tripartite.

I. Fabius Pictor narrated in great detail (although not annalistically) the mythical pre-history and foundation of Rome together with the associated period to about 450 BC.[3] On the one hand, one may argue with Petzold [Bibl. §2.] against Timpe [Bibl. §3. and §2.: "Mündlichkeit"] that Rome's pre-history and naturally the foundation itself, but not the time subsequent to the foundation would have been included. One may also conclude from authors dependent on Fabius Pictor, such as Dionysius of Halicarnassus (*Roman Antiquities* 1.5.2–6.2; see below, Ch. 5.2.2, p. 115), that immediately after the foundation of Rome a new epoch, the "early history" (*archaiología*), of the city had begun. On the other hand, we find support for Timpe's position in a fragment of Fabius Pictor composed according the rules of Greek rhetoric that narrates in great detail the establishment of Rome's chief festival (*ludi magni* or *Romani*) in the transitional period between monarchy and republic, that is, a period well after the foundation of the city (*FGrH* F. 13 = *HRR* F. 15f. = *AR / FRH* F. 19f.). Timpe argues that here the author continued to follow the same source as he had for the history of Rome's foundation. Both periods accordingly constitute a literary unity for him.

The first part of Fabius' narrative organized individual events and significant accomplishments around the figures of Aeneas (arrival near the mouth of the Tiber River), Ascanius (the foundation of Alba Longa), and Romulus (foundation of Rome). In doing so, Fabius Pictor (*FGrH* FF. 1–4 = *HRR* FF. 3, 4, 6, 5 = *FRH* FF. 3, 5, 8, 7) followed the Greek author *Diocles* of Peparethus (*FGrH* 820) whose name and work survive only in the brief mention made of them. For the pre-history, foundation, and earliest history of Rome Pictor certainly did not go back to Roman documentary sources, but instead reached for (and retold) the ready-made and polished literary work of a Greek author. To the extent that Italian traditions found a place in the history of Rome's foundation, that place may be attributed to the earlier efforts of Greek authors. Fabius Pictor was certainly not the first to include them. The legend of Rome's foundation that would eventually become canonical does indeed include material from mid-Italy, but in general this is a literary achievement that belongs not to the Romans, but to the Greeks (see above, pp. 42f.). The Roman Fabius Pictor was merely a literary intermediary who wrote at the scene of his history's action (Classen [Bibl. §3]; followed by Petzold [Bibl. §2]; and Timpe [Bibl. §2: "Mündlichkeit"]; the latter opposed to von Ungern-Sternberg [Bibl. §2]).

II. Fabius Pictor's early history of Rome extended either from the monarchy (Petzold [Bibl. §2]) or, more likely, from around 450 BC (Timpe [Bibl. §2: Mündlichkeit]) to just before the outbreak of the First Punic War in 264 BC (see above, p. 43). According to Dionysius (cited above), earlier Greek and Roman authors, including Fabius Pictor in particular, treated this portion of Roman history only summarily. For "summarily" Dionysius uses the word *kephalaiodós*, "according to the main points" or "essential aspects" (for the formal Latin equivalent, *capitulatim*, see below, Ch. 3.2.1, pp. 53f.). Modern scholars understand the term as follows: Fabius Pictor and the earlier annalists did not narrate this portion of Roman history in annalistic fashion. We surmise from this that no narrative Greek source was to be had, and that no suitable materials from Roman family traditions or priestly notices were available (see above, Ch. 2.1, pp. 34ff.; Ch. 2.2, pp. 37ff.). In any event, until late in the first century BC, Greek-language historiography provided only sketchy historical information for early Roman history, despite the fact that Mucius Scaevola had constructed a detailed and unbroken narrative in Latin from the Roman point of view late in the second century BC (see above, Ch. 2.2, pp. 38ff.).

III. Fabius Pictor was able to tell the history of recent and contemporary events in detail and according to the calendar of yearly offices, i.e., in annalistic fashion, with the assistance of witnesses and his own experience. This is the only portion of his work to which we may apply the Latin term *Annales* (*FGrH* 809 T. 5a–c). Two fragments testify that Fabius identified years by means of consuls: the year 225 BC is so identified partially in 19b *FGrH* (preserved in Eutropius 3.5 = *HRR* note to F. 23 = *AR* / *FRH* F. 30a) and definitely in 19c *FGrH* (preserved in

Orosius 4.13.5 = *HRR* F. 23 = *AR / FRH* F. 30b). Then again, do the late authors who preserve these fragments present Fabius without subsequent additions? We must interrogate especially closely the citation of both consuls with three-part names in the version of Orosius, which most likely does not derive from Eutropius. We do not know what concluding date Fabius aimed at or actually reached.[4] The latest preserved fragment dates from 217 BC, early, therefore, in the Second Punic War (*FGrH* F. 22 = *HRR* F. 26 = *AR / FRH* F. 32), and may for this reason derive from well before the planned conclusion to his work.

The quality of the three parts of Fabius' Roman history thus varied greatly in terms of sources, subject matter, and narrative presentation. Cicero censured the works of Fabius and other early annalistic writers on the ground that they distinguished themselves in their linguistic and stylistic sterility (*De oratore* 2.51–53 and *De legibus* 1.6), but Cicero's observation can pertain only to the second and third parts of the *Romaiká*, because the narrative of the first part was worked up according to the rules of Greek rhetoric, as various fragments on the foundation of Rome and its early history clearly demonstrate (e.g., *FGrH* F. 4 and 13 = *HRR* F. 5 and 15 = *AR / FRH* F. 7 and 19ff.; see above, p. 44). Fabius must have pursued diverse aims vis-à-vis his Greek or Greek-reading audience in the three parts of his work as well. The Greeks had (as they customarily did with the "barbarians" they encountered) written the Romans into their myths and thus brought them into their world. They even provided the Romans with Greek ancestry, and this had a bearing on the prehistory of Rome and the history of its foundation (see above, p. 44). As a result, Fabius needed only to make use of ready-made accounts in the first part of his *Romaiká*. In the second part of his work, he had to narrate Rome's expansion on the Italian peninsula and justify, above all, Rome's annexation of the Greek cities of southern Italy. In the third part, the real task was to refute the hostile work of *Philinus* of Agrigentum (*FGrH* 174), a Sicilian Greek, who had argued that Rome was at fault for the outbreak of the First Punic War because it had violated its treaty obligations. Similar efforts were required concerning the outbreak of the second Punic war to rebut Greek partisans of Hannibal, *Silenus* of Caleacte (*FGrH* 175) and *Sosylus* of Sparta (*FGrH* 176). The works of these two authors may be considered the real occasion for the genesis of Fabius Pictor's *Romaiká* and thus for the first historiographical composition from a Roman pen. The similar aims of the second and third parts of the work were easily combined in a general self-justification that would become canonical: Rome had always and ever fought godly and just wars (see above, Ch. 1.3.1, p. 25).

To what extent Fabius succeeded in making his arguments before his intended readership must remain uncertain, given the wretched state of our sources. We may, however, cite the presence of a copy of Fabius' history in the library of the Greek city of Tauromenium in eastern Sicily, which presupposes the audience he envisaged in the second half of the second century BC (*AR / FRH* F. 1; see above note 3, p. 44). Fabius' special task in the first part of his Roman history, namely, to prove vis-à-vis the Greeks that the Romans had from the beginning been participants in Greek culture, had been made relatively easy by the earlier efforts of Greek authors in the same direction. It remains questionable to this day, however, to what extent Fabius' project was successful in his own day and how influential his argument was among his successors. The answer to this question depends on how we assess the claim made some two hundred years after Fabius by *Dionysius* of Halicarnassus who wrote that he was the first to offer to the Greeks the cultural incorporation of the Romans as Hellenes. To what extent may this claim have actually corresponded to the perceptions of *Dionysius'* day? Was it merely a rhetorical device to arouse the curiosity of his readers (*Roman Antiquities* 1.5.1; see below, Ch. 5.2.2, pp. 114f.)?

In addition to Fabius' aims vis-à-vis foreign readers, we find domestic Roman purposes. The pursuit of Roman readers in a work composed in Greek may astonish, but is easily explained by the sure command of the language of Greek literature enjoyed by the Roman ruling class of Fabius' day. Fabius Pictor was grounded in the very well-established traditions of his clan (*gens*) and stood firmly on its side in its differences of opinion and contemporary disputes with other noble clans and their clients (see below, Ch. 3.3, p. 62). Fundamentally, he approved of and supported the political leadership enjoyed by the Senate and its majority. This attitude sometimes led him to criticize explicitly the discussions and decisions of Rome's citizen body in their assemblies and the behavior of individual Roman magistrates. Fabius expresses such censure, for example, on the question of a military intervention in Sicily in 265/4 BC, which in turn led to the First Punic War (Polybius 1.10f.). He likewise censures Gaius Flaminius, whose politics were, from the Fabian point of view, demagogic, and thus opposed to the *mos maiorum* as well as dangerous for Rome. Fabius makes him, as consul, responsible for Rome's catastrophic defeat by Hannibal at Lake Trasmine in 217 BC: Flaminius was both incompetent and arrogant (Polybius 2.21–22 with 3.80–85 and Livy 21.63 with 22.1–7, who follow Fabius Pictor's account).

Fabius Pictor was not just the first Roman historical writer; he was the original founder who *stamped* several decisive qualities on all Roman historiography. In Rome, history became the domain of members of the senatorial class, something written by statesmen. Authors pursued political aims in their works that reflected their own social and political status. For this reason, they never wrote world history, but instead wrote Roman history (see above, Ch. 1.2, pp. 12ff.). Most writers began their history with Rome's beginnings, and they brought that history down until their own day. Later authors sometimes tried variations on this theme by appending their own work to that of a predecessor, so that, by way of continuation or supplement, their work became (and their pred- ecessor's remained) one that treated Roman history from its beginnings to the present day (*historia continua* or *perpetua*; see below, Ch. 4.1, p. 69). For the archaic period, Roman historiographers first followed Greek exemplars of the Hellenistic age; later they imitated Roman products, which, for their part, had appropriated Greek works. Later authors too followed the example of Fabius in their justification of Roman expansion and policies. Even the Greek Polybius did so, although he clearly recognized the bias Fabius' apologetic aims had engendered in his work (1.14).

3.1.2 Later authors (from Cincius Alimentus to Postumius Albinus)

Lucius Cincius Alimentus (*FGrH* 810, *HRR* I CI / 40, *AR* I LXXIII / 54, *FRH* 2) was a contemporary of Fabius Pictor and perhaps even his elder. Around the middle of the Second Punic War in 210 and 209 BC, Cincius served as a *praetor* in Sicily, and in 208 BC he led a failed siege operation against the city of Locri in southern Italy. For a time, he was Hannibal's prisoner of war. He wrote a Roman history from the founda- tion of the city (which he reckoned at 729/8 BC) to his own time and included his own imprisonment (*FGrH* F. 5 = *HRR* F. 7 = *AR* / *FRH* F. 10). Compared to Fabius' account of the events in the war against Hannibal, Cincius' offered a distinct advantage in the author's personal military experience, his personal knowledge of the theaters of war, and his own involvement with the action. Nevertheless, Cincius' history was read by far fewer than was Fabius'.

The victor over Hannibal's son and namesake – whose clan (*gens*) was politically opposed to the Fabian – *Publius Cornelius Scipio* (*FGrH* 811) was, in consequence of a sickly physical constitution, not politically active. According to Schmitt ([Bibl. §3.] 279–282 and *passim*), traces of his historical work are preserved, insofar as they touch on the Second Punic War, in Polybius and Livy. Scipio appears as an exception to the

Roman historiography of his day: he narrated the perspectives of both sides in the war.

In the midst of levying troops for Rome's bloody wars in Spain, *Aulus Postumius Albinus* (*FGrH* F. 812, *HRR* I CXXIV / 53, *AR* I LXXIX / 59, *FRH* 4) was, as consul in 151 BC and together with his colleague, arrested by the tribunes of the *plebs*. Just after Rome's victory in 146 BC, he participated in a senatorial commission to settle affairs in Greece. As a result, he must have come into contact with the most important Greek historian of Roman expansion, Polybius, whom we have already frequently mentioned. In many respects, Postumius was demonstrably sympathetic toward the Greeks. In his Roman history, he apologized for his inadequate command of the Greek language, for which apology he was straightaway taken to task by his contemporary *Cato* (*FGrH* F. 1b = *HRR* Cato F. 1 and Nepos (vol. II) F. 14 = *AR* / *FRH* F. 1b: here without Cato's censure). He presumably wrote a work about the arrival of Aeneas in Italy as well.

Aemilius Sura (he does not appear in the editions of fragmentary historical authors) and his work, *The Years of the Roman People* (*Anni Populi Romani*), are hardly known at all, although his work may have appeared before Polybius' *History* and before Cato's *Origines* and would thus presumably have been composed in Greek. Velleius Paterculus tells us, however (1.6.6), that Aemilius Sura was the first Roman author to reckon Rome and its rule over other nations and countries as one empire in a series of world empires.[5] This partly Greek, partly Near Eastern theory of a succession of world empires and the place Rome came to hold in it, would much later, in Christian historiography, take on the greatest significance (see below, Ch. 7.3.3, pp. 233ff.).

3.2 Early Annalistic Writing (II)

Roman historians after Fabius at first imitated his use of the Greek language. After *Cato*, however, this would change. Cato indeed introduced innovations, some of which were appropriated by his successors, while others were destined to remained unique. Latin became in this way the language of general choice. Roman historians thus abandoned the audience that had occasioned the rise of Roman historiography (see above, Ch. 3, p. 42), and exclusively addressed their fellow citizens and their Italian allies. This had been the practice of Roman epic poetry from its inception (see below, Ch. 3.3, pp. 60f.). This shift from one language to another with its accompanying change in audience would have been unimaginable without a significant alteration in the aims and purposes of Roman historiography. On the one hand, the successful conclusion of their wars against Carthage as well as against the kingdoms of the Antigonids and Seleucids had relieved the Romans of the immediate need to justify their policies. Another factor was the gradual erosion of the high regard in which the Romans had held the Greeks. Many decades of intensive, but nevertheless often unsuccessful, diplomatic efforts to reshape the political organization of the Greek world had initially required explanations, but this need too had disappeared. In choosing Latin, Roman historiography returned to the purpose that remembrance of the past had served in Rome before the rise of historical writing: self-discovery and self-definition of what it meant to be Roman in relation to family (*gens*) and to community (see above, Ch. 2.1, pp. 34ff.).

An important change, both in content and in form, took place at the conclusion of the series of historians we treat here and at the beginning of a "new" period in Roman history (Rome's civil wars and the disintegration of Rome's nobility): current events became the preferred, if not the only, historical subject. This practice resulted perhaps from the rapid assimilation of the Greek author *Polybius* (circa 200–120 BC) whose historiography took up recent events exclusively and in whose work Rome's political and military actions were central (see below, Ch. 3.2.2, p. 58; Ch. 4, pp. 65f.; Ch. 4.1, pp. 66ff.). This alteration in Roman historiography's focus may also have led to a differentiation in terminology: *Annales* for narratives of the distant past; *Historiae* for works on so-called contemporary history. The distinction never, however, became entirely rigid, and could not, for linguistic reasons as well (for Tacitus' *Histories* and *Annals*, see below, Ch. 6.1.3, p. 138). Just as narratives concerned exclusively with contemporary history could simply clip the last part from continuous accounts, the *historical monograph* could similarly excerpt any number of thematically related years from the midst of a continuous narrative. The relationship of both historiographical types to *historia continua* or *perpetua* is thus analogous. It is therefore no surprise to find that the historical monograph develops around the same time as the narrower focus on current events or contemporary history. Although such monographs were at first written about events some generations removed from the present, they later took up themes primarily concerned with contemporary history (see below, Ch. 3.2.2, p. 58; Ch. 4.5.1, pp. 86f.). The monographic treatment of a topic could impose changes and limits on the practice of annalistic reporting, but it did not fundamentally exclude annalistic methods.

3.2.1 Marcus Porcius Cato

Marcus Porcius Cato (234–149 BC; Schönberger, *HRR* I CXXVII / 55, *CC*, *FRH* 3) came from the city of Tusculum in Latium and grew up in the countryside. He was one of the few men without senatorial ancestry who achieved political careers and thus gained admission as "new men" (*homines novi*) to Rome's ruling class. Cato, who had served as a soldier almost from the beginning of the Second Punic War, even managed to attain the highest offices. Already in 195 BC, he enjoyed administrative and military successes in Spain as a consul. His constant advocacy of the *mos maiorum* befit his attainment of the *censorship*, a post he won against great competition in 184 and that led to his acquisition of the cognomen *Censori(n)us* (see below, Ch. 3.2.2, p. 55). At a time of significant and continuously increasing Greek cultural influence in mid-Italy, Cato appeared time and time again as the spokesman for those leading politicians who opposed this trend. In this capacity, he secured the speedy departure from Rome in 155 of a Greek embassy whose number included philosophers. Despite these efforts, Cato did not escape Greek influence. He even claimed that he had himself derived much profit from his study of the Greeks and their culture, though remaining at a distance from them (Schönberger F. 356), and for this reason supported against innovation and new fashions what he considered ancient, tested, and true. Cato energetically opposed negative aspects of the nobility's ascendancy. With the exception of Carthage, he displayed an unbending sense of justice not only toward those who had been conquered by Rome, but also toward those who were not willing to subject themselves to Rome without a fight. All this made him over time an opponent of the Cornelii Scipiones. His combative style led to Cato's involvement in an extremely large number of trials as a defendant, but he allegedly defended himself successfully every time.

In court, but also in the Senate, Cato delivered numerous speeches, and he subsequently published written versions of them. Copies survived and were still read a hundred years later in the age of Cicero. His literary productions included more than speeches. He also wrote letters. He collected and edited maxims, which, despite his ostentatious dismissal of Greek culture, he often translated from Greek. He composed technical treatises, and because it survives in its entirety, his most important treatise for us is his *De agri cultura* (*On Agriculture*). As a strict and dutiful father concerned for his son's education, he wrote "*Books for my son Marcus*" (*Libri ad Marcum filium*). These volumes provided educational guides to farming, medicine, oratory, and Roman history. From about

170 BC he composed a history of Rome entitled *Origins* (*Origines*). We may assume that among all these literary productions Cato maintained a basic consistency and tenor in topics and details. Cato even incorporated some of his own speeches in his history (Schönberger FF. 91 ff., 112ff.). With the insertion of speeches Cato did something that had long been taken for granted in the Greek historiographical tradition, but which in Roman historiography had until then been unusual.

Cato wrote his *Origines*, as he had his other writings, in Latin, the first Roman history by a Roman author not composed in Greek. As Cato remarked in his criticism of his contemporary Postumius Albinus' Greek annals: one was not compelled to write in Greek (see above, Ch. 3.1.2, p. 49). This was, of course, true, so long as one no longer *primarily* aimed to have Greeks as readers of Roman historiographical works. The exclusion of such readers suited Cato's general attitude toward the Greeks (which we have just sketched), and all later authors whose native language was Latin followed Cato's lead in using Latin for historical writing (except Publius Rutilius Rufus who wrote a Roman history in Greek around 90 BC; *FGrH* 815, *HRR* I CCLIV / 187, *AR* III X / 2, *FRH* 13). In short, through his literary efforts Cato became the creator of Latin prose.

According to the admittedly rather cursory summaries available to us in the biography of Cato by *Cornelius Nepos* (3.2–4; see below, Ch. 4.4, p. 82), Cato, like his predecessors, began his seven-volume historical work with the origins of Rome, and he treated all of Roman history until far into his own day. In fact, according to the dating of the trial described in fragments 112ff., he brought his history down to the year of his death in 149. Book 1 was devoted to the pre-history of Rome in the story of Aeneas, the foundation of the city by Romulus (here 751 BC), and the monarchy to its end 244 years later. The total time elapsed for all this, according to the conventions of Cato's day, was seven hundred years. Books 2 and 3 handled the Roman Republic until the year before the First Punic War (507 to at most 265/264 BC). Cato included foundation legends (or histories) of the cities and peoples of Italy, hence the title of the work, *Origines*, in the plural. With this expansion in his subject matter, Cato compensated for the poverty of the inscriptional evidence on offer in the priestly almanacs, a poverty he had himself deplored, for the early history of Rome (see above, Ch. 2.2, p. 37). Cato set a new tone with his view beyond Rome to its nearer and farther neighbors and by treating them on par with Rome itself in terms of form and content. Indeed, Cato was ahead of his times: the peoples of Italy would be unable to achieve equal political and legal rights with the Romans for another two or three generations after Cato and then only after overcoming a deep-seated opposition in Rome itself. Each (foundation) history included geographical and ethnographical descriptions (Schönberger FF. 33ff. = HRR FF. 31ff. = CC / FRH 2.1ff.). Cato did not follow a chronological, and certainly not an annalistic, approach, but instead organized his material geographically according to locations. This procedure raises the question of how much chronological continuity might have existed within these two books. Petzold [Bibl. §2] conjectures a large gap in the history of Rome itself from 450 to circa 264. Flach [Bibl. §1.3], however, has pointed out that Cato treats the Gallic invasion of 390 BC in either his second or third book, and that Cato must have narrated its beginnings in connection with the Etruscan city of Clusium (indications for this may be found in Schönberger FF. 34ff. = HRR FF. 34ff. = CC / FRH 2.3ff.).

On the one hand, Books 1–3 form a group with their account of origins. Books 4–7 form another. These latter books treated the great international developments of the recent past and present that precipitated or ensured Rome's expansion from the First Punic War to the Spanish wars. Here too the main organizational principle was not arrangement according to annual office, but instead according to wars, their theaters, and their significance (according to Nepos Cato 3.2–4 passim). As opposed to Fabius Pictor (see above, Ch. 3.1.1, pp. 43f.), Cato's thematic organization and consequent departure from a purely annalistic scheme were motivated not by the poverty of his sources, but arose instead through the conscious choices he made in the arrangement of his materials. Cato's later volumes are similar to his earlier ones in this way too. They speak a great deal about "land and people," as we may observe in his description of the Carthaginian constitution (Schönberger F. 82 = HRR F. 80 = CC / FRH 4.3).

As with his somewhat later Greek contemporary Polybius (1.1.5), we generally see Cato's true narrative goal in the defeat of the Macedonian monarchy in 168/167 BC. He must have reached this point by the end of the fifth volume. According to this logic, Cato would have composed Books 6 and 7 as supplements to what he had originally planned on covering. Analogously, Polybius continued his work beyond the "landmark" of 168/167 to another historically convenient endpoint: 146 BC. Nevertheless, a difference demands our attention. As we noted earlier, the year of Cato's death and the last year reached by his history coincide. We must conclude from this that, unlike Polybius, Cato continued to write without a new and well-defined goal, thus reaching 149 BC at the latest. We cannnot therefore answer the question of whether Cato completed his *Origines*, and, given the circumstances under which he was writing, we cannot even ask what endpoint the author may have set as his goal. Cato's successive continuations remind one of Ennius, who composed his epic, the *Annales*, before Cato (see below, Ch. 3.3, pp. 61f.). A further problem is occasioned by Cato's title for the work – *Origins* (*Origines*) – in light of the scope of the entire work. If one conceives of the Greek *ktisis* as "foundation history," then the title suits not even Books 1–5 (contra Flach [Bibl. §1.3] pp. 71ff.), but instead only Book 1 (on Rome) and Books 2–3 (on Italy). Did Cato at first wish only to write foundation history and the early history of Rome and Italy? In that case, he would have summarized the *ktisis* (which the Greeks always wrote for just one city at a time) for a number of histories of cities and peoples, and, in doing so, he would have combined numerous foundation stories into a novel whole. He would thereby have originated yet another innovation in Roman historiography (see above, Ch. 3, pp. 42f.).

Cato's main focus was on political events (Nepos *Cato* 3.3: *quae fierent*). We may add to this category another category that may seem surprising in so sober a Roman as Cato: "things that amaze or worthy of admiration" (Nepos: *quae viderentur admiranda*). Of course, under the category of *admiranda*, Cato (as opposed to many ancient writers) did not collect sensational events so much as morally exemplary and heroic deeds. These deeds were not always free of drastic reversals of fortune, as, for example, the story of a certain Roman tribune, who was ready to sacrifice his life in Sicily during the First Punic War, but, contrary to expectation, survived. Unlike the Greek Leonidas, he received scant praise for his proven heroism (Schönberger F. 83 = *HRR* F. 83 = *CC / FRH* F. 4.7a). Cato's moral exemplars are not at all forced or overly dramatic, but instead provide sober and simple representations of objective conduct. This derives primarily from the fact that Cato's praiseworthy examples do not serve to praise individuals. In the example we cited above, Cato speaks continuously of "a (military) tribune" without mentioning his name. This is even more striking when we consider that he compares the unnamed Roman tribune with a well-known hero of Greek history, whom he naturally calls by name: Leonidas. Cato's basic approach to past Romans follows the same pattern as his treatment of this tribune: he never calls them by their names, but instead continuously identifies them through the political and military offices that provide the key to their place in Rome's civic and social hierarchy, but which fail to individualize them (Schönberger FF. 85 and 88 = *HRR* FF. 88–86 = *CC / FRH* 4.11 and 13; Nepos *Cato* 3.4).

In the portion of the *Origines* devoted to contemporary history, Cato's impersonal praise for historical actors stands, however, in stark contrast with his bitter denunciation and even personal attacks on select individuals. These denounced individuals, as opposed to those praised, are named by Cato. This is made possible formally by the incorporation of Cato's own speeches (as discussed above) into the structure of his historical work. Cato consciously uses this means to smear more permanently his contemporary, the former praetor, Publius Servius Galba, who was acquitted by a Roman court (wrongly in Cato's opinion) on a charge of violating international law. But more stands behind these personal attacks on select contemporaries than mere disapproval of individuals. Cato believed that during his own lifetime the Romans had turned from long-enduring and generally sound values to corrupting influences, and it was always these that he attacked passionately and bitterly again and again, even if in vain (Livy 34.1–8; Plutarch *Cato* 16.7 and 19.4; Schönberger F. 325). As subject matter for narrative history, such moral critique was something new in Rome.

As a writer of history, Cato thus brought numerous innovations: in language, by making the transition from Greek to Latin; in subject matter, by treating social, religious and moral critique as topics in their own right and by emphasizing the Italian peninsula as opposed to just Rome; and in form, by moving away from the annalistic principle in favor of a primarily thematic organization and by integrating a large number of speeches. Greek historiography offered models for his two formal innovations, so Cato's choice of Latin as a literary language was certainly not motivated by a move away from the Greek literary world, whose influence in Rome would reach its peak in the mid- and late first century BC (see above, Ch. 1.1, pp. 10f.). Cato's *Origines* exerted considerable influence. Nevertheless, their many innovations in content and form failed to find wholesale adoption. The work later became a treasure trove for quotation, although later, at a time when tastes had changed, it was criticized as fundamentally lacking in *doctrina* (Nepos *Cato* 3.4), which most likely means that Cato's work lacked erudition in the sense of a Greek philosophical outlook. Cato's preferred method of organizing his material primarily according to theme might have led others to produce historical monographs, but, as such, his work served as a model for hardly a single historian. The narration of all Roman history, or long stretches of it, generally remained chained to the annalistic scheme.

3.2.2 Other authors (from Cassius Hemina to Sempronius Asellio)

Gaius Cassius Hemina (*HRR* I CLXV / 98, *AR* II IX / 2 *FRH* 6) wrote *Annals* in four books: (1) the early history of Italy and the saga of Aeneas,

(2) Rome's foundation and early history to the sack of the city by Gauls around 390 BC (?), (3) Rome's subsequent history to the outbreak of the Second Punic War, and (4) the Second Punic War. On the other hand, a fragment that would fall under the year 146 BC raises questions about possible continuations as well as about the final endpoint and the date of his work's composition (*HRR* F. 39 = *AR* / *FRH* F. 42). Certain features recall Cato: an interest in religion (*HRR* FF. 18 and 20 = *AR* / *FRH* FF. 21, 23), an interest in social and cultural themes (*HRR* F. 13 = *AR* / *FRH* F. 16), and an interest in the foundation of cities in Italy (*HRR* FF. 2 and 3 = *AR* / *FRH* FF. 2, 3). We may add etymological explanations (*HRR* FF. 2, 3, 4 = *AR* / *FRH* FF. 2, 3, 4) and the linking of Italic-Roman chronology with the Greek chronology of Homer and Hesiod (*HRR* F. 8 = *AR* / *FRH* F. 12). Aside from a citation by just one late historian, Appian, Hemina was otherwise consulted only by antiquarians interested in the history of Rome's cults in the distant past, and he was cited by them for this purpose (see below, Ch. 6.2.2, pp. 164f.; Ch. 4.6, pp. 96f.). This religious focus may have been, but was not necessarily, characteristic of his work in general.

Lucius Calpurnius Piso (*HRR* I CLXXXI / 120, *AR* II XIX / 18, *FRH* 7) earned the cognomen "Frugi" for honesty and integrity and, like Cato, the cognomen "Censorius" for his fundamentally rigid moral outlook. As a tribune of the *plebs* in 149 BC, he was responsible for establishing a permanent commission on extortion in order to combat more efficiently a principal evil in Rome's contemporary administration of the provinces: the plundering of subjects by their governors. As consul in 133 BC, he opposed the agrarian reforms of Tiberius Sempronius Gracchus and fought in Sicily against rebellious slaves. His stylistically plain *Annales* extended in seven volumes from the origins of Rome to 146 BC. He displays antiquarian and mythological interests, and he freely criticizes and reinterprets the myths and legends of early Roman history on a rational basis (cf., e.g., *HRR* F. 5 = *AR* / *FRH* F. 7, where he justifies Tarpeia). He also makes an effort to correct the chronology of the Roman kings (*HRR* F. 15 = *AR* / *FRH* F. 17: Tarquinius Superbus is not the son, but instead the grandson of Tarquinius Priscus). Such efforts did not, however, prevent him from including interesting anecdotes (*HRR* FF. 8, 27, 33 = *AR* / *FRH* FF. 10, 30, 36).

Piso's moralizing contrast of earlier competence with contemporary corruption could well have had Cato's moral critique of his own times as a model. Piso was nevertheless the first historian who not only identified Rome's falling away from the *mos maiorum*, but also pinpointed it with an exact date. Later historians followed his lead in this effort (one that strikes us today as odd), although they always employed of necessity more recent (that is, later) dates for the Romans' *turning point* from good to bad behavior. It could be that Piso even differentiated two turning points: one possibly in connection with the influx of luxury and Rome's addiction to it in 187 BC (*HRR* F. 34 = *AR* / *FRH* F. 37) and the other in 154 BC when Rome's loss of all shame was made explicitly manifest. During the censorship of Marcus Valerius Messalla and Gaius Cassius Longinus, a palm tree collapsed that had grown after the final triumph of the Romans over the Macedonian kings (168 BC) from the altar of the chief god Jupiter on the Capitol, and had served as an icon of victory. A fig tree, the manifest symbol of sensuality, sprouted in its place (*HRR* F. 38 = *AR* / *FRH* F. 41). For this author, the occasion for the decisive turn from modesty to shamelessness appears to have been the effort by the two censors of 154 BC to build a theater of stone (sena-torial opposition successfully prevented them from doing so). These censors, rather than adhering to the duties of their office, i.e., insisting upon and upholding the *mos maiorum*, had attempted to introduce unconventional, and thus immoral, ways. It is no surprise that Piso found the youth of his day immoral, especially in relations between the sexes (*HRR* F. 40 = *FRH* F. 43), and just as unsurprising that Piso found literary imitators when they assessed the youth of their own day (cf. Sallust *Catiline* 12–14, esp. 14.2; discussed below, Ch. 4.5.1 pp. 87f.).

Gnaeus Gellius (*HRR* I CCIV / 148, *AR* II XLIX / 71, *FRH* 10) proved that it was possible to provide a detailed narrative of more ancient Roman history, despite a complete lack of reliable information and before the publication of *Scaevola's* priestly almanacs (see above, Ch. 2.2, p. 38). His Roman history ran from its beginnings to at least the year 146 BC. In his second book, he described the capture of the Sabine women shortly after the foundation of Rome (*HRR* / *AR* / *FRH* FF. 10–13), and by the 30th or 31st book, he was just beginning to narrate the year 216 BC (*HRR* F. 26 = *AR* / *FRH* F. 27). He also (or perhaps even primarily) filled the books devoted to early Roman history with general historical information and antiquarian details, that is, from a modern point of view, with cultural developments such as the inventor and the origin of the alphabet, of building with clay, of smelting metal, and of weights and measures (*HRR* FF. 1–6 = *AR* / *FRH* 1–5; see below, Ch. 4.6, pp. 96f.). It remains uncertain whether Gellius' work appeared in exactly 97 volumes (*HRR* F. 29 = *AR* / *FRH* F. 30/31), of which, however, over sixty were devoted to the most recent seventy years (or a bit longer). His influence on later narratives of early Roman history, including most likely Scaevola's edition of the priestly almanacs, could have been profound (see above, Ch. 2.2, p. 39). Dionysius of Halicarnassus clearly used his work for the early history of Rome (see below, Ch. 5.2.2, p. 115).

A *Gaius Fannius* (*HRR* I CXCIII / 139, *AR* II XXXIII / 44, *FRH* 9) was the son-in-law of Laelius. Laelius, for his part, was the close friend of the younger Publius Cornelius Scipio. This Scipio was the destroyer of Carthage and Numantia (the center of Spanish resistance), and the opponent of his relative Tiberius Sempronius Gracchus' agrarian reforms. In 146 BC, Fannius fought as a soldier in the conquest of Carthage and later in Spain. In 122, he was consul and, for a time, allied with Gaius Sempronius Gracchus, but he parted from him in a difference over the question of extending Roman citizenship. Fannius was active too as a lawyer and advocate. The Roman history of this same (?) Fannius ranged from the origins (?) of Rome to his own day. Multiple mentions of the city of Drepanum / Drepana in Book 8 (*HRR* / *AR* / *FRH* F. 3) could apply as easily to the First Punic War (264–221 BC) as to either of the two Sicilian slave wars (135–132 and 104–101). As a result, very different reconstructions of his work are possible.

Lucius Coelius Antipater (*HRR* I CCXI / 158, *AR* II XLI / 50, *FRH* 11) was, as we conclude from his Greek third name, likely the descendant of a non-Roman ex-slave who had been granted citizenship. As a grown man in the 120s BC, he was personally acquainted with Gaius Sempronius Gracchus. He was active professionally as a jurist and as a teacher of oratory, which at that time in Rome was an exclusively Greek occupation. After 120 BC, he wrote Latin literature's first *historical monograph*, a history of the Second Punic War in seven books. Like Hellenistic historical works on Alexander the Great, it had a main hero: Hannibal's conqueror, Publius Cornelius Scipio Africanus. To the extent that Antipater exceeds his chronological limits, he does so from time to time in internal digressions. It can be no accident that he dedicates the work to his contemporary, Lucius Aelius Stilo, the founder of Latin philology, inasmuch as Coelius made use of many and varied linguistic and stylistic devices in conformance with current rhetorical and literary fashions. Cicero considered him "the first real author among Roman historians" (von Albrecht [Bibl. §1.3] p. 307), and of this he was completely convinced (Cicero *De oratore* 2.5ff.; *De legibus* 1.6). *Cato* had incorporated into his Roman history speeches that he had himself delivered and which were thus authentic. Coelius was likely the first Latin historiographer to follow Greek usage, rewriting or, in the worst case, completely inventing speeches (see above, Ch. 1.3.1, pp. 21f.). Coelius did not shy away from invention even outside his speeches, if such invention corresponded to the contemporary taste or served to heighten the drama or permitted the gods to play a role and intervene in earthly affairs (for this last example, see *HRR / AR / FRH* F. 11, where Coelius follows the Greek historian Silenus, and *HRR* F. 20 = *AR / FRH* F. 20b). Only Coelius, for example, has the fleet brought by Publius Cornelius Scipio from Sicily to North Africa driven off course by a violent storm shortly before land-fall, almost sinking, and the soldiers piteously scrambling to land in disorder and without weapons (*HRR* F. 40 = *AR / FRH* F. 47). We must, however, credit Coelius with achievements of a different order: exact study of the sources. Approximately eighty years after the events he described, he made use of orally transmitted testimony as well as reports even from the enemy side, as, for example, the work of *Silenus* of Caleacte (see above, Ch. 3.1.1, p. 46). In general, he adhered to the accounts of *Polybius* and *Cato*. From time to time, he told the same event several times in succession according to the versions of divergent sources, as, for example, the death of Gaius Claudius Marcellus in 208 BC first according to oral tradition, then according to the written version of a funeral oration delivered by the fallen commander's son, and then accord-ing to his own researches (here he does not name his sources; *HRR* F. 29 = *AR / FRH* F. 36). Coelius' influence on late republican and impe-rial literature was considerable; it is immediately perceptible especially in Livy (see below, Ch. 5.1, pp. 104f.).

As a young man, *Sempronius Asellio* (*HRR* I CCXLII / 179, *AR* II LIV / 84, *FRH* 12) – not to be confused with Lucius Sempronius Tuditanus (*HRR* I CCI / 143, *AR* II XXVIII / 40, *FRH* 8) who com-posed a work on political offices and public institutions – served as a military tribune in the war against Numantia (until 133 BC). Of his sub-sequent career in public service, we know nothing. Decades later he was the first Roman to write purely contemporary history, most likely under the title *Rerum gestarum libri* (*Books of Deeds Accomplished*) or *Historiae*. It apparently extended from 168 or 146 BC to at least (?) the assassina-tion of the tribune Livius Drusus in 91, which was the signal for revolt, and the Social War of the Italians against Rome (91–89). One can explain this restriction to the most recent of events as a result of the annalistic method. Its application compelled exact attention to details that existed in worthwhile abundance only for the recent past. Of course, an annalistic and chronological scheme was not Sempronius' goal, but it does serve to link the actions of various principal figures in a variety of places and different areas as well as the presentation of intent (*consilium*) and moti-vation (*ratio*) for each action (*HRR / AR / FRH* FF. 1–2). Behind all this we may perceive Asellio's obvious intent to employ historiography as a means to teach political behavior in general and to promote patriotic conduct in particular. This goal, as the author makes clear, could hardly be achieved through a mere collocation of facts.

Sempronius is polemically caustic when he opposes "the writing of history" (*historias scribere*) to "telling stories to little boys" (*fabulas pueris narrare*), under which rubric he deprecates the genre of *Annales*. This makes it difficult, on the one hand, to identify the historiographers he means, and should not induce the reader to look for precise authors or works (*contra* Flach [Bibl. § 1.3], p. 83). On the other hand, it enables us to classify this historian in a general literary and rhetorical way as well as a within a specific historiographical tradition. Sempronius' irreconcilable twofold division of true "history" from false "children's stories," apparently leaves no room for a mediating "poetic truth" in the customary tripartite division: *historia, argumentum*, and *fabula* (see above, Ch. 1.3.2, pp. 26f. with note 7, pp. 256f.; and below, Ch. 3.3, p. 62). Asellio's polemical criticism of Greek historiographers of the Hellenistic period, follows the lead above all of Timaeus of Tauromenium (*FGrH* 566), and even more of *Polybius* with his harsh attacks against many of the historians who preceded him, and in particular against Timaeus (see especially Polybius Book 12). The substantial similarity or rather almost identical conception of "pragmatic" historiography in Polybius (11.18a; cf. 19a) and in the fragments Sempronius (1–2) demonstrate that the author of the latter was acquainted with the former, agreed with one of his central priciples, and adopted it as his own. Sempronius likely also followed Polybius in his disdain for rhetorically embellished historical writing. Perhaps this attitude, which ran counter to then-prevailing fashion, was the reason for the limited influence of Sempronius' *Res gestae* (but compare below, Ch. 4.1, p. 69, on Cornelius Sisenna).

3.3 Early Historical Epic in Rome (Naevius and Ennius)

At the same time as Roman historiography, the epic poetry of the Romans took up historical subjects. One is sometimes tempted to see a parallel development and perhaps even complete analogy. Nevertheless, we may also discern essential differences between early Roman historiography and epic. One crucial difference: the authors of these poems with historical content (like the early poets in Rome in general) did not belong to Rome's ruling class. In fact, they were not from Rome or even Roman citizens. Of course, they participated after their fashion in Rome's political life, and fought on Rome's side in the period's major wars. These poets wrote for Romans, and therefore from the beginning did not use Greek, but instead the Latin language. Like later annalistic authors who wrote in Latin (see above, Ch. 3.2, p. 49), they wished to make the Romans of their day aware of their own actions and ancestors, not convince the outside world of the justice of Rome's actions. From the point of view of style and form, the development of our two surviving examples of Roman historical epic ran a course exactly opposite to that of early annalistic writing (in prose): first the monograph – with, of course extensive pre-history – and then a complete history constructed on an annalistic scheme. The question must remain open whether this is simply coincidence.

Naevius (circa 265–200 BC; in the edition of Barchiesi) was a Roman soldier in the First Punic War. In his poetry, he attacked the family of the Caecilii Metelli, which belonged to the nobility, and he ridiculed Scipio Africanus. He composed stage plays and an epic, the *Bellum Punicum*. In his epic, he related not just the Punic War itself, but also through excursuses its pre-history, beginning with Aeneas. We find recent events with historical references to the distant past. The style of the fragments is partly poetic, partly simple and concise, and to that extent reminiscent of the kind of chronicle one finds on contemporary grave inscriptions (see above, Ch. 2.1, p. 35).

Quintus Ennius (239–169 BC; in the edition of Skutsch) participated in the Second Punic War on the Roman side where he was "discovered" by Cato, who brought him back to Rome. He was soon associating with such important politicians of the time as Publius Cornelius Scipio Africanus (Major), whose deeds he celebrated. We are told that, after his death, his statue was placed in the tomb of the Scipios. In the capacity of poet, he accompanied the consul Marcus Fulvius Nobilior in 189 BC on his campaign against the northwestern Greek Aetolians. He finally became a Roman citizen in 184. Ennius narrated the history of Rome from Aeneas to his own day in 18 books of *Annales*. Corresponding to the availability of source material and with results like those of his prose-writing colleagues, Ennius provides ever-increasing detail as he approaches his own day. By the beginning of Book 7, Ennius had already reached the beginning of the First Punic War. He sketched it only briefly, presumably because he had in mind Naevius' poem, which had already covered this ground. Only afterwards and most likely first with the Second Macedonian War (about 200 BC) did his presentation become expansive. The endpoint he reaches in Book 18 was not his original goal. As the beginnings of Books 7 and 10 show in particular, he composed and published successive installments with varied and extended aims.

Under the influence of Homer, who represented the epitome of epic, and relying on him for poetical technique and diction, Ennius wrote history in an elevated epic style. Ennius may well have used the *Annales* of *Fabius Pictor* (see above, Ch. 3.1.1, p. 43), but, in light of his high praise for Scipio Africanus, he did so, in respect to the most recent past, in spite of Fabius Pictor's inherent pro-Fabian and anti-Scipionic bias (see above, Ch. 3.1.1, p. 47). Ennius, who was a popular and favorite author, could well have served as a source for later writers of Roman history.

Even though we are able to compare only fragments of early epics with fragments of early prose histories, and despite the differences we have just noted, the correspondence of subject matter and principal aim is apparent. In light of the peculiarities of ancient literary production, this requires explanation only for modern readers of Greek and Latin literature. Ancient literary and rhetorical theory did not oppose poetry's concept of truth to history's. What was "fictional," and therefore "impossible" or "unreal," was not contrasted with what was "true." Instead, poetry posited a middle way: that which was "invented, but in conformance with reality as we experience it" (in Roman parlance, this was the *argumentum*, the mediating term between *fabula* and *historia*: see above, Ch. 1.3.2, pp. 26f.). This middle way corresponded to poetic practice well before the development of literary and rhetorical theory. Just as historiographers hoped not just to teach, but also to entertain, poets too aimed not only to give pleasure (*delectare*) and to engage the emotions (*movere*), but also to teach (*docere*). They accomplished these goals insofar as they attempted in their fiction to imitate reality or "life." This imitation resulted sometimes in the appropriation of material directly from life, even though invention, the very thing that distinguished the content of poetry from other genres, was lost in the process. For this reason, works of poetry could offer not just general philosophical enlightenment and ethical teaching, but also instruction in such practical matters as agriculture. The genre of didactic poetry, which corresponded in form to epic, arose very early for the express purpose of education and instruction. Although we cannot, without restriction, view the works of early Roman epic as didactic poems, these works did indeed provide theoretical knowledge in a specific area; and this instruction was apparently the aim of their poets – just as it was for those who composed history in prose.

4

The Historiography of Rome between the Fronts of the Civil Wars

The political activities of the brothers Tiberius and Gaius Sempronius Gracchus (133–121 BC) met with great resistance: protest movements, threats of violence, assassinations, and civil wars. Contemporaries experienced these events, and regarded them, as fundamentally different from those of earlier times. A fissure opened in Rome's ruling class that would not be closed for some one hundred years. Optimates approved the continued predominance of a purely senatorial regime. Populares favored a regime that included significant participation of tribunes and popular assemblies. These divisions among the citizenry led to contradictory evaluations of both recent and current events within historiography. The Roman historiographer could hardly come to these events objectively in a spirit of non-partisan and scientific inquiry. Instead, he derived his point of view for the most part either directly from his own position in the senatorial order or indirectly through his dependent status as a client to a particular senatorial clan (compare above, Ch. 1.3.2, pp. 31f.; Ch. 2.1, pp. 34f.; Ch. 2.2, pp. 36f.; Ch. 3.1.1, pp. 47f.). As a result of this rift (from then on omnipresent), Rome's ruling elites lost their generally unified vision of what constituted "truth," and what had formerly been the consensus view became just one of many possible positions, diverging from one another in various degrees or even standing in opposition to one another. This also permitted portions of the more remote past to be viewed from other and sometimes extremely different angles. The struggle of the orders of the fifth to fourth centuries BC, for example, were interpreted, and reinterpreted, according to one's view of the effect

Roman Historiography: An Introduction to its Basic Aspects and Development,
First Edition. Andreas Mehl.
© 2014 Hans-Friedrich Mueller. Published 2014 by Blackwell Publishing Ltd.

of the Gracchi's efforts at reform. A personalization of political debate quickly ensued in Rome that included both verbal assaults and acts of violence, as well as increasing concentration on the deeds and careers of just a few "great" men. A corresponding historiography arose geared to this trend or, in some cases, oriented even to one man in particular. Even contemporaries criticized the one-sidedness of most works composed under the temporary dictatorship of Lucius Cornelius Sulla (82–79 BC). This more recent *annalistic* writing (so-called) was either indebted or opposed to him. A few generations later in the early Principate (and consequently an age that faced similar difficulties in treating its own recent history), the outbreak of the civil wars was identified as the time when Roman historiography first began to lose its dedication to truth (Seneca, *De vita patris*, *HRR* II, 98. F. 1).

Similarly, just as the Roman republic lost its ideal unity in contemporary political practice as well as in the historical understanding of it, so also could it slip from view as a possession that was worth preserving. At the very least, doctrines derived from Greek philosophy (which from that time on was very much pursued at Rome) could result in treating the Roman state in relative terms. With the Epicurean theses that our world is not unique, that many worlds appear and disappear without divine intervention, and that religion consists of an inner attitude, not ritual, the didactic poem of Cicero's contemporary Lucretius (*De rerum natura* 2.1084–1092; 5.1198–1203) rocked two foundations of traditional Roman thinking about the nature of the world and the state. Although he edited and published Lucretius' poem after the poet's death, Cicero could nevertheless cling steadfastly to the uniqueness of the Roman state, and contemporary historiography could likewise continue to describe state ritual. The Roman republic, however, no longer played a role in the calculations of many leading politicians – even if, in contrast to Caesar, they did not say so openly (Suetonius *Caesar* 77; for Caesar's contemporary antagonist Pompey, compare, for example, Cicero *Letters to Atticus* 8.11). In the midst of a crisis that could lead to complete despair, one poet searched for, and obtained, inner freedom through philosophy (Lucretius), and another through his personal lifestyle (Catullus), unleashing thereby new values of individuality and subjectivity in personal poetry (this as early as Lucilius), but many politicians and intellectuals instead searched for the restoration of inner self-confidence in ancient Roman virtues. For this very reason, Cicero and Sallust directed their gaze back toward early Rome. And, for this reason too, Cicero sketched the history of the Roman constitution in the second book of *On the State* (*De re publica*), a treatise outlining his political philosophy.

Both *Cicero* and *Sallust* stressed the intrinsic value of literary endeavors. Like Lucretius, the first among the poets to do so, they developed and promoted a new, more interior conception of fame. Aside from triumphal imagery, this conception had nothing in common with the traditional celebrity of the conquering Roman general. Both authors thereby distanced themselves from that traditional incentive to participate actively in public life and on behalf of the community, which, as a consequence of their arguments concerning early epochs of Roman history, they would have had to advocate. Contrary to their intentions, they effectively proved that antiquity could no longer be rendered useful or relevant to the present, but served instead simply for nostalgic reminiscence.

Shifts in historical interests and focus as well as changes in the manner in which Roman history itself or individual periods and their historical contexts were viewed and treated also resulted in formal or generic innovations. At the beginning of the civil wars, that is, from a literary historical perspective, still in the era of earlier *annalistic* writing, we find departures from a strict scheme of annual reports (see above Ch. 3.2, pp. 49f.; Ch. 3.2.2, pp. 55ff.). This trend grew more pronounced in subsequent decades. Authors narrated early Roman history either in abbreviated fashion or abstained from it altogether, sometimes appending their own narratives to existing works as a sort of continuation (*historia continua* or *perpetua*). Increasingly popular too was the *monograph* which focused exclusively on a select historical topic. Possible subjects abounded in the events and circumstances of the civil wars. Indeed, they called out for treatment. Many such works and their authors are known today only by their names and titles (but compare Ch. 4.5.1, p. 86, on Sallust). All the historiographical variants we mention here had one thing in common: significant, or even exclusive, attention of historical writers to recent history and the events of their own lifetimes.

In the epochs we treat here increasing focus on individuals led to the development (in the following order) of autobiography and biography, and, in order to meet the need for self-justification, a new type of *commentarius* (the Latin word could refer to sketchbooks, memoranda, and memoirs as well as personal commentary). These literary genres did not represent (at least not necessarily) historiography, but not only did they provide material for historical writing, they were also very similar to it. Because the ancient world considered it self-evident that historiography should be classified as literature, *literary* and *rhetorical* criteria determine to what extent we consider a work with some general historical content a piece of historical writing per se (see above, Ch. 1.3.1, pp. 17ff.; and below, Ch. 4.3, pp. 79ff.). How closely an author's (auto-)biography or memoirs resembled "historiography" depended not on the extent or intensity of his documentary researches (*Quellenforschung*), but was instead above all a function of how his report reshaped and expanded his materials and how impressively he made the transition from mere documentation to dramatization. In this regard, Cicero and Caesar's accomplishments were substantial. Because of the possibility in principle that works of such literary genres might become historiographical works, we include these genres as part of our study (see above, Ch. 4.2, pp. 69ff.; Ch. 4.3, p. 81).

4.1 Later Annalistic Writing: Optimates vs. Populares and Traditional Annalistic Writing vs. Contemporary History

Later annalistic writing (so-called) is, despite the partisanship we have just discussed and its consequent sacrifice of historical trustworthiness, extraordinarily important for us. The complete presentation of Roman history that became *classical* was *Livy's*: archaic Rome, the monarchy, and the Republic until the dictatorship of Sulla, therefore the single largest stretch of Roman history by far in a single work, and one that reached into the Augustan period. All of this rested on the work of these later annalistic writers (see below Ch. 5.1, p. 104).

Quintus Claudius Quadrigarius (*HRR* I CCLXXXV / 205, *AR* III XXIII / 13, *FRH* 14) was likely the client of an important family and was optimate in outlook (*HRR* FF. 79 and 83 = *AR* / *FRH* FF. 80 and 84). In an unconventionally abrupt style, with the introduction of anecdotes (*HRR* FF. 40 and 80 = *AR* / *FRH* FF. 40a and 81) and, as noted already in antiquity, with a propensity to supply exaggerated casualty figures for all Rome's enemies (*HRR* / *AR* / *FRH* FF. 62 and 63), Claudius also aimed to entertain his readers (*HRR* / *AR* / *FRH* F. 10b). To the extent that we identify him with the "Claudius" mentioned by Livy (25.39 and 35.14), he appears to have reworked an early annalistic source composed in Greek by Gaius Acilius. He seems, moreover, to have omitted the period before the Gallic invasion on the grounds that it was too legendary, but to have used Acilius' work for the period up to the 180s and then to have continued the narrative into his own times, i.e., to (minimally) the time of Sulla's dictatorship. From our own point of view, it must remain an open question whether or not Claudius' estimation was correct about the reliability of the source material after the decisive break he drew at the Gallic invasion. This break has, however, directly or indirectly influenced some modern presentations of Roman history. The structure of Claudius' work reveals a definite preference for contemporary history. Of his 23-volume history, he devoted five books to the approximately two centuries from the Gallic invasion to the Second Punic War, whereas another five books treat the brief ten- to twenty-year period from the conflict between Marians and Sullans at the beginning of the 80s to the end of the dictatorship of Sulla in 79 BC or perhaps to events after it (*HRR* F. 95 = *AR / FRH* F. 96; 80 or 73 BC). This practice, which annalistic writers repeatedly employed as a compromise between the generic requirements of packaging historical events in equivalent and sequential yearbooks and the demands of writing up contemporary history, resulted in detailed accounts of current events that often proved very useful sources for subsequent historical writers. For this reason, Livy frequently cites the *Annales* of Claudius Quadrigarius, although never from their first five books.

*Valerius Antia*s (*HRR* I CCCV / 238, *AR* III LXIII / 104, *FRH* 15) wrote the history of Rome in 75 books from its beginnings to the outbreak of the Social War ("War with the Allies") in 91 or to Sulla's resignation of the dictatorship in 79 or perhaps even to his death in 78 BC, but in all events as high praise to his own *gens* (clan). Borrowings from his work that appear in Dionysius of Halicarnassus, Livy, and Plutarch demonstrate that he bestowed political offices on Valerii that the general historical tradition ascribes to members of other *gentes* (clans). He also attributed heroic deeds to Valerii in Rome's wars against the Sabines. In fact, only Valerius describes these wars from the end of the sixth to the middle of the fifth century at all (compare especially Dionysius of Halicarnassus 5.37ff.). We may at present view them with great certainty as inventions. At least to the same extent as Claudius Quadrigarius, Valerius exaggerated the numbers of fallen enemies (*HRR* FF. 29 and 32 = *AR / FRH* FF. 30 and 33). Valerius held even more steadfastly than Claudius, however, to the principle of reporting events according to a yearly scheme, though he did sometimes collect the events of several years together and, like Claudius, brought in all manner of stories for entertainment. Valerius was an important source for Livy.

Gaius Licinius Macer (*HRR* I CCCL / 298, *AR* III L / 89, *FRH* 17) was a tribune of the *plebs* in 73 BC, a time when the restrictions placed on the office by Sulla were still in effect. Macer agitated for the restoration of the rights of the people's tribunes as a way to restore the honor of the Roman people (for his speech to this effect, see Sallust *Historiae* 3.48). Prosecuted and convicted on the charge of extortion before Cicero (as praetor) in 66, he committed suicide. He left behind an incomplete historical work that already in its second book was narrating the war the Romans fought against the Greek city of Tarentum in southern Italy and King Pyrrhus of Epirus from 282 BC (*HRR* F. 20 = *AR* / *FRH* F. 21). Because this fragment cannot be dismissed as a preview or excursus, we must consider untenable Frier's considered inference ([Bibl. §2], p. 154) that Macer aimed at, or achieved, an endpoint with the *Lex Hortensia* as a conclusion to the conflict of the orders in 287 or even earlier (Flach [Bibl. §1.3], p. 89], is not clear on this point). Just as his political career proves him a *popularis*, this point of view appears repeatedly throughout his historical work, even among events and persons from early Roman history, especially in his narration of the conflict of the orders in the fifth and fourth centuries BC. The author also tells the story of the rise of plebeian *gentes* to the nobility, and he does not neglect the achievements of members of his own *gens* on the side of the *plebs*. He does this (and may on this account be compared with Valerius Antias) even against the prevailing historical tradition (*HRR* F. 16 = *AR* / *FRH* F. 17). This aside, he exercised practical reason in his estimations of myths and legends, and, for early Roman history, he examined the available documents, including the so-called *libri lintei* (inscribed linen bands likely akin to those of the Etruscan "Mummy of Agram"), which were stored in the Temple of Juno Moneta and contained official lists (*HRR* FF. 13–15 = *AR* / *FRH* FF. 14–16).[1] Livy used Macer's work especially for early Roman history. This use cannot derive from Macer's extremely short summary of the first centuries of Roman history, but must be ascribed instead to Macer's distinctly partisan presentation, which seems to have attracted Livy, although (or perhaps because) it offered a perspective very different from his own.

Lucius Cornelius Sisenna (*HRR* I CCCXXIV / 276, *AR* III XXXVIII / 50, *FRH* 16) was a praetor in 78 BC, and died in 67 on Crete while serving as a lieutenant (legate) of Pompey in the war against the pirates in the eastern Mediterranean. Sisenna was apparently indeed on friendly terms with the popularly oriented Licinius Macer, but was himself deeply optimate in his basic outlook: Quintus Hortensius Hortalus and Lucius Licinius Lucullus numbered among his friends and, although in vain, he even assisted Hortensius in defending the former governor of the province of Sicily, Verres, against Cicero's prosecution in 70. Sisenna's *Historiae* followed a Hellenistic Greek stylistic model, Cleitarchus' Alexander history, and its emphasis was even more clearly on current events than was the Roman history of Licinius Macer: Book 1 of 12 (or perhaps even 23) extended from Rome's pre-history to the Social War or "War with the Italian Allies" (*HRR* / *AR* / *FRH* FF. 5 and 6; 90

BC). In the following 11 (or 22) further books Sisenna reached Sulla's resignation of the dictatorship in 79 or his death in 78 (*HRR* F. 132 = *AR / FRH* F. 134; 82 BC). This distribution allows us to conclude that Sisenna continued the Roman history of *Sempronius Asellio*, which had extended to the murder of the tribune of the *plebs*, Livius Drusus, that had precipitated the Social War (see above Ch. 3.2.2, p. 59). While Asellio actually wrote purely of current events, Sisenna adhered to a traditionally complete annalistic history of Rome, but summarized the longest period of Rome's development in a rudimentary abridgment. That Sisenna chose the time of Sulla's actions as his main object of study may be related to their common membership in the clan of the *Cornelii*. Fully a generation later, Sallust clearly saw his own point of view as utterly opposed to Sisenna's fundamentally optimate and pro-Sullan views, but nevertheless acknowledged Sisenna's careful work as an historian, at least in relation to the work of the other more recent annalists, and what is more, he explicitly chose to continue Sisenna's *Histories* (Sallust *Bellum Iugurthinum* 95.2; see also below Ch. 4.5.1, p. 88).

About a generation later, we find a very likely intentional exception to the trend of the times in the work of the *eques*, businessman, and publisher *Titus Pomponius Atticus* (*HRR* II XX / 6, *FRH* F. 19; 109–32 BC), who was the literary friend and financial advisor and supporter of Cicero as well as a friend to other eminent political and literary figures of the day. In his *Liber annalis*, he proceeded from the foundation of Rome to his own day, and identified, from the beginning of the Republic, each year through the names of its chief (i.e., eponymous) magistrates, and to each year appended foreign and domestic affairs, reforms, significant legislation, as well as genealogical and cultural notices. From Greek history, he subjoined indications that would permit its synchronization with Roman history. The work must have been more a bare chronicle than a full-fledged narrative or interpretive study (compare below Ch. 5.2.4, p. 120). *Cornelius Nepos* achieved something similar, but much more extensive, in his *Chronica*, although, on the other hand, he also wrote biographies that featured the interest of his own day in personalities (*HRR* II XXXX / 25; see below Ch. 4.4, p. 82).

4.2 Autobiographies, Memoirs, *Hypomnemata*, *Commentarii*, and their Influence on the Historiography of Current Events

These four literary genres are not only similar to one another, but are also very much like writing the history of current events. In *autobiography* as well as in the less strict accounting of one's life history demanded by *memoirs*, a Hellenistic emphasis on individual personality appears side by side (and in interaction) with a self-conscious awareness of being Roman, noble, and master of the world. Romans first began to write about themselves in the period of the civil wars. This likely resulted from a need to measure themselves additionally or even exclusively according to individual and subjective standards before the wider audience of their fellow citizens and the much more restricted circle of their social class, inasmuch as traditional collective standards no longer sufficed (see above Ch. 4, pp. 64f.). Although no longer absolute, the *mos maiorum* still represented a real force, and, in the late Republic, autobiography could therefore be a means not only to describe, but also to defend, one's own conduct and lifestyle. *Memoirs* were even more conducive to this purpose, and offered their author the chance to choose a single suggestive episode from his life that was especially suited to justify him either before the general public or a select readership. Already in the fourth century BC, the Greek author Xenophon had presented his own participation and role in larger political and military affairs through memoirs in which he aimed to justify himself before the public (*Anabasis Kyrou*). Insofar as the emphasis in autobiographies and memoirs lay on the author's prior conduct, especially in political and military matters, in Rome such works could also carry the title *Res gestae* (*Deeds Accomplished*). This was the title of Sulla's memoirs. The testamentary report that Augustus provided of his deeds was intended for posthumous publication through inscriptions, and, when it was indeed published as planned, the term *res gestae* came to signify a definitive self-presentation.

In the Hellenistic period, Greek politicians directed *Hypomnemata* as recollections and justification toward fellow citizens of their own city as well as interested parties in other cities. They published them during or after their term of office (for example, Demetrius of Phalerum *FGrH* 228 or Aratus of Sicyon *FGrH* 231). Roman politicians composed *commentarii* (also *libri*) during their year in office, and published them at the end of their term as reports on their activities and experiences that often included basic principles, guidelines, and instructions for the office they had held. These were intended for an office holder's successor as well as for the state's two primary institutions: the Assembly of Roman Citizens and, above all, the Senate. To the extent that they were published at all, this took place at the end of the year in office. As we may discern from these observations, there were some significant differences between *hypomnemata* and *commentarii*. *Hypomnemata*, as private sketches and explanations, could be shaped by authors as they saw fit. They could address longer periods of time, and were thus appropriate for exploring larger political connections and circumstances. And, to the extent that they were composed after the fact, they could be used for *ex post facto* interpretations of earlier events in light of subsequent events, and were well suited to just such uses. They are in this respect related to *memoirs*, but go beyond them, insofar as the author can present their explanations and justifications of previous political decisions as guidance for the future use of the community. *Commentarii*, on the other hand, were official and part of one's public duties. Their formal bounds and content are set by the office, its duties, and the duration of its term, which was generally just one year. These facts and the requirement of immediate publication rendered impossible any interpretation and reinterpretation in the light of subsequent events. On the other hand, Caesar's *Commentarii* arguably retained the features of *hypomnemata* (see below Ch. 4.2.2, pp. 72ff.). During the time of Rome's civil wars, these literary categories of self-representation, which were hardly defined unambiguously, began to take on a more mixed character.

4.2.1 Self-representations until Cicero

Even *Gaius*, the younger of the two *Gracchi* brothers, wrote about his own political activity. *Marcus Aurelius Scaurus* (*HRR* I CCXLVI / 185, *AR* III LXXXVIII / 161), consul 115, Censor 109 BC, defended himself against accusations of greed and bribery in his three-volume autobiography, portraying himself as the representative of ancient Roman values and sparing no self-praise. *Quintus Lutatius Catulus* (*HRR* I CCLXII / 191, *AR* III XCVII / 170), elected consul in 101 BC after three previous failed electoral bids, composed a memorandum on his consulship, so that the fame of his victory over the Cimbri at Vercellae would not accrue solely to his co-consul Gaius Marius, who had already been a respected and successful general for years. *Publius Rutilius Rufus* (*FGrH* 815, *HRR* I CCLIV / 187, *AR* III X / 2 and XCIV / 164, *FRH* 13), consul in 105, worked to protect the residents of the province of Asia from exploitation while he served as legate to the governor Quintus Mucius Scaevola in 94 BC. As a direct result, Roman equestrians who had experienced discomfiture as tax-farmers prosecuted him in 92 for extortion of the provincials, and secured a conviction. Rufus chose the allegedly mistreated province of Asia for his exile. From this location he settled accounts with his opponents in at least five books *De vita sua* (*Concerning his own Life*), and described a life lived according to the principles of the Stoic philosophy that he had learned at a young age from study with Panaetius. This work earned him great fame in later ages for his character. *Lucius Cornelius Sulla* (*HRR* I CCLXX / 195, *AR* III XCIX / 172), consul in 88 and 80, dictator 82–79, had reached the 22nd book of his *Res gestae* (*Deeds Accomplished*) at the time of his death in 78 BC, and it was completed by his freedman Epicadius. This work, dedicated to his younger comrade-in-arms, Lucius Licinius Lucullus, offered a summation of an eventful and successful political career. In Sulla's self-presentation, his successes accorded with his cognomen *Felix* ("the one blessed with luck"), and derived from the goddess Tyche/Fortuna's interventions in his favor. Many later historians and authors with diverse viewpoints and attitudes, including Sallust, Diodorus, Livy, Plutarch and Appian, used his account.

Marcus Tullius Cicero (*FGrH* 235, *HRR* II III / 3, Courtney 149) carefully plotted the literary immortality of his consulate (63 BC) and its greatest accomplishment, the discovery and suppression of the Catilinarian conspiracy in Rome. He wanted others to compose this tribute, but they evaded his request (see below Ch. 4.3, p. 77). So Cicero did more than simply gather the material for such a work: he finally wrote it himself, and more than once. In 63 he sent a detailed letter on his performance as consul to Gnaius Pompeius Magnus, who lingered in Asia after his various military and organizational successes. In 61/60 Cicero composed an epic poem in Latin, *De consulatu suo* (*On my Consulship*), as well as a prose piece in Greek on the same topic (Plutarch *Crassus* 13). Inasmuch as he still hoped for full historical treatment from another hand, Cicero called this last effort merely *Commentarius* and *Hypomnema*, although the piece was, in his opinion, full of Isocratean and Aritotelean elements, i.e., he had crafted it rhetorically and dramatically. Cicero aimed for wide readership in the "cultural capital" of Athens as well as other Greek cities. He relied on his friend Titus Pomponius Atticus for publication and distribution (*Letters to Atticus* 1.19.10 and 2.1.1–2). Cicero sent copies to friends and relatives too, and wanted to produce a Latin version (*Letters to Atticus* 1.19.10 and 1.20.6). Plutarch used this Greek *Commentarius* as one of his sources for his biography of Cicero. In another work that he began composing after 59, but did not publish during his lifetime, Cicero defended his politics in general (*De consiliis suis* [*On my Political Choices*]). His exile in 58/57 served as the main theme of another epic poem that he wrote in three books: *De temporibus suis* (*On my [Unhappy] Times*).

4.2.2 Caesar's *Commentarii*

Gaius Julius Caesar, consul in 59 and dictator as well as consul until his assassination on March 15, 44 BC, emerged early as an opponent of the

Sullan restoration. From the time of his return from his propraetorship in 60 he demonstrated an unusually intense drive for power that did not shy away from open illegalities. In 60/59 he made a tactical alliance with two other ambitious politicians, Gnaeus Pompeius Magnus, widely acclaimed, as well as attacked, for his generalship and organizational achievements, and Marcus Licinius Crassus, the richest man in Rome. Because Caesar pursued his career in the face of decided opposition among significant sectors of the nobility, he was led, if not compelled, to compose justifications of his conduct. He profited from his considerable education in languages, literature, and philosophy, which he had acquired very much like Cicero, and he demonstrated his literary talent in this endeavor (his *Commentarii*) as well as in other works. Lack of time, coupled with a desire to keep Rome informed about his successes as quickly as possible in hopes of exerting influence on public opinion, meant that Caesar himself did not write parts of his final report, leaving this task instead to others (compare what follows here with pp. 74f.). Two multi-volume works of commentary may be traced in this way to Caesar.

Caesar's attack on Gaul, which he initiated on arrival in his assigned province and which required many years of wide-ranging warfare (58–50 BC), derived from his personal ambition rather than at the behest of the Senate or as a necessary defensive measure to protect the area. One could even accuse Caesar of war crimes both in his initial attack and in his conduct of the ensuing war. His opponents in the Senate were well aware of these facts, and based on them their plan to neutralize Caesar, at least politically, as soon as his unusually long governorship came to an end. For this reason, Caesar worked hard to show in his *Commentarii de bello Gallico* (*Commentaries on the Gallic War*) that he had been compelled to wage war outside the boundaries of his province. For the same reason, it was crucial for his survival to spell out that public opinion viewed his war no differently from Rome's other wars of conquest, namely, completely positively. This is why we find Caesar tagging such conclusions to the ends of his books as the one we find at the end of the last one he composed solely with his own hand: "When these events (the successes of the year 52 BC and his victory over Vercingetorix) were reported by letter at Rome, a twenty-day period of thanksgiving was offered" (*BG* 7.90.8; cf. 2.35.4 for 57 and 4.38.5 for 55 BC).[2]

Aside from one letter inserted, according to Suetonius *Caesar* 56, at the beginning of Book 8 by a third party, Caesar's share of the *Gallic Wars* runs to 8.48.9, and therefore encompasses the events from 58 to the winter of 51/50. Beginning with 8.48.10, we find a few chapters written by Caesar's lieutenant Aulus Hirtius, which serve as a bridge to Caesar's second work of commentary on the civil war.[3] As a result of the gradual composition of the *Commentarii de bello Gallico* over time, we can trace increasingly exact information about Celtic and Germanic peoples and their differences. On the other hand, some anticipation of, and references to, later events point to a late and rapid redaction of those parts of the commentary that Caesar had composed himself. This only appears to involve us in contradiction, inasmuch as the final product consists of yearly reports, which Caesar sent to Rome each winter in his official capacity as governor, but which he also reworked in accordance with his political and literary ambitions (for the first point, see above Ch. 4.2, pp. 70f.).

In the *Gallic Wars* each book covers a single year of the war. Because, however, Caesar's lieutenants were often operating simultaneously on various battlefields against various foes, we find attention to the chronological progression of events within a year combined with the principle of explaining larger connections and contexts. As a result, Caesar will recount simultaneous actions successively, but mark them as chronologically parallel with such expressions as "at about the same time" (e.g., 3.20.1). It is therefore the choice of the author that determines in what order he presents two or more simultaneous events. On occasion, Caesar appears to shift the end of a year, so that he does not have to conclude his report with renewed rebellion and war, but may instead close with success. For example, the Alpine campaigns of Caesar's legate Sergius Sulpicius Galba are reported not at the end of Book 2, but instead at the beginning of Book 3. Whether or not this peculiarity was a feature of his original annual reports must remain an open question. Although geographical and ethnographic surveys such as the excursus on Gauls and Germans in 6.11–25 or 28 are connected in time to the year the annual report addresses, they transcend whatever occasion justified their inclusion to support Caesar's conception and representation of the larger forces that determine the action. In this respect, his work's organizational principles most resemble the Alexander history of the Macedonian general and Egyptian king Ptolemy I (*FGrH* 138): background – the development of the situation – reflection and decision – action and result. We may for this reason and on formal grounds explain such passages as well as Caesar's introduction of speeches in direct quotation as generic borrowings from historiography where both excursuses and speeches were standard elements. On the other hand, in Caesar's work they also serve the function of providing the causes and justifications required by a *Commentarius*.[4]

The other books of commentary are devoted to the civil war that Caesar began against the majority of the Senate, which rallied around Pompey. In light of the unequivocally negative connotations of "civil war" to his contemporary audience, the title we generally give the work today, *Commentarii de bello civili*, can hardly have been the author's choice. Three of the books penned by Caesar himself describe the events that begin with the outbreak of civil war following the meeting of the Senate on January 1, 49 BC (a date that coincidentally imposes an annalistic stamp on the beginning of the work), and continues to the inception of the Alexandrian War after the defeat of Pompey at Pharsalus and his flight to Egypt in 48. The narrative ends with the murder of Pompey upon making landfall in Egypt and the execution of his murderers by order of Caesar upon his subsequent arrival in Egypt. It alludes only indirectly to related events and further developments in the escalation of hostile elements around Caesar (at the end of Book 3).[5] This hardly represents the conclusion to a book or even a year. There follow three more books composed by Hirtius (whom we just discussed above) and Gaius Oppius or perhaps others. These books describe the events of 48/47 to 45. Only the first of these additional books lives up to the stylistic standards set by the section composed by Hirtius at the end of Book 8 of the *Gallic War*. These findings make it impossible to offer precise answers to questions concerning the method and timing of the publication(s) of Caesar's *Civil War*. But they do allow us to conclude that a whole staff of collaborators may have worked on the composition and publication of the *Commentarii de bello civili*. Important as this self-representation was to Caesar, he simply lacked the time to complete it himself.

We can, however, recognize and understand the purpose of these *Commentarii*. Because his opponents had already begun their propaganda campaign to demolish Caesar before his march into Italy, the first task his explanations faced was to defend himself: Caesar represented reason, he had not desired years of civil war, his actions were justified, the views of his blinded Roman opponents, on the other hand, were weak, brittle, and crumbling. Furthermore, Caesar aimed to portray himself as a person who operated according to ethical principles for political goals and to make his dictatorship – a form of government unworthy of his ancestry – acceptable to the Roman people. He fought for his rightful place among his peers in the ruling class (*dignitas*), for the welfare and tranquillity of Rome, Italy, and the empire, for leniency (*misericordia*) toward his domestic opponents, for success through the strength of his character (*virtus*) combined with supernatural assistance or "fortune" (*felicitas*: compare above Ch. 4.2.1, p. 72, on Sulla). These *Commentarii* on the civil war were addressed to the ruling class, to local elites, and, not least, to Caesar's own army and its soldiers. They serve as a sort of book of public praise for an army that needed moral assurance for its actions and that received as much negative criticism as its leader (cf. La Penna [Bibl. §4], p. 203). We must also view them in the context of the numerous memoranda and messages the dictator addressed to the communities of Italy in the first year of the civil war in order to win their favor.

Although an important and critical contemporary voice reckoned that both commentaries displayed more errors and carelessness on Caesar's part than they did intentional distortions (Asinius Pollio *HRR* II 68 F. 4), moderns sometimes tend to the view that Caesar definitely lied. This may be true to the extent that Caesar of necessity wanted to use his commentaries to excuse and justify himself at (almost) any cost (see above, pp. 72f.). In his so-called *Civil War*, in which the stakes were from the outset life or death for Caesar, we discern the author's partisanship and desire to justify himself much more readily than we do in the *Gallic War*. In the case of the latter, it was possible to compare the original annual reports Caesar had submitted to the Senate (these reports were open to inspection, especially by Roman elites) with the commentaries Caesar subsequently published. This fact would have made it difficult, if not impossible, to make later substantive alterations to the material. Too many eminent Romans, not all of them necessarily favorable or on his side, had witnessed Caesar's decisions and responses during the Gallic War as well as to some extent the Civil War. Caesar was thus in no position to convince the Roman people that any given "x" was actually a "y." That said, in addition to the deft choice of *commentarius*, a literary genre that would have seemed harmless enough to his readers, other cosmetic applications remained available for dressing up the truth, including clever coloring, exaggeration, simplification, omissions, and from time to time selection of the variant most convenient to Caesar from among plausible versions of events. These finer methods were capable of achieving some substantive results, perhaps even better than those through systematic falsification.

Caesar offered his "truth" in a clear style and in a seemingly innocuous narrative of his actions always in the third person, leaving the reader with an impression of objectivity rather than partisan subjectivity, in spite of the fact that other contemporary self-presentations immediately alerted readers that they should not expect the pure truth (see above, Ch. 4.2.1, p. 71). Livy, who used sources from opponents in addition to

Caesar's *Commentarii* (see below, Ch. 5.1, p. 103), confirms this to the extent that he lavished praise on Pompey, Caesar's main opponent in the first phase of the civil war, and thereby allegedly earned the epithet "Pompeian" from Augustus (Tacitus *Annals* 4.34.3). On the other hand, it is precisely this self-presentation of Caesar that contributed substantially to his fame in his own lifetime as well as again from the fourteenth century to the present. It is interesting for the development of historiography as a genre that we cannot avoid the conclusion that contemporaries had already drawn about Caesar's commentaries: rather than providing building blocks for historical writers, they constituted an *historiographical work* in their own right, thanks to their formal and literary qualities (Cicero *Brutus* 262, see below Ch. 4.3, p. 81).

4.3 The History of Current Events Made to Order and Contemporary Concepts of Historiography (Cicero)

During Rome's civil war, historical works on current events could sometimes come into being through a rather peculiar route. In his dialogue devoted to the history of Roman eloquence, Cicero's partner in conversation, Marcus Junius Brutus, remarks, as if it were self-evident, that with his commentaries Caesar aimed to provide material for historians of current events (*Brutus* 262). This corresponds to Cicero's own view of what purpose obliged him, along with other eminent politicians, to compose memoirs in the widest sense of that term (see above, Ch. 4.2.1, pp. 70f.; Ch. 4.2.2, pp. 72ff.). It was also possible that one might send someone one's own treatment of one's actions along with hints, or even an outright request, to work it up as an historical narrative or perhaps an historical epic. From about 100 BC, we know of more than a few instances of just such histories and epics published at the request of politicians, generally based on their memoirs. The Greek poet (Aulus Licinius) Archias of Antioch wrote for Gaius Marius (*FGrH* 186). His competitor, who wrote for Quintus Lutatius Catulus, was the Roman poet Furius Antias (Courtney 97). Lucius Licinius Lucullus wrote for Lucius Cornelius Sulla (*FGrH* 185). Archias wrote for him too, as he did also for Quintus Metellus Pius. Gnaeus Pompeius Magnus enjoyed the services of the Greek poet (Gnaeus Pompeius) Theophanes of Mytilene (*FGrH* 188).

Archias, in blatant competition with Pompey's poet, was to resume his historical poem on the topic of Cicero's handling of his consulship, but he never completed the epic. Cicero then tried the most famously learned man of his day, *Posidonius* of Apameia or Rhodes. His main historical work extended to 85 BC (*FGrH* 87), and he was to write another on the basis of memoirs Cicero sent to him, but he declined, arguing that Cicero's memoirs satisfied all literary requirements and to that extent themselves represented a work of historiography (Cicero *Letters to Atticus* 2.1.1–2; early June 60 BC). Posidonius thus expressed the same opinion of Cicero's memoirs, although on different literary and rhetorical grounds, as had Marcus Junius Brutus (at least according to Cicero) of Caesar's *Commentarii* (see above Ch. 4.2.2, p. 78). And lastly *Lucius Lucceius*, who began writing history after his failed bid for the consulship in 60 BC, worked at writing up recent history until at least 56 BC. At Cicero's urging and with the help of materials Cicero made available that covered his political career from the beginning of the Catilinarian conspiracy to his return from exile, he was supposed to give these events wider scope in his work, once he had advanced far enough in time. Better yet, he was supposed to write a monograph on the topic immediately (Cicero *Letters to his Friends* 5.12(13); June 56 BC). This laudatory narrative from the quill of a third party likewise failed to appear. We should also put Cicero's request to Lucceius in the context of the fact that four years earlier, in 60 BC, Cicero had already received a report on his consulship in Greek from his friend *Atticus*. This report, however, did not meet Cicero's literary and rhetorical standards for an historical work, and he thus characterized it as merely a *Commentarius* (*Letters to Atticus* 2.1.1).

Cicero strove to accomplish what many of his contemporaries likewise aimed to bring about under the same conditions. But, whereas Cicero failed, others had no difficulty becoming figures (and, if possible, the central figures) in historical works and historical epics within their own lifetimes. This may strike us as strange, but this phenomenon was one of the distinguishing features of this period of civil war, and we must classify such efforts as part and parcel of "outward displays of individual achievement" and "self-justification." This behavior may also be traced, albeit under changed circumstances, in the *imperial* period: the *princeps* seeks to promote his fame by commissioning historical works that will glorify his military accomplishments as well as help legitimate his (quasi-)monarchical position. We may observe this not uniquely, but especially well, in the correspondence of the famous orator *Marcus Cornelius Fronto* with his former students, the jointly ruling emperors Lucius Verus and Marcus Aurelius, regarding the Parthian war they conducted from AD 161 to 166. *Lucius Verus* entered into his own letters copies of official correspondence, his written instructions, his speeches before the Senate, his addresses to the soldiers, and his negotiations with his opponents. Moreover, he charged two military commanders, Avidius Cassius and Martius Verus, with the preparation of *commentarii*. All this he sent to Fronto as the basis for an historical work he was to compose. The emperor indicates that he is also himself willing to write a *commentarius*, if Fronto should ask, and he gives detailed instructions for the presentation of his achievements in the Parthian War.[6] In light of the crippling handicaps posed by the lopsided preponderance of power in such relations, panegyric history in praise of the reigning emperor was the only viable option (compare below Ch. 6.1.1, pp. 129f.).

Why were politicians of the civil war period – and later Roman emperors – not content with memoirs and other such works that they themselves composed? Why did they want third parties to compose historical narratives about them? The answer to these two questions is on two levels. In the first place, epic and historiography were considered elite literary genres, and, as such, the linguistic and stylistic standards were so high that not every active politician was necessarily up to the task. Many lacked talent, education, or time. Secondly, writing one's own history failed to satisfy historiography's generic demand for objectivity, the concept of which was tied to the person who did the writing. Those who wanted their histories told wanted above all a lot of praise. This was hardly problematic if someone else wrote the work. But whoever wrote his own history had to restrain himself from too much praise or else risk quickly losing credibility with his readers and thus the effect of the praise (Cicero *Letters to his Friends* 5.12(13).8). In bestowing praise, what mattered was not how justified or unjustified it was in fact or how credible its effect, but instead who the person was who did the praising, i.e., the source of the praise. Because of the serious function generally ascribed to it, historiography was obligated to guarantee its objectivity – or at least appear to do so. At the same time, a distinction between author and subject matter (or person described) was normally the case, and considered the general rule for historical writing about contemporary events. It is for this reason that authors of histories of their own times were so meager in their remarks about themselves, and when they did make mention of themselves, they offered an apology for having done so. This applies to a *Thucydides* as much as it does to a *Tacitus* (Tacitus *Annals* 11.11.1). *Ammianus Marcellinus* was the first to depart from this pattern, thus partly imparting to his work the character of *memoirs*, a distinctly lesser literary genre in the opinion of antiquity (see below Ch. 7.2, pp. 209f.).

In spite of this superficial expectation of objectivity, the Romans of the civil war period, and especially *Cicero*, had more than just the one-sided and restricted interest in historiography that we have just sketched. We may understand what historiography represented for them or what it was supposed to be and what consequences this had for the historian's task, if we piece together Cicero's statements from works of diverse genre and purpose (in their chronological order of appearance: *Letters to Atticus* 1.19.10 and 2.1.1–2; *Letters to his Friends* 5.12; *De oratore* 2.51–64; *De legibus* 1.5–10; *Brutus* 252–255 and 261–262). Although Cicero's conclusions and requirements may not have represented the norm in all details for educated Romans of his day, we may view the result as at least a fair cross-section.

Three requirements that historical writers were obligated to fulfill competed with each other, the peculiarity of which modern historians, despite their familiarity with Cicero, only discern with difficulty. Above all, historiography portrays political events. It is consequently desirable that the historical writer have real political experience, which, in Rome, invariably includes speeches before the public courts (1). Nevertheless, as the Greek examples cited by Cicero demonstrate, it is also possible to write history without this personal background. The reason for this astonishing sacrifice of a seemingly necessary requirement lies in a warrant that is much more important than any guarantee for the material accuracy of an historical representation: the creation of suspense according to the very rules drama employs (see above, Ch. 1.3.1, p. 19). This demands of the historiographer very different capacities and qualities, namely, poetic power and rhetorical skill (2). The ethical demands Cicero makes for the historian to adhere to the truth pale in comparison (3). They do so precisely because it is permissible to transgress the boundary that divides the literary genre of historiography from *eulogy* or *panegyric*. Truth and objectivity (as demands made of historians) are understood here in very simple terms indeed, without any philosophical underpinning, and as purely moral in scope, inasmuch the historian's real political experience – an absolute requirement as seen from the modern point of view – could be forfeited without qualms.

Other demands were made of historical writers in addition to these three requirements. First, as Cicero reckoned in his assessment of Caesar's *Commentarii,* the erudition that derives from the study of "abstruse and choice literature" and its presentation (*Brutus* 252: ... *litteris ... reconditis et exquisitis*). With this requirement Cicero satisfies the common ancient practice of inserting passages (excursuses) into historical narratives, in which the author demonstrated his further knowledge and wider reading that went beyond the historical subject immediately at hand (see above, Ch. 1.3.1, p. 23). Finally, rhetorical skill and/or rhetorical practice are best combined with historiography. One narrates in proper sequence and in what manner something was planned, done, and accomplished. One sketches the characters of the persons involved, and one describes the scenes of the actions. Language flows accordingly and easily. At this point, a difference becomes clear: political and forensic speeches frequently require vehemence and polemic, but just these techniques are withheld from historians, especially in their judgments of actions and actors, lest they diminish their seeming objectivity. Truthfulness thus loses even more value when weighed in the balance against demands for expertise and the ability to give the narrative dramatic shape: truthfulness is reduced to a subjective element and a facade.

All this provides the lens for Cicero's assessment of Greek and Roman historiography and the development of the latter down to his own lifetime. The single criterion Cicero employs to judge Roman historical writers down to Macer and Sisenna is exclusively their language and style: with one half-hearted exception all these authors are judged unsatisfactory. The result is that Atticus has words put in his mouth demanding that Cicero compose an historical work, the first from a Roman pen that would not have to stand below Greek works, inasmuch as the task absolutely requires rhetorical accomplishment (*opus ... oratorium maxime*; *De legibus* 1.5). All Rome's previous historians lacked the proper schooling, but Cicero, of course, enjoyed oratorical training, talent, and experience (see above, Ch. 1.3.1, pp. 22f.).[7] The stipulation of a requirement for an historiographical work's rhetorical perfection does not result in Cicero's actually providing clear instructions about its linguistic and stylistic shape. Instead, two widely divergent and opposed styles emerge as ideal possibilities, and both of them were in fact realized in Cicero's day. One could transform a *commentarius* or *hypomnema* into an historiographical work, insofar as one deployed all available rhetorical means to dress it up, just as Cicero himself did and desired that others likewise do (see above, Ch. 4.2.2, p. 72; Ch. 4.3, pp. 77f.). But one could also, as Caesar did, make a show of renouncing all such means – a rhetorical demonstration in itself – and thereby achieve the stylistic level demanded of an historical work (*Brutus* 262). With this we return to the central issue: again and again and above all it is through literary and rhetorical means, primarily linguistic and stylistic in form, that Romans and Greeks produced a work of historiography.

4.4 Biography (Cornelius Nepos)

Although Romans had long been acquainted with biographies composed by Greeks, it was not until Rome began to take autobiographies, memoirs, and the like for granted (see above, Ch. 4, pp. 65f.; Ch. 4.2, pp. 69ff.), that they too composed biographies, which then very soon appeared in large numbers. We must first mention the politician and, more importantly, the learned antiquarian and poet *Marcus Terentius Varro* (*HRR* II XXXII / 9; 116–27 BC; compare below Ch. 4.6, pp. 96f.) whose biographical collection of older Roman poets together with a huge collection of seven hundred biographies of Greeks and Romans (*Hebdomades vel de imaginibus*), who had excelled in diverse fields of endeavor. Of his biographies only the most pitiful fragments survive. When in 47 BC Varro began writing a three-volume biography of Pompey shortly before his murder, incorporating people and events in accordance with the rapidly changing situation of the then-raging civil war, he was likely the first to write a *political* biography of a subject in the present that was exactly and formally parallel to writing a political history of current events (see above, Ch. 4, pp. 64f.; Ch. 4.1, pp. 66ff.; below Ch. 4.5, pp. 84f.).[8] On the other hand, in antiquity biography would hardly ever be conceived of as a typical means for describing the *political* aspects and conduct of someone's life (see below, Ch. 6.4.2, pp. 185f.). This is true even for the biographies of Roman emperors as well (see below, especially Ch. 6.3.1, p. 167).

The biographical work of the only somewhat younger *Cornelius Nepos* (circa 100 until sometime after 27 BC) survives at least in part (*HRR* II XXXX / 25). He came from the region north of the Padus (Po), lived privately in Rome, and was especially active in the same social circle as Cicero's renowned friend Titus Pomponius Atticus. Like Atticus, he wrote a *Chronicle* (see above, Ch. 4.1, p. 69) as well as a collection of *Exempla* (see below Ch. 6.6, p. 198). He exchanged letters with Cicero. He published biographies of historically important men as well as contemporaries (*De viris illustribus*) in various thematically organized collections, who had achieved eminence not only in political and military affairs, but also in the literary world, namely, as historians, poets, philosophers, language teachers, and scholars (*grammatici*). As Greeks, Carthaginians, Persians, and Romans they represented diverse nationalities. Nepos describes not only their culturally specific customs and practices, but also assesses them according to their own native value system. He specifically judges Greeks, for example, according to their own, and not according to Roman, standards (*Lives of Outstanding Commanders of Foreign Peoples, praef.* 1.1–3). Like Varro's biography of Pompey, Nepos sketched his biography of Atticus very close in time to the events of his subject's life as they unfolded. Of the biographies that have survived, his lives of Atticus and Cato (which we put to much use above;

see Ch. 3.2.1, pp. 52ff.) are, because of the subjects they treat, of the greatest literary and historical interest. In fact, through his biography of Cato, Nepos may also be considered a primary source for the history of Roman historiography.

Nepos, who recognizably lays importance on the artistic and aesthetic merits of his biographies, bases them on such diverse sources as annalistic historical narratives, official biographies, eulogies, and funeral orations. These biographies show great formal variety too: chronological sequences of events can give way to episodic narratives, which can serve the purpose of sketching through anecdotes the character of the personality under review. Personal judgments are sometimes implied by the narrative itself or sometimes stated directly in the foreword or afterword. The biographies do resemble each other, inasmuch as Nepos organizes each life (in all the thematic areas he treats) according to virtues (*virtutes*) or vices (*vitia*). In this respect, his biographies show similarities to the genre of *exempla*, a genre in which he, of course, himself composed a work (see below Ch. 6.6, p. 198), and they sometimes approach eulogy, as we may observe in parts of his *Life of Atticus*. Specifically Roman elements in his presentations include the qualities of commanders and the topical separation of personal conduct according to public and private spheres (*vita publica / privata*). All this demonstrates that Nepos did not wish to write "history" – neither in the modern sense of the term nor according to ancient ideals of the genre. For him, history merely provides material and illustration. And, with these two, he aims to produce a "picture of his subject's conduct and life" (*Epimonandas* 1.3).[9] This picture is not necessarily rooted primarily in the political sphere. Nepos expressly guards against this idea that he should be considered an historian who, rather than a "life" (*vita*), describes the "actions" (*res*), of his subject (*Pelopidas* 1.1), i.e., "principal acts undertaken for reasons of state" as required by an historiography that, since the time of Thucydides, had focused on politics as its proper theme.

Today we are well aware of the tendency of many ancient historians since the time of Xenophon to distance themselves from pragmatic and political history, allowing their narratives to drift away from the historical and chronological continuum and to disintegrate into episodes and ethically determined examples. From this perspective, Nepos, along with all other ancient biographers, actually stood very close indeed to the basic goal, as well as the results, of a segment of ancient Greek and Roman historical writing. We must differentiate here between ancient self-criticism that seeks to enhance its prestige through overt delimiting of its goals and modern criticism that looks at the genre as a whole. Nor may we blur the distinction maintained throughout antiquity between history and biography, inasmuch as the decisive consideration for ancient biography was its focus from its inception directed toward a person in a way that was specifically neither historical nor chronological in motivation. If one wished to understand the philosopher Socrates fully, one examined the relationship between his teaching and the conduct of his life until the last moment of his death in order to find manifest examples of his principles (Plato and Xenophon). The peripatetic school of philosophy founded by Aristotle had a hunger for empirical knowledge that was close in methods and interests to Hellenistic and Alexandrian biography and very much concerned with documenting the various possibilities for realizing human potential or *conducting a life*. As a consequence, they were much more interested in "intellectuals" than in politicians or generals. Such works did not depend as much on chronology or on the political significance of actions, but instead on their suitability for more general conclusions concerning typical modes of behavior and the essential traits of a human being. This method alone led to the representation of a person's *ethos* or character as the true goal of biography, as Plutarch would later make especially clear (see below, Ch. 6.4.2, p. 185). To the extent, however, that ancient biography pursued this aim, it ran the risk of removing historical personages from history, thereby sinning against historiography as conceived by a Polybius or from a modern perspective.

4.5 The Experience of the Collapsing and Ruined Republic

The end of the Republic was the period, once again unstable and especially bloody, between Caesar's assassination and the beginning of constitutionally settled government under the de facto autocracy of Augustus. For many contemporaries in these years as well as those that immediately followed the restoration of domestic peace, these innovations at first appeared uncertain in scope, but soon proved unmistakable. An extremely intensified inner ambivalence coupled with a conscious awareness of the new political dichotomy provided the context for the creation of historiographical works that were especially influential.

4.5.1 Gaius Sallustius Crispus

In the last years of the Republic, Gaius Sallustius Crispus composed historiographical works that are today the period's most famous.

According to the later imperial consular and historian, *Cornelius Tacitus*, he was Rome's most important historian (*Annals* 3.30.2). In fact, the language and style of Tacitus owe quite a lot to the genre-shaping example of Sallust (see above, Ch. 1.3.1, pp. 22f.). Soon after Tacitus, literary devotees of archaism praised Sallust's diction, and imitated it. Sallust's was the only work of Latin historiography ever translated into Greek. And precisely because Christians could summon Sallust against classically religious society and its customs as an unbiased witness of unsurpassed lucidity, they praised him as an "historian of truth rendered noble" (Augustine *City of God* 1.5 *nobilitatae veritatis historicus*).

Sallust, who was born in 86 and died in 35 BC, enjoyed a rather short political career marked by vicissitude. The few accomplishments of his most successful years he owed to Caesar. In 52, as Tribune of the *Plebs*, he opposed the politician and gang-leader Titus Annius Milo who agitated on Cicero's side. Two years later, the censor, Appius Claudius Pulcher, expelled him from the Senate. In 49, and thus during the first year of the new civil war, Sallust was, thanks to Caesar, invested with a second quaestorship, and became once more a member of the Senate. After this, he held several military commands as Caesar's agent in Illyria, Campania, and Africa with varying degrees of success. In 46/45, after Caesar's victory at Thapsus (south of Carthage) over the so-called senatorial party who had arrayed themselves against him there, Caesar appointed Sallust pro-consul of the province Africa Nova (which he had formed from King Juba's likewise defeated kingdom of Numidia), even though Sallust had never even held the post of praetor or consul. Sallust enriched himself shamelessly, and he was threatened with prosecution. Caesar, however, protected him. After Caesar's murder, Sallust withdrew quickly and unmolested from politics, and lived as a very wealthy private citizen, who owned, among other properties, two stately villas formerly belonging to Caesar, each of which commanded majestic gardens and grounds, one in Rome and the other in Tibur (Tivoli).

During his politically active phase, Sallust on several occasions published works that engaged with current affairs. Around 54, he attacked Cicero with an invective and in 50 and 46 he directed two letters to Caesar, in which he offered advice on current events and recommended reforms in government with an aim toward moral improvement. Finally, in retirement, Sallust turned to the writing of history. But he did not do so at the conclusion of a political career that had seen him successfully attain every office in the *cursus honorum* (the standard sequence of political offices). He thus wrote not as an epilogue to his political career, but as a substitute for it – although he would not have wanted to acknowledge this. Just as he generally reckoned intellectual and moral accomplishments worthier than physical ones, he regarded historiography (in contrast to its traditional ranking) as an intellectual activity of the first order, and thus at least as worthy as the orator's or the politician's (*Catiline* 1–4; cf. above Ch. 4, p. 65). Based on this calculus, Sallust ascribed to historical knowledge an educational and moral force that corresponded to ancient Roman values (*Jugurtha* 4).

Sallust wanted to adhere to the special demands placed on historical writers: as a private man, he kept himself free from hopes, fears, and political factions (*Catiline* 4.2 *a spe, metu, partibus rei publicae*). Here we encounter for the first time in Roman historiography (at least to the extent that we may discern from what remains) that abstract and fossilized formula, exclusively formulated by denying the historian's subjectivity as a way to guarantee his objectivity. We find its "classic" form in Tacitus as *sine ira et studio* ("free from angry resentment and eager partisanship"; *Annals* 1.1.3). Still, Sallust's third stipulation that the historian not toe a party line at a time of bitter factional strife must be considered decisive – even when, or especially because, it was nearly impossible to fulfill in light of a Roman historian's integration into his society (see above Ch. 4, p. 63). Nor did he approach his new occupation without additional preparations: Sallust commissioned an outline of Roman history from the philologist Lucius Ateius as part of his collection of materials for his own work (*HRR* II LVII / 41). He thus farmed out investigation of the sources by having someone else sift through historical texts in advance. One should not forget that the rich sources available for Sallust's historical writings included Punic texts (*Jugurtha* 17.7). Sallust also had a collection made of archaic Latin vocabulary and idioms as well as grammatical forms. As the representative of traditional morality, Sallust wanted to demonstrate in his own language and with the pointed consistency of his rhetorical rules his return to what was old and therefore good. We may observe the results of these efforts in the many linguistic archaisms we find throughout his historiographical works.

Sallust wrote three historical works. All three of them were devoted to the period of the civil wars, partly to recent history (*Jugurtha*) and partly to events that took place during Sallust's own lifetime (*Catiline* and the *Histories*). They belong to two diverse genres. The *Histories* differ from a general history in the annalistic tradition only insofar as they restrict the period of time covered. His two earlier compositions were both monographs (*Catiline*, *Jugurtha*). As Sallust himself expresses it in the first of these works, he approaches his themes *carptim* ("selectively;" *Catiline* 4.2),[10] that is, he chooses his material from among numerous possibilities. He does this according to how noteworthy the incidents and the historical actors in them were in the context of larger sequences of events, although he does not himself explicitly describe the reasons for his selections. In this same work, at least by the time we arrive at his assessment of Caesar and Cato (*Catiline* 53.6), Sallust does, however, reveal his criteria: *ingens virtus* (conduct far excelling customary stand-ards) and *mores* (moral principles and the moral conduct that derives from them). In the final analysis, then, it is the power of the exemplary, both positive and negative, that occasions Sallust's selection of topic for a monograph. Because this may be perceived most clearly in the conduct of individuals, Sallust composes his works, or at least large parts of them, around individual Romans and, in the case of the dictator Sulla, around the lasting impact of his actions.

With occasional forays into the recent past, Sallust addresses political events surrounding the central character of Lucius Sergius Catilina (born circa 108 BC) in his first historical effort, *The Catilinarian Conspiracy* (*De Catilinae coniuratione*). These events began in the city of Rome toward the end of 66, and concluded in spring 62 with armed conflict between a Roman army and rebels under Catiline. The height of the crisis occurred during 63, the year of Marcus Tullius Cicero's consulship (*Catiline* 5–61, esp. 25–55). General knowledge of Catiline's conspiracy and its adherents derived from the speeches and publications of Cicero, the same man who, as consul, first detected the existence of the con-spiracy and subsequently took the initiative in its suppression and the punishment of the conspirators. He undertook all of these efforts in the full conviction that he thereby saved Rome from complete destruc-tion. Sallust wishes to offer a corrective to the necessarily vested personal perspectives in the publications of the consul of 63, especially his four speeches against Catiline, but also his later retrospective representations of his conduct in prose and poetry (see above Ch. 4.2.1, p. 72; Ch. 4.3, p. 78). Above all, Sallust hardly views Cicero as the omni-competent statesman who determines all outcomes. The greatest impression is con-sequently left not by Cicero, but by Caesar and Cato with their opposing speeches before the Senate on the punishment of the Catilinarians impris-oned in Rome (*Catiline* 51–52: two extremely long chapters). Both men make a case for exemplary conduct based on moral values (*virtus*), but each offers a definition incomplete and to that extent one-sided in its own way. As a result, however, each is worthy of admiration for his con-ception of *virtus* (53.6).

The *Catiline* begins with a general section on the opposition of body to mind and spirit together with a discussion of the relative merits of political activity and the writing of history (*Catiline* 1–4; see above, p. 86). Sallust provides a solid example of his thinking in the person of Catiline whose mind and spirit he then proceeds to describe. Catiline in turn is placed in the context of contemporary as well as past standards of Roman conduct. This enables Sallust to engage in moral critique: he condemns the conduct of his own day and recent past, while praising the moral standards of earlier times (*Catiline* 5.9–13.5; and again 36.4–39.5). The contemporary degeneracy of political life, exemplified by the conspiracy of Catiline, is in this analysis the result of a recent collapse in moral standards, the aspects of which are illustrated in Sallust's portraits not only of Catiline himself (5.1–8 and 14.1–16.5), but also of Sempronia, a woman belonging his circle (25.1–5).

Moral and political judgment combine to condemn an entire class: the Roman nobility, which had recently produced criminals like Catiline. The dictator Sulla plays the lead, and is made responsible (5.1–8 with 11.4–12). Not without reason does Sallust backdate the conspiracy of Catiline to the year 64, and report at the end of 66 his supposed conspiratorial machinations, which we might even consider ahistorical. Sallust does this to unlink Catiline's conspiracy against the state both chronologically and, to the extent that he can, causally from Catiline's failures in the elections of the 60s. At the same time, Sallust brings Catiline's candidacies as close as possible to Sulla's dictatorship together with its fatal attendants, graft and murder, in all of which Catiline, as a young man, had played his part. For Sallust, Sulla's dictatorship had an epochal impact that went well beyond Catiline. It was a major cause and the final tipping point in the collapse of Roman morality (see also below).

Sallust's second historical monograph (*De bello Iugurthino*) displays the same authorial motivation as the first. Their introductions are especially similar insofar as both deploy the opposition of body to mind and spirit as the theoretical foundation for historical judgment and for his estimation of writing history as an intellectual activity with the potential to edify its readers (*Jugurtha* 1–4; see above pp. 85f. and 87). Sallust then turns to a description made possible partly by his own military and political experiences in North Africa. He sketches the early history of the Numidian royal house (5–26), includes an excursus on the region (17–19), and relates the progress of the war against the Numidian king Jugurtha from 112 to 105 BC: Jugurtha inflicts a number of embarrassing defeats on the Romans, but, thanks to the efforts of his quaestor Sulla, Marius captures Jurgurtha and wins the war (27–114). The progress of this war is narrated in close parallel to events in Rome, i.e., with the formation of factions, their conflicts, and the maneuvers of individuals, all of which are animated by ambitions materially harmful both to the common good and to the conduct of the war against Jugurtha. Illustrative of factional conflict are Quintus Caecilius Metellus Numidicus, commanding general against Jugurtha 109–107 BC, who represents the nobility, and Gaius Marius, who represents the people. Metellus also serves as an example of individual ambition. Sallust wishes to demonstrate that these domestic factions and the corruption of the nobility's leaders so endanger Rome's foreign relations that external enemies can recognize and exploit their own opportunities in this situation (cf., e.g., 35.10). Against all this, Sallust sets the success of Marius, who rose from the lower orders to conquer for the first time ever "the arrogance of the nobility" (5.1: *superbia nobilitatis*).

Sallust's *Historiae* survive only in fragments (Maurenbrecher [Bibl. 1.2]). In five or more books they treated Roman history as a continuation of the *Historiae* of *Cornelius Sisenna* from 78 to at least 67 BC (see above Ch. 4.1, p. 69). By continuing the history of a predecessor Sallust was able to write annalistically without having to slog through all prior Roman history (see below Ch. 4, p. 65). What amazes, however, is Sallust's choice. He chose to continue an author who belonged to the opposite "party." Even if we grant the unusual respect that, according to Sallust, Sisenna had earned for trustworthiness, this instance of *Historia continua* appears as a purely technical exercise: a means to write comprehensive Roman history without having to make the effort oneself.

In his *Histories*, Sallust narrated various foreign and domestic wars as well as domestic developments, including the partial revisions of the Sullan constitution during the consulate of Pompey and Crassus in 70 BC, and the extraordinary career of Pompey, who made of himself an indispensable military commander and organizer, and ascended to the consulate directly from the *equites* (i.e., without having first entered the senatorial class through election to a lower office, as constitutionally required). Sallust's aim is also in this work a critique of the nobility, and, for this reason, the oppositional figure of Quintus Sertorius is important. Sertorius, until his assassination in Spain in 72, maintained for the *populares* a kind of anti-Rome with its own senate. Among the fragments of this work, speeches and letters are especially prominent. They survived separately as conspicuous examples of rhetoric (see above Ch. 1.3.1, p. 22). The speeches of three Roman consuls from the years 78 to 75 and of the tribune of the *plebs* Licinius Macer derive from the debate on whether to overthrow the Sullan constitution. Three speeches favor change. One opposes. (For Licinius Macer, see above Ch. 4.1, pp. 67f.).

In all three works Sallust makes crystal clear his antipathy for the nobility of his own day as well as for the recent past. On the other hand, he considers the people and their leaders equally corrupt (*Catiline* 37f.; *Jugurtha* 40f.), and already during his active political career he had concluded that, "for the people, cleverness was superfluous" (*Second Letter to Caesar* 10.6).[11] In this same letter, composed when Sallust was still in a subordinate political position, we also find an application of the antithesis between body and mind/spirit that features so prominently in his later historical work: Sallust compares a senate that fulfills its duty to mind/spirit (*animus*) and the common people (*plebs*) to the body (*corpus*), and states that the latter must obey the former. From this perspective, Sallust was perfectly consistent when, despite his negative view of the Sullan settlement, he disapproved of the complete restoration of the plebeian tribunate in 70 (*Catiline* 38). So too the rise of men from the people could only signify for him emergency assistance made necessary by an incompetent nobility. What Sallust wanted therefore was not the substitution of popular for senatorial rule, but instead a different senate and a different nobility, adorned with the moral standards that he considered essential. Sallust was to this extent no *popularis* at all, and, despite the dependence of his career on Caesar, he was not without reservations about the man, and thus, at least as an historian, held an independent political position that straddled the split between Optimates and Populares.

Cicero was probably the first in Rome to take notice of the Greek historian *Thucydides* (Cic. *De oratore* 2.56 and 93). While Cicero admired (in a rhetorical work on public speaking) Thucydides' style, Sallust imitated the *language* of this Greek historian. According to one later Roman critic, Sallust actually excelled his model in the pregnancy and compressed brevity of his expressions (Seneca *Controversiae* 9.1.24.13). But the Romans never adopted or developed Thucydides' historical methods, and, even among Greeks, only a small minority made the attempt (see above Ch. 1.3.2, pp. 27f. and 30).[12] Sallust did not arrange his historical material according to Thucydides' methods. Instead, his writing is stamped with its author's own Roman character, by an intense individuality (not to be underestimated), and by the rhetorical, dramatic, and mimetic methods of Hellenistic historiography, which stand in stark contrast with the methods of Thucydides. This becomes evident when, in examining historical causation, we find not political and pragmatic explanations, but instead basic moral principles (see above, Ch. 1.3.1, pp. 24ff.). Whereas Thucydides assumes that the basis for human behavior remains constant over long periods, Sallust sees in the historical process profound change to it that manifests itself concretely in the collapse of moral standards.

The collapse of Rome's moral standards may seem typical of Sallust, but he is hardly the inventor of this concept nor of its defining characteristic, the supposed revolution from virtuous to immoral conduct that occurred at one specific point in time, the so-called *turning point*. Even before Sallust this historical practice must have become manifestly questionable, the idea that one could identify a turning point not just in the fundamental moral conduct of an individual, but even of a society and with chronological precision: *Lucius Calpurnius Piso Frugi* described the moral collapse that took place in Rome with a turning point in the year 154 BC, but, then again, eventually already in the year 187 and thus with a different causality (see above, Ch. 3.2.2, pp. 56f.). Perhaps *Gaius Fannius*, reckoned so highly reliable by Sallust, did the same thing, albeit with a different turning point (see above, Ch. 3.2.2, p. 58). Even the Greek *Posidonius* (mentioned above in connection with Cicero: Ch. 4.3, p. 78), who died in 50 BC, saw a turning point in the moral conduct of the Romans or even several of them, at least to the extent that we can discern from the fragmentary remains of his works: the destruction of Carthage in 146 and the defeat of the Cimbri and Teutones in 102/101, insofar as external pressure was thereby removed from the Romans. We find also the destructive agitation of the Gracchi 133–121 as well as the tribunate of Livius Drusus in 91 BC, the successes and failures of which widened the gulf between Rome and Italy and exacerbated the divisions between the Senate and people of Rome (Diodorus 34/35.24–30 and 33.4–6; 37.1.5–2.2 and 3.1–5 after Posidonius' *Histories*).[13]

In his persistent efforts to understand Rome's moral collapse and its effects, Sallust arrived at three different dates and, accordingly, at three different combinations of events and, more significantly, three different explanations (*Catiline* 10.1–2; 11.4; cf. 36.4–39.5; *Jugurtha* 41–42; *Histories* fragments 11 and 12). According to all three works, the destruction of Carthage in 146 BC freed the Romans from fear of their enemies. A shift from virtuous to immoral conduct was the result. Behind this explanation stands the idea (as with Posidonius) that outside pressure has the effect of maintaining moral conduct. In contrast, the other two turning points have purely domestic causes. Sallust sees one in the work of the Gracchi as well as (here differently from Posidonius who adopted the perspective of the Optimates) to an even greater extent in the actions of their opponents from 133 to 121 BC (though, logically enough, not in his *Catiline*). The other turning point is the work of Sulla, especially during his dictatorship 82–79 BC (but this, understandably, not in the *Jugurtha*). In fact, the conspiracy of Catiline has its origins in this last variant (see above, pp. 88f.). In each of his two monographs there are consequently two turning points: the first, which would become the "classic" turning point in ancient literature, is the destruction of Carthage, and the second for each is a combination of circumstances that antedates by just a little, and thus explains, the main subject of each monograph. The disruptions of the Gracchi and their opponents lie behind the conduct of the war with Jugurtha and Catiline's conspiracy grows out of Sulla's dictatorship. This is intentional. We cannot know whether the *Histories* offered the sum of three "turning points," but it is conceivable. The peculiarity of two (somewhat different) turning points in the *Catiline* and *Jugurtha* lead to the conclusion that Sallust worked up the concept of turning points in moral collapse as a systematic model for understanding historical development. This conclusion as well as many details in his prefaces and remarks in digressions have implications beyond the short periods of Roman history that he treats.

Sallust can hardly have overlooked the problem of whether or not two or three "turning points" could still be considered turning points. A twofold dilemma becomes manifest: in the first place, Sallust must have harbored some doubts about the possibility of a sudden and punctual arrival of moral collapse, because, in spite of joining two correlated turning points in each of his two smaller works, he describes, even before the fall of Carthage, a tendency toward corruption in Roman morality. Only two periods in Roman history were truly virtuous domestically: the period of Rome's battles against the Etruscans and the approximately seventy years from the Second Punic War to the destruction of Carthage (*Histories* frags. 11 and 12). In the second place, as we have just discussed, Sallust was confronted with several moral collapses conceived of as turning points in Roman historiography, and could even, in the work of a single author, read of two or more sudden changes from virtue to immoral conduct. This too should have led to real doubts about any "turning point." The idea of a turning point was, however, surely a fascinating one, and it was always well suited as a device for dramatizing sequences of historical events. After Sallust, *Tacitus* too used this principle for shaping his compositions, although he did so with a specific and characteristic variation. Sallust gives us moral corruption and turning points not for individuals like Catiline, but rather only for social groups and society, the effects of which, in turn, become manifest in the conduct of individuals. *Tacitus*, on the other hand, who lived under, and wrote about, the conditions of monarchy, clearly outlines turning points in the circumstances of individuals, namely, the Roman emperors, especially two of them: Tiberius and Nero. Also in the description of their lives and regimes, one turning point will hardly suffice (see below Ch. 6.1.3, p. 147).

The thesis that the destruction of Carthage had an absolutely negative impact on the Roman people rests on the assumption that external pressure is required to bring about and maintain morality. This idea cannot be combined with the conception that human beings are capable of remaining virtuous on their own. For many later Christian authors, this was exactly the point at which they began their critique of Rome's classically religious morality, and Sallust was, as an adherent of traditional Roman religion, for this reason viewed as an eminently qualified witness (see especially Augustine's *City of God* 2.18 with its various citations from Sallust's work). But the explanation of "outside pressure" works for only one of Sallust's three turning points. In regard to the others, one must look to changes in the Romans themselves and must, in this respect, assume that they have the capacity for good as well as evil. We must also take care to note that Sallust, no matter how severely he criticizes or exposes, in no way aims at the simple condemnation of groups and individuals who have failed to live up to the moral standards he demands. Rather, again and again he offers psychological explanations for moral deviations. He stands very close in this practice to the teacher, historian, and philosopher *Posidonius* (whom we just mentioned above) whose theories of decadence and turning points had become popular among Roman intellectuals of the age. Psychological explanations for moral degeneracy appear typical of Posidonius as well. With such explanations, conduct becomes plausible and probable, but may nevertheless be portrayed as neither compelled nor unavoidable. Thus, in Sallust's view, just as in Posidonius' diagnosis, Rome's moral collapse was not triggered mechanically as some automatic consequence of Rome's successful extension of political power. On the contrary, Rome's military success offered enormous opportunities to the men and women of Rome's leading families for the easy pursuit of power, honor, and wealth, but it hardly compelled them to pursue these things. To this extent, Sallust clearly recognizes the responsibility of individuals for their own actions. He spells this out quite clearly in the introductory chapters to both his monographs (*Catiline* 1ff. and *Jugurtha* 1ff.). And it is just this ascription of personal responsibility that affords ethical weight to Sallust's judgments of individuals and a tragic quality to his narrative.

4.5.2 Gaius Asinius Pollio

Just as the Republic was transformed by many small steps into a de facto monarchy, many gradual changes took place in Roman historiography, above all, in the treatment of the recent past and current events. Some Romans who later became historical writers traversed the entire *cursus honorum* (or prescribed sequence of political offices) under political conditions that might still be described as republican: internal conflicts may have been dominated by just a few, whose influence was disproportionate, but, on the other hand, not of long duration, and all affairs were not yet dependent on the will of a single person. But as these men grew older, they found themselves increasingly enmeshed in the congealing rule of Octavian-Augustus. Under significantly changed political circumstances, they now wrote the history of events that they had themselves lived through and had a hand in shaping. Among these historians, we find *Gaius Asinius Pollio* (76 BC–AD 5; *HRR* II LXXXIII / 67). He rose first as a military adherent of Caesar and then of Mark Antony, became consul in 40, and then, after his triumph in 39 over an Illyrian tribe, retired from active political and military life. Conspicuously, he took no side in the conflict between Octavian and Antony toward the end of the 30s. He had spent some time in his youth among rebellious (so-called) neoteric poets, and lived since his retreat from politics, like Sallust, for art and literature. Like his famous contemporary Maecenas, he played the role of benefactor and patron. He permitted himself the liberty to support literary artists who were out of favor with Augustus such as the historian *Timagenes* of Alexandria (*FGrH* 88). In addition to poetry and speeches, he also composed *Histories*. This latter work he composed with help and advice of Sallust's former research assistant Lucius Ateius (see above, Ch. 4.5.1, p. 86). The work most likely proceeded, as a continuation of Sallust's *Histories*, from the year 60 and the immediate pre-history of the so-called first triumvirate and consulate of Caesar to the victory of Antony and Octavian over the assassins of Caesar at Philippi in 42. Pollio wrote this recent history shortly after Octavian conquered Antony and Cleopatra.

Unusual narrative techniques and a unique style are typical traits of Pollio's historical work. He characterizes events through a sort of spotlight effect cast by brief utterances spoken by the historical actors themselves. He attaches reputations to the dead according to categories that read like slogans. He combines objective narrative – as will *Tacitus* later (see Ch. 6.1.3, pp. 149f.) – with the mere suggestion of an unfavorable appraisal of the person described, and to this extent avoids direct censure. He does all this in heavily poetic language with short, choppy sentences, and in this resembles Gaius Gracchus before him and subsequently Tacitus.[14] Like Sallust, Pollio too had an impact on the later shape of the language of historiography in Latin (see above 1.3.1, pp. 22f.). Among Pollio's purposes and goals was to correct *Caesar* in his *Commentaries*, although, contrary to his customary practice, Pollio criticized Caesar rather mildly (F. 4; compare Quintilian 10.2.25; see also above Ch. 4.2.2, p. 76). He was more straightforward in censuring his somewhat younger historiographical colleague *Livy* for "provinciality," a charge that likely referred not to the substance, but to the literary qualities of Livy's work (*patavinitas*: Quintilian 1.5.56 and 8.1.3). Most important for us, however, is Pollio's nuanced moral appraisal of the legacy of *Cicero* (F. 5). He fully recognizes Cicero's talent and industry, but finds him wanting in his ability to cope with fortune and misfortune, his consistency toward his enemies, and his conduct in the face of death. Cicero's career mirrored Pollio's own in political activity alternating with literary effort, in his search for freedom for the community, and – an increasingly important trend of the times – in the search for a free scope for his own personality (compare Pollio in: Cicero *Letters to his Friends* 10.31(30).5). If, in the context of the circumstances of his times, the political and social life of a Cicero was possible only at the price of inconsistency and the necessity of placing personal interests above other considerations, this rule prevailed even more strongly for a Roman of the highest senatorial rank in the perhaps even more difficult times in which Pollio lived. In this respect, Pollio was related to all later generations of senatorial historical writers who again and again under a succession of emperors were subject to similar circumstances and risks.

All this may have obscured an important point. As an historian, Pollio was courageous, because, with the history of the last decade of the civil war, he had taken on a minefield, and this at a time when in Rome the memory of the recent past was still fresh. For many it was painful or embarrassing, and the inclination to forget and keep silent was great. Moreover, with the effective concentration of power at Rome, public opinion derived almost exclusively from a single point of view. In the ode that he dedicates to Pollio, Horace, a poet frequenting Augustus' circle, calls the *Histories* "a work rich in risks" that has its author "walk through fires, that still glow under deceptive ashes" (*Odes* 2.1.6–8; published 23 BC).[15] This does not represent the poetic hyperbole of praise, but instead the perspective of a contemporary witness who had as a young man himself fought on the defeated side during the civil wars, and had since come to know the new regime from close and long-standing personal relations with the powerful, but who nevertheless had not become one of their uncritical panegyrists. Horace hinted not only at what might happen to literary artists, especially historians, but also at what actually happened to Titus Labienus the younger (*HRR* II C), whose works were banned by the Senate and whose suicide was more or less compelled. This was a consequence not of the civil wars, but instead the manner in which they were brought to an end, not through a compromise between warring factions, but instead through the nearly complete victory of one side. The writing of history and its publication became in extreme cases a potentially life-threatening danger, something the Romans had not experienced before. But it would remain just that under the empire (see below Ch. 5.1, p. 103; Ch. 6.1.2, pp. 133f.).

4.6 Antiquarian Writings

In addition to the various genres of historical writing and related literary disciplines dedicated to the distant past and recent events, much study was from the second century BC to the third century AD devoted to the study of Roman antiquities and archaic Latin. This genre, which we call antiquarianism, experienced a real efflorescence during the civil wars. (For the second century BC, see above 3.2.2, pp. 57f.) The authors engaged in such researches were attempting to obtain a broad view of their own Roman culture. Studies of this sort compelled them to delve into distant times, into the origins of Rome's religious cults, into "primitive" social relations, and into early phases in the development of the Latin language. These things had nothing in common with the research and writing of political history. Nevertheless, and especially in the first century BC, antiquarianism did not necessarily represent an escape from the horrors of the recent past or the current civil war, which would have been an understandable enough motivation (see below, Ch. 5.1, pp. 106f.). When, for example, the history of state and private furnishings over the centuries is adjudged a degeneration from functionality and usefulness (*utilitas*) for the sake of developing luxury (*luxuria*), as Varro argues in his *De vita populi Romani (On the Life of the Roman People)*, this analysis aims its critical gaze at the present. This combined use of the distant past and present did not differ in principle from Sallust's historiography of current events (see above Ch. 4.5.1, p. 86). For this reason, not all antiquarian reports are as unsuspicious or immediately trustworthy as some modern students of ancient history have sometimes supposed.

The most important antiquarian works were composed by the author we just mentioned, *Marcus Terentius Varro* (116–27 BC), who combined the investigation of antiquities with linguistic analysis especially effectively. Many authors who composed exclusively antiquarian works spent their entire lives in their study-chambers, but this was not the case for Varro. He enjoyed a long political and military career, and he was especially adept in biographical works, but not just about earlier Greeks and Romans. With his three books on Pompey, he demonstrated his capacity for contemporary biography as well (see above, Ch. 4.4, p. 82). To this extent, then, the greatest antiquarian of the age was no different from contemporaries who composed annals and monographs on current events. Like them, Varro was subject intellectually to all the circumstances and pressures of that age.

5

Augustan Rome, Roman Empire, and other Peoples and Kingdoms

The victory of Octavian in 30 BC over Mark Antony, the last of the powerful associates who had shared in the struggles against Caesar's assassins, brought an end to the civil wars and, depending on one's perspective, either a return to the republican constitution or the beginning of monarchy. The former point of view was repeatedly upheld by the sole ruler, the Princeps Augustus, and he published this view posthumously in his *Record of my Deeds* (*Res gestae*: see above, Ch. 4.2, p. 70). The second point of view was taken up not just by those who came later. From the perspective of their own times, later authors saw in Augustus – if not already in Caesar – the first founder of the imperial order, and they saw the institutions of that order congealing, or already firmly fixed, around these first Caesars. But even contemporaries of Augustus sensed, or explicitly recognized, the momentous revolution that had occurred in the political order that, in particular, robbed the nobility irrevocably of their previous privileges. Some welcomed this state of affairs, some rejected it, some took it well, some poorly. For this reason, despite almost universal longing for peace, some contemporaries could not reckon the *Pax Augusta*, the "Augustan Peace," as a purely positive development. The assessments of the new order and the man who had ushered it in were, to be sure, just as diverse and divided.

If one did not accept the new conditions or Augustus, a return to the "free" Republic always beckoned. And those who adopted this attitude, but did not know the Republic either from their own experience or from the accounts of eyewitnesses, ran the risk of viewing Rome's previous constitution as an idealized antithesis to the present. Those, on the other

Roman Historiography: An Introduction to its Basic Aspects and Development,
First Edition. Andreas Mehl.
© 2014 Hans-Friedrich Mueller. Published 2014 by Blackwell Publishing Ltd.

hand, who understood the old Republic as it really existed in the previous generation, namely, convulsed with civil wars, had a much easier time accepting the new order of things. An acceptance of the new constitution and reality could nevertheless paradoxically arise from the same cause as an idealized veneration of the old Republic. As has been recognized at least since *Tacitus*, the tendency of many Romans during the early impe-rial age to live privately and quietly, thus in effect supporting the regime, resulted from the long period of Octavian-Augustus' de facto sole rule, which was unchallenged by serious rivals from 30 BC to AD 14. A new generation had grown up that had no memory of the Republic (*Annals* 1.3.7). We find diverse attitudes mirrored in the historiographical works that were composed during the Augustan age toward the recent past and toward a present stamped by Octavian-Augustus. Their remains, espe-cially the surviving portions of *Livy*, whose work practically consigns his contemporaries to oblivion, provide an unsatisfactory, because one-sided, impression. This impression can be corrected by consideration of *Asinius Pollio*. But he composed his work – early – in Augustus' reign, and, at least in his political career, belonged to a previous generation (see above, Ch. 4.5.2, p. 94).

For contemporary historiography there was, however, one further consideration for assessment: despite the all the turmoils of the civil wars, Octavian-Augustus, but also other powerful men before him from Marius to Caesar, had managed through the entire period of the civil wars to maintain, and sometimes even to expand, the territory that Rome con-trolled or at least influenced. And, with Octavian's conquest of Egypt in 30 BC, the circle of subjugated peoples round about the Mediterranean had, more crucially, been closed. The Mediterranean represented for Greeks and Romans alike the world, and this entire world was now ruled by Rome alone. The world vis-à-vis Rome's world domination would of necessity become a topic for historiography, especially as Augustan propa-ganda trumpeted precisely this, the achievement of world domination, as an accomplishment of Augustus, and used it (among other arguments) to justify his preeminent role in the state. Roman world domination could in principle be observed and assessed from two points of view: from Rome and by Romans or from the perspective of those subject to, and ruled by, them. On the other hand, the appraisal of Roman expansion and the relations of Romans with other peoples and states, as well with their rulers and ruling classes, did not necessarily lead non-Romans and those newly Roman to assessments that contradicted the verdicts on those same events rendered by Romans of Roman or Italian ancestry (see below, Ch. 5.1, p. 110; Ch. 5.2, p. 111).

5.1 Titus Livius: Roman History from Romulus to Augustus in its Entirety

Titus Livius' Roman history was considered *the* history of Rome, and was much read and widely used, from the time he wrote it through the conversion of the Roman empire to Christianity and subsequently during the Middle Ages, the Renaissance (by, for example, Niccolò Machiavelli), the European Enlightenment, and, finally, well into the French Revolution. And yet, among the ancient writers of Roman history, Livy was unique and an exception. Born around 60 BC in Patavia (Padua), he came from a provincial town that had first acquired Roman rights when Livy was already a young man. Livy thus derived from a class that was establishing itself in the life of Rome around the time the civil wars were drawing to a close. Unlike the previous ruling class, these people came not from Rome and mid-Italy, but instead from Italy's borderlands. Nonetheless, after his arrival in Rome (most likely some time after Octavian's victory over Antony and Cleopatra), not only did he fail to enter politics, he became a writer of history without ever having served in a single office, and therefore lacked his own military and administrative experience of public affairs. Livy is thus a special case in Roman historiography, which is dominated both before and after him by senators. In spite of, or perhaps because of, his political abstinence, Livy soon found himself in the company of Augustus and his family, together with such men as Vergil, Horace, and Maecenas, and he received from these connections the income to support himself. Among Augustus' family members, he later inspired the young "prince" *Claudius* to write history (see below, Ch. 6.1.2, pp. 133f.). Above all, Livy soon wrote, in the vicinity of the *princeps* himself, and from the beginning of the 20s BC, a Roman history that extended from earliest times to his own day. He published the work in successive installments, through which he became famous. Livy likely died in his native city around AD 17, i.e., three years after Augustus.[1] Given the context in which it was composed, one wants to see in Livy's work a point of view in simple agreement with Augustus. And we can muster as evidence Livy's positive appraisal of the peace and of Augustus' religious politics as well as Livy's adoption of new and contemporary ethical values into the fabric of his history (see below, pp. 107f.). But such an assessment, as it does likewise for the Augustan poets, falls short.

Only Books 1–10 and 21–45 of Livy's Roman history survive intact. These books include the early history of Rome and the decades from the beginning of the Second Punic War in 218 to immediately after the end of the Third Macedonian War in 167 BC. Of the other books, that is, from more than three quarters of the original 142 books, we have only ancient abridgments (*Epitomae*) and summaries (*Periochae*) as well as some fragmentary excerpts that preserve the original wording.[2] This wretched transmission of the text renders general statements about Livy's work as a whole by no means worthless, but certainly tentative, and this holds true especially for general accounts of his methods of composition, his consistency in, or deviations from, certain views as well as for his general aims as an author. The name of the work, *Ab urbe condita* (*From the Foundation of the City*), which is based on the work's first sentence, identifies the actual beginning of the history only approximately, inasmuch as Livy also treats the pre-history of Rome. On the other hand, Livy makes it clear that he is an author in the annalistic tradition who will write all Roman history, and that this customarily includes the remote origins and first beginnings of Rome. Like others before him, Livy treats these topics rather summarily (see above, Ch. 4, p. 65): he dedicates just one book to the pre-history and foundation of Rome together with the 250-year history of the monarchy to 510 BC. He reaches recent history and the beginning of the civil wars in 133 BC as early as Book 58 and subsequently, in Book 109, the civil war between Caesar and the majority of the Senate under Pompey's leadership in 49 BC. Some 34 books were thus available for narrating the events of the last 41 years through 9 BC. In calculating the number of books to the number of years, we can observe that Livy devoted proportionally more space to this final period than he had to all previous times. Thanks to the *Periochae*, which are almost completely preserved, we can discern in Livy's work, more readily than is the case with earlier lost annalistic works, that annalistic narratives of Roman history in its entirety are like a stream that from its source to its mouth grows continually wider.

As it existed in antiquity, the *Ab urbe condita* ended after 142 books with the death of Augustus' stepson Drusus in 9 BC as the result of an accident. Livy can hardly have aimed at this conclusion, inasmuch as this event is significant neither in the history of Rome and its empire nor in the reign of Augustus. We should leave it an open question whether Livy, as has sometimes been argued, intended to bring his work down to the death of Augustus, and for one reason in particular: Livy could not pursue such a plan until after the man had actually died. In light of the compass of his work and the decades he spent at work on his account of all Roman history, we should perhaps grant Livy a certain open-endedness in regard to planning or perhaps reckon that he successively aimed at what became a series of conclusions, as was similarly already the case with Cato's much shorter *Origines* and was certainly possible in annalistic historiography in general (see above, Ch. 3.2.1, pp. 53f.).

Successive installments of the work according to a set scheme, as many have postulated for the *Ab urbe condita*, can only have negative, not positive, consequences. To the extent that Livy subdivided his work into groups of either five, ten, or fifteen books (*pentads, decades, pentekai-decades*), we must assume on formal grounds that the author aimed at a corresponding total of 145 or 150 books. This much-advocated scheme can only be demonstrated under certain conditions. Books 6, 21, 26, and 31 represent indeed the beginning of groups of books, but we find deviations from the system in Books 35 and 36, and in the section devoted to contemporary history there are real difficulties. The victory of Octavian over Antony and Cleopatra, the natural conclusion to a section, is dealt with not in Book 135, but as early as Book 133. Neither Book 136 nor 137 has survived either among the *Periochae* or *Epitomae,* but, judging from the contents of 135 and 138, the Secular Games of 17 BC must have fallen between them, and marked either the end or the beginning of a group of books. In the narration of the last 150 years of Roman history, it is conceivable that large sections of the work were not arranged according to proportional composition, but instead around eminent politicians and generals: Scipio Africanus the younger, Marius, Sulla, Pompey, Caesar, and Octavian-Augustus. The ancients had already begun calling this section of Livy's work, the eight books devoted to Caesar's civil war (109–116), the *Civile bellum*, partly after Caesar's three (or perhaps six) books of commentary, the *De bello civili* (a name, incidentally, not bestowed by their author). Ancient readers also gave this selection of books its own special numeration (see above, Ch. 4.2.2, p. 75). Unfortunately, the surviving *Periochae* do not permit us to draw more detailed conclusions.

Because the *Periocha* of Book 121 (which describes the events of 43 BC) contains an introductory remark that the book was first published after the death of Augustus, we know that Livy had already published the greater part of his work by AD 14. In the some forty years that elapsed from the time of the publication of the first book between 27 and 25 BC, Livy had thus published 120 books at a pace of approximately three books per year. On practical grounds, one may assume that he likely began more slowly, and that his rate of book production increased gradually. We find confirmation of this in the date for Book 9 – before 20 BC – and for Book 28 – after 19 BC. On the other hand, the preparation and composition of 22 books (121–142) in the three remaining years of Livy's life seems unrealistically high. Livy must then have already proceeded by the time of Augustus' death much farther with his narration of the age of Octavian-Augustus than we would otherwise conclude from the date of publication provided for Book 121. Of course, the notice to Book 121 does not preclude the possibility that, at the time of Augustus' death, Livy had already composed, or at least prepared, more than the 120 books he had published.

A gap between the composition and publication of a literary work that appears in installments over a period of many years can certainly result from an author's work methods. In Livy's case, more delicate considerations may have applied. With the events that dated from Caesar's assassination and his testamentary adoption of Octavius, the historian had entered the last phase of the civil war. The man who became Augustus was actively involved in these events (from Book 116). This was by far the most sensitive part of his entire history. The aged Augustus had already (though not in unfriendly fashion) branded Livy a partisan of Pompey for his narrative of the phase of the civil war immediately before Caesar's murder (Tacitus *Annals* 4.34.3). Augustus was gentle then because, in his later years, he expressed neither entirely positive views of his deified "father" Caesar or entirely negative views of Pompey (compare Cassius Dio 56.34.2–3). Livy's representation of Caesar as the great destroyer and a positive appraisal of Pompey would therefore not necessarily have provoked the wrath of Augustus (on Caesar, compare Livy in Seneca *Naturales quaestiones* 5.18.4). The phase of the civil war *after* Caesar was another matter entirely (44–28/27 BC). At the beginning of the *Pax Augusta*, one could not speak freely on the topic without real risk to one's personal safety. The poet Horace, who was a member of Augustus' inner circle and enjoyed relationships with other people close to Augustus, including Livy, confirms this (see above, Ch. 4.5.2, pp. 95f.). Decades later, at least while Augustus still lived, these circumstances continued to prevail. Livy had encouraged the young Claudius, step-grandson of Augustus, born around 10 BC, to write history (see above, p. 100). Claudius began his narrative immediately after the assassination of Caesar. After being repeatedly and harshly reprimanded by his mother and grandmother, who monitored his work as it progressed, Claudius abandoned the project, and turned to a new and likely safer period: the years that followed the official end of the civil war in 28/27 BC (Suetonius *Claudius* 41). This may well have served as a warning for Livy. He was likely not as venturesome as his older contemporary Asinius Pollio (see above, Ch. 4.5.2, pp. 94f.), preferring instead to delay publication of as many of the potentially offensive books as possible until after the death of Augustus.

In face of the mass of materials available to him, Livy had to approach the preparation of his materials economically. For most of the past, he did not have to investigate primary sources, but could instead employ relevant narratives irrespective of how distant or close the authors had themselves been to the events they described. Livy thus used for the Second Punic War, 218–201 BC, the monograph of *Coelius Antipater* (see above, Ch. 3.2.2, pp. 58f.), and, for the events in the East from 201 to 146, he used the detailed narrative of the Greek author *Polybius* (see above, Ch. 3.2, p. 50). For longer sections of early Roman history as well as for parts of more recent Roman history, he used the Roman histories of earlier or later *annalistic* writers (see above, Ch. 4.1, pp. 66ff.). For long stretches, Livy could follow a single author, consulting other authors from time to time to check or supplement the first (not that we can discern a regular pattern to this practice). Livy's use of his sources, together with his fundamentally general and thus vague practices in citation, has some consequences that have set up a stumbling block for philological and historical investigation. The same historical works can be found in various states of refraction throughout Livy: directly rewritten by Livy, but also rewritten in consultation with the account of a later author, whose own work, in turn, Livy will use directly without intermediary check. It sometimes happens that Livy will narrate the same event twice (so-called doublets) – albeit varying the details – because he follows more than one author. On occasion Livy reports something only to correct it (and thus himself) later because he now follows a different author. One should never lose sight in all this that Livy's ability to assess military and political affairs neither derived from personal experience nor was acquired growing up as a member of republican Rome's ruling class (see above, pp. 99f.). Livy barely understood the intricacies of senatorial rule. Especially alien to him were the social and economic circumstances as well as the power politics of the personal relations of the Nobiles and the various interest groups that surrounded them. One must thus confront in Livy an idealized Senate and a corresponding censure of the Roman citizen-body as well as Roman politicians as soon as they strike out independently, departing from whatever the will of the Senate may have been at the time. And this, despite his own status as man of the periphery and, again, his sympathy for parvenus and outsiders.

Livy fulfills *Cicero's* demands for a literary and rhetorical Roman historiography (see above, Ch. 4.3, pp. 79ff.; cf. Livy frags. 59f., ed. Jal [Bibl. §1.1]). For this reason alone, *Thucydides* can hardly number among those who taught him historical methods (see above, Ch. 1.3.2, pp. 27f.).

Nevertheless, this Greek author offered Livy a *literary* model in one instance. Whereas, for the former, his topic, the Peloponnesian War, was, "of all wars, the most worthy of study," for the latter, it was the Second Punic War that presented monumental themes on a world stage (compare Thucydides 1.1–2 with Livy 21.1.1–2). Although Livy's historiographical methods may not be especially interesting, his work's linguistic features are another matter altogether. From the beginning to the end of his work, his shaping of the conclusions to his sentences (*clausulae*) imitates Sallust. On the other hand, we find his Latin style archaic only at the beginning. Later it is unexceptionally classical and Augustan. Three factors are reflected in this change: (1) for earlier and later portions of his Roman history, Livy made use of sources whose authors derived from various epochs and thus often from diverse places in the evolution of the Latin language. (2) In the transition from the Republic to the Principate of Augustus, which took place during the first decade of his composition of the *Ab urbe condita*, the aesthetic sensibilities of both literature and the decorative arts had changed substantially, under the influence of Octavian-Augustus and the artists around him. (3) A rhetorical rule specified that linguistic style should adapt itself to its theme both in detail and in general. Livy followed this rule with some restraint. He did adhere to another, somewhat contradictory, rule more closely: just as a politician should always maintain his dignity and seriousness of purpose, an historian should always avoid giving offense either with his language or in his narrative (compare *Ab urbe condita* 7.10 with the version of Claudius Quadrigarius *HRR* I 207ff. F. 10b = *AR / FRH* 10b, who does not follow Livy's maxim).

Livy's work makes clear that annalistic historiography, despite proceeding year by year (and this holds true for Livy too), does not have to result in slavishly moronic proportionality in the narrative of important and unimportant details or in refraining from interpretation and from constructing broader contexts of meaning (but compare above, Ch. 3.2.2, p. 60). The collection of various books around closely related and important events represents interpretation through composition. Leitmotifs can hold small details as well as large themes together and at the same time separate them from other unities, as, for example, the theme of *libertas* (freedom) at the beginning of Book 2, which serves as a contrast to the verdict rendered in Book 1 that branded the monarchy unfree. Especially important events like great speeches, declarations of war, battles, and triumphs are placed in prominent positions, namely at the beginning, middle, or end of a book. The various consequences of an event are themselves dramatized individually, and, in comparison with his sources, Livy made his narrative tauter (especially in respect of the emotions of his main actors), sometimes remodeling it, and thus what cannot be portrayed as a whole through annual reports stretching across centuries is accomplished in such details (see above, Ch. 1.3.1, p. 19). Livy also makes use of a wide palette in portraying personalities, sometimes directly and sometimes indirectly. He can paint individual portraits, just as he can also render his characters as types. He will, for example, take a certain characteristic belonging to a clan (*gens*) of Rome's ruling class, and ascribe it time and again to individual members of that clan. Examples include the arrogance of the Claudii or the brave self-sacrifice of the Decii. Despite the typecasting such constants represent, Livy treats his characters as individuals, whose conduct does not appear uniform in diverse situations, but, on the contrary, frequently appears to depend on circumstances and context. We find this again in Tacitus (see below, Ch. 6.1.3, pp. 146f.).

In light of the long period of time, some forty years, over which the books of the *Ab urbe condita* successively appeared, we must reckon with the possibility that the author's attitudes and views changed from Book 1 to Book 142, and that his values may have shifted. The preface to the entire work, at once full of feeling and complex thought, was already written *before* the publication of Book 1, to which it is prefixed. In all events, it was not written *after* the publication of Book 142. This preface presents the feelings and thoughts of Livy in the 20s, that is, a time still close to the civil wars. We may thus use it as a measure only for early, not later, books, and certainly not for the entire history. In principle, this holds true for those books that have survived as well, Books 1–10 and 21–45, whose events are remote from Livy's own lifetime. The ancient abridgments and summaries (produced, we should add, according to subjective criteria) can in their reduction of a rich narrative to dry lists of dates and major events hardly help us discover Livy's fundamental attitudes and views and their eventual transformation over time. But we do get some help in the few anticipatory remarks Livy makes in his early books about contemporary events. Insights into Livy's attitudes and views gleaned from surviving pieces of his work provide only random spotlights, whose transfer to the work as a whole may well be unproblematic in some details, but nevertheless must in others remain *sub judice*, and in still others will surely prove misleading or inapplicable.

Even the expression *nostra aetas* ("our age"), which we find in the preface before Book 1 (*Preface* 5), as a term for the period of the Roman civil war or, more precisely, for its last phase, would, by the time Livy arrived at his narrative of that (last) phase of civil war, no longer have been immediately appropriate. There is a simple reason for this. After more than thirty years under the Principate of Augustus, although the civil war remained a volatile topic, Livy's approach would surely have been less emotional than it was when he composed the first book and the preface. At that time, ancient Roman history represented for him a refuge from working on the history of his own times, even though he supposed that his readers would have preferred the opposite (*Preface* 4–5; compare above, Ch. 4.6, p. 96). Furthermore, Livy considers the collapse of moral standards a fact (*Preface* 8–12). In contrast, however, to *Sallust* and other historians, Livy does not find the Romans' path into decadence marked by just one turning point. Instead, it runs at first a rather level course, declining more and more steeply over time until finally its downward curve becomes precipitously sharp (see above, Ch. 4.5.1, pp. 91ff.; and below Ch. 8, pp. 246f.). The real moral decline had entered Roman life much later than it had the societies of other peoples, and its nadir, in which "we can bear neither our faults nor their cure," had been reached only in the present (*Preface* 9).[3] It is difficult to imagine that Livy would have offered this same assessment of present conditions at the end of Augustus' reign. In other words, Livy would have been unable to confirm the exclusively pessimistic judgment we find in the preface before Book 1. The present moment that, at the end of the civil war, was marked by the complete collapse of moral standards would, by the time Livy got round to narrating this epoch, have actually been the beginning of a new era, which, even if one did not like it, was nevertheless very different from, and perhaps also better than, what had gone before. These last considerations are less hypothetical than might appear at first glance. We find in Livy not just decadence, but also progress. And both, not just the former, are processes over time. Both the external expansion of Rome and the evolution of Rome's moral values are for Livy the results of long developments. After the moral quicksands of the civil wars, gradual improvement was therefore not inconceivable.

Livy's religiosity is blatant. We must consider it to have been a constant in his life and work. The social function of religion and cult is for him, as for most Romans, self-evident (compare, for example, Cicero *De republica* 2.26f.). As a result, Livy countenances, on the one hand, pious deception, but, on the other, condemns sects and thus any private religion or religious groups that may possibly represent a danger to the state. Examples include, on the one hand, the second king Numa and the nymph Egeria (1.19.4–5) and, on the other, the Bacchanalia and their suppression (39.8–19). Livy is skeptical of gods who intervene in human form, and, in his careful way, he puts us on notice as early as his *Preface* (7–8) that he will leave the question open as to whether or not the god Mars really sired the twins Romulus and Remus. He signals that his attitude toward the gods is more like the attitude of the poets who call on the gods for inspiration at the beginning of a work when he too calls on the gods (*Preface* 13). The respect that this Roman author displays for the numinous when he is confronted with unusual occurrences that cannot be explained otherwise than through supernatural forces binds him more than anything else to the distant past: "When I describe these distant events, my whole spirit becomes somehow archaic, and a reverence for the sacred compels me to register (supernatural events) in my annals," writes Livy immediately before recording the odd occurrences (prodigies) of the year 169 BC. In Livy's view, these prodigies offered real insight into the future, and he contrasts ancient attitudes with contemporary indifference toward the numinous, an indifference that had left – harmful – traces in historiography (43.13.1ff.: quote from §2).[4] Did Livy continue to consider religious and cult practices neglected even after he had praised Augustus' renovation of crumbling temples (4.20.7) and even after Augustus' reforms of cult practice? Or was this earlier evil state of affairs now happily repaired?

Livy announces directly in his *Preface* (9–10) that he intends to offer moral instruction and that he will do so with positive and negative moral examples. He also repeats this on many occasions throughout the surviving books of his historical narrative. He hopes to accomplish this, on the one hand, by offering historical models of conduct worthy of imitation, and, on the other hand, by offering examples that should be avoided. The conduct of historical personages has an impact not only on those who later study it and take it to heart, but also an immediate impact on historical contemporaries. Morality is always illustrated through conduct, rather than through abstract and general rules or through maxims. Conduct is, of course, bound to specific situations. And this is what provides the rationale for what we have just observed about Livy's practice of exploring individual character in its specific historical context. The values Livy extols are, on the one hand, traditional in Rome. Among them, the virtues of the soldier stand out as well as a very formal and ritualistically conceived sense of justice that provides ready pretexts for Roman conduct in relations with others. In addition to these virtues, we find, on the other hand, contrasting virtues that result from the experience of the civil wars and the concomitant suppression of unrestrained belligerence and ambition: a readiness to make peace and to work together for social harmony as well as those values that were propagated from a proper appreciation of the general mood in the circle around Augustus. This is why immediately after the customary praise of Rome's reputation for war (*Preface* 7) at the beginning of Livy's historical narrative and thus at the beginning of Roman history, we find the story of Aeneas' arrival, leading the Trojan remnants, on the coast of Latium. War threatened to break out between these Trojans and the natives under King Latinus, but it was averted by a treaty of peace and friendship. Livy tells this story at length quite movingly, dismissing the other version, with which he was quite familiar, in just a few words: that only an initial defeat in battle convinced Latinus to conclude a treaty with Aeneas (1.1.4–9). And in his high praises of Rome's second king Numa's achievements in peace, Livy weaves in Augustus' recent achievement of a comprehensive peace (1.19.3). As a practically oriented preacher of morality, Livy does not concern himself with contradictions in the values he exhorts or whether logic renders them mutually exclusive.

Non-Romans too had, of course, aimed frequently at the composition of complete histories of Rome and this continued into the Augustan period. Two items are of interest in this regard: when Livy chooses to cite the testimony of non-Romans and, above all, how he cites non-Romans and with what sorts of value judgments. Livy states in his very first sentence that he will write the *res populi Romani* ("deeds of the Roman people;" *Preface* 1). He consequently passes over non-Roman affairs, to the extent that they have no importance for Rome (e.g., 39.48.6). His manner of describing non-Romans is predicated on his simple conception of the moral – and not necessarily technical or practical – victory of the better side over the worse. Rome's complete victory and the accomplished fact of Rome's unquestionable world domination gave Livy room for generosity to mention explicitly, on the one hand, Roman mistakes along the way to world domination and, on the other hand, to furnish Rome's enemies (especially the Carthaginian Hannibal) with noble qualities, so that Livy could offer them up too as objects of admiration and, more importantly, as models – although naturally only in part – worthy of imitation. This is made even easier for Livy because, in his view, even if non-Romans occasionally surpass individual Romans, Rome's supremacy demonstrates that Romans have, in sum, proven superior to non-Romans. Both the *Ab urbe condita*'s partial critique of Roman conduct toward others and its partial praise of non-Romans thus contribute to the construction of a patriotic work in praise of Rome.

5.2 World History, the History of the World beyond Rome, and Roman History by Non-Romans and New Romans

The Civil War demonstrated just how closely the "world" (or, more accurately, the Mediterranean area together with territories on its borders) was bound to Rome. Every region and almost every country, even those "free" territories not yet ruled and administered directly by Rome as provinces, were sucked into the maelstrom of the conflicts between Romans, becoming thereby natural targets for requisitions and recruitment as well as battlefields in the contests between Roman armies. Rome's dominion over the entire Mediterranean became an accomplished and unalterable fact with the end of military conflict at the conclusion of the civil wars and with the decades-long peaceful rule that continued to prevail under the reigns of Augustus and his successors in the Principate. Roman history had to this extent become world history and world history had become Roman history.

Historians and chroniclers whose ancestry was non-Roman could no longer close their eyes to the fact that their world had become Roman. In analyzing and judging events, these historiographers could still shift their emphasis, view Rome's hegemony from the point of view of one of the many peoples subject to it, or even treat its establishment by Rome critically. But in doing so, they could not realistically imagine, expect, or even hope for fundamental changes in the relative balance of power or the conditions of Roman rule. Non-Roman and newly Roman historiographers alike recognized this. On the other hand, Greek historiographers as well as those educated in Greek culture could deploy ideas formulated in an already distant past about the unity of humankind and the *oikoumene* (i.e., those portions of the Earth inhabited by human beings). These writers could thereby easily describe the Roman empire as the fulfillment of the purpose of world history. And one could, of course, simply resign oneself contentedly to life under Rome's rule, and thus assess it positively without any close questioning of how the empire came to exist. It is also no coincidence that all the historiographers we shall discuss or introduce in the pages that follow spent time – and many of them many years – in the city of Rome. Whether stated explicitly or silently assumed, Rome did double duty as a reference point for authors of non-Roman derivation: as the empire and as its center (see above, Ch. 1.2, pp. 12ff.). These observations will remain valid for a much later admirer of the Roman empire as well: *Appian* (see below, Ch. 6.2.2, pp. 162ff.).

5.2.1 World History and Roman History (from Diodorus to Juba)

As early as the second century BC *Polybius,* one of the greatest of the Greek historians, had, despite his criticism of its various aspects, approved in principle of Rome's hegemony. *Posidonius* of Apamea (and a citizen of Rhodes), who continued Polybius' history, in the first century BC held the same opinion. The Sicilian Greek *Diodorus,* who, drawing in part on Posidonius, wrote between 60/50 and 30/20 BC, imbued his *Library of History* with the Stoic and Cynic conception that all the peoples of the Earth shared a common ancestry, and thus set as its proper sphere all time and all inhabited space or, as Diodorus put it, world history as if it were "of just a single city" (1.1.3: καθάπερ μιᾶς πόλεως; cf. 1.3.2 and 6).[5] His history accordingly includes events beginning with the creation of the world and humankind. Diodorus fulfills his geographical goal of including the entire Earth when he first describes early mythical times, but he soon loses this wider view – and naturally so from Greek and Roman perspectives – when he begins to concentrate on Greek and Roman history, although he regains it again when he reaches recent and contemporary events, especially Rome's massive expansion up to the beginning of Caesar's command in Gaul, which forms the conclusion to his world history. Because Diodorus' work has not come down to us complete and because we possess only fragments for the period of Rome's expansion throughout the Mediterranean, we must refrain from formulating specific criteria for evaluating this author's views. We must instead content ourselves with the general observation that for Diodorus too the world appeared to have achieved political unity through Rome (1.4.3), and the author, on the basis of his conception of the world as a single city or polis, welcomed this. In light of the importance he attached to an individual's ethical conduct, we can also surmise that Diodorus assessed at least some Roman politicians positively (e.g., 33.28b). We can only answer hypothetically the question why Diodorus would have ended his work with an event so unsuited to it: did he perhaps wish to spare himself the last two phases of Rome's civil wars, whose events were closely connected with each other and were truly waged world wide, for the sake of his own personal safety? (Compare above, Ch. 4.5.2, pp. 95ff.; Ch. 5.1, p. 103.)

Timagenes of Alexandria (*FGrH* 88) likely did not share the attitudes of Polybius, Posidonius, and Diodorus toward Rome. He came to Rome as a prisoner of war in 55 BC, and lived there as a free man in the circle of Octavian-Augustus. Much later, after he had fallen into disfavor because of unfriendly remarks he had made, Asinius Pollio took him into his circle (on which, see above, Ch. 4.5.2, p. 94). To the extent that we may view *Livy's* criticism of "irresponsible Greek authors" as applicable to Timagenes too, his work *On the Kings* (*Peri basileon*; the portions dealing with Augustus and contemporary events were allegedly, according to another source, burnt by Timagenes himself) gave prominence to the Parthian empire and Macedonians (especially Alexander the Great) to the disadvantage of Rome and Romans (Livy 9.18.6; *levissimi ex Graecis*). It is the considered opinion of many scholars that *Pompeius Trogus* adopted Timagenes' negative assessment of Rome, although this cannot be confirmed from what survives of Trogus' historical work in the epitome of Justin (see below, Ch. 5.2.3, p. 117).

During the reign of Augustus, as well as to some extent during the reign of his successor Tiberius, other men too who were born in neither Rome nor Italy wrote Roman history, or "world history," in Greek. Nicolaus of *Damascus* (*FGrH* 90) tutored the children whom the last Ptolemaic queen, Cleopatra VII, had with Mark Antony. Nicolaus later became an advisor to the Jewish king Herod I, a favorite of Augustus, and thus found his way to Rome and to Augustus. He became an historian at Herod's instigation. Nicolaus collected odd ethnic customs (FF. 103–124). This may be connected with the peripatetic orientation that he experienced in his own life, which he treated as a topic in his autobiography (FF. 131–139). His 144-volume *Historiai* likely extended to the death of King Herod in 4 BC. Of the approximately one hundred fragments (FF. 1–102), at least seventy of them (many quite long) belong to Books 1–7. They demonstrate that the work was a "synchronically arranged world history" (Lendle [Bibl. §1.3], p. 245). The few surviving fragments, however, that deal with recent history provide no keys to its presentation. Nevertheless, taken together with another of Nicolaus' compositions, his panegyric *Life of Augustus* (*Peri tou biou Kaisaros*: FF. 125–130; written already by about 20 BC), we may infer that his world history too would have changed into "court history" as it approached the present. In other words, it would have concluded with high praise of Herod (and Augustus).

Strabo of Amaseia (circa 64 BC–AD 23; *FGrH* 91), who came from the small kingdom of Pontus in northeast Asia Minor and settled eventually in Rome, composed two major works: *Geographika* and *Historika Hypomnemata*. The latter work's surviving portions offer spare and one-sided testimony. In about 39 or 43 volumes (our two best guesses), this work seems, like many works of Roman annalistic history, to have run briefly through the great length of more remote ancient history (Books 1–4 reached approximately 145 BC.) and then – continuing *Polybius* – to have treated in great detail recent history and current events possibly to the end of Rome's civil wars (Books 5–39 or 43; see above, Ch. 4, p. 65; Ch. 5.1, pp. 100f.). In a sober narrative, Strabo appeals to his readers, who, like him, should be "well-rounded, free citizens, schooled in philosophy," whom he wishes to educate "politically for the general benefit of all" or "as a contribution ... toward their ethical and political philosophy" (F. 2 = *Geographika* 1.1.22f.).[6] On the one hand, this senti-ment is similar to Polybius'. On the other, Strabo completely lacked any connection to practical political engagement, was thus very different from Polybius, who had himself been both a political magistrate and a military officer. The similarity of instructive purpose in both Strabo's *Geographika* and *Historika Hypomnemata* allows us to substitute the former for the latter in another respect as well: in the concluding chapter of the *Geographika* (17.3.24), Rome's empire is described as the largest and most powerful in the Mediterranean up to that point. In a short descrip-tion of its extent, he also mentions those territories of the *oikoumene* (or inhabited Earth) that Rome did not rule. These areas he characterizes, of course, as small, miserable, barely settled or inhabited exclusively by "savages," and consequently meaningless for the *oikoumene* or not quali-fied for inclusion in it. In contrast to these territories, to the extent that Strabo mentions extra-Roman territories inhabited, and ruled, by people with such still formidable names as the Parthians, the Indians, the Ethiopians, among others, he stresses the ongoing historical process that will convey them too into Roman possession. The not yet quite one hundred percent domination of the Earth by Rome will thus soon be completed. In this way, Strabo reflects the official language that insisted on Rome's dominion over the whole world, and thereby proves "Augustan."

Gaius Julius Juba (circa 50 BC–AD 23; *FGrH* 275) was the son of a Numidian king who was raised in Rome as a prisoner of war and subse-quently placed as king on the throne of Mauretania by Augustus. He wrote ethnographic, cultural, and natural histories, some of which the elder Pliny used for his own *Natural History* (*Naturalis historia*), as well as a merely two-volume *Romaïké Historia* (or, alternatively, *Romaïké Archaiologia*). The few fragments of the latter (FF. 9–12) do not permit us to draw conclusions about his political inclinations. From the point of view of genre, however, Juba's *Roman History* may be viewed in its brevity as a precursor to imperial and late antique compendiums of history (see below, Ch. 6.5, pp. 186ff.).

5.2.2 Dionysius of Halicarnassus: early Rome and the Greeks

Dionysius of Halicarnassus composed a peculiar Roman history specifically for Greek-speaking readers. Born around the year 60, he lived from 30 BC at Rome as a teacher of Greek rhetoric who enjoyed connections to Greek and Roman intellectuals. He wrote various stylistic treatises on Herodotus, Xenophon, Theopompus, and, especially noteworthy, Thucydides. His historical works include a *Chronicle*, in which he coordinated dates for Roman history with dates from Greek history (see below, Ch. 5.2.4, p. 120), and a twenty-volume *Romaïké Archaiologia* (*Roman Antiquities* or *The Early History of Rome*). We possess Books 1–10 of this latter work in their entirety, parts of Book 11, and Books 12–20 only in excerpts and quotations. In this work, Dionysius offered Roman history from earliest times to just before the First Punic War in 265 BC (1.8.1–2). In this way, he supplemented the work of an earlier historian, whom he mentions frequently: *Polybius*. Dionysius thereby followed a practice customary from the time Greek historians had begun composing continuations to Thucydides' *History of the Peloponnesian War*. Among Roman annalistic writers too, it was common practice to compose one's work as a continuation to some predecessor (see above, Ch. 4, p. 65). What was unusual, however, was that Dionysius focused his work on an earlier historical period than that of his predecessor. Polybius, of course, had composed a history of the great phase of Roman expansion from the time of the Second Punic War, i.e., from 220 to 168 (or perhaps 146) BC, furnishing it with a prelude beginning in 264 with the First Punic War. (Compare in this regard Tacitus below in Ch. 6.1.3, p. 139)

In his extensive preface (1.1–8), Dionysius formulates the assumptions on which he bases his work. Greeks are either unacquainted with the early history of Rome or falsely informed about it, as in, for example, the claim detrimental to Rome's reputation that its first settlers were former slaves (1.4.2). Dionysius opposes this with the thesis that the Romans were of Greek descent, for the truth of which his narrative of early Roman history will supply the proof (1.5). This thesis accords with a common Greek practice in dealing with non-Greeks, but, more significantly, long before Dionysius Greek authors had made this argument by interlacing history with myth, and later, but still a good two hundred years before Dionysius, the first Roman historian, *Fabius Pictor*, had adopted this position when presenting Rome to a Greek and Greek-speaking public in order to absolve Rome of its barbarian status (see above, Ch. 3.1.1, p. 47). Dionysius' project is thus in principle hardly new, and one suspects that this teacher of oratory will extol the object of his labors in rhetorical fashion. Nevertheless, his thesis may well have represented something new for his intended audience, inasmuch as those earlier Greek-language authors who wrote of the Romans' Greek ancestry had, in the meantime, fallen out of fashion and into oblivion. On the other hand, Dionysius' very approach presupposes that the libraries of his day could still supply him with works of the sort that helped him arrive at his view of the Romans' descent, and offered the proof he required.

Greeks as the founders of Rome represented for Dionysius not some mere fact from a long-forgotten past, but rather, above all, a means for arguing his case in the context of recent developments in power politics that had shaped his present world: Rome had achieved dominion over the world, thereby eclipsing all the previous (world) empires that Dionysius lists and briefly describes (1.2f.).[7] Dionysius wished to demonstrate to the Greeks of his time (the closing years of the first century BC) that, although they – like everyone else – were subject to Roman rule, Greeks were ruled not by an alien people, i.e., by barbarians or inferiors, but instead by their own kind, and, furthermore, as Dionysius often stresses, by a morally and culturally advanced elite of their own kind. Ultimately, Dionysius aims to reconcile Greeks with the loss of their independence under Roman rule, and to establish Rome's status relative to the Greeks on a more abstract level. Granted, this too is hardly new, but – keeping in mind the very different balance of power that prevailed at the time – rather like the method of the first Roman historian, *Fabius Pictor* (see above, Ch. 3.1.1, pp. 43f.).

Dionysius certainly surpassed Pictor, however, in shaping the contents of his work, above all in regard to his complex stylistic and linguistic aims, so that it would meet the needs of three distinct groups within his intended Greek readership: politically active citizens, together with the local governing class in Greek cities, secondly, those with philosophical interests, and, finally, those who simply looked for entertainment (1.8.3). To all these groups he broadcast the good news of Rome's Greek status and what this implied for Greeks under Roman rule. Consequently, Dionysius, unlike Fabius Pictor, did not aim exclusively at an immediate political effect, but instead at shaping Greek public opinion more generally, which, although it could indeed express itself to some extent directly in political action, resulted in other more indirect kinds of expression too. If we consider that, despite all the inscriptional evidence loudly proclaiming steadfast loyalty to Rome and its political leadership, power politics, and thus Rome itself, remained remote from the intellectual experience of those who inhabited Greek cities and areas under Greek cultural influence, then we begin to understand Dionysius' aims.

The variety of the *Romaïké Archaiologia* both in form and content requires, on the one hand, as the author himself concludes, that he cannot employ a single historical genre (1.8.3), and thus offers a – typically Roman – blending of genres (see above, Ch. 1.1, p. 11, and below, Ch. 6.1.3, pp. 136f.). This implies, on the other hand, that Dionysius must describe "all aspects of life in ancient Rome," and offer, in particular, constitutional, legal, moral, and cultural history (1.8.2).[8] Dionysius prepared himself for this extensive program by studying relevant Greek historians as well as Roman historians who wrote in Greek, and, after learning the Latin language, also early as well as more recent annalistic writers, of whom he mentions a quite a few (1.6–7). Despite his diligence, the final product does not entirely satisfy. Some important reasons for this may be found in Dionysius himself. He possessed neither political or military experience nor any feeling for historical or critical analysis. Both faults induced him to fall repeatedly for the frauds of more recent annalistic writers (an example may be found above in Ch. 4.1, p. 67). He did not recognize the historically unique or singular, and thus compared Roman and Greek institutions, especially Athenian institutions, without ever at least mentioning deep and lasting differences. To compare the Roman Senate with the Athenian Council (*Boulé*) is fatally flawed. Finally, Dionysius' rhetorical profession enabled him to compose, i.e., invent, speeches in abundance. Still, we must keep an important point in mind: what the Greek Antiochus of Syracuse had long ago begun (*FGrH* 555) was subsequently taken up and elaborated above all by other Greco-Sicilian historiographers, and it was this that Dionysius pursued to its logical conclusion: Rome, and, indeed, all Roman history from its very beginning, had to be considered an essential element in any Greek conception of history.

5.2.3 Pompeius Trogus: world history round about Rome

As early as the reign of Augustus, Pompeius Trogus wrote a peculiar sort of world history under the title *Historiae Philippicae*. His ancestors had belonged to a southern Gallic tribe, the Vocontii. His grandfather had become a citizen while in the service of Pompey, whom his uncle had served as well, and his father had enjoyed the confidence of Caesar. Trogus' family may thus serve as an exemplary case of Romanization brought about during Rome's civil wars, characterized by service to, and integration within, the power structure dominated by one or another of Rome's "great men." The general conception of morality, as well as the belief in gods and fate that is discernible in his history, also testify to his intellectual Romanization. Trogus appears to have prescribed for himself a life devoted to literature and erudition, inasmuch as, in addition to his history, he composed a work *On Animals* and perhaps another *On Plants* as well. Although large chunks of Livy's *Ab urbe condita* survive in the original, together with a nearly complete listing of its contents composed at a later date (see above, Ch. 5.1, pp. 100f.), the 44 books of Pompeius Trogus' *Historiae Philippicae* were completely eclipsed by a third (?) century AD abridgment prepared by one Justin. In addition to fragments of the original, we have so-called *Prologi*, very short, likely original, listings of contents book by book. We may discern content and overall scheme as follows: Books 1–6: Assyrians, Medes, Persians, Scythians, and Greeks; Books 7–40 (by far the greatest part of the work): the kingdom of Macedon and its successors, especially the empires of Alexander the Great, the Antigonids, the Seleucids, and the Ptolemies, and, in connection with these, the smaller Hellenistic states like the Pontic Kingdom of the Mithradates, until the destruction, or rather annexation, of all these kingdoms by the Romans; Books 41–42: India and, above all, the empire of the Parthians until its treaty settlement with Rome in 20 BC; Book 43: Rome's early history until King Tarquin the Elder, together with histories of the Greek city of Massilia (Marseille), the Ligurians, and the Gauls; and Book 44: Spain from the supremacy of Carthage to its subjection by Augustus.

What the work offers is precisely *not* a history of the subjugation of other nations and empires by Romans, but instead the history, as well as the geography and ethnography of these other peoples until the moment they were absorbed by the Roman empire, or, in the case of the Parthians, who were never conquered, until they came to a negotiated settlement with Rome. It is thus a world history round about Rome, and, as such, unique in ancient historiography. At the same time, it depicts the successive transfer of world domination from one power to the next in chronological sequence: Assyrians – Medes/Persians – Macedonians (– Romans). In this regard, it is within Greek and Roman literature an early witness for the concept of the succession of universal empires. The content of this work, together with just what it does not contain, has given rise to the suspicion that Trogus rejected Roman annexations and the Roman empire (compare above, Ch. 5.2.1, p. 112). But we do not find this attitude in those excerpts scholars have identified as pro-Gallic, nor does it jibe with Trogus' representation of early Rome as the embryo of its later empire or his characterization of Rome in this very context as his "native land" (*patria*: Justin 43.1.1–2). The assumption of a critical or even hostile attitude toward Rome on Trogus' part contradicts, moreover, his high praise of Augustus as the conqueror and civilizer of Spain and the whole world that we find in the last sentence of Justin's abridgment (44.5.8). With this twofold concept of conquest and civilization he summarizes the very Roman and Augustan ideology described in the famous lines of Vergil (*Aeneid* 6.851–853). This sentiment indeed represents the highest praise for Rome – in short, we find absolutely no trace of either a critical or hostile attitude toward Rome. Justin, as a much later author, was under no compulsion to pay Augustus such homage in a place so prominent that it seems almost like a dedication to its object of praise, which can be only a living person. This high praise of Augustus – and (with him) of Rome – at the end of Justin's abridgment thus likely derives its content and probably even its formulation too from Trogus' original. It is therefore impossible to agree with those scholars who argue that Trogus' comments on Roman victories or even on Roman expansion itself and his argument for a *fortuna Romana* or his recognition of the Parthians as rulers of the eastern half of the world or a few remarks that are critical of Rome all represent hostile assessments (Justin 28.2; 29.2.1–6; 30.4.16; 31.5.2–9; 38.4.7; 39.5.3; 41.1.1). We might also reflect that Sulla and Caesar had likewise appealed to the "fortune" or "good luck of the Romans" in accounting for their successes, and that Trogus' (or Justin's) appeal to the same can thus hardly be construed as negative, but connotes rather something highly positive. It confesses a conviction that Romans enjoy the protection of the gods.

We will have to seek elsewhere for the reason why Trogus did not describe Rome's conquest of the world, and we find it in the distinctive features of ancient literary practice: ancient historians often continued, and thus expanded, the works of earlier historians (see above, Ch. 4, p. 65; Ch. 4.1, p. 69; Ch. 4.5.1, p. 89; Ch. 5.2.2, p. 114; and, below, Ch. 6.1.2, pp. 135 and 139). In their works ancient authors and poets continually incorporated references – sometimes obvious, sometimes covert and accessible only to cognoscenti – to the works of other authors, and such referencing was, in fact, standard practice among Augustan poets. Trogus wrote his historical work fully aware of *Livy's* history of Rome, that is, of those books that had recently appeared (Justin 38.3.11). Livy consciously avoids narrating events, their consequences or their contexts, unless they have some connection to Rome (see above, Ch. 5.1, pp. 109f.). It was a natural step for a Roman of recent non-Roman derivation to expand on Livy's work. Roman history with its unavoidable extension to the entire Mediterranean, together with non-

Roman history in this same region on its geographical borders, resulted in true world history. According to the peculiar nature of ancient literary practice, Trogus himself, otherwise unknown and apparently a member of no known literary circle, may well have hoped through his supplement to share in the fame that immediately greeted the *Ab urbe condita* and its author.

Trogus addressed his topics with extremely varied degrees of intensity and breadth. The availability of older representations will not alone explain this. We must rather posit an intention on the part of the author. Trogus devotes by far the largest portion of his history to the monarchies of Macedonian royalty and other kingdoms in their vicinity from south-eastern Europe to Asia Minor, Egypt, and Central Asia. In this context we may note the work's much-discussed title, *Historiae Philippicae* (*Philippic Histories*). One Philip (Philip II, 359–336 BC) stood at the beginning of Macedon's rise to power. In 197 BC another Philip (the Antigonid Philip V, 222/1–179) was the first monarch of Macedonian ancestry conquered by the Romans. His grandson Philip lost the throne of Macedon because in 168 Rome deposed and imprisoned his father Perseus (Justin 33.2.5). A false Philip stirred up trouble in Macedon for a short time in 150–148, until he too was conquered by the Romans. Two kings bearing the name Philip, father and son, stand at the end of the Seleucid dynasty. The younger of the two was deposed in 66/65 by the Roman general Pompey. In 56 he was nevertheless supposed to become king in what was then still Ptolemaic Egypt, but it was again yet another Roman who prevented this. Trogus therefore used monarchs of Macedonian ancestry named "Philip" to denote the rise and fall of the so-called Hellenistic states. Trogus considered political Hellenism especially important not only for its own sake, but also for the growth of the Roman empire, and thus too for Livy's history – and we may say: he was right to do so.

5.2.4 Universal chronology (Castor and Dionysius)

The diachronic comprehension of the past in as terse a linguistic short-hand as possible as well as the organization and presentation of ordered time in a visually obvious way, in short, chronography, which had been practiced by the Greeks from the fifth-century BC, could hardly escape the first-century BC trend that saw the "great" historical narratives appending Roman history to Greek and other foreign history in order to create universal history (see above, Ch. 4.1, p. 69). The Greek author Castor of Rhodes (*FGrH* 250; first half of the first century BC) established his chronology for history from 776 BC on the basis of the Greeks' Olympic games. He synchronized the dates of the kings of Assyria and the later kingdoms of the Near East with the dates of the rulers, priests, and high officials of the three Greek cities of Sicyon, Argos, and Athens; as well as with the dates of the kings of Rome's predecessor Alba Longa and, of course, with the dates of the kings and then consuls of Rome itself. By ancient reckoning, the world's first empire was the Assyrian, with Ninus its first king. Castor made this same year the first year of Aegialeus in Sicyon, thereby winning for Greece an antiquity equal to the first of the famous ancient Near Eastern kingdoms (FF. 1–2). Because the ancient Near East, like both Greece and Rome, commonly conceived that what was old was intrinsically better than anything more recent, Castor's measure had enormous consequences: arguments on the basis of greater antiquity were made in Hellenistic times as well as during the early Roman empire by Jews and later by Christians too against their neighbors (see below, Ch. 6.2.1, p. 159; Ch. 7.3.2, pp. 223f.). Castor brought further synchronizations down to the conclusion of the political and administrative reorganization of Asia Minor and the Near East by the Roman general Pompey in 61/60 BC. Castor's chronology therefore had many strands, these strands were synchronized with each other, and Rome was from its very beginning woven into the system. The elements of this first synoptic view, or rather synchronized universal chronology, served to render previous chronologies obsolete as well as to offer a model for subsequent chronologies.

Dionysius of Halicarnassus, the author of *Roman Antiquities*, followed another path in his *Chronology* (*FGrH* 251; cf. above, Ch. 5.2.2, pp. 114ff.), but one that likewise conformed to the trend of the times. He based his chronology on dates from Roman history, but he also expressed these dates in terms of Olympiads – as had the Romans *Atticus* and *Nepos* before him (see above, Ch. 4.1, p. 69) – and he provided equivalents from Greek history too, yielding, for example, the first pair of consuls in Rome = Isagoras as archon in Athens = the first year of the 68th Olympiad (F. 2 = *Roman Antiquities* 1.74.6). Dionysius was thus able to link Greeks with Romans not only in his *Roman Antiquities*, but also by employing means offered by the genre of "chronology."

6

Imperial History and the History of Emperors – Imperial History as the History of Emperors

During the imperial period, and especially so in the imperial city of Rome itself, historical writing, its composition, its reading, and its reception, continued to remain primarily the domain of men from the senatorial class who were actively engaged in service to the state, as well as the domain of those from the equestrian class who from the age of Augustus were drawn into administrative positions in increasing (and increasingly active) numbers that eventually surpassed those of senators. For this reason, there was no break in the fundamental assumptions of Roman historiography, even though, within just one or two generations, the new distribution of power had brought about far-reaching changes in the social structure of Rome's elite, and transformed it. As a result, the "living tradition" gradually disappeared (cf. Peter [Bibl. §6]). The equestrian, but from now on the senator too, ultimately worked for the emperor, and his career depended heavily not only on the emperor's favor, but frequently on his systematic support and intervention. The senatorial office holder's activities were merely administrative. Very little political content remained, because each post was bound by extensive instructions. The emperor made truly important decisions in consultation with a small circle of advisors whose discussions were closed to public view. He constituted his council however he pleased, and commonly included senators, but, on the other hand, did not make his selections according to elite republican criteria: one's rank in the Senate or whether one was a senator at all did not matter. Senators, individually or as a group, no

Roman Historiography: An Introduction to its Basic Aspects and Development,
First Edition. Andreas Mehl.
© 2014 Hans-Friedrich Mueller. Published 2014 by Blackwell Publishing Ltd.

longer decisively shaped or influenced public opinion. With the establishment of monarchy in Rome, public opinion, long polarized during the
civil wars, was transformed into a monopoly belonging to the emperor.
All of this induced in the ruling class neither unmixed gratitude nor
unmitigated hostility, but rather muted and altogether conflicted feelings. Robbed of their traditional opportunities to rule, the senatorial class
nevertheless was now indispensable for administration and continued to
enjoy a status that was socially superior to equestrians. To this extent
their place in society was assured, and they soon accommodated themselves to it in a manner that has been termed "half-reconciled to monarchy" (cf. Flach [Bibl. §1.3] pp. 166 and 169 on the tenor of senatorial
historiography of the early empire).

Because the *princeps* controlled both the reins of power and public
opinion, any opposition could make use of neither the general public nor
meetings of the senate in their efforts against the emperor, but instead
had to rely exclusively on the conspiratorial seclusion of small groups.
But this is just what irritated the emperor. This irritation, coupled with
its disastrous consequences in the conduct of so many emperors, served
to amplify the already conflicted attitude toward the reigning emperor
among that portion of the Senate that was hostile and disaffected. In this
context, it is remarkable that the Senate only once out of hostility to the
emperor, after Caligula's assassination in AD 41, formulated a plan to
restore the Republic. The plan was, however, not pursued with real
determination, and was, in all events, opposed by stronger elements who
acted decisively. Apart from this instance, opposition to an emperor was
not the rejection of a system, but merely the rejection of one man and
sometimes his entire family. This is the case too for the so-called Stoic
opposition among senators that scholars have sporadically overrated especially for the reigns of Nero (AD 54–68) and Domitian (AD 81–96).
Moderns have called this opposition Stoic because the senators they class
under this rubric held general views concerning political power and rulers
that were imbued to some extent with Stoic ethics, but their so-called
"opposition" constituted neither a unified movement in itself nor did
these senators pursue political goals, let alone real constitutional objec-
tives. Instead, individuals who enjoyed a small following of adherents or
admirers displayed their hostility and contempt for a misguided emperor
in a way that condemned them to failure in advance. One occasionally
demonstrated one's attitude despite the danger and with the knowledge
that one thereby sacrificed one's social standing or even one's life. Of
course, for this very reason the "Stoic opposition" would also receive
echoing acclaim from a segment of contemporary literature.

Because we have lost so many early imperial historical works, we find our first real view of a contemporary awareness of the consequences of the new political order for historiography in statements by *Tacitus* and the even later *Cassius Dio*[1] (see especially Tacitus *Histories* 1.1 and *Annals* 1.1; Dio 53.19.1–5;[2] below, Ch. 6.1.3, pp. 143f.; Ch. 6.1.4, p. 154). Their mutually supplementary agreement, however, about the effects on historians and senators suggests that these perspectives and critical judgments must go back already to the first generations of the imperial age.[3] The consequences of the new organization of state power were immediately noticeable in the treatment of any number of themes, and they were ever-present and all too obvious in historical writing that treated current events. The writer of history, belonging in general to the senatorial or equestrian class who was active (or formerly active) in government, possessed too little familiarity with the Roman empire (itself difficult to comprehend in its vast extent), its government, or the principles and details of its administration, inasmuch as full knowledge of these things was available to very few people beyond the emperor himself. This came about in a twofold way: much information, and important information especially, reached the *princeps* and his closest advisors exclusively, and this small circle took care that this remained the case. The emperor thus enjoyed in effect a monopoly on information. What is more, significant issues were no longer debated in the Senate or in the assemblies of the people, and hence in an accessible way, but instead were discussed and decided in the seclusion of emperor's cabinet and council. For this reason, important policy decisions as well as many decisions on smaller points could really no longer be properly understood by contemporary historiography. The historian of the Principate, who wrote a history of his own times, thus restricted his reports, on the one hand, to what transpired among senators and equestrians, relating above all what they did in *open* view, that is, what political and administrative issues the emperors handled in the Senate, the depressing high points of which were the treason trials that they conducted in the Senate against fellow senators. On the other hand, the historian also related unverified news (because unverifiable), which was not infrequently mere "gossip and scandal," about the emperor, the imperial family, and their court.

As a result of all this, and not just because the senatorial and equestrian gaze was fixed on Rome, the empire was not the central theme, but instead the city of Rome and the affairs of the emperor's court or the emperor's relations with the Senate or even individual senators. Because all decisions ultimately proceeded from the emperor, general political historiography was redirected to the head of the empire, and becomes *biographical history of the emperors* or *imperial biography* (see below, Ch. 6.1.1–4, pp. 130ff.; Ch. 6.3, pp. 165ff.). Senators and equestrians fulfilled in this an extremely practical need for an understanding of recent history and current events with a focus on the person of the emperor in which they would seek answers to questions like these: how can I get along with the emperor and his household, including the empress, imperial slaves and freedmen, the court, and his advisors? How may I recognize as soon as possible dangerous traits in an emperor? How may I survive a bad emperor without losing respect and self-respect? The focus of historiography on the emperor may, however, have had another cause, one that required the greatest tact: emperors and their dependents were naturally interested in historical writing about themselves, and wished just as naturally to be depicted positively. Their position also made them capable of warning potential authors or the historical writers they had themselves chosen, and regularly issuing orders to them or simply prohibiting whatever they found unacceptable (see above, Ch. 4.3, p. 79; below, Ch. 6.1.3, pp. 133f.).

The transition to an historiography concentrated on a person had consequences for the literary form. These were, however, easily dealt with, because *annalistic historiography* was not required to depart from its previously established generic principles, which, from the beginning, had organized material according to consular years, subdividing events further, above all, as to whether they fell under the rubric of domestic or foreign affairs (see above, Ch. 1.2, pp. 12f.). This formal division of material within the account of a given year could easily be adapted to a narrative whose central theme was the emperor. The content of contemporary historiography, on the other hand, remained fundamentally problematic. Despite their justifiable necessity, the history of emperors and imperial biography were a paradox, precisely because contemporaries lacked reliable information about the motives for the emperors' actions and conduct (see above, p. 123). The dilemma confronting imperial biography and historiography in the imperial age could not manifest itself more clearly.

Because the possibility for historians to form independent judgments was from this point forward severely restricted by an irreparable lack of information, the previous ideal of independence from partisanship gave way to a new ethical position that called for the impartiality of the historian toward the emperor (see above, Ch. 4.5.1, p. 86). We must consider, however, their justifications, which they based on a claim to emotional neutrality, in light of how dependent their public careers were on the will of the emperor and his administration: their statements reflect their wishes rather than reality, and likely represent (self-)deception. Only a freely offered admission, free of any self-justification, that one's own career has been promoted by the emperor and by other powerful persons in his circle, can be accepted as an accurately and objectively honest state-ment by an imperial historian of the senatorial or equestrian class (see below, Ch. 6.1.1, pp. 130f.; Ch. 6.1.3, pp. 140f.).

For the vocation of the historical writer these new social conditions add up in such a way that he, as a senator or as an equestrian, no longer enjoys the earlier advantage of comprehensive expert knowledge, and, from this point on, he can never escape the disadvantage of his existential dependency. He thus lacks two conditions which he himself deems essential for writing history. These restrictions, to which historians and historiographers are now alike subject, can lead to, and often may have had as a consequence, the writing of historical breviaries or short histo-ries: both summaries of comprehensive extant works as well as the composition of independent compendiums, which would not suffer from their lack of access to detailed knowledge (see above, Ch. 5.1, p. 100; Ch. 5.2.1, p. 113; below, Ch. 6.5, pp. 186f.). This awkward situation for the research and description of recent history and current events led already to the contemporary conclusion that the best men no longer became historians (... *magna ingenia cessere*: Tacitus *Histories* 1.1.1). Here too we find of course paradoxes. This realization does not appear just anywhere, but instead in an imperial historical work, whose composi-tion was subject to just those restrictions that had led the best to turn away from historiography. The man who, strictly speaking, rendered this negative judgment about himself, is, as the author of several works about the early imperial period, one of the most brilliant exemplars of his craft, and he may – despite the various demerits one may (or must) assess against his originality – be counted even today among the most fascinat-ing of all historians precisely because of the conditions under which he wrote history.

Once their exclusion from information became final and permanent, it was all but impossible for historians to offer an original assessment of individual emperors. Ignorance must then be replaced by conjecture. This results in the construction of motivations for the emperors' actions and behaviors according to psychological patterns that can be reduced to the simplest of clichés. Where proof is lacking, it is sufficient to assume, suspect, and insinuate. The flattery bestowed while an emperor reigns and lives will become posthumous praise or, if an emperor's administra-tion ends horribly or a successor makes a sharp break with his imperial predecessor, it will be abruptly transformed into its complete opposite:

malicious criticism and condemnation. The second possibility actually occurred more frequently: in the early Principate with all Julio-Claudian emperors after Augustus and again later with Domitian. In all events, the judgment rendered one way or the other immediately after the accession of an emperor's successor generally remained fixed. If necessary, later historical tradition offered nuanced variations on this judgment, but confirmed it on the whole. In those rare instances when opinion on an emperor was at first divided or uncertain, the historical tradition soon offered an unambiguous evaluation that turned it decisively in one direction or the other. In this way, for example, the initially unsettled judgment of Nero was very quickly simplified into negative stereotypes (Josephus *Jewish Antiquities* 20.154f.), and the still diffuse judgments of the first *princeps* Augustus among contemporaries were posthumously quickly distilled into a mostly positive evaluation, which, in spite of Caligula's malice toward his great-grandfather, never again budged (Suetonius *Caligula* 23.1 and 25.1). Nevertheless, voices did on occasion arise later to criticize and disapprove of Augustus' actions, and in fact did so from different, sometimes even opposed, perspectives. *Dio* and *Eutropius* viewed Augustus' reign as establishing liberty for, or restoring it to, the Romans (see below, Ch. 6.1.4, pp. 155f.; Ch. 6.5.2, p. 195), while *Tacitus* and the *Historia Augusta* saw it as tyranny (see below, Ch. 6.1.3, pp. 139f. and 149; Ch. 6.3.3, p. 172). As the founder of the monarchy in Rome (not, we may note, as the restorer of the Republic, which is how he wanted the outside world to see him), Augustus eventually became the undisputed great exemplar. His greatest fame, however, would be granted to him only by a Christianized Roman historiography that made him a central character in God's plan for the salvation of this world (see below, Ch. 7.3.3, pp. 232 and 234f.). We must not forget that late antique Christian historiography was dependent on much earlier and already long-fixed judgments of Roman emperors, and was therefore capable only of adding a Christian perspective to them.

The obstacles we have here laid out that the political and social conditions of Rome's imperial period put in the way of historiography can mislead us into disparaging its value as well as deceive us about its status in the history of Roman literature. In truth, historiography composed in Latin actually reached its zenith at exactly this time (see above, Ch. 1.3.1, pp. 22f.). The explanation for this is provided by the circumstance that ancient historiography in general and to a greater extent Roman historiography in particular consisted of – evaluative – narration rather than original research (see above, Ch. 1.3, pp. 17ff.). This is also precisely what reduces the negative impact of a lack of detailed information in the imperial period and what simultaneously allows the literary qualities of this genre to stand out all the more prominently. Imperial historiography developed moreover many subgenres, which is why Chapters 6 and 7 of this book's account have been systematically organized according to genre as well. On the other hand, various links run throughout this self-imposed system of organization between historical writers of diverse subgenres in terms of their social ranks, their political and moral out-looks, and their linguistic-stylistic aims. In the following pages, these links will be made clear through explicit comparisons, references, and cross-references. Readers of Chapters 6 and 7 must likewise always keep in mind that they will be confronted with a diversity of authors who pos-sessed individual characteristics, and clearly differed from each other according to all manner of important literary criteria, including self-understanding, intended readership, claims, and intellectual or literary level. They differed, in fact, in many more respects than we have time or space to illustrate in this brief account.

6.1 Empire and "Republic:" Senatorial Historiography

In the following pages, we discuss historiography penned by Roman senators or those of the equestrian class who were allied with them intel-lectually. Because of Roman historical writing's deep social roots, most narratives from the early to the late imperial period clearly depict a gulf between emperor and senators. Although the latter advocated on behalf of the ancient Republic, their actual knowledge and awareness of how this previous form of government worked to a great extent evaporated, as did, concomitantly, the institutional memory of the republican Senate's place in it. Because of their experience with Hellenistic monarchies and Hellenistic ruler worship, Greek members of the Senate would have been more comfortable with Rome's transition to monarchy as well as with emperor worship along Hellenistic lines, which was adopted quickly in the East, but only after some hesitation in the West. Greek senators were in large measure unburdened with the intellectual "ballast" of the Roman Republic, and thus did not find the transition to the new conditions of governance as problematic as did their fellow Roman senators. All this, together with the contemporary realization that many emperors pos-sessed only limited qualifications (or even none at all) either for their position or for their duties had the consequence that competent senators were thought and styled not so much defense attorneys for the previous constitution as they were more capable of imperial rule than was the actual emperor. This rendered them (at least in the opinion of others) rivals of the reigning emperor. It could be considered a vestige of the republican constitution that emperors did not enter the succession simply by inheritance, but had to be confirmed by the Senate too. This in turn enabled a favorite fantasy among historical writers of the early imperial period that an incompetent *princeps* could and had to be replaced by another, better person, naturally a senator. Such thinking preserved the illusion that even then, as in republican times, one served in an elite ruling collective, from whose ranks the most suitable need only be selected.

The reigning Caesar could himself make just such a selection, making use of adoption as a means to name his successor. The Roman nobility was long accustomed to this practice from its common use during the time of the Republic, and the method thus counted as aristocratic and republican. From the time of Nerva (96–98), one thought that this "ersatz Republic" (*loco libertatis*, Tacitus *Histories* 1.16.1) had become reality, because Nerva selected Trajan, to whom he was not related, as his successor. One had previously seen too the – failed – attempt of Galba, who had become emperor by rebelling against Nero, to secure his rule with the adoption of a distinguished young Roman by the name of Piso in January AD 69.[4] As we see in the words of Tacitus just cited, the Republic stood in early imperial historical writing for "liberty." Indeed, it was a synonym for Rome's previous constitution, which, from the point of view of the senatorial order, implied manifold possibilities for political action with a concomitant advancement of one's own public career and the acquisition of prestige. Opposed to this state of affairs, however, the less-dignified *loco libertatis* or "substitute for republican freedom" referred to just one political act by a single person, the emperor. In other words, even in the most favorable situation, the conditions of the Principate could, from a distance, resemble, but never equal, those of the Republic. Liberty in the constitution of the Principate could only be decidedly less than it had been in the Republic. As other statements from historians of that time demonstrate, liberty meant no more than the unrestricted and, to that extent, free expression of opinion. This was, of course, a necessary precondition for writing and publishing history, especially of recent and current events (Tacitus *Agricola* 2–3; and below, Ch. 6.1.3, pp. 142f.). Freedom of speech would have seemed even more important, moreover, as the other fundamental requirements for historiography could no longer be procured (see above, Ch. 6, p. 123; below, Ch. 6.1.3, pp. 142f.).

It is nevertheless hardly possible when we study the historiography of the early Roman empire to comprehend thoughtful reactions to the loss of political liberty and its replacement by a rather different, severely restricted liberty in terms of intellectual development because the loss of almost all contemporary Julio-Claudian and Flavian narratives means that we can reconstruct the course of early imperial historiography and its literary near-relations and dependents only inferentially (see above, Ch. 6, p. 123; below, Ch. 6.1.2, p. 133). The negative consequences of these shockingly wide gaps are obvious for our understanding of *Tacitus*, whose works represent the earliest and most complete historical writing to survive in the tradition of these authors (see below, Ch. 6.1.3, pp. 147f.).

No matter how narrowly or widely one defines senatorial historical writing in respect of the social rank of the author and his attitude toward liberty (and thus his greater or lesser bias toward the conduct of the emperor and perhaps the imperial system), this genre ceased, according to the usual view, either immediately after *Tacitus* or, at the latest, with the death of *Cassius Dio* (see below, Ch. 6.1.4, pp. 151f.). A senator of the old school was originally, as a magistrate and later, as a representative of the emperor, active in both civil *and* military affairs. As a consequence, however, of imperial reforms in state service, from the middle of the third century officials of senatorial rank were restricted to purely civil affairs, and, in the fourth century, a senator of the late Roman empire saw his sphere reduced even further to the affairs of one or the other of the two cities of Rome or Constantinople. Senators and officials of senatorial rank rested their entire prestige vis-à-vis those holding important and supreme military offices in the only domains left to them: law and rhetoric. During the fourth century the number of "barbarians" holding military offices steadily increased; in the fifth they held even the top positions in the military command structure in the western half of the empire. Hostility toward the military was, among civilians, eventually connected therefore with an anti-barbarian and, above all, an anti-German posture. Even such historical writers as *Eutropius* and *Ammianus Marcellinus*, who had themselves risen through military careers, made this civilian view their own.

Under these circumstances, the goal of a senator was no longer safe-guarding a vestige of the Republic or, more properly, quasi-Republic, within a monarchically constituted state, but instead preserving or, wher-ever possible, strengthening civilian as opposed to military interests, which in reality were always growing within and around the imperial office, no matter who the emperor was: one hoped thereby to secure the social and ceremonial precedence of civilian (especially senatorial) ranks above the military orders (see below, Ch. 6.5.2, p. 195; Ch. 7.2, pp. 212f.; compare also Ch. 7.1, p. 205). One may view this shift in persuasive aims, rooted as they were in the central importance of social rank, as the manifestation of a completely new intellectual orientation, and, accordingly, place the end of senatorial historiography as a genre before it. If, however, one views this shift as a development *within* the circle of people belonging to the senatorial class, a development corresponding to the objective and subjective changes they had experienced as a group, then senatorial historiography did not end at all before antiquity itself came to an end or changed rather into a new state of affairs (see below, Ch. 7.3.4, pp. 241f.).

We must, however, by no means stamp all historiography of the early and late empire with the die of a "republican" and senatorial point of view. We see this already in *Velleius Paterculus*, the first representative of imperial historiography, whose work for the most part survives. He composed his narrative as praise for the reigning *princeps*, Tiberius (see the next section for details). Many authors must therefore have likewise written narratives of recent events that praised all too highly the currently reigning emperor, and criticism of just such historical works and their authors is one of the main objects of the satire *How to Write History* by Lucian of Samosata (third quarter of the second century AD). We may reckon it as self-explanatory to classify narratives of recent history composed at the behest of emperors under the category of laudatory and sycophantic historiography (see above, Ch. 4.3, pp. 77ff.).

6.1.1 Gaius (?) Velleius Paterculus

Velleius Paterculus (circa 20 BC to at least AD 30) hailed from the urban nobility of Campania. His grandfather and father had served under Pompey and Augustus in mid-level military ranks. Velleius' family and Velleius himself were linked to Augustus and his stepson, adoptive son, and ultimate successor, Tiberius, but also to the Vinicii, a senatorial family likewise hailing from Campania, whose members had climbed senatorial ranks during the last decades of the civil war, and had obtained elevated and the elite posts in the service of Augustus. Velleius likewise entered military service, doing so on the career path of an equestrian, and served under Publius Vinicius, under Augustus' grandson Gaius Caesar, and, most significantly, under Tiberius. On the occasion of his triumph in AD 12, Tiberius rewarded Velleius lavishly. At that time he had just become a senator, and would later advance as far as the praetorship (in AD 15) – as a candidate backed by the *princeps*, his election was guaranteed. All this we learn from Velleius' historical work, which was published in AD 30, and dedicated to Marcus Vinicius, who was consul that year and the son of Velleius' former commanding officer. Velleius also further flattered him in an otherwise unusual way: he dated events in terms of years before Vinicius' consulate in AD 30 (1.8.1 and *passim*). Velleius likewise paid homage to the man who, at the time of the work's publication, was the most powerful man in Rome, prefect of the praetorian guards and trusted agent of the reigning emperor Tiberius: Aelius Sejanus (2.127f.).

Velleius' historical work, whose original title has not come down to us, consists of just two books. Book 1, which does not survive in its entirety, offers world history, flowing from the Trojan War into Roman history. Book 2 moves in the opposite direction, beginning, with the destruction of Carthage, as Roman history and expanding its purview to world history. With increasing detail, Velleius arrives at the Principate of Tiberius. His description of the achievements of the reigning emperor, his erstwhile commanding officer in the military and benefactor, by the end of his work sings the praises of Tiberius' successful care for peace, order, and material prosperity (2.126–130). Whereas *Livy* wished at the beginning of his Roman history that it were customary for historians to bless their work with a prayer, Velleius actually concludes his work with a prayer on behalf of principate, realm, and the reigning emperor Tiberius (2.131; see above Ch. 5.1, p. 108). Inasmuch as the author, who himself profited from the new settlement, and did not hide this fact, dedicates his work to a highly placed person, whose family had derived benefits during the transition from the earlier to the now permanent constitutional settlement, and inasmuch as he proclaims that Roman as well as world history alike are fulfilled in the person of the then-reigning Tiberius, we may consider him a supporter of the new "system," which was monarchy. Even when the author takes the side of the senate against the people and the *populares* in his Roman history of the republican period, his account and his commentary remain extremely distant from, and downright opposed to, the aims pursued by early imperial historical writing. As a result, neither contemporary nor later senatorial historiography took notice of Velleius' work.

Velleius' moral position results from a conventional emphasis on *virtus* as combination of morality and competence. On the one hand, Velleius accepts the recently established model positing the destruction of Carthage as the sudden turning point in the moral development of the Romans (2.1.1–2; in the same context 1.11.5; see above, Ch. 4.5.1, p. 91). On the other hand, we may discern many decisive ruptures in his history after that date: 50/49, 30/27 BC, and AD 14, the latter oriented toward

Tiberius. Both of the last two dates mentioned, in contrast with the first, mark positive turn-arounds and developments or even greater improvements. Despite his manifest indignation, à la Sallust, at Rome's total moral collapse after 146 BC, we find little substantiation for this negative assessment in Velleius' account: Romans are excused their atrocities against others and among themselves partly through manipulation of facts and partly through assessments that play facts down, render them more attractive, or pass over them in silence. In this way, responsible parties are absolved.

Velleius naturally uses this method for the reign of Tiberius: we do not find in his history the ultimately lethal persecution of the senator and historian *Cremutius Cordus* in 25 BC (see below, Ch. 6.1.2, pp. 132f.). Velleius denounces ingratiating flattery as an accompanying symptom of too great a concentration of power, and thus the current constitution with emperor and imperial family, in whose circle Velleius himself spent so much time (2.102.3), but the author fails to recognize that, in offering this criticism, he strikes himself too.

In its concision, Velleius' historical work is the first surviving brief history in Latin literature, and prefigures a trend that will a few generations later become quite popular (see above, Ch. 6, p. 125; and Ch. 6.5, pp. 186f.). And, if, in spite of its brevity, it displays quite a few characteristics of annalistic writing, the continuity of the narrative is nevertheless broken up by a number of interwoven stories, many *exempla*, biographical passages, and – we must confess, thoroughly fascinating – literary notices, in which the social climber demonstrates his cultural refinement, and how, from a literary perspective, he numbers among the elite of his day. Velleius even formulates a literary theory: competitiveness (*aemulatio*) among authors leads to the early perfection of a genre. Once this happens, subsequent authors, inasmuch as they can no longer satisfy their ambition, turn to another genre. This leads to the decline of the first genre, while the second is again brought quickly to perfection, and so the pattern continues. This same motivation, however, can also lead to a premature transfer of talent from one area to another, thereby preventing the perfection of the first (1.16–17). Velleius does not, of course, explicitly apply his theory to political history or, for instance, the historical development of the constitution, although he could have tried, given his willingness to explore so many decisive historical turning points and ruptures in such a brief space (for a rather different analysis of Velleius' approach, see Schmitzer [Bibl. § 6] p. 82). Granted, this would have relativized the quality of Tiberius' administration by reducing it to the status of a link in the ever-varying chain of historical development. It was, however, precisely this that Velleius' historical work could, according to the conception of its author, in no way permit, a work in which even Augustus grows pale when compared to his successor.

6.1.2 Authors of the Julio-Claudian and Flavian period (from Cremutius Cordus to Pliny the Younger)

The deplorable state of the surviving literary tradition permits us to review briefly here just three authors and their (lost) works (see above, Ch. 6, p. 123 with note 1, p. 260; and Ch. 6.1, pp. 128f.). The senator *Aulus Cremutius Cordus* (*HRR* II CXIII / 87) wrote a history of the civil wars and the age of Augustus. Because he neither praised highly nor criticized severely Caesar and Augustus (although he did denounce the senate for its sycophancy toward the emperor already in the age of Augustus and praised Caesar's assassins, Brutus and Cassius, as the "last of the Romans"), he did not offend Augustus, in whose presence he had even read from the work. Only much later did Aelius Sejanus, whom Cremutius had earlier offended, use his powerful position as praetorian prefect and favorite of the emperor Tiberius to lodge a charge of treason before the Senate on the basis of his statement regarding Brutus and Cassius. Fully aware of the condemnation and death that awaited him, Cremutius defended himself, and then took his own life. His historical work was burned by the state, but some copies were preserved by Cremutius' daughter, and in AD 37 with the express approval of Caligula an edition was published that had, in the meantime, been toned down (F. 3 = Tacitus *Annals* 4.34–35; cf. further Quintilian 10.1.104; Suetonius *Tiberius* 61.3 and *Caligula* 16.1; Dio 57.24.2–4). The case of Cremutius is an exemplary demonstration of the uncertainty in which historians of the imperial period found themselves when they wrote about the recent past. What failed to offend one powerful man could displease another or serve as a convenient legal weapon against an author. It was not merely the attitude of the emperor that mattered, but equally the opinions of the important people around him. The situation became thereby that much more unpredictable. And a statement that others routinely repeated without endangering themselves could suddenly serve as the occasion of one's ruin (see above, Ch. 4.5.2, pp. 95f.; compare Ch. 6, p. 122).

Even a member of the imperial family could find himself in trouble when he tried his hand at writing the history of recent events. This happened to *Tiberius Claudius Nero Germanicus* with his history from the death of Caesar (10 BC to AD 54, emperor from 41; *HRR* II CXX / 92; see above, Ch. 5.1, pp. 100 and 103). We may identify two issues that set this trouble apart from others: Claudius did not arouse the ire of the *princeps*, but instead of his mother and grandmother. As a result, he retreated to a time even closer to the present than the topic that originally occasioned offense. Despite its proximity to the present, his new topic was nevertheless free from danger or at least less dangerous. Claudius wrote many historical accounts, some while he was still a prince, others when he was emperor (Suetonius *Claudius* 41–42). In addition to his incomplete history of the conclusion to the civil wars, he wrote, in Latin, 41 books on the history of the period after the end of the civil wars as well as, in Greek, twenty books on Etruscan history and another eight books on Carthaginian history. We may reckon historiographical in a wider sense Claudius' eight books of autobiography and his defense of Cicero against Asinius Pollio. Even though almost none of Claudius' historiography has come down to us, we must not forget that this author, as emperor, had the power to ensure that his work was promulgated. He thus had his Etruscan and Carthaginian histories preserved in the Museum of Alexandria, which remained the most renowned location for scholarship and learning, and had them read aloud there publicly as well.

Together with statements Claudius made on historical topics connected with his administrative work as emperor, especially in his so-called Speech to the Gauls (*Inscriptiones Latinae Selectae* 212), fragments and references to his historical works allow us to glean a few insights into his preferences and thinking as an historian. Claudius knew early Roman history in great detail as well as in its many recorded variants, which he could weigh against each other with intelligence. He was scrupulous in this, delving into complexities at length, even at the cost of clarity. In general, he seems to display interest in, understanding of, and even sympathy for the vanquished and for non-Romans sacrificed to Roman expansion, just as he does for those on the losing side of the civil war among the Romans themselves. In Roman history, Claudius sees two opposing principles of historical development, sometimes in parallel and sometimes in tandem, at work through the centuries: (1) From the beginning, Romans accepted foreigners into their city, and made them citizens. This is an abiding principle that does not change in new situations, or even develop with the progress of affairs: it conforms rather to a well-known Roman way of thinking. (2) From the beginning, Romans adjusted the constitution of their community and of their state in accordance with the needs and necessities of the moment. This statement expresses the principle of constant renewal and change, and this is astonishing in the context of a city that so loved to represent itself as hostile to change. In arguing for the admission of distinguished Gauls into the Senate (or senatorial order), Claudius views this act as the most recent link in a long chain of historical events combining these two principles, and he establishes thereby a singular view of historical evolution that went well beyond the conceptions common in Rome (see below, Ch. 8, p. 245 with note 1, p. 263). Although, since his own day, he has been saddled with the ill repute of a fool, Claudius deserves credit within Roman historiography for especially thoughtful originality.

Gaius Plinius Secundus (the elder Pliny: *HRR* II CXXXXVI / 109) was a commanding officer of equestrian rank, who was stationed with the fleet at Misenum and was killed during the eruption of Mount Vesuvius in AD 79. He is famous today for his 37-volume *Natural History*, which survives, but he also wrote twenty books on the *German Wars*, which are the only historiographical work cited by Tacitus in the first six books of his *Annals*, as well as 31 books of *Roman History* (*A fine Aufidi Bassi* or "From the End of Aufidius Bassus"), which continued the unknown work of an obscure author by the name of *Aufidius Bassus*. This latter work occupied Pliny from at least AD 55 until 77. In accordance with the wishes of its author, it was published posthumously. Because Pliny was compelled in a work on recent history to discuss the reigning emperor and his sons under a monarchical form of government, he easily, if not inevitably, attracts charges of sycophancy for the purpose of advancing his own career. In order to avoid this charge, he purposely refrained from publishing his work during his own lifetime (*Natural History* Introduction § 20). Pliny's conduct reveals another dilemma of imperial Roman historical writing on contemporary events (compare above Ch. 6, pp. 122ff.): authors of such works must decide whether to risk disrepute or, if, like Pliny, they refrain from publishing during their own lifetimes, refrain from enjoying literary renown. Fame for one's writing during one's own lifetime – a natural goal for all ancient (and modern) authors – became impossible in this situation, and this too we must reckon a consequence of the new political conditions that prevailed from the age of Augustus.

Granius Licinianus, who wrote annalistic Roman history during or after the reign of Hadrian, no longer belongs to this group. Fragments of his work were first discovered in 1853. They cover the years 163 to 78 BC, and derive from Books 26–36 of what must have been an extensive work. Granius prefers purely descriptive, as opposed to interpretive, historiography, and, for this reason, censures *Sallust* (Book 36). As far as we can determine from the excerpts that we find in later authors, Granius depicted ancient customs, and, in this respect, closely resembles antiquarian writers (see above, Ch. 4.6, pp. 96f.). We cannot determine more precisely either the endpoint of his work or his sources, among which, however, we may at least reckon Livy, whether directly or indirectly.

6.1.3 Publius (?) Cornelius Tacitus

Cornelius Tacitus, who has been famous throughout the centuries, although he has also been chastised as the disillusioned diagnostician and critic unmasking the exercise of monarchical power, certainly did not derive his lineage from the ancient and patrician Cornelii of the city of Rome, but instead hailed from an area north of the Padus (Po) or from southeast Gaul. Born around or after AD 55, he studied rhetoric, possibly with Quintilian, the most famous instructor of the time, and entered on a senatorial career. Around 78, he married the daughter of the senator Gnaeus Julius Agricola, who was entrusted under the three Flavian emperors with important administrative and military posts. Under these same rulers, Tacitus advanced as far as the praetorship (88) and was selected for one of the most prestigious priesthoods, the *XVviri sacris faciundis* (the priestly college of 15 men in charge of the Sibylline books). He became a consul (and was perhaps already selected for the post by Domitian) during the Principate of Nerva in the course of the year 97. In this capacity, he delivered the funeral oration for his predecessor in office, Lucius Verginius Rufus, one of the most important senators of the age. In the year 100, together with his boyhood friend Pliny the younger (who was the nephew of the historian), Tacitus prosecuted the former proconsul of the province of Africa, Marius Priscus, for extortion of the inhabitants. The prosecution took place before the emperor Trajan who served as presiding judge. We may conclude from this that Tacitus and Pliny both belonged to the inner circle around Trajan. Sometime after 110, Tacitus administered the province of Asia as proconsul. After this, he disappears without a trace. As an historian, Tacitus devoted his work to the history of the Principate from AD 14 until his own times.

In his first work *De vita Iulii Agricolae* (*On the Life of Julius Agricola*), we find the life, achievements, and career of his stepfather Gnaeus Julius Agricola (AD 40–93) especially involved with circumstances prevailing under Domitian and with a description of Britain. It was in the administration of this province, as well as its pacification and Rome's attempt to expand it, that Agricola rendered his greatest (and last) service on behalf of emperor and empire (cf. *Agricola* 13–38; circa AD 77–84). The *Agricola* is a typical example of a free (but for Romans not unusual) use of multiple genres within a single work (see above, Ch. 1.1, p. 11): we find in it elements of moral biography, funeral oratory, panegyric, and ethno-geographic description, together with political history. As a result, the work far surpasses the usual tendencies of the age for mixing histo-riography and biography (see above, Ch. 5.2.2, p. 116; Ch. 6, p. 124; below, Ch. 6.3, p. 164). Tacitus does not, of course, join jarring elements forcibly, but rather works with features that, whatever their ultimate derivation, have stood in proximity to, or even been a traditional part of, historical writing.[5]

In spite of the difficulties and persecutions Domitian occasioned for Agricola in the eyes of the author, including even (suspected) poisoning, Tacitus, both in his mixing of genres and in refraining from casting the hero of his biography in the role of a martyr, intentionally contrasts the *Agricola* with the martyrs' biographies then commonly circulating among members of the Senate's so-called Stoic opposition (see above, Ch. 6, p. 122). We may already recognize in this early work linguistic and stylistic features as well as basic ideas of the Tacitus whom we know from his later great annalistic histories.

In the *Germania* (*De origine et situ Germanorum* / *On the origins and circumstances of the Germans*), Tacitus first takes up the Germans' common characteristics and institutions (1–27) and then the peculiarities of individual tribes (28–46). He does this without reference to a particu-lar time period. As a result, the characteristics he describes lack any historical anchor and thus also the possibility of being identified and then related to each other as stages in a historical process. As is customary in ancient ethnography, the past is presented as if it is as valid in the present as it ever was before (see below, Ch. 6.4.1, p. 183). Seemingly timeless characteristics, as broad stereotypes, are, of course, well suited for com-parison with others that differ from them or are perhaps even their opposites. And this is what Tacitus aims to do: by comparing Romans to the (supposedly) wild, uncivilized, more natural Germans, he will challenge the Romans of his own day who differ so much from them. To the extent that, through ethnological findings or facts, he aims to instruct and to improve on a foundation that is at once psychological and moral, Tacitus stands very close to the Stoic scholar and historian *Posidonius* (compare, for example, *FGrH* 87, FF. 15 and 31).

The *Dialogus de oratoribus* (*Dialogue on Oratory*) differs quite mark-edly linguistically and stylistically from his other four works, resembling instead Ciceronian Latin quite closely. On these grounds it is often rejected as Tacitus' work, but these criteria are in themselves insufficient, inasmuch as a writer schooled in ancient rhetoric would have practiced and mastered adjustments of style to genre as well as the imitation of the language and style of other authors. In the *Dialogue on Oratory* various men, among them Tacitus' instructor in rhetoric, deliver speeches and discuss the recent corruption of contemporary eloquence. Comparison of ancient with contemporary eloquence (14–23), criticism of current educational practice and praise of Ciceronian educational ideals (28–32), comparison of earlier proximity to the practice of the forum and the goal of preparing speakers for public debate of policy differences, with contemporary oratorical practice devoted to topics far removed from real life (33–35, followed by some large breaks in the text) lead finally to the introduction of the political and social conditions necessary for oratory. During the Republic political and judicial speech in the public sphere were bound up with its freedom as well as with its civil wars. The security and peace of the Principate no longer require argumentative speeches of this kind (36–41: concluding with the speech of Maternus who reconciles the previously prevailing positions with one another).

The two works of Tacitus that are historical in the narrower sense of that word treat Rome's early imperial period and bear the titles *Histories* and *Annals*, neither of which is original, although both are ancient, even if they do not derive unambiguously from common usage (see above, Ch. 3.2, p. 50). The *Histories* treat the years 69 to 96, in other words, "the year of four emperors" (Galba, Otho, Vitellius, and Vespasian) and the reigns of the three emperors of the Flavian family (Vespasian, Titus, and Domitian). Of the original (and most likely) 12 books, only Books 1 through the middle of Book 5 survive. Of these, the first three deal solely with the vicissitudes and bloody circumstances of the extremely eventful year 69. The rest of the surviving work treats the after-effects of the battles between the pretenders to the throne in Roman Germany and Gaul with the revolts of the Batavi and Treveri and the suppression of them, the normalization of affairs in Rome and Italy after the recognition of Vespasian as the new emperor as well as the continuing suppression of the Jewish revolt, henceforth under the command of Titus, the son of the new *Princeps* Vespasian. All this encompasses just parts of the years 69 and 70. We know nothing about the organization of topics in the books that have been lost (but for the use of these books by Orosius, see below, Ch. 7.3.3, p. 236).

We do not know whether Tacitus' last work, the *Annals*, was completed. Eighteen volumes seem to have been planned for the period from the death of Augustus to the death of Nero and the beginning of Galba's Principate (AD 14–68). Surviving portions of this account include only Books 1 through the beginning of 5, 6 (without its beginning), 11 (without its beginning), and 12–16, which lacks its conclusion. The years

29–31, 37–47, and 66–68 are missing either in whole or in part, and therefore lack essential connections and context. We can nevertheless discern the general structure: Books 1–6: the Principate of Tiberius, Books 7–12: Caligula's and Claudius' Principates (most likely Books 7–8 and 9–12 respectively), and Books 13–18: the reign of Nero and the beginning of Galba's Principate.

Notices in and relationships between Tacitus' five works as well as indirect indications allow us to determine their chronological sequence: *Agricola–Germania–Dialogue on Oratory–Histories–Annals.* Composition must have spanned the years 96/97 to some time after 110. Tacitus twice announced works he would write, but he changed each of these plans, and then worked on topics different from those he originally projected as his next undertakings. The work he promised in *Agricola* 3.3 about past slavery under Domitian (81–96) and, by way of contrast, present felicity under Nerva and Trajan (from 96 or 98) became instead, with the *Histories*, an account of the year of four emperors and the resulting rule of the Flavian dynasty that ended with Domitian's assassination (69–96). Tacitus next announced in his *Histories* 1.1.4 that he planned to treat the period of Nerva and Trajan (which he had not yet dealt with) as its continuation in a separate work, but with the remark that he had "set the task aside for old age" (*senectui seposui*), and thus made clear that he would not take up contemporary history immediately after finishing the current work. In fact, rather than continue working toward the present, Tacitus turned instead to the more distant past: the history that led up to the year of four emperors and the Flavian period, composing in his *Annals* an account of the reign of the Julio-Claudian dynasty (14–68) that begins with the Principate's first transition of power from Augustus to Tiberius, and that accordingly attempts to demonstrate that even then one already found oneself in a hereditary monarchy.

Scholars have surmised that these two (or perhaps multiple) changes of plan were occasioned by Tacitus' gradually growing dissatisfaction with the Principate of Trajan as a regime that was not in fact so different from the previous "bad" reigns. If this had been the case, Tacitus would have convicted himself of the grossest sycophancy with his second notice of a plan to write about the Principate of Nerva and Trajan, coupled in the same breath with conspicuous praise for both rulers, something his contemporaries would have seen through immediately. One thus prefers an alternative explanation: as an intellectual who accepted the Principate grudgingly, but who was viscerally dispirited by it, Tacitus could not avoid the realization that the "liberty" granted by Nerva and Trajan represented merely a cosmetic repair of the Principate, and that such tyrannies as Domitian's were not accidents at all, but remained rather a possibility actually favored by the system's basic structure. As a result, rather than proceed toward the present, it was necessary to push back to earlier conditions and stages of the Principate. Among these, proceeding back from Domitian, we find the first stage in the struggles for power after the death of Nero (68–69), which led to the establishment of a new dynasty, namely, the Flavian. We have to see a decisive earlier stage in the reinforcement of the Principate as the rule of a single person and an imperial family in the transition of power from Augustus to Tiberius in AD 14, but even here we do not of course arrive at the root of the Principate. For this, one would have to go even further back to the establishment of autocratic rule by Augustus after his victory over Antony, his final opponent in the civil wars (30/27 BC). This Tacitus did not do in his *Annals*, although he recognized the need for such a project. He had already demonstrated this awareness in the foreword to his *Histories* (1.1.1) with the observation that Roman historical writing had as a consequence of the accumulation of power in a single hand "since Actium" (31 BC) markedly diminished in quality. As he commenced work on the *Annals,* Tacitus must therefore have felt quite clearly the inadequacy of employing AD 14 as the beginning of his account. We can discern this from the outline of the reign of Augustus which serves as a preface to his death and succession (necessary too for the sake of even basic clarity), and which, despite its brief compass, is particularly rife with numerous aperçus, political judgments, and critical commentary directed against Augustus (*Annals* 1.2–4). We do not know, alas, whether Tacitus ever planned or perhaps even set about a third work on the history of the Principate that would have covered the age of Augustus.

Tacitus' biography is significant for understanding his work, although it does not of course explain it exclusively or completely. As a boy or youth Tacitus lived through the death of Nero, the bloody year of four emperors, and the ultimate success of Vespasian. He fully participated in the political affairs of the Flavian period. His senatorial career advanced steadily and apparently without setbacks, even under Domitian, whose reign Tacitus condemned immediately after his assassination, and it continued to flourish under the new regime. Tacitus makes no effort to deny this, and he adds to his account of his own career under the Flavians a generally formulated demand that every historian is duty-bound to objectivity, and that he must thus write without prejudice. The historian must, in other words, be free from emotions either friendly or hostile toward the ruler whose reign he will describe, and Tacitus makes clear that he will adhere to this demand or at least intends to (*Histories* 1.1.3).[6]

Assuming Tacitus' intent was sincere, various fatal, but never sufficiently proved, suspicions leveled against the emperor Domitian (in his first work, the *Agricola*) already show that the Tacitus fails to meet the seemingly simple standard he had set himself, but instead had deluded himself in respect to his capacity for objective description of (contemporary) history. He was hardly the only one to do this (see above, Ch. 6, pp. 124f.). This error concerning one's supposed freedom from partisanship vis-à-vis a contemporary ruler seems to have been common among early imperial historians, and is readily comprehensible as a consequence of the conflicted feelings then typical of those belonging to the senatorial order (see above, Ch. 6, pp. 121f.).

Tacitus suffered, possibly his entire life, from the contradiction between his inner distancing from, or perhaps even opposition to, and his actual participation in, the administration of Domitian, and this inner conflict would have accused him, and unmasked him, before his own conscience as one who, although he may have been induced or enticed, had not been compelled to collaborate. If Domitian really had compelled him, the later reaction of the historian would have proved much simpler, straightforward, and immediate. If his "experience of Domitian" is a fact, about which we should have no doubts, then neither should we doubt its impact on his portrait of this emperor. We should nonetheless separate his characterization of Domitian from his characterizations of earlier emperors, although they are in principle of the same type, especially those of Tiberius and Nero. Tacitus had no need to project his "Domitian" onto Tiberius and Nero: there were enough historians of the early imperial period who had personally experienced both emperors, and the way they coped (or even failed to cope) with their experiences intellectually and emotionally in their accounts of recent history, despite their likewise stipulated ideal of non-partisanship, could well have influenced Tacitus. He needed only to help himself to these portraits of rulers readily available in the historical accounts of the Julio-Claudian emperors. He could do this even more easily to the extent that he found in them items corresponding to his own negative portrait of Domitian and to his difficulties in working through a phase of his own life. If Tacitus very early on read the accounts of the Julio-Claudian period and its emperors offered by senatorial historiography, these accounts may well have influenced his characterization of Domitian, with the result that he produced a mixture of his own experiences combined with the literary influences of others, and this would also mean of course, that his own literary product was partially topical. In this way too, we may resolve a dispute that has over some decades exercised especially those scholars writing in

German and that is associated especially with the names of Flach [Bibl. §6 and §1.3 on the literary tradition] and Urban [Bibl. §6 on Tacitus' own experience].

With the short Principate of Nerva (96–98) and the subsequent reign of Trajan lasting almost twenty years (until 117), changed conditions ensued both domestically and in foreign affairs that would be of special significance for Tacitus and other senators of the period. From the threats of Dacians on the lower Danube and from the offensive in Northern Britain undertaken under Domitian, Trajan turned to the conquest of Dacia and eventually also to a massive campaign of conquest against the Parthians and annexation of territories in Mesopotamia. Tacitus represented himself as an expansionist in terms of foreign policy, which accorded well with Rome's elite senatorial tradition, and for this reason did not assign great value to peace, because peace leveled what was unequal (*Annals* 12.12.1). He was thus unable or simply refused to understand why some, though certainly not all, previous emperors adhered to the defensive policy outlined by Augustus in his last will and testament, and he was especially incredulous when Domitian ordered (though well justified strategically) a withdrawal from the conquests made by his father-in-law Agricola in Britain. On the other hand, unlike Appian, he refused to acknowledge the actual expansion of Roman power that took place under Julio-Claudian and Flavian emperors in southern and mid- Britain as well as in southern Germany (see below, Ch. 6.2.2, p. 163). He attributed what in his view was as an exclusively defensive posture to the incompetence of the emperors and to their resentment of the military capacity possessed by members of the senatorial order. Trajan's new foreign policy must therefore have occasioned some satisfaction for Tacitus, as it did for Florus (see below, Ch. 6.5.1, p. 189). Domestically, the free expression of opinion that Nerva granted and Trajan confirmed released members of both upper classes from life-threatening danger that had been partly latent, partly open, and from a silence that had embarrassed and compromised them to the extent that it left them open to a charge of cowardice. From the distance of just a few years, the historian characterized his relief after Domitian's death this way: "… it is a rare happiness of our times that we may think what we wish and say what we think," and he uses this statement to characterize the quality of the "liberty" he enjoyed during Nerva's Principate (*Histories* 1.1.4).[7] This liberation was for Tacitus at that moment the most critical: his hyperbole welcomed this newly created situation as a circumstance that had until then been impossible under the Principate's constitution. In fact, the commencement of freedom of expression marked for Tacitus the beginning of his own historical writing: he immediately composed his biography of Agricola, whose career culminated during the reign of Domitian (*Agricola* 1–3).

Tacitus nevertheless recognized at the commencement of this new state of affairs that there was a definite boundary to the use, and thus also to the usefulness, of their newly won freedom of expression. People were far too deeply sunk in slavery. The persistent and long-lasting silence that had been compelled by terror was comfortable: "Together with our voices, we would have lost our memories, if we had been as capable of forgetting as we were of keeping quiet" (*Agricola* 2.3;[8] compare 45.1). It was simply impossible under these new conditions to find one's way out quickly from a silence that had long ago hardened into habit and posture. Tacitus must have suffered from this especially, because he affirms this difficulty conspicuously and profusely in word and image. He was also well aware that the Republic had not been restored with Nerva, but instead that he had given the imperial system a more human face, insofar as its new incarnation now included freedom of expression (*Agricola* 3.1–2). This was the extent of it, and nothing more. What was on offer here, as wonderful as it may have seemed after the events of the most recent past, remained but a small element of the former liberty of the Roman Republic and – to an even greater extent – of a freedom bordering on pure anarchy, and Tacitus, who frequently mentioned them, had ideas about both. As it was, this one small element of liberty that had appeared in his time remained precarious, because this freedom had not been won or decreed by the Roman people or by the Senate, but instead had been granted by a ruler. The emperor retained the power and, in his view of things, also the right to suspend temporarily or rescind permanently his gift of restricted liberty (see above, p. 6.1, p. 128).

Freedom of expression did not necessarily improve an historian's access to information. If Tacitus' knowledge about the Roman empire benefited from the new conditions, it was not so much because of the liberty afforded by the Principate, but because he was personally close to the rulers Nerva and Trajan, and he thus had access to information flowing from the regime's most inner circle. This was the case at first only for the present and the near future, and, secondly, was, as a regular aspect of monarchical rule, in principle nothing new or even different from what had occurred under Domitian. For the past, Tacitus could only have taken advantage of access to the archives, but access was not then (and certainly not now) included in the concept of freedom of expression, not to mention the fact that archive work – as opposed to browsing obscure literature for an excursus – was not viewed in antiquity as a duty to be consistently pursued by an historian (see above, Ch. 1.3.2, pp. 28f.; Ch. 4.3, pp. 80f.). That the new political situation brought no advantage to the historian writing about the recent past and current events, Tacitus seems to have realized at least later, when he states in the foreword to his *Histories* (1.1.1) that general "ignorance in matters of state" (*inscitia rei publicae*) begins with the autocratic rule of Augustus, but fails to terminate even with the reigns of Nerva and Trajan, and thus runs uninterrupted (compare Ch. 6, pp. 123ff.). Nevertheless, the conditions that prevailed from 96/97 until the first years of Hadrian's reign (after 117) saw the publication of several historical works on the recent past and current events, in particular the works of Tacitus and the imperial biographies of *Suetonius* covering almost exactly the same period of time (on the latter, see below, Ch. 6.3.1, p. 166). To this extent, the expectations Tacitus entertained at the very beginning of this "new age" were fulfilled. At the same time, historical research, composition, and publication were revealed to depend – as so often in history – on prevailing political conditions.

If we wish to understand Tacitus' attitude in his works correctly, we must become aware of another condition that formed part of the wider context: the extended absences from Rome of the emperor and a number of people around him that were occasioned by Trajan's major wars, which he led himself, and then even more by the long trips that his successor Hadrian undertook to inspect the empire. This continued – and increased in extent – under later emperors. Such absences had negative consequences both for whatever senators and equestrians were left behind as well as for the city of Rome and the entire region. As Rome and Italy gradually lost their previously pre-eminent position, from the second century AD, they also lost their attractiveness. The magnificent buildings erected in Rome by the emperors could hardly conceal this fact. Social life in Rome lost luster. Pliny the younger and Tacitus would, for a very long time (in fact, for centuries), be the last important authors to reside in Rome. Tacitus was a man for whom the city of Rome was, as his historical accounts testify, the natural center of the Roman empire. His topographical knowledge of the *urbs* was exact, and he demonstrated profound interest in it, if not affection for it. For someone like Tacitus, the discernible devolution of Rome and Italy in his day must have been depressing, and, in view of their ideal importance, perhaps even a sign of the decline of the empire under monarchical rule.

Both the *Histories* and the *Annals* follow the annalistic tradition (see above, Ch. 1.2, p. 13; Ch. 3, p. 41; Ch. 3.1.1, pp. 45f.), although in detail Tacitus departs markedly from the genre. The *Histories* commence with an enumeration of the consuls for the year 69 (1.1.1), and, after the foreword (1.1) and a very general introduction to the situation and some notice of what extraordinary and horrifying material readers may expect (1.2–5), slip unnoticeably back into a report on the year 69 from its beginning (still in 1.5). But Tacitus departs very quickly from the annalistic mode. He fills several volumes with the main characters and places of the various events of the year 69, and fails to conclude the year at the end of a book, nor does he mark the beginning of the year 70 with the new *consules ordinarii* (regular consuls), but instead mentions them – Vespasian and Titus – in the midst of a partial report (4.3–4: reactions of the Senate to the letters of Vespasian and his assistant Gaius Licinius Mucianus). This quickly ensuing shattering of annalistic chains in the *Histories* did not, however, induce Tacitus to do so from the very *start* of his work, and thus to begin at some other time according to objective historical considerations. He thus sacrificed the opportunity to commence his account at an historically meaningful point in time: in June of the year before, i.e., 68, with the death of Nero and the recognition of Galba as emperor. For this reason, when Tacitus later wrote the *Annals*, he could not end with Nero's death, but – provided he got this far – had to continue reporting new events and circumstances until the end of the year 68. On the other hand, he began his historical report in the *Annals* not with the first of January in the year of Augustus' death, AD 14, but instead with the death of Augustus in the month of August (1.5ff.) and accordingly without indicating the year in which this occurred. Before this, however, he inserted a not especially chronological outline of the changes in the state of affairs ushered in by Augustus' long autocratic rule (1.2–4). Within the *Annals*, the beginnings of books sometimes correspond exactly with the beginnings of years and sometimes they do not. The distinctive features we have just discussed as well as other conspicuous departures from annalistic practice, as in, for example, summing up several years in his reports on a province, may serve as evidence that Tacitus had clearly freed himself from annalistic constraints, but that this was not the result of a gradual development from slavishly following to willfully avoiding the annalistic scheme. Individual departures from the annalistic scheme may indeed be justified by the concrete goals of the account and composition, but we cannot derive from this a general explanation for Tacitus' handling of the annalistic system – apart from a very general one, that, for Tacitus, structuring a work according to a chronological scheme could not take precedence over the circumstances that bound together people and important events and developments.

Tacitus portrays the actions and conduct of the *Roman emperors* in much the greatest detail, and through both of these he portrays their character traits. He thus follows a characteristic trait of imperial historiography (see above, Ch., 6, p. 123; below, Ch. 6.3, p. 165). Formally, Tacitus puts the emperor in the foreground. He does this by generally reporting at the beginning of a consular year on the emperor and those in his immediate circle, i.e., the imperial family and their court. He also sometimes marks conclusions and beginnings of books with changes in emperors (*Annals* 6/7: Tiberius/Caligula; 11/12: Claudius/Nero). The *principes* and their foils, whom Tacitus describes, commonly (but not necessarily) represent types, such as tyrants (Tiberius, Domitian), tragic heroes (Germanicus, Agricola) or even the fool (Claudius). Whatever significance some characters like Agricola, Germanicus, and Corbulo may take on as actual figures or even just as literary foils to a given emperor, they all pale in comparison with the *princeps*. The constitution of the Principate and its development disappear behind the emperors' fear and envy of highly competent men, which serves as the (supposed) chief motive of their actions. Although Tacitus is at least aware of the importance of the provinces for imperial power, the fortunes of the empire with its provinces receive extremely summary treatment, and frequently with several years lumped together in one report. Some centuries later Tacitus would be reckoned not unreasonably the author of imperial biographies (Jerome, *Commentary on Zechariah* 3.14; see below, Ch. 6.3, p. 165).

Because of the state of the texts that have come down to us, we may best observe in the six books devoted to Tiberius and his reign (*Annals* 1–6) the effect that the similarly biographical structure of both *Histories* and *Annals* had on their composition, and thus on Tacitus' account of the history of that period. The biographical, moral, and psychological interest of the historian manifests itself in a peculiar way: Tacitus generally presents non-imperial personages as characters varying according to the exigencies of circumstances, just as Livy had done before him (see above, Ch. 5.1, p. 106). Tiberius, however, appears with a character (*ingenium*) that is not only unchanging, but rather from the very beginning remains consistently vicious and furtively scheming. His character gradually reveals itself as external circumstances and possibilities change, and especially as chains to his conduct (*mores*) are successively cast off (mostly as a consequence of the deaths of close associates), and it manifests itself in correspondingly typical actions.[9] We thus find a logically constructed and precisely dated series of stages in the changes of Tiberius' conduct. These are summarized by Tacitus in his concluding portrait of Tiberius, and are marked by the following deaths (*Annals* 6.51.3): (1) the death of his nephew and adoptive son Germanicus in AD 19 at the end of Book 2; (2) the death of his own son Drusus in AD 23 at the beginning of Book 4 (i.e., 4.7–8; see below); (3) the death of Livia in AD 29 at the beginning of Book 5; and (4) the death of his favorite, and briefly the most powerful man in Rome, Sejanus, in AD 31 at the end of Book 5 (or the beginning of Book 6).

The theme of deterioration (by way of successive revelations) intersects, however, with that of change from good to bad at a single great turning point, a mode long entrenched well before Tacitus in Roman historiography (see above, Ch. 3.2.2, pp. 56f.; Ch. 6.1.1, pp. 131f.). With a verbal echo, Tacitus takes this tipping point from a work of *Sallust*, who served as his model in so many things, (*Annals* 4.1.1 and *Catiline* 10.1: see above, Ch. 4.5.1, p. 91). Tacitus, however, does not apply the concept of a turning point, as his predecessors did, to all Romans as a group, but instead to just one person, the emperor Tiberius and the evolution of his conduct. In this construction, moreover, the decisive moment, which Tacitus once more strives to date precisely (AD 23: *Annals* 4.1.1; cf. 4.6.1), comes not from the falling away of people through death, but instead the rise and (fatal) influence of a single person, the praetorian prefect, Sejanus. Even in the first eight chapters of the fourth book of the *Annals*, when Tacitus joins, not unskillfully, the fates of Sejanus and Drusus as antipodes, it is clear that the combination of two fundamentally divergent representations cannot lead to a result without inherent contradiction. More concretely, in the version with one turning point, our perspective on the death of Drusus (as an act of murder by Sejanus) changes from a view that sees a moment that triggers further action into one that views an event already triggered beforehand. For this reason, the murder does not stand at the beginning of Book 4, but is instead, in standard annalistic fashion, included in the running commentary on the year's events (4.8), while fundamental remarks about the relationship between Sejanus and Tiberius are, as programmatic elements determining the action, placed at the beginning of the book before the murder (4.1–2).

Nero's conduct and administration likewise display in Tacitus, on the one hand, a division into a period that was at first good and another period that was later bad (*Annals* 14.1: AD 59). On the other hand, these events reveal several stages, and thus correspond to the mode of explanation we observed in the books on Tiberius with their combination of various patterns for the evolution of an emperor's conduct. But the two variations in accounting for change do not combine as clearly for Nero as they did for Tiberius, although this could result from our loss of those books of the *Annals* recounting the concluding years of Nero's Principate and life. We find the division of Nero's Principate into five good years (the *quinquennium Neronis*) and into a subsequently bad period also in other authors independent of Tacitus (Aurelius Victor *Caesares* 5.2). We likewise find independent traces in Suetonius of both a turning point in the reign of Tiberius' administration and in the gradual revelation of his true character, i.e., the deterioration of his conduct in several stages (*Tiberius* 26.1; 33; 42.1; 57.1; 61.1; 62.1; 67.1). We must therefore conclude that Tacitus took from early imperial historiography both the principle of a single turning point and also the principle of gradual deterioration. Both of these principles are, from an historical perspective, doubtful and unlikely, but an attempt to fuse them even more so. This may represent a singular achievement by Tacitus, but his artistry in composition would then distinguish him more as a dramatist than as an historian.

Source criticism (*Quellenforschung*) plays an important role in the modern assessment of Tacitus' two (more narrowly) historical works as well as of his contemporary biography, the *Agricola*. Because, however, devastatingly few written records survive and because Tacitus cites his sources unsystematically and seldom mentions authors or their works by name, we rarely progress beyond speculations in listing earlier imperial authors and works, as, for example, Cluvius Rufus and Fabius Rusticus (compare above, Ch. 1.3.2, p. 28; Ch. 5.1, p. 104). More productive comparisons include Suetonius' *Lives of the Caesars*, which appeared at almost the same time as Tacitus' final work, the *Annals*, and the Greek author Cassius Dio's *Roman History*, which was deeply indebted to the annalistic traditions of Roman historiography (see below, Ch. 6.1.4, pp. 153f.; Ch. 6.3.1, p. 168). In the case of Suetonius, however, our task is complicated by the difference in genre and concomitant literary aims. In the case of Cassius Dio, incomplete transmission of the text and its composition in a different era complicate the identification of similarities as well as distinctions between them. After discussions and controversies that have spanned several generations of scholars, we may hold fast to one most probable conclusion: Tacitus makes use of the same early imperial materials as do Suetonius and Cassius Dio, and he does so in the same way that they do. He consequently stands neither nearer to, nor farther from, an awareness of the problems or the judgments of the main currents of early imperial senatorial historiography than do *Suetonius* and, above all, *Cassius Dio* (see above, Ch. 6, pp. 121ff.).

Tacitus possessed exceptional verbal artistry. On the one hand, he conveys (seeming) certainty by means of insinuation characterized by bald statements, often free-floating logic, and syntax strung along in the "ablative absolute" (a grammatical construction liable in Latin to ambiguity). On the other hand, he returns devastating verdicts with the fewest and tersest words possible. And, thanks to his fondness for these means of expression, Tacitus traced the prescribed lines more sharply, and thereby rendered his judgments clearer and more one-sided not only than those of the two authors we compare him with here but also than those of the Roman historians who preceded him. For an example of this, we may compare how differently Tacitus (*Annals* 11.9.1–10.7) and *Cassius Dio* (*Roman History* 56.43–44) each handles the positive and negative verdicts of individuals in the so-called "Final Judgment" of the deceased Augustus, which each found as a setpiece in the historiography of the first century AD. Only Tacitus' version can occasion in readers a profoundly negative assessment of Augustus or, more correctly, can seduce them to one (see below, Ch. 6.1.4, pp. 155f.). These arts have led many modern classicists (and, indeed, philologists more commonly than ancient historians) to the deceptive conclusion that Tacitus' judgment of emperors and empire was his alone and based exclusively on his own research or his own experience. Tacitus does not stand, to be sure, as the undisputed representative of the historical writers who preceded him, but neither does he depart fundamentally from them with opposing verdicts grounded on the basis of independent sources amassed for that purpose. The value of the historical testimony of his writings does not therefore differ fundamentally from the value of the works of early imperial historical writers that he used.

What stand behind Tacitus' unalleged, but rather merely slyly insinuated, "facts" and behind the pointed formulations of his verdicts are then by no means always ingenious and deep insights, but rather, to the contrary, often crass misinterpretations, as in the case of *Annals* 6.6, which, like Suetonius *Tiberius* 67.1, reports on a letter of the emperor Tiberius to the Senate. Tacitus at first in a manner similar to Suetonius reinterprets the letter in such a way that, rather than offer the writer's reaction to a specific situation, reveals the writer's inner character. But in the pointed emphasis of his verdict Tacitus goes significantly farther than the biographer, and thus likely farther too than their common sources, inasmuch as Tacitus categorizes Tiberius' statements according to the tropes for tyranny common in antiquity. In this psychologizing fashion he ascribes the darkest possible inner life to Tiberius, despite the fact that the situation in which Tiberius wrote the letter, a context Tacitus himself included in his account, should have kept him from just such nonsense. In those places where Tacitus draws his own interpretation from commonly available sources, much of what he presents is historically (even) less credible than the linguistically simpler and intellectually less complex descriptions and interpretations of parallel accounts by other authors.

We must in sum see Tacitus as a deeply skeptical intellectual whose views were self-contradictory. This historian longed for Rome's Republican past; yet he was aware of the weaknesses and errors of the Republic as well as its subsequent transformation. He agreed with the purpose, with the positive effects, and thus with the necessity of the Principate's constitution, but only resignedly so, sunk as he was in nostalgia for the Republic. In all events, he had his doubts about every possible constitution and its theoretical basis. He completely failed to appreciate the appropriateness of the emperors' defensive strategy for then-prevailing domestic conditions as well as for foreign affairs because he saw behind it nothing more than the aim of blocking republican competition among the elite. He wavered between accommodating himself to the "system" and withering criticism of every attempt at accommodating one's conduct. At both the beginning and the end of his career as an historian – and thus most likely throughout – Tacitus praised citizens in high office whose conduct toward the emperor and his regime displayed a middle way "between rude intransigence and ugly subservience," although he must have himself been aware that he praised something that was at once vague and fundamentally impossible, and that, to this extent, what he formulated was merely an excuse (*Agricola* [as a whole]; *Annals* 4.20.2–3 [for the quote]).[10]

What Tacitus considered evil, he detested deeply, but he was at the same time so fascinated by it that he devoted more of his descriptive powers to such topics than he did to anything else. In his conception of gods and fate, Tacitus wavered between superstition and agnosticism. Nevertheless, he believed that he, as an historian, "could recognize not only chance occurrences and outcomes of events, but also their inner logic and causes" (*Histories* 1.4.1).[11] He was deeply rooted in tradition, but he could and did approve of innovations. We should, or rather must, expect from such a person a literary work that demonstrates for long stretches indeed a consistently negative characterization of its protagonists, the emperors, but which in all other respects exhibits not intellectual consistency, but instead a wealth of emotional and intellectual perspectives. Like no other historiographical writing from a Roman pen, Tacitus' work is tragedy in prose with reversals of fortune, its actors' blindness, and other elements typical of the genre (see above, Ch. 1.3.1,

p. 19). Those who search through Tacitus' historical works above all, or even exclusively, for historical truth that emerges as a result of Tacitus' reasonable investigation of the sources, engage in an undertaking with only limited rewards. Indeed, Tacitus' subsequent influence, which first appeared in late antiquity, notably in both classically religious and Christian authors, and, since the Renaissance, above all and understandably so, among so-called "moralists," has been characterized less by "what" he wrote and much more by "how" he composed his accounts. As a result, his literary influence lies more in his work's ability to fascinate than it does as an example of sober acquisition of knowledge. (For Tacitus in late antiquity, see below, Ch. 7.2, pp. 209ff; Ch. 7.3.2, p. 228; Ch. 7.3.3, p. 236.)

6.1.4 Lucius Cl(audius) Cassius Dio Cocceianus

Cassius Dio was a native of Nicea in Bithynia (circa AD 155–235), and belonged to the elite of the Roman empire from the time he was born to a father who was a Roman senator, holding high offices up to and including a consulship and pro-consulship. Dio himself came early to Rome, where, like his father, he became a senator (under Commodus; 180–192), and a consul (under Septimius Severus; 193–211). Dio took part in Caracalla's (211–217) expedition to the East, and then, under Macrinus (217–218), became a curator, i.e., an imperial administrator and supervisor of finance, for the cities of Pergamum and Smyrna. Under Alexander Severus (222–235), Dio administered the provinces of Africa, and then Dalmatia and Pannonia Superior. In AD 229, he was awarded a special honor: an ordinary consulship (i.e., the eponymous consulship that gave its name to the year), which he held together with the emperor. Soon afterward he withdrew from official duties, and retired to his native city. Dio enjoyed an altogether extraordinary career that was apparently made possible by his close association with that emperor and his family who after the death of Commodus was able to win the imperial throne in the various struggles against and among his rivals. We find this mirrored in various parts of Dio's writing.

The biography Dio composed of his fellow countryman Arrian, who was likewise active historiographically, is not extant (see below, Ch. 6.4.1, p. 181). As a favor to the emperor, who was himself evidently a believer in oracles and miracles, Dio compiled oracles and omens that presented Septimius Severus' seizure of power as divinely prefigured, and he attached to it an objective account of the turmoil and battles for the imperial throne from the murder of Commodus on December 31, 192 to Septimius' entrance into Rome on June 9, 193 or perhaps beyond even

this event to the defeat of his last rival for the throne in AD 197. Dio
later incorporated this material in his *Roman History*. Dio prepared for
his major work, the *Romaïké Historia*, most likely only after 211, that
is, after the death of Septimius Severus, with ten years devoted to col-
lecting sources. He then spent another 12 years writing, bringing the
work up to the death of Septimius. Dio then set the work aside, but
picked it up again later, and continued it. In the end, he wrote eighty
books that extended to the year of Dio's ordinary consulship in 229
(72[73].23; 80.5). Only Books 36–60 are, however, extant, covering the
years 68 BC to AD 47. For the rest of the work, we must rely on
the collections of excerpts compiled in the tenth century at the order
of the Byzantine Emperor Constantine VII Porphyrogenitus, which were
taken from ancient Greek historical accounts and arranged according to
topics. Also extant are excerpts made by the Byzantine monks Joannes
Xiphilinus in the eleventh century and Joannes Zonaras in the twelfth
century.

Dio strove for a factual account of Roman history (46.35.1), but he
also dramatized events, and his own rhetorical training allowed him, like
so many ancient historians both before and after him, to compose
speeches. Most conspicuous among them is the extremely long discussion, that Dio has Agrippa and Maecenas conduct in advance of the
dramatic changes made to the Roman constitution in January 27 BC and
in Octavian-Augustus' presence on the relative merits of "democracy"
(the Republic) and monarchy (55.2–40: 29 BC). This clearly stands in
the tradition of the likewise inauthentic debate conducted in the Persian
empire on democracy, aristocracy, and monarchy that we find in the
Greek historian Herodotus (third quarter of the fifth century BC): in one
author, it was the principle of literary invention, in the other, literary
imitation that shattered the links to historical facts. In Dio's case especially, his division between Agrippa-Republic and Maecenas-monarchy
lacks any foundation in what we know about the behavior of either man
in the vicinity of Octavian-Augustus. Agrippa, for one, assisted more than
any other contemporary in ultimately establishing Octavian-Augustus as
sole ruler. In the words Maecenas speaks in favor of a humane monarchy
we listen to the voice of Dio himself.

Dio's *Roman History*, as an extensive general account of Roman
history from its prehistory and the beginnings of the city of Rome to the
lifetime of its author, was of a type no longer common at the time of its
composition, belonging in fact, to a subgenre that had been defunct since
Livy's *Ab urbe condita* (see above, Ch. 4, p. 65; Ch. 4.1, pp. 66ff.; Ch.
5.1, pp. 100f.). Because we possess only the books that cover the period

from about one hundred years before the end of the Roman Republic to the early imperial period, we cannot determine the structure of the work or the organization of the material with great precision. We can say that the *Romaïké Historia* was organized in distinctly annalistic fashion. This method intersects nevertheless with a thematic organization of materials according to topic. As opposed to Dihle [Bibl. § 1.3 p. 358], we should see in this less a mixture of Roman and Greek historiographical traditions, and much more the specific challenges faced by an historical account that devotes most of its attention to events in Rome as the center of the empire with the Senate, magistrates, and later, as first priority, the emperor, his family, and his inner circle, but that also describes occurrences throughout the empire in the provinces and above all along border regions in all directions. Dio was not the only one who had to cope with the problems resulting from such an account. *Tacitus* faced them too, and attempted to solve them in the same way, inasmuch as there were in principle no viable alternatives (see above, Ch. 6, p. 123; Ch. 6.1.3, pp. 144f.). Dio's whole work may have been divided into groups of ten books (decades). Book 41, which survives, begins with the civil war between Caesar and Pompey, with the majority of the Senate supporting Pompey. Book 51, which also survives, begins with the autocratic rule that Octavian-Augustus achieved through his victory at Actium. Only approximately can we conclude from the extant excerpts of lost books that Book 11 may have begun with the First Punic War, Book 12 with the Third Punic War, Book 31 with the first Mithradatic War, and Book 71 with the administration of Marcus Aurelius. Nevertheless, it is problematic to infer consistent principles of division for a work that its author continued beyond his original goal, as we can also see from the works of *Cato* and *Livy* (see above, Ch. 3.2.1, p. 54; Ch. 5.1, p. 101).

Another division of the work (or, more correctly, the account of the general history of Rome contained in it) and one not based on arithmetical units may be taken from statements made by Dio. This division is together with its justification informative for his thinking as an historian. Dio's most important statement in this regard is the summary that he places immediately before his report on the measures Octavian-Augustus and the Roman Senate took after the victory over Antony and Cleopatra in 31/30 BC, and especially in January 27 BC, to reorganize the constitution and the political life of Rome: Rome, for the sake of its own well-being, could no longer remain a republic. The new shape of the administration, however, had implications for how well informed the common public as well as historians would remain. Earlier, in the Republic, all the affairs of the Senate and assemblies of the people were common knowledge. For this reason, one could know everything and set it down in historical works and check subjective portraits with the help of statements made by others as well as with documentary evidence. After the measures taken in January 27 BC, however, everything was kept secret, and, when real information nevertheless leaked out, one mistrusted it because it was impossible to check its veracity, suspecting that it was misinformation spread at the behest of those in power. What happened or even did not really happen therefore no longer corresponded at all with what was reported or kept quiet. Even Dio could thus, in proceeding further with Roman history, report only what he found, and then formulate his own opinion (53.19). Just as Tacitus and, obviously, pre-Tacitean historical writers had before him, Dio's observation identifies the grave consequences of the Principate for the investigation and composition of Roman history during the imperial period (see above, Ch. 6, p. 123; Ch. 6.1.3, p. 143).

If we supplement Dio's observation in 53.19 with a short remark he makes for the period after Commodus' death in 192 (72[73].4.2), we are led to a threefold division of his work on Roman history to his own times: after the regal period, which here represents an uninteresting prelude, we find (1) the Republic as a time of open, generally accessible, information, followed by (2) the imperial regime until about the time of Commodus' accession (180) as a period lacking in good information and providing misinformation, and finally (3) Dio's own day when, as an adult, he enjoyed his own immediate access to information. On the one hand, Dio's description is superficially technical, insofar as every historical account depends on the quantity and quality of surviving information, but, on the other hand, it offers a subtle appraisal of the epochs. And neither is as simple as it may appear at first glance.

We may consider it certain that Dio, like other authors of general Roman histories, treated the first centuries of Rome only briefly, and that his account grew more detailed as he went on (see above, Ch. 3.1.1, p. 45; 4.1, p. 65; Ch. 5.1, p. 101). After some ten books for Rome's first five hundred years, including its pre-history too, another seventy books follow for the second five hundred years. Nevertheless, according to Dio 53.19 the amount of information available was not continuously increasing as he approached his own day. In fact, the 25 books or so devoted to the one hundred years of the civil wars (133–31/30 BC) provide a significantly more detailed account than the twenty books or so for the next approximately 190 years of the imperial period from 31/30 BC to circa AD 160. Dio's basic observations are thus confirmed in his historiographical practice in terms of the quantitative ratio of the later part of the first epoch to the major part of the second epoch. As opposed to the second epoch, we must, in accordance with Dio's remark for the third epoch, reckon with another increase in the available amount of information. Ten books, however, for the almost seventy years from circa AD 160 to 229 do not provide anything like the detail devoted to the account of the civil wars – this does not astonish. Nothing had fundamentally changed in administrative affairs since 27 BC. Only Dio's access to information for current events had improved thanks to his close ties to the Severan dynasty. But we may presume that he could not make limitless use of that information without thereby endangering his own person. No one could tell whatever he liked about the machinery of power and its secrets. For this reason, we can demand full disclosure in contemporary history and the joy of detail connected with it from neither *Tacitus* nor *Suetonius* nor Dio (see above, Ch. 6.1.3, pp. 143f.; below, Ch. 6.3.1, pp. 168f.).

Dio 53.19 offers an unmistakable appraisal of epochs, but this can, however, occasion misunderstandings. It also follows from Dio's other observations that, in respect of the availability and credibility of information, his verdict on the third epoch cannot differ fundamentally from his verdict on the second. Freedom may well serve as a criterion in the appraisal of epochs we find in Dio 53.19, as it does also for other late Greek authors who, like Dio, consider "democracy" the equivalent of the Roman "Republic," associating it with the time before Augustus, but the only criterion Dio actually spells out is the general accessibility and reliability of information. With this criterion as our measure, things look bad for epochs two and three. Nevertheless, Dio reduces the absolute value of this criterion for a general appraisal of his epochs when he introduces his fundamental observations in 53.19 with the acknowledgment that the end of the Republic was absolutely necessary, and that the new system of government, which he had just described in some detail, was better and more salutary for Rome and its empire (βέλτιον καὶ ... σωτηριωδέστερον: 53.19.1). After almost two hundred years of imperial rule, neither freedom of information nor its reliability represented absolute values for someone who had been all too closely associated with a dynasty that, like no other before it, had pressed ahead with the transition to a military monarchy.

Even so, if we label Dio a monarchist, but do so without "ifs and buts," we fail to comprehend him. On the one hand, his "Last Judgement" of the deceased Augustus rests on the basis of the same sources as *Tacitus'* account, but, in contrast to *Tacitus*, Dio dismisses all charges against the first emperor, and justifies all his acts (Dio 56.43f.; Tacitus *Annals* 1.9f.;

see above, Ch. 6.1.3, p. 149). On the other hand, Dio describes the establishment of the new constitution in 27 BC as an awkwardly staged undertaking afflicted with internal contradictions (53.2ff.). And in Dio's version of the "Last Judgement" of the deceased Augustus' great contribution in the view of his contemporaries lies ultimately not in his establishment of the monarchy itself, but instead in his combination of monarchy with "democracy," of order and security with freedom (56.43.4). We may compare this with what Tacitus recognizes as the achievement of Nerva and Trajan, but simply refuses to grant to Augustus (see above, Ch. 6.1.3, pp. 142f.). Even if Dio might have followed his source's views more closely than corresponded with his own, the possibility nevertheless remains that his monarchical convictions, under the influence of works of early imperial senatorial historical writing, were not as firmly established as his remarks elsewhere in his historical account would seem to suggest. In this case, Dio would be less a monarchist from enthusiasm for monarchy as a system of government, and more from insight into the long since inalterable course of the Roman empire's development.

6.2 Rome and Foreign Peoples

The processes of Romanization and Hellenization indeed brought acculturation to the Roman empire, but it nevertheless failed to produce a unitary Greco-Roman culture across the entire empire. In addition to the persistent linguistic division of the empire into (predominantly) Latin and (predominantly) Greek halves, scattered, but significant, regional (or rather national) peculiarities in language, religion, administration, and economy persisted. For this reason, the relationship between the central authority of Rome and individual regional or cultural groups within the Roman empire as well as the characteristics of one of these groups could continue to serve as topics worth taking up. Beyond this consideration, such topics could take on sudden relevance when regional conflict arose within the Roman empire. One would otherwise be tempted to shift one's gaze from the generally slow, and thus hardly perceptible, changes of the imperial period to the more remote past when relationships between Rome and other peoples altered dramatically, often in regular stages, and almost always in Rome's favor and to the disadvantage of others, i.e., the period of Rome's great expansion. In treating the more distant past as well as closer, problematic events requiring sensitive assessment, an historical writer could or would have to reveal his attitude toward Rome's world domination.

6.2.1 Josephus/Flavius Josephus: Jews and Others

Jews of the Hellenistic period had developed an extensive literature in Greek for a Greek and Hellenized audience. This literature placed Jewish history on an equal footing with Greek history, both in its wider and narrower senses, and set forth the special career of the Jews and the people of Israel under their God. This phase of ancient Jewish literature ended around AD 100 when Jews rejected Hellenistic-Roman culture, although this culture had likely always been controversial, leading to occasional disturbances. Apart from *Maccabees* 1–2, which became part of the *Bible*, Jewish-Hellenistic historical accounts have come down to us only in fragments (*FGrH* 722–737) with the exception of one author who appeared at the end of this extraordinary phase of Jewish literature. *Josephus* (AD 37/38 – circa 100), who was later called *Flavius Josephus* after he acquired Roman citizenship, offered an historiographical response to the Jewish revolt against Roman rule over Judaea. The revolt, which was accompanied by violent internal divisions, was suppressed by the Romans, and terminated with the capture and destruction of Jerusalem, including its Temple (AD 66–70).

As the son of an elite priestly family, Josephus was well acquainted with the main streams of Judaism of his day, Pharisees, Sadducees, and Essenes, and joined the Pharisees, whose rules for conducting one's life he compared to the doctrines of Greek Stoic philosophers (*Autobiography* 2.12; see below, p. 161). He came to Rome for the first time in AD 64 as part of a mission sent to assist in the defense of some of his fellow countrymen in court. During his stay, he met, and won the trust of the emperor's wife Poppaea. And, although, upon returning home, he opposed (at least according to his own words) the revolt of oppressed Jews against incapable and corrupt Roman governors, he very soon took over their organization in Galilee. By spring 67, Josephus had become a prisoner of the Romans. He must have found himself in Vespasian's presence, however, because he predicted to Vespasian that he would ascend to the imperial throne. When in AD 69/70 Vespasian had actually emerged as emperor from the wars of the various pretenders to the throne after Nero's death, Josephus received his freedom and Roman citizenship, but remained with the Roman army, now under the command of Titus, Vespasian's elder son, until the conquest of Jerusalem in AD 70. He lived afterwards as a well-respected man, and was supported by an imperial pension in Rome.

With the encouragement of Epaphroditus, a freedman who likely acquired his freedom and honors under Nero, Josephus wrote Israelite and Jewish history in Greek, so that his people, who faced difficult and depressing conditions after the revolt, might be portrayed in a positive light. His works were laid up in one of Rome's public libraries, and he was himself honored with the erection of a statue. Josephus thus received more attention and recognition from the state than almost any other Greek or Roman historical writer of any period. Most likely, however, these accolades were aimed less at him directly and, as behooved Roman political aims, more at pacifying and gratifying those Jews who had settled across the entire empire. This was an objective of the Roman government especially after the suppression of the revolt in Judaea. The imperial administration failed to recognize, however, that, in this instance, Josephus was despised – as could hardly have been otherwise – by many of his fellow countrymen as a traitor to the Jewish cause, while others despised him for his initial hostility to Rome, and that, as a result, he remained extremely controversial.

Josephus composed an account of the Jewish revolt and its suppression (AD 66–70) together with a rather extensive historical prelude in seven books (probable title: *Perí tou Ioudaïkoú polemou*, perhaps with the addition of *pros Romaious*; *The Jewish War* with the addition *against the Romans*), another general account of Jewish history in twenty books (*Ioudaïké Archaiologia: Jewish Antiquities*), an autobiography (*Iosep[h] ou Bios*; *Autobiography of Josephus*), and a two-volume work *Against Apion or on the Great Antiquity of the Jewish People* (original title likely just *Perí archaiotetos Ioudaion*). With the two smaller works, which he composed only after *The Jewish War*, Josephus defended both himself (*Autobiography*) and his people (*Against Apion*). His fellow countryman *Justus* in the city of Tiberias, located in Galilee, where Josephus had been active at the beginning of the Jewish revolt, was from the start a supporter of Rome, and, for this reason, fled at an early stage. In reaction to Josephus, Justus wrote his own *History of the Jewish War* as well as a *Chronicle of the Jewish Kings* (*FGrH* 734). Justus brought the latter work down to his patron Marcus Julius Agrippa II, who, as the great-grandson of Herod, had been permitted by the favor of Rome to govern several territories of Palestine in succession, and who, until the Jewish revolt, supervised the Temple. Justus charged Josephus with insubordination against Rome for portraying himself in *The Jewish War* as taking up arms during the Jewish revolt. Josephus then portrayed himself in his

Autobiography as someone who had stood on the Roman side from the very beginning, devoting 68 of the work's 76 chapters to his conduct during just those two years (AD 66–67).

From the beginning of Hellenism, Jews defended themselves against literary attacks on their people, their religion, and their way of life in writings composed in Greek (and labeled "apologetic" by moderns), in which they justified Judaism. In this effort, they could, of course, be successful only if they to some extent accommodated the intellectual world and conceptions of non-Jews, and portrayed those peculiarities of their religion and way of life that had attracted unfavorable attention in such a way that non-Jews, especially Greeks, would be able to comprehend them in terms of their own culture. The only text of this sort to survive is Josephus' *Against Apion*. Josephus defends the Jews against Apion's charges and against the charges of earlier anti-Jewish authors of diverse ethnic and cultural backgrounds as well by resorting to a method of argumentation that generally commanded respect in the ancient world: Josephus aims to prove that the Jewish people are among the most ancient, and therefore among the best, of all civilized peoples, and that, in particular, Greek philosophers depend on Moses, who lived and worked much earlier than they did, and that Jewish law is consequently insuperable (compare above, Ch. 5.2.4, p. 120). The Jews in general and Josephus in particular found themselves in a situation vis-à-vis the wider world around them, in which Christians too would likewise soon find themselves, partly as an outgrowth of Judaism and partly as an independent religious group. They would react no differently than had the Jews before them (see below, Ch. 7.3.2, pp. 224f.).

Josephus first wrote the *Jewish War* in Aramaic, which was at the time the language common in Syria-Palestine, and between 75 and 79 produced a Greek version with some assistance. The work relies on sketches Josephus had made, beginning with his time in the Roman headquarters outside Jerusalem, when he took notes on his own experiences as well as the stories of defectors and others (*Against Apion* 1.49). With close access to events thus guaranteed, the work met additionally with the approval of Vespasian and his son Titus, when Josephus presented it to them. The account also reportedly pleased Agrippa II, something which, however, in light of the reaction of Agrippa's favorite Justus, seems less than certain (see above). In the fourth century, the *Jewish War* was translated into Latin. This version preserves the name "Hegesippus" (likely a mangled form of "Josephus") as its author, and was attributed to the church father Ambrosius, bishop of Milan (circa 340–397). A Slavic translation was also produced very early, likely from the original Aramaic.

The allocation of blame and merit, of praise and censure, in the *Jewish War* was not simple. Josephus was indeed able to denounce some Roman atrocities against the Jews, but was in general compelled to praise the Roman army, and express his admiration for it (for an example of an extensive excursus, see 3.70–109). In his extended description of the prelude to the Jewish revolt against the Romans, Josephus was able to remove the assignment of blame from the Jews and ascribe it, above all, to the Seleucid King, Antiochus IV (175–164 BC), who had already been controversial during his own lifetime and whose reputation was low among the Romans. When he arrived at the events immediately leading up to the revolt as well as the revolt itself, in light of the prevailing balance of power, Josephus was unable to assign the blame to Rome's provincial administration, but neither did he wish to ascribe it all to his fellow countrymen. Responsibility for the terrible events of the years 66–70 thus fell on a few Jewish fanatics, the "Zealots" and the "Sicarii," who had criminally assaulted Rome, whose destiny it was to assume world domin- ion in recompense for its competent efficiency. This was a theme then current for justifying Roman rule, and one that would also be adopted in the second century by the Alexandrian Greek Appian (see below, Ch. 6.2.2, pp. 162f.). Josephus, however, instrumentalizes the theme here against others subject to Roman rule, even though he too was subject to Roman rule, the difference being that he, of course, had fully accom- modated himself to it. He thereby manages to exclude the "Zealots" and the "Sicarii" from the circle of citizens and subjects of the Roman empire, and, to the extent that Rome represents the world, to exclude them from any human community whatsoever. The famous verse of the Augustan poet *Vergil* about Rome's destiny to rule the world (*Aeneid* 6.851–853) demands that Rome suppress all those who fail to submit. The brutality of this verse is never more plainly manifest than when one who is non- Roman by birth deploys its content against his fellow countrymen.

The *Jewish Antiquities* were finished circa AD 93/94, and relate Israelite and Jewish pre-history and history from the creation of the world (accord- ing to the *Books of Moses*) down to the Roman emperor Nero (AD 54–68). They intersect therefore parts of the *Jewish War*, which Josephus takes advantage of through various references he makes in the later work to the earlier one. The similarity of the title *Jewish Antiquities* to the title of the *Roman Antiquities* by the Augustan Greek author Dionysius of Halicarnassus is no accident, but is instead by design (see above, Ch. 5.2.2, p. 115). Just as the latter had grafted the Romans in their origins to the Greek world, Josephus likewise joined the people of Israel and the Jews through their history to the peoples of the Mediterranean, and, in the East, to communities predominantly Greek or (sometimes heavily) influenced by the Greeks. It was Josephus' aim, as it had been already in *Against Apion*, to portray the distinctive attributes of Israel and the Jews as outstanding accomplishments of human culture, and, at the same time, to accommodate Jewish teachings and institutions to the intellectual world of cultured Greeks (see above). In this way Josephus turns the three main theological streams of late Hellenistic Judaism, which were also social and political movements, into philosophical schools analogous to the three classical Greek schools of the Academy, the Lyceum, and the Stoa (13.171–173 with references to the more extensive account in the *Jewish War* 2.119–166). Books 1–11 bring the history of Israel and the Jews down to the time of Persian rule and its dissolution by the Macedonian Alexander the Great according to a Jewish tradition in an exegesis that Josephus had learned in school. Books 12–20 integrate the Jewish history of the Hellenistic and Roman periods into the general history of the ancient world. Josephus follows both Jewish sources (such as the first book of *Maccabees* and documents detailing the sequence of the high priests from the Age of Alexander the Great [336–323] until the destruction of Jerusalem and the Temple in AD 70) as well as Greek and Roman-Greek authors (such as Nicolaus of Damascus or Strabo; see above, Ch. 5.2.1, pp. 112f.). He also mixes dating schemes: traditional Jewish dating with Macedonian names for months as well as the Roman system. Quite a few of the documents Josephus weaves into his account by, or for the benefit of, Jews have occasioned scholarly debate as to their authenticity (or lack of it).

Because Josephus also depicts the period when Jesus and his apostles were active, scholars have long asked whether or, possibly, how he, as a devout Jew, handles this difficult subject, which had given Roman administrators and officials trouble. The question cannot, however, be posed in this way. The famous passage on Jesus as a teacher *and* Messiah in *Jewish Antiquities* 18.63f., the so-called *Testimonium Flavianum*, can no longer be viewed as the first testimony about Jesus from outside the *Bible*, but is rather, according to current scholarly consensus, a later Christian interpolation. Nevertheless, a statement about Jesus formulated by Josephus may once have occupied the same place in the text, one that Christians deemed unacceptable, and that they therefore altered or replaced. Just such manipulation is suggested by the removal or abbreviation of a passage in another spot. The Greek theologian Origenes (first half of the third century) cites from *Jewish Antiquities* 20.200f. a passage about Jesus' brother Jacob that did not appear in the manuscripts available to him (*Against Celsus* 1.47). We find the reason for the omission of the passage in the tenor of the statement as established by Origenes: its author did not believe that Jesus was the Messiah. This view, which is one that we might assume in advance that a devout Jew would take, could hardly have permitted him to portray Jesus elsewhere (18.63f.) as the Christ, i.e., the Messiah. We cannot tell whether other passages in the *Jewish Antiquities* were subject to similar interventions nor likewise whether just one interpolator was at work or perhaps more and at different times. We are equally unable to explain how such manipulations could possibly have been inserted into the entire manuscript tradition, at least to the extent that we still have access to it. We can only point in general to the efforts of Byzantine and medieval interpolators who worked in accord with Christian doctrine, and also to similar interpolations Christians appear to have made elsewhere, as, for example, in the *Historia Augusta* (see below, Ch. 6.3.3, p. 175 with note 15, p. 261). Josephus represents, nevertheless, a special case. He was not classically religious, but rather a Jew, whose written work was posthumously Christianized through later interventions. As a contemporary witness to earliest Christianity in Jerusalem and among the Jews, Josephus must have appeared indispensable to later Christians.

6.2.2 Appian of Alexandria: a retrospective view of the establishment of Rome's world domination

Appian of Alexandria makes his appearance as a late admirer of Rome's world domination and the establishment of its dominion (circa AD 90/95–165; see above, Ch. 5.2, pp. 110f.). He was active as a rhetorician and in the courts first in his native city, and then, while still in his youth, in Rome. Here he found a patron in the famous rhetorician and court pleader *Marcus Cornelius Fronto*, who from 138/139 educated the later co-emperors Marcus Aurelius and Lucius Verus and was himself consul in 143. It was perhaps through this connection that Appian advanced to the status of procurator. He was therefore a Roman citizen (or became one), and, as such, belonged to the equestrian class. In addition to a lost autobiography, he composed a *Roman History (Historia Romaïké)* in 24 books. Of these, we possess only the *Preface*, Books 6–7, Books 12–17, parts of Books 8, 9, and 11, and excerpts and fragments of the other books.

Appian's historical work focuses on Rome's foreign affairs and its aims in terms of those states, peoples, and dynasties ultimately conquered by Rome and subjected to its rule. Appian's high esteem for the Roman people and their leaders induces him to describe the military and diplomatic sequence of events that made Rome master of the world, a status approached by no previous empire (*Preface* 1.1–12.47 *passim*). Rome earned its successes, in Appian's view, through the intelligence, competence, and tenacity of the Romans (*Preface* 11.43ff.). In contrast with Tacitus, and even more plainly with Florus, who writes at about the same time and about the same topics as Appian, Roman expansion does not end for Appian with Augustus and then not begin again until Trajan (see above, Ch. 6.1.3, p. 142; below, Ch. 6.5.1, p. 189). Appian, in other words, does not admire Rome's imperial expansion as a phenomenon located merely in the past, nor even as one located in the past and resumed again in the present with a definite interval separating the two periods. Instead, Appian views Roman expansion as a continuous process from the most distant past until his own times. For this reason, he admires past emperors as much as he does contemporary emperors. In the context of this fact, together with the connection we have already mentioned between Appian and Fronto, we may surmise that Appian must have had close relations with the imperial house, and that he wrote his historical work at the request or suggestion of the emperor or that it was perhaps the idea of someone from the emperor's inner circle to bring the work down to the present or even, in the most extreme case, that Appian wrote a history "made to order" (see above, Ch. 4.3, pp. 77ff.). Nevertheless, according to Appian's own statements, which we have no reason to doubt, his *Roman History* was created over a very long stretch of time, and his work on it thus began many years before Marcus Aurelius and Lucius Verus' accession to power in AD 161. It is therefore impossible that the idea for Appian's historical work could have derived from the Parthian War of 161–166 and the request directed to Fronto by the emperor Lucius Verus to celebrate the war with an historiographical account (see above, Ch. 4.3, pp. 77f. with note 6, p. 259).

Appian's *Roman History* is remarkable for an unconventional organizing principle. The author concludes that a chronologically organized narrative that has to deal with simultaneous events in multiple locations is the root cause of confusing shifts in location when narrating complex action. Appian counteracts this problem, after a bit of obvious experimentation, by fixing his gaze on only a single scene of historical action, or, more precisely: by focusing on actions extensively connected to the same distinct location (*Preface* 12.46f.). In practice, this thematic approach allows Appian to portray an opponent to Rome from its first contact with the Romans to its final subjugation by them. He does this, however, without synchronizing or otherwise connecting the events of his narration to other actions simultaneously undertaken by Romans and other opponents (*Preface* 13.49; 14.58). Appian also joins other sets of events to his geographical scheme, namely, early Roman history and Rome's civil wars. The strange structure of his historical account is reflected in the names individual books receive according to their content. Most books, but certainly not all of them, have geographical names. Others indicate content or name the main characters.

We may view the result in the following arrangement, singular for a history of Rome, which makes Appian's likewise unusually extensive justification almost necessary (*Preface* 14.53–60): 1: *Regal Period*, 2: *Italy*, 3: *Samnites*, 4: *Gauls*, 5: *Sicily*, 6: *Spain (Iberia)*, 7: *Hannibal*, 8: *Carthage (Libya)*, 9: *Macedon*, 10: *Greece and Ionia*, 11: *Syria*, 12: *Mithradates*, 13–17: *Civil Wars* (13: *Marius and Sulla*, etc.), 18–21: *Egypt* (additional books on the *Civil Wars*), 22: *A Century* (conquests from Augustus to Domitian), 23: *Dacia* (conquests under Trajan), 24: *Arabia* (more conquests under Trajan), and, likely planned, but not completed, at least one more book on the Parthians (likewise under Trajan). Nevertheless, this scheme still leads to what Appian decried in the customary chronological and synchronous methods he did not employ: doublets of the same events, cross-references, and gaps. We find this especially in the wars between Rome and Carthage, which were fought in both Sicily and Spain, and, in the Second Punic War, basically around Rome and throughout Italy, with the result that the difficulties we mentioned crop up in his books on *Sicily*, on *Spain*, on *Hannibal*, and on *Carthage*. We must concede, of course that the obstacles placed in the way of a smooth and unified narrative by the customary sequencing of an historical account were hardly a mere phantom of Appian's imagination. Even Polybius experienced difficulties representing in his account his accurate knowledge of the various links in world politics.

Appian evidently used many sources for his chronologically and geographically comprehensive work of history, including, of course, sources in Latin. Given the extent of his account's many topics, it is self-evident that Appian, like Livy, was dependent on the quality of his sources (see above, Ch. 5.1, p. 104). Furthermore, his main sources seem to be reflected also in variations in his manner of narration and even in his style. Appian seldom cites a source, but, when he does, the citation is so accurate and so exact, that we can check it against its original, or use it to supplement a fragmentary work (compare, for example, F. 18, of Appian's *Gallic* book with Caesar *Gallic War* 4.12–15, and his book on *Carthage* 132.628–631 with *Polybius* 38.22[39.6]). Although earlier scholars condemned Appian as utterly worthless (at least in Germany where negative criticism reached its zenith around 1900), Appian has long since been categorized as a trustworthy source, and, indeed, for the period between the end of Polybius' work and the age of Cicero, he is an indispensable historical writer.

6.3 Imperial History as Imperial Biography

Just as the Roman empire induced authors of Roman history to write the history of emperors, and thus brought them into the precincts of imperial biography, biographers who took up emperors as their theme were led into the vicinity of historiography. The church father *Jerome* (before 350–circa 420) realized both these points when he described, on the one hand, *Tacitus*, the early imperial historian, as the author of *Lives of the Caesars* (*Vitae Caesarum*) and, on the other, *Suetonius*, the biographer of early emperors, as *historicus* (*Commentary on Zechariah* 3.14; *Preface* to his continuation of Eusebius' *Chronicle* p. 6 Helm; see above, Ch. 6, p. 123; Ch. 6.1.3, p. 146). And for the reviser and editor or certainly for one of the authors of the *Historia Augusta*, there appeared to be no distinction any longer between the historians and the biographers of the imperial age (*Probus* 2.7; see below, Ch. 6.3.3, p. 177 with note 18, p. 261). In both genres – in one of which the task was to relate and describe not a way of life, but acts, and in the other where the task was not to relate deeds, but to tell the story of a life – the tasks were blended, an indication of the political situation after Augustus and in general of the reality of a monarchy, in which official events were bound up with what rulers did and left undone (see above, Ch. 6, pp. 121f.). The sources too were likewise for the most part the same for both genres, as a three-way comparison of *Tacitus–Cassius Dio–Suetonius* demonstrates (see above, Ch. 6.1.3, p. 149). Basic differences between both literary genres were nevertheless preserved, and these influenced what was presented and how it was presented as well as what was left out. In historiography in general, and among Roman writers in particular, who were heirs to the annalistic method, we find chronological accounts that proceeded annually to the extent that they could (see above, Ch. 1.2, p. 13). In biography, we find a tendency to formulate topical categories and, above all, an effort to comprehend people and their characters through events and personal conduct independently of any political implications that these may have. Imperial biography thus remained true to the criteria antiquity had established for "biography" (see above, Ch. 4.4, pp. 82f.; below, Ch. 6.4.2, pp. 185f.).

6.3.1 Gaius Suetonius Tranquillus

At about the same time that Tacitus was writing the only historical account on the early imperial period to survive more or less intact that was composed at a time close to it, another Roman, not coincidentally, was composing biographies of *principes* corresponding to almost the same period, specifically the time from Caesar to Domitian (see above, Ch., 6.1.3, p. 144). *Suetonius*, born around AD 70, learned the profession of a *grammaticus* (grammarian and philologist) as the student and dependent of the younger Pliny, and rose socially as the protégé of the equestrian official Gaius Septicius Clarus, who climbed to the rank of praetorian at the beginning of Hadrian's reign. Thanks to his powerful patron, Suetonius too – on the career path of an equestrian – secured a series of exalted secretarial posts in departments appropriate to his training: *a studiis* (records), *a bibliothecis* (library), and, finally, *ab epistulis* (correspondence). In the last post, he was responsible for the emperor's written communications. When in AD 122 Hadrian dismissed many men from his inner circle, both Septicius and Suetonius were affected.

Suetonius composed many works on primarily historical and cultural historical topics that do not survive. In his biographical works, his subjects were, somewhat like those of Cornelius Nepos (see above, Ch. 4.4, pp. 82f.), partly poets, orators, historical writers, grammarians, and rhetoricians (*De viris illustribus, On Famous Men*), and partly Roman rulers (*De vita Caesarum libri VIII*). We possess individual sections of the first collection, and of the *Eight Books on the Lives of the Caesars*, we possess the entire work except its preface and the beginning of the *Life of Julius Caesar*. Inasmuch as the work is dedicated to Septicius, we may surmise that at least its first books appeared before the wave of dismissals in 122. His *Lives of the Caesars* were therefore composed (or at least prepared) at a time when Suetonius, thanks to his official position, could make use of the imperial archives.

Suetonius' imperial biographies adhere to a much stricter pattern than do those of *Cornelius Nepos* (see above, Ch. 4.4, pp. 82f.): family relationships, birth, education, assumption of the *toga virilis*, early career or beginning of the reign, deeds in war, conduct of private life, omens and prodigies, death, last will and testament. These sections vary from biography to biography only according to their relative importance. For this reason, Caesar's long road to dictatorship takes up much space (1–33) while the "portrait" of Vitellius, who ruled only briefly, is interwoven with the report of his death (17). The point at which a new organizing principle shapes the narrative will sometimes be announced explicitly (e.g., *Nero* 19.3). Within the various categories, we find recurring sub-sidiary topics such as sex life, so-called last words, or even the emperor's own literary activity as well as his interest in literature more generally and his influence on its development (for the latter, see, e.g., *Augustus* 89.3: cf. *Life of Horace* 2–3). Both official acts and private deeds are sorted according to categories of "good" and "bad." All in all, Suetonius' arrangement results in the combination of a crude and only perfunctory chronology with thematic rubrics that serve as the decisive organizing principle (as Suetonius himself observes in *Augustus* 9.1). As a whole as well as in its particular points, the arrangement makes only limited sense from a modern perspective, and it is, moreover, incomplete. Sometimes a rubric and its content fail even to correspond (as, for example, good and bad deeds in the *Life of Nero*).

In Suetonius history inevitably disintegrates into stories and a life and career into disconnected fragments. Whoever would read Suetonius as an historian (and this, according to ancient biography's own self-characterization would, of course, be unjustified [see above, Ch. 4.4, pp. 81f.; below, Ch. 6.4.2, pp. 185f.]), will criticize Suetonius' method of composition, above all, the way he collects individual stories, thereby dismembering the sequence of events and disconnecting actions from causes and effects. And, as a consequence of this, our critic will note with some displeasure that many of the examples that Suetonius uses to fill up his topical categories are questionably filed or even misfiled altogether, inasmuch as the author has himself lost sight of their sense in the wider context, in which he originally found them (or would have found them). This in turn demonstrates that Suetonius' approach is unproductive even from a biographical point of view. The fatal flaw in his scheme for arranging his material thus resides in the impossibility of finding a common denominator for chronological narration and topical reportage and in the fact that his rubrics do not allow readers to comprehend an an emperor's personal development, at least from the time he reaches adulthood. On the other hand, sporadic indications in some of the biographies reveal that Suetonius was at least not completely unaware of changes and evolution in conduct or character (see above, Ch. 6.1.3, pp. 147f.).

The various small sections arranged within a Suetonian biography are sometimes artfully constructed, but, unlike an emperor's reign as portrayed by *Tacitus*, they fail in sum total to create dramatic tension, and certainly do not amount to tragedy (see above, Ch. 6.1.3, p. 150). On the other hand, they may culminate with, or take their beginning from, a verbatim quotation. The biographer recalls, for example, the words of the dying emperor Vespasian, which have the effect almost of satire: "Alas, ... I believe I am becoming a god!" (*Vae, ... puto deus fio!; Vespasian* 23.4). The words remind us of the man's improbable path to the imperial throne and, at the same time, draw our attention to his consistently simple and naïve manner even at the moment when he is faced with the final and greatest consequence of his imperial sovereignty. Unlike our historian, who assiduously avoids verbatim quotation, Suetonius makes ample use of this possibility, above all as a way to permit his various "heroes" to characterize themselves. Suetonius even inserts quotes in Greek into his Latin text. His work thus demonstrates, on the one hand, a considerable variation in style as a result of these inserted quotations. On the other hand, the author's own prose displays choice diction, which he combines with intentionally unobtrusive elegance, avoiding dark expressions and bold imagery – in all these points the opposite of the historian's style and especially that style that Suetonius expressly mentions, namely *Sallust's*, as well as the style of the biographer's near contemporary *Tacitus* (*On Grammarians and Rhetoricians* 10.7; compare *Caesar* 56.2 and *Augustus* 86 on the style of these men; see also above Ch. 1.3.1, pp. 22f.; Ch. 4.5.1, pp. 85 and 90; Ch. 6.1.3, p. 149).

In view of the state of our sources for the early Roman imperial period, modern scholars have repeatedly undertaken comparisons between *Suetonius, Tacitus,* and *Cassius Dio* (see above, Ch. 6.1.3, pp. 148f.). Because Suetonius considers Caesar the first of the Roman emperors, whereas Tacitus (*Histories* 1.1.1; *Annals* 1.1.1; 1.2.1; 3.28.1–2) stresses the short duration of Caesar's rule, and considers Augustus the first monarch, we must infer from this discrepancy that a divided tradition existed from the early imperial period, and also continued long after (see below, Ch. 6.3.3, p 172; Ch. 6.5.2, p. 195; Ch. 7.3.3, pp. 232 and 234). With the archival material available to him as a result of his official position, but not available either to Tacitus or Dio, Suetonius is able on a few occasions to correct and refute versions that turn up in the senatorial historiography that we find in Tacitus and Dio: that Augustus selected Tiberius for his successor because he considered him bad or that Nero was untalented in poetry (compare *Tiberius* 21.2–7 with Tacitus *Annals* 1.10.7 and Dio 56.45.3 or *Nero* 52 with *Annals* 14.16.1). None of this should imply, however, that the biographer made consistent use of this material and certainly not that Suetonius, Tacitus, and Dio made systematic comparisons of literary records available to them at the time.

Divergent (but in no case contradictory) individual and summary assessments of the emperors rest not on different sources or sources of different types, but result instead, in the first instance, from the formal differences in the narrative styles of the historian and biographer, which include different ways of selecting and handling facts. Their different social positions also had an impact. It does not surprise us that such equestrian-friendly emperors as Claudius and Otho receive kinder judgments from the equestrian Suetonius than they do from the senator *Tacitus*. In general, however, Suetonius diverges from the basic characterizations he found already formulated in the historical tradition as little as does Tacitus. This is the case too for such details as the turning point in the reign of Tiberius and his gradual degeneration as the unmasking of his true character – with one difference: Tacitus, as an annalistic historian, feels obligated to date events precisely, whereas Suetonius, as a biographer presenting catalogues, obscures chronology (see above, Ch. 6.1.3, p. 147). For the sake of his rubrics, Suetonius generally had to adjust and rework chronological accounts much more extensively than did historical writers.

Suetonius' biographies are unified by the consistency of the author's basic views on the exercise of monarchical power, including such values as social harmony (*concordia*), moderation (*moderatio*), and many others. These values were hardly Suetonius' invention. They were conventional, and may be compared to the so-called virtues (including the physical qualities) of a ruler likewise identified by Suetonius (this is especially clear in *Augustus* 31; 42.1; 51; 79; etc.; compare Pliny *Panegyricus* 3.4). We cannot expect from Suetonius an evaluation of the Principate as a system. He does not focus first and foremost on the political sphere, but instead on people of the highest rank and in the highest offices and on their conduct within their surroundings, including, for example, their family, the imperial court, the Senate under pressure from other people. For this reason, he does not, on the one hand, report an event as important as the fall of Sejanus, but instead merely alludes to it in midst of reporting on some completely different official business of the emperor (*Tiberius* 48.2). Agrippa is missing from Octavian-Augustus' side at the battle of Actium, not to mention his strategy and the other battles successfully waged on behalf of Octavian-Augustus (*Augustus* 17.2). On the other hand, Suetonius relates in happy detail intimacies of the emperor with close personal relations of both sexes. In general, we obtain decidedly less useful knowledge for understanding political history from Suetonius than we do from *Tacitus* in particular. Then again, his emperors have many more facets to them than do Tacitus', and their characters therefore appear more open, and are thus more likely closer to the historical truth than Tacitus' pointedly enhanced *principes* with their few, bizarre, and even more frequently evil, character traits. As a biographer of monarchs, Suetonius continued to exert great influence in later times similarly imbued with the spirit of monarchy, as were the Middle Ages and Renaissance. We may observe this, for example, in Einhart's *Life of Charlemagne* (*Vita Caroli Magni*).

6.3.2 Marius Maximus and Herodian

Lucius Marius Maximus Perpetuus Aurelianus composed biographies of emperors from Nerva to Elagabalus, that is, for the years AD 96 to 222 (*HRR* II CLXXX / 121). Unlike Suetonius, Marius was a senator. He served several terms as provincial governor, was in AD 217/218 prefect of the city of Rome, and in 198 or 199 and in 223 held the consulship. Only fragments of his work survive. All of them (2–27) except the first (1) derive from the so-called *Historia Augusta*, which is to say from antiquity's most dubious and least trustworthy historical work (see below, Ch. 6.3.3, pp. 171ff., especially p. 176). We hardly dare draw conclusions from this work. We shall nevertheless make two observations: if Marius continued *Suetonius'* series of biographies, which had ended with Domitian (up to AD 96), and – in addition to this – imitated him, then this likely represents the first instance in Roman *biographical* literature of *historia continua* over a longer period of time, which was achieved by appending one's work to an older account (for the practice in annalistic historical writing, compare above, Ch. 4.1, p. 69). And, if the relevant remark in the *Pertinax* of the *Historia Augusta* (15.8 = HRR F. 18) is correct, then Marius attached official records to his biographies as appendices. If this were indeed his practice, Marius, as a biographer, far excelled every historian with his insight into the importance of sources and documentary evidence for history.

Herodian (circa AD 180–250) held a low-level post in Rome's civil administration. He lived intermittently in Rome. His *Imperial History after Marcus Aurelius* (*Metá Markon basileias historia*) narrates in eight short books the often rapid changes in emperor, the simultaneous reigns of various pretenders who mutually fail to recognize each other, their battles against one another, and the frequently strange personalities of the emperors between AD 180 and 238. He thus offers the *history of emperors*. The history of the empire is only a part and merely a function of his history of the emperors. Biographical criteria for the emperors, above all their age upon accession, have, according to Herodian, a great influence on how they rule (1.1). Herodian's choice of recent events and the present for his account lead inevitably to a pathology of imperial rule:

unworthy men, even insane men, indulge themselves (1.15 Commodus; 4.6ff. Caracalla; 5.5ff. Elagabalus). This sort of analysis leads to exaggeration, although Herodian's history is in truth far less fantastic than what we find in the *Historia Augusta* (see below, Ch. 6.3.3, pp. 172f.). His moral values are those of the educated class of the Greek-speaking citizenry. This may have kept him from straining too much after sensationalism for cheap effect. Nevertheless, an anti-oriental attitude is discernible in his work that may reflect the attitudes of a Syrian Greek.

6.3.3 *Historia Augusta* / *Scriptores Historiae Augustae*

Probably the most mysterious work of ancient literature, and in all events the most dubious and least trustworthy piece among ancient works of historiography and biography, is the collection of imperial biographies that, since the edition of the text published by Isaac Casaubon in 1603, has gone by the name of *Historia Augusta* (*HA*) or *Scriptores Historiae Augustae* (*Imperial History* or *Writers of Imperial History*). Its original title had been rather *Vita(e) principum* (*Lives of the Emperors*) with the addition of the names of the first and last emperors treated by the collection.[12] It is precisely the fog of uncertainty surrounding the *HA* that has elicited scholarly literature in an abundance that has rarely been granted to any other ancient literary work. All these many efforts have, however, failed to solve the puzzles of this work, and, as things stand, future investigations are just as likely doomed to failure.[13] The authorship is dubious and quite controversial, as are the date (or dates) of its composition, perhaps also of its revision, furthermore its point of view regarding the late antique battlefield between classical religion and Christianity, and finally the many sources cited in its biographies – not to mention all the important defining characteristics of an historiographical and biographical work. Investigation of the *HA* is further complicated first by the tendency of the work's seemingly clear and credible testimony to prove deceptive time and time again, and, secondly, by the impossibility of ever clarifying any of its parameters individually. Instead, the literary variables that determine its shape remain interdependent. As a result, we always suspect that at least one more lurks unseen or that we fail to take into account some uncertain, but very important, thing. Nevertheless, there is no way around the *HA*. At least for the emperors who can no longer be found in the works of *Cassius Dio* and *Herodian* (those after 229 or 238), we must, for lack of anything better or more detailed, use the evidence of the *HA* (see above, Ch. 6.1.4, p. 151; Ch. 6.3.2, p. 170; compare below, Ch. 6.5.2, p. 193).

In its current state (and in this it remains the same as it was in the Middle Ages; see note 12, p. 261), the *HA* contains thirty books of imperial biographies that begin with Hadrian (117–138), end with Numerian (282–284), and are drawn up as accounts encompassing an individual, a pair, a group of three, or a larger group of emperors. The *HA* provides accounts not only for legitimately recognized emperors, but also for princes and, under the label *tyranni* (a term used elsewhere in the Latin literature of late antiquity in the same way), for usurpers and pretenders to the throne. Under the latter category we also find fictitious persons. In their biographies, but also in those of real people, uncertainty about facts is compensated for by anecdotes, miracles, fable, and gossip. The *HA* organizes its material neither chronologically nor according to definite topics, but instead randomly, which may be the result of a lack of real information, but it could well also be intentional (see below). From a political and social point of view, the *HA* aligns itself with the emphasis on liberty we find in senatorial historiography, and its observation that Augustus was the one to put an end to liberty links the work closely with the historian *Tacitus* and differentiates it at the same time from the assessment of Augustus we find in *Cassius Dio* and *Eutropius* (*Carus...* 3.1; see above, Ch. 6, p. 126; Ch. 6.1.3, pp. 139f. and 149; Ch. 6.1.4, pp. 155f.; and below, Ch. 6.5.2, p. 195). The attitude of the *HA* toward Christianity and classical religion, which has become the central focus of a great deal of recent scholarship, appears in *Severus Alexander* 29.2; 43.6; 51.7f. as an acceptance of both sides, a position possible only for adherents of traditional religion, but the attitude can be construed differently in other biographies (see below, pp. 174f.).

To the extent we suppose that the *HA* bypassed *Marius Maximus*, and aimed to continue *Suetonius*, whose last biography was of *Domitian* (81–96), then we also conclude that *Nerva* (96–98) and *Trajan* (98–117) must have been lost (see above, Ch. 6.3.1, p. 166; Ch. 6.3.2, p. 170). There is indeed no preface. And, within the collection itself, in addition to smaller bits and pieces of text in the biography of the two Gallieni, we are missing in particular the emperors of the years 244–253, namely, Philip the Arab (244–249) and Decius (249–251) in their entirety, as well as the beginning of the biography of the elder Valerian (253–260), the first chapter of which today begins in the middle of a sentence. Here too we will want to suppose that we have suffered a later loss in the literary tradition, particularly in light of *Aurelian* 2.1 where we learn that one of the (alleged) authors of the collection, Trebellius Pollio, composed biographies from the two Philips, father and son, to Claudius and his brother Quintillus (268–270). Of course, the uncertainties of the

HA also allow the possibility that people and subjects were intentionally omitted. In regard to the gap in the work, it is also significant that the historical tradition reckoned Philip the Arab as well disposed toward Christians, and even regarded him as a Christian, that Decius instituted the first empire-wide persecution of Christians, and that the elder Valerian also persecuted Christians, which is simply not recorded in the surviving portion of his biography. One immediately realizes that, if the two emperors were omitted intentionally, two opposed points of view had to be at work. If one nevertheless seriously considers the possibility that the so-called gap was inserted intentionally at the first creation of this col-lection of biographies, then one must perforce assume that the work is deeply enigmatic: one considers it possible that the classification of the work's worldview should be rendered more difficult, and that traces of its authorship should be obscured. In light of the literary and historio-graphical games the *HA* plays with its readers, this assumption is not off the mark (see below, pp. 175f.).

The most protracted scholarly controversy was kindled by the *question of authorship* in connection with *dating*. According to remarks in the work itself, six men are named as each having written several biographies that often, but not always, immediately follow each other in sequence. The dedications of individual biographies to emperors increase in number around Diocletian (284–305) and Constantine (306–337). *Aurelian* 1–2 names (Gaius) Junius Tiberianus, who was city prefect in 291/292 or 303/304, as patron of the work. Some of the biographies written by "Pollio" and by "Vopiscus" mention, or presume, that the father of Constantine, Constantius Chlorus, who died in 306, is still alive. From indications in the text itself we would thus conclude that the literary activity of the six authors corresponded with the end of the third and the first third of the fourth century. But ever since the publication of two articles by Hermann Dessau in the journal *Hermes* in 1889 and 1892, the indications provided by the *HA*, both as to authorship and date, have been questioned.

There are no linguistic or other stylistic differences or commonalities in the biographies that point to six authors as assigned and specified by the text of the biographies themselves. Scholars concluded for this reason that the six authors were invented, and that a single author hides behind them. There were to be sure voices that rose time and again to attempt to refute this extreme reduction of authors to a single individual, but the question was immediately posed: if not one, then, of course, six or how many would it be? After a first essay published in 1992, Burkhard Meissner relatively recently conducted an examination that was similar, but not identical, to work conducted by others (see Meissner [Bibl. § 6] 1997). Meissner analyzed the frequency of small structural words like *et* and *in* first in Suetonius and then in the individual biographies of the *HA*. He compared the results for each according to the best statistical methods, and arrived at astonishing results. On the one hand, various biographies assigned by the text to a variety of authors could well have been written by a *single* author. On the other hand, there are biographies in the *HA* that are assigned to a single author, but could well have been written by diverse authors. Although ancient linguistic virtuosity, schooled as it was in grammar and rhetoric, offers room for doubt in the face of results gathered through linguistic statistics, another article by Meissner (see Meissner [Bibl. § 6] 1993) demonstrates that some biographies approach past, present, and future differently, diverge in their assessments of emperors, and offer different accounts of the emperors' personal qualities. This is especially the case between the first and last biographies, and within the pieces attributed to "Julius Capitolinus." The result of all this may not yet have won the approval or recognition of the established scholarly consensus on the *HA*, but it will be difficult to refute. There are several authors, but they are neither the six authors named by the work nor do they correspond to the biographies as ascribed by the text, and they were at work in different periods. Somebody collected the biographies for publication, and in the process revised individual texts. The collection must thus, as Theodor Mommsen already surmised, have emerged in two stages. These could lie far apart in time. The creation of the work and its revision might therefore be located in very different periods which could in turn account for the different points of view we find within the *HA* as well as the divergent attitudes toward Christianity and classical religion.

Doubt about the six authors the work names and doubt about its dating are interdependent. To be sure, skeptics are united only in dating the work later than Constantine I, i.e., after 337. Their estimates vary widely, however, between the reign of the last classically religious emperor Julian the Apostate (361–363) and the period immediately before AD 525, which was the year of the execution of Quintus Fabius Memmius Symmachus, who reputedly wrote out the entire *HA* for his own Roman history (Jordanes *Getica* 15.83ff.). If they suppose there was a single author, these divergent estimations of a date must deal merely with one time period. This appears at first as an advantage, but proves to be a disadvantage, usually when we situate the *HA* in the literary polemics between adherents of traditional religion and Christians, and attempt to establish it as the composition of *one* author writing at *one* time with *one* point of view.[14] It is precisely this point of view or "bias" that scholars locate in the text, and then employ as evidence in a circular argument to establish a date, that remains, in fact, not at all clear (see above, pp. 172f.). Inasmuch as the respective authors of the biographies fail to state openly their personal ideology or bias, scholars proceed on the basis of their hidden messages. This immediately raises questions. How do we recognize and describe what it is we look for? What consequences result for the still vague dating of the work? Can we both determine the work's general attitude and date it using methods that are not purely subjective? And further: is there in the *HA* just one point of view in the battlefield between classical religion and Christianity? If there are indeed several attitudes or at least if it is possible that there were, where do they come from? Perhaps, if we follow Meissner and other scholars who have made similar arguments, from multiple authorship and a later recension made with an eye to publication? Or perhaps from a medieval Christianization that took place hundreds of years after the *HA*'s original composition and publication, a fate that subsequently befell other writings of classically religious and, in one instance, Jewish antiquity (see above, Ch. 6.2.1, pp. 161f.)?[15]

The *HA* frequently cites individual documents and various types of records. We find this, granted, above in the biographies of unknown or historically questionable personages and under dubious accompanying circumstances. Aurelian supposedly kept a diary in "linen books." Linen books are otherwise known only for lists of magistrates in early Roman history, and for this purpose from only one author, *Licinius Macer*. Modern scholars are skeptical too about this use of them (*libri lintei*: *Aurelian* 1.7; see above, Ch. 4.1, p. 68 with note 1, p. 258). In the biography of the emperor Tacitus (8.1–2), we find mention of "ivory books," which supposedly contained relevant decrees of the Senate. This was the case for the decree making him emperor as well: one could find it oneself with the signature of the emperor in just such a *liber elephantinus*, and this volume was stored in the sixth cabinet of the Ulpian Library. If this exaggeratedly exact and simultaneously nonsensical statement does not appear suspect, then perhaps this statement from *Probus* 7.1 will arouse suspicion: the (supposedly) same author, after citing a letter of the emperor Aurelian to his general Probus, the content of which defies belief, and after likewise questionable historical statements about his predestination for the office of emperor, relates that he could not find the senatorial decree on Tacitus' election as emperor! In light of such sleight of hand in dealing with "documents," it is not surprising that the unverifiable "documents" that the *HA* supposedly took from the work of *Marius Maximus* likewise arouse suspicion (see above, Ch. 6.3.2, p. 170). We cannot even verify the authenticity of the content and formulation of the otherwise credible abuse shouted chorus-like through the Senate upon the death of Commodus, details of which, we are told, were provided by Marius Maximus in excerpts from the *Acta diurna* or *Acta urbis* (*Commodus* 18–19; compare 15.4; on the *Acta urbis* or *Acta senatus*, compare *Probus* 2.1). This too could easily have been invented.

The *HA* makes use of a whole series of literary sources in Latin and Greek from *Marius Maximus* (problematic, of course, precisely because he appears in the *HA*) to, most likely, *Aurelius Victor* (see above, Ch. 6.3.2, p. 170; below, Ch. 6.5.2, p. 193). To the extent that one accepts *Eutropius* as a source, the composition of the *HA* or at least sections of it must be placed after the emperor Julian (see below, Ch. 6.5.2, pp. 194f.). And, if one wishes to see *Ammianus Marcellinus* or remains of the lost historical work of *Nicomachus* in the *HA*, then the creation of the *HA* or individual sections of it cannot be dated before the conclusion of the fourth century (see below, Ch. 7, p. 200; Ch. 7.2, pp. 207ff.). Here too we find two criteria linked to each other that are decisive for understanding the *HA*. As with other works of ancient historiography in general, so also in the *HA* more authors and works could have been used as sources than are cited altogether in the relevant biographies. Nevertheless, with the *HA*, we also have to reckon with the opposite possibility, because the *HA* cites authors for whose existence we have no other testimony: authors who could not possibly have been used in the *HA* because they did not exist! In the arrangement of the biographies of the emperors, the *HA* follows Suetonius, which it expressly cites as a model on several occasions only in the use of the rubrics of "good" vs. "bad," but not in the use of topical rubrics (see above, Ch. 6.3.1, pp. 166f.; for the reason for this, see p. 172). To the extent that Marius Maximus actually attached documentary appendices to his biographies, and the *HA* borrowed from them, the *HA* diverges from this model, because, like Suetonius, the *HA* provides the documents within the biographies themselves as immediate evidence for a statement (see above, Ch. 6.3.1, pp. 168f.; Ch. 6.3.2, p. 170).

When we look at the *HA*'s treatment of models and sources – whether documentary or literary – it is above all clear that the *HA* wants to be understood as, and probably enjoyed, playing with literary and historiographical conventions. It is astonishing that a document introduced as important and consequential, one that in the context of an exact account is supposed to defend the author against an anticipated charge of "blindly following some or other Greek or Latin author" fails to turn up. But this is divulged only later and in another biography (*Tacitus* 8.1–2; *Probus* 7.1: see above, p. 175).[16] What remains then of the historian's pretension that he will take great care in his efforts "not to allow earlier deeds to vanish"? When the author makes a distinction between earlier authors of the sort, whose works he wants to follow "in his treatment of the life and times of the emperors," and those, whom he, on the other hand, does not want to follow, and when he names manifestly fictitious authors for those of the first sort, whom he wants to follow, among whose names we also find the "authors" of the biographies of the *HA*, but we find among those not chosen as models an historian like Tacitus whose work would be relevant to the subject matter in addition to those who like Sallust, Livy, and Trogus were in terms of their period and subject matter actually precluded from having anything to say about emperors, he then makes a mockery both of the custom and near cult among ancient (and late antique) intellectuals of appending their work to and imitating earlier authors as well as of the working method of historical writers and biographers who were always bound to their sources.[17] Inasmuch as the same author rejects higher stylistic ambitions for his own undertaking, and dismisses as "extremely eloquent" the authors he rejected, but classifies those he chose as models as "not so eloquent as they are lovers of truth," he adopts, to be sure, a stance with which ancient historians time and again defended their seriousness of purpose, but he discredits that stance at the same time as mere pretense: for he himself, on the one hand, professes to report according to sources that he does not know or that he knows do not exist, and, on the other, like so many other works of ancient historiography and biography, he adorns his work with linguistic and stylistic refinements and pointed interpretive remarks (*Probus* 1.6–2.2; 2.6–8).[18] When the *HA* wanders back and forth between truth and fiction in such a sophisticated way, often recognizable only at second glance, and asserts this as the chief characteristic of historiography (*Aurelian* 2.1–2: see above, Ch. 1.3.2, pp. 29f.), we can hear the author or the editor and reviser of these biographies of emperors roaring with laughter.

What then is the *Historia Augusta*? At the end of a long series of historiographical and biographical works that strive continually to be taken seriously, it is a persiflage of ancient historiography, or, more precisely, of that which represents itself as such through its own assertions. This may well represent the primary purpose of the *HA*. We should therefore not expect the work to take a side in the conflict between classical religion and Christianity, and the modern inquiry into this question proves irrelevant to the most significant aims of the author or the editor and reviser of this collection of biographies. The usefulness of the *HA* for primarily historical purposes is rather restricted, and it is thus a work that irks us, but simultaneously entertains us, because its wit hits its mark.[19]

6.4 Personal History and Biography in the High Empire beyond Roman Emperors

Curiosity about Roman emperors could extend to other rulers and to other personalities in political life more generally as well as to persons in other times. An ethically motivated interest in the conduct of real people had in any event likely never abated in any period.

6.4.1 Curtius Rufus and Arrian of Nicomedia: histories of Alexander

Alexander the Great elicited especially intense interest during the imperial age. Early on, Octavian-Augustus demonstratively honored him by visiting his grave in Alexandria and by occasionally using his image as a seal (Suetonius *Augustus* 18.1 and 50). Alexander, like the mythical hero Herakles/Hercules, served as a generally available ideal type, whose currency was as valid in the Latin West as in the Greek East. For this reason, it does not occasion surprise that, during the Roman imperial period, at least two, apparently independent, works were devoted to this Macedonian king and founder of universal empire. Like their many, centuries older, predecessors, in whose tradition they followed, both works were organized not according to the thematic categories of ancient biography, but instead proceeded according to chronologically narrated actions. Both works are thus classified as "Alexander histories," a term also used for earlier works that narrated the deeds of Alexander the Great in the same fashion (compare *FGrH* 117ff.). Inasmuch, however, as all earlier works on Alexander have been lost (apart from the sketch of Alexander within *Diodorus'* universal history), and now exist only in fragments, Curtius' and Arrian's accounts represent our decisive sources for Alexander, and, as such, likewise provide insight into earlier Alexander histories. But they also mirror for us the cultural concerns of the period when they were composed, a period characterized by monarchy and Rome's universal empire. The object of their inquiry may have lain far removed from the authors in time, but, in respect to the concerns of their age, it likely provided a topic of current interest.

A certain *Quintus Curtius Rufus* wrote in Latin the *History* (or *Histories) of the Macedonian Alexander the Great* (*Historiae Alexandri Magni Macedonis*). But, although we find two bearers of the name "Curtius Rufus" in the works of Tacitus, the younger Pliny, and Suetonius, the date and identity of this historian of Alexander remain uncertain. The thoroughly classical style of the work provides no assistance in establishing a date. The author mentions that he lived through a time when several pretenders to the throne fought one another in a civil war that threatened the empire with collapse and ruin, but that fortunately only one man survived, who then, as a true monarch, led the Roman people into a new and happy age. In light of the emphatically grateful admiration the author expresses toward this emperor, he must have been ruling at the time Curtius composed his history of Alexander (10.9.1–6). Because the political situation described corresponds with more than one period in the history of the Roman empire, the author's contemporary allusion does not really help us in dating his work. Scholars most commonly assign the situation Curtius describes to the year of four emperors after the death of Nero and the final victory of Vespasian (see below, pp. 180f.).

Curtius portrays Alexander's life and deeds in ten books, of which, however, Books 1 and 2, the beginning of 3, the end of 5 and the beginning of 6, as well as parts of 10 are missing. The literary tradition regarding Alexander was divided into two camps. Curtius, along with Ptolemy Soter, Cleitarchus, Aristobulus, and Timagenes, made use of the works of three Greek authors of the fourth and third centuries BC and one of the first century BC, that were partly friendly, partly hostile, and to some extent objective in their accounts of Alexander, but also, as was so often the case in accounts devoted to the theme of "Alexander," partly inclined toward the fabulous and miraculous. Curtius thus exercised a free choice in selecting events and assessments. Beyond this, we also find evidence for a knowledge of diverse authors from Herodotus and Thucydides to at least Livy, an acquaintance Curtius would have acquired through the literary and rhetorical education then customary. Curtius tells his story according to contemporary precepts of "tragic" historiography: he paints scenes, and thereby sometimes relegates what is historically significant to the background, changes chronology for the sake of effect, and turns geography and real landscapes into idylls or places of horror to accord with whatever action he narrates. He fashions speeches in diverse styles, and this is especially manifest in paired speeches, to accord with their speaker. This practice utterly fails, however, to bring these speeches even within the vicinity of authenticity.

Curtius casts Alexander in an overwhelmingly negative light: he is, above all, sickly, addicted to conquest, ruthless, and murderous. To this extent, the author merely follows one strand of the tradition available to him. At the same time, Curtius' portrait of Alexander may include references to contemporary emperors, and thus also clues as to the date of the work's composition, which, nevertheless, will remain elusive (see above, p. 179): one might, for example, compare the burning of Persepolis with Rome, and thus Alexander with Nero (5.7.2ff.; Tacitus *Annals* 15.38ff.). We also find an older Roman point of view regarding Alexander prominently on display: this Alexander, who, together with his army, was morally degenerate, could never have conquered the collectively brave and morally upright Romans. Alexander had already long been, in this respect, an anti-hero to the Romans (cf. Cicero *Republic* 3.24 and, for extended discussion, Livy 9.17–19, among others). As a result, Curtius has a "barbarian" prince deliver a speech in Alexander's presence about the discrepancy between his enormous outward success and his lack of inner greatness (7.8.12–30; compare 7.9.1 and 17). With this he expands on a favorite theme of the rhetorical schools (Seneca *Controversiae* 7.7.19 and *Suasoriae* 1). His characterization of Alexander also serves a peculiar literary purpose: the division of the work into two halves. In the first half (to the end of Book 5), Alexander pursues his still-living external enemy Darius III. In the second half, Alexander faces no real opponents other than himself, and wages his predatory campaign across Asia, thereby meeting his own demise. As the programmatic preface to the second half puts it (6.2.1): "The man whom the weapons of the Persians could not break was conquered by his own vices."[20] In reviewing Alexander's entire life, Curtius would, of course, arrive at a summary judgment that (while also displaying his admiration for the Macedonian king and world conqueror) differentiated between, on the one hand, Alexander's great talents, and, on the other hand, the fortune that spoiled or even corrupted him at such a young age (10.5.26–37, which follows the report on Alexander's death).

Monarchy is for Curtius the natural state of affairs. The assessment of whether it is good or bad or at least tolerable depends, in his view, on whether or not two conditions are present, and met. On the one hand, Curtius had himself experienced the bloody wars between pretenders to the throne, and, on the other, he relived in literature the wars of the Diadochi (or "Successors") after the death of Alexander. The catastrophic impact that he saw in such a situation led him to conclude his Alexander history not with the death of the king and a final appraisal of him, but instead to continue with a description of the outbreak of the wars of the Diadochi in connection with the fate of Alexander's corpse that, with an outburst of rhetorical emotion, he then interweaves with his own experience of Rome's civil war and its unexpectedly quick and happy resolution, an experience that differs so markedly from the wars of the Diadochi that flared up time and time again for some two generations (10.6–10, especially after 10.9.1). For Curtius, the essential point about both sets of circumstances is that monarchy only functions when there is a single ruler, because "monarchical rule cannot be shared" (*nam ... insociabile est regnum*: 10.9.19). Secondly, Curtius refuses to extol absolute monarchy, and he rejects above all the worship of a living monarch as a god. Callisthenes, who represented this position with cleverness and courage, although in vain, in opposition to Alexander, is termed the "defender of public liberty" (*vindex publicae libertatis*: 8.5.20; compare above, all of Ch. 5). We may be certain that Curtius wanted his readers to make the connection with Rome, inasmuch as the worship of living emperors as gods frequently recurred as topic of current interest. Curtius' point of view aligns with that of many Roman senators. In addition to Callisthenes, Curtius paints Alexander's opponents in the brightest possible colors. We may thus profitably compare him with early imperial historians, especially Tacitus, without thereby suggesting or establishing direct literary influence in one direction or the other. Certainly, one thing is clear: Alexander represented for Curtius no remote object of inquiry, but instead a theme depressingly relevant for the Rome of his own day.

More important than Curtius' work for our knowledge of Alexander, and at the same time less pointed in its relation to the events of the time in which the author lived is the *Anabasis of Alexander* by *Arrian* of Nicomedia in Bithynia (born circa AD 85/90). A Greek, he studied philosophy with Epictetus, who taught the philosophically inclined laity of the upper classes. Epictetus employed succinct ethical admonitions, very similar to the instruction we find in the *New Testament*, to enable his students to conduct their lives accordingly and to provide them with a moral framework for their future service in the imperial administration. Arrian wrote up and published Epictetus' lectures. He also composed an *Encheiridion* ("vade mecum") as a guide to it. He owed his public career primarily to Hadrian (117–138), the most philosophically educated of the emperors and a lover of Greek culture. Consul in 129 or 130, Arrian spent the next six years governing the border province of Cappadocia. He settled later in Athens, where he became a citizen, held several offices in the city's administration, and was, in all events, very productive in his literary efforts. Besides, however, his *Anabasis of Alexander* and another historical work (the *Indiké*), his other works exist only in fragments (*FGrH* 156).

Arrian's writings reveal their author's peculiar mix of mental attitudes. He was politically a Roman; in native feeling, he was Bithynian; and, as an educated citizen and philosopher, Athenian, with a predilection for the Athenian classical period. He thus swam in the currents of contemporary Atticism and the Second Sophistic, and was additionally an admirer of *Xenophon*. As his literary successor, Arrian likewise writes an *Anabasis* (see below, p. 182) and an *Art of Hunting* (*Kynegetikós*) and even calls himself by Xenophon's name in one of his writings (*Alanike* = F. 156; FF. 12.10 and 22). Some of Arrian's writings convey military and administrative content, and stem from his activity in Asia Minor and in the Black Sea region. Other works are partly biographical, partly ethnographical and historical. Finally, we may mention the eight books of the *Bithyniká* about his native land and its history until its testamentary transfer to Rome in 74 BC. Three works are devoted to Alexander the Great, his personal milieu, and his deeds: the *Anabasis Alexandrou* (literally "Alexander's Campaign" through Asia, but more generally: *History of Alexander*) in seven books, the continuation of which was the ten-volume *History of the Diadochi* (*Ta met' Alexandron*), of which unfortunately only scanty fragments survive (*FGrH* 156 FF. 1–11). As an appendix to works treating Alexander's admiral Nearchus and Megasthenes, a sometime functionary of the Seleucids, Arrian composed the *Indiké*, partly describing the land and people and partly describing Alexander's return journey from the Ganges to Persia.

The *Anabasis of Alexander*, conforming to Xenophon's *Anabasis*, its literary model, which likewise has seven books, does not mark clearly the division between books in terms of content or purpose or even theme, but instead runs through events from Alexander's accession to power in 336 to his death in 323 BC, and then to a concluding summary evaluation (7.28–30). By going back to older works that seemed to him more trustworthy, Arrian aimed to present not only an objective, but also a positive, portrait of the Macedonian king and conqueror who, in his opinion, had not yet received an appropriate evaluation (*Anabasis* preface to Book 1 and 1.12.2–5). The method he used was reasonable, especially his practice of reproducing what the authors he considered most reliable agreed on in their own reports, and he drew too on own his military and political experience when exercising his choices among his sources. This experience helped him differentiate between the probable and implausible. Nevertheless, his work loses value, inasmuch as he places the secondary author Aristobulus on the same level as the combatant

Ptolemy Soter, and he allows individual scenes from works he himself acknowledges as less reliable to take their place in his main narrative. His fashionable adherence to the literary orientation toward classical Athens also leads him to avoid technical terms in administrative and military matters, and in the *Indiké* even leads him to make use of an old literary dialect of Ionian Greek as the archaizing successor of the ethnographer and historian Herodotus. Literary influences thus had a powerful effect on him, but he was by no means alone in this: probably at about the same time an almost completely unknown Cephalion composed his *Various Histories* (*Pantodapaí historiai*) which reached the age of Alexander likewise in the Ionic dialect.

The writings revolving around Alexander as well as several others are geographically devoted to the East. The area from Asia Minor across Syria to Mesopotamia and into Iran encompassed territories that during Arrian's lifetime stood at the center of the difficult and varied relations between the Romans and the Parthians as they struggled for supremacy. For a Roman writer interested in Roman power and as an inhabitant of the eastern part of the empire, Trajan's war against the Parthians (113–117) would have represented a high point. India had likewise become an area of interest, especially to those inhabiting the Eastern Mediterranean, on account of the trade then carried on across (what we today call) the Red Sea past Arabia, and from there to the Indian Ocean. In this sense, Arrian addressed a contemporary need – but with a limitation astonishing from a modern perspective: the ethnographic part of his *Indiké* was a purely literary exercise. It relied on a source that was four hundred years old, and for just this reason failed to convey facts about contemporary maritime trading. Arrian sacrificed the possibility of conveying real information on current affairs on the altar of literary tradition, and, in doing so, took a position that was in ancient ethnography generally considered a matter of course. This approach sometimes resulted from a more general aim at moral instruction (see above, Ch. 6.1.3, p. 137), but this was, in all events, not the case for Arrian.

6.4.2 Plutarch of Chaeronea: *Parallel Lives*

Plutarch (circa AD 45–120) lived his life as a member of the local ruling class and a sometime office holder in his tiny native city of Chaeronea in Boeotia. Out of conviction, he took on a priestly office in Delphi. Belief in traditional religion and philosophical speculation were for him not mutually exclusive. In fact, he strove to reconcile them. His philosophical education led him to Athens as a youth for an extended period, and later trips brought him to Asia Minor and Italy. In Rome he acquired lasting friendships with senators, and, through these connections, Roman citizenship. At home, he presided over a considerable library of his own, instructed young people privately, represented in his own person a destination for the philosophically educated (even from Rome), and, making use of his collection of books, composed a large number of writings.

Plutarch's works may be classified into two main categories. What we today call the *Moralia* treat moral philosophy, sometimes theoretically and systematically, and sometimes from a practical perspective. Some of these texts offer advice for political careers according to the premises of a philosophically grounded ethics. As with other Greek intellectuals of Rome's high imperial period during the so-called Second Sophistic, this to some extent involves making use and providing accounts of previous literature, much of which presupposes a state of political and constitutional affairs that the passage of time had long ago rendered obsolete. Plutarch nevertheless demonstrates through the official posts he held in his own city that he, as an educated man and as a philosopher, could also cope with the issues and circumstances of his own day that restricted the political development of citizens in the provinces to such a great extent. He was perhaps helped by his own fundamentally apolitical personality, which led him in a comparison of the two most famous Greek authors of comedies to prefer the apolitical Menander over the political Aristophanes. Other writings of Plutarch are devoted to antiquarian details of Greek as well as Roman antiquity, partly for their own sake, but partly in comparison of what is Greek with what is Roman. Still others are devoted to comparative "parallels" in the events of Greek and Roman history. Three of his *encomia* treat historical themes from an ethical point of view.

Plutarch's other significant group of works comprises biographies in three series: (1) biographies of Roman emperors to Vitellius, of which Galba and Otho still survive, (2) a varied mix of collected life stories, of which we still possess only one about the great king of Persia, *Artaxerxes* II, and another about *Aratus* of Sicyon, and (3) originally 23, but today just 22 pairs of *Bioi paralleloi*. These *Parallel Lives* were dedicated to a Roman friend of Plutarch's, Quintus Sosius Senecio, who was himself a friend of Trajan (98–117), with whom he served several times as consul. In these unusual biographies Plutarch pairs a Greek and a Roman (except in one case where he compares two Greeks and two Romans, the latter the two Gracchi brothers). Plutarch presents his pairs in a way that allows comparison of life circumstances, achievements, or character traits. Some of these double biographies include, at the conclusion of both, a short comparison (*synkrisis*) whose authorship is debated. The conception for these parallel biographies represents nevertheless the same comparative project we find in some of Plutarch's other writings. In comparing Greece with Rome or Greeks with Romans, Greeks and Romans appear as equals and equally important. The former do not appear solely as "poets and thinkers" while the latter do not appear solely as politicians and military men, but instead both appear as both, and to this extent complete. Like *Dionysius* of Halicarnassus (see above, Ch. 5.2.2, p. 115), Plutarch thus makes a contribution to the unity of the Roman empire in terms of its two most important political and cultural groups. Behind this attitude stands the self-confidence of a cultured and prosperous Greek, who lived well under the Roman empire and who profited from his acquaintance with Rome's leading personalities, even though he had himself faced no need to offer his service on behalf of empire and emperor.

Even if we discount Plutarch's treatment of such "persons" as Theseus, whom moderns would classify as belonging to the realm of myth, enough biographies remain that were devoted to historical personages and whose historical content Plutarch extracted from historiographical writings. His biographical work is especially important for the glimpse it provides into Hellenistic historiography, which has come down to us in only fragmentary ruins (*FGrH* 154ff.). We should not let this, however, obscure our awareness that Plutarch is not an historian nor does he desire to be one. He is rather a biographer whose literary aims partly contradict those of an historian. Nevertheless, his aims do correspond precisely with those of other ancient biographers (see above, Ch. 4.4, pp. 81f.; Ch. 6.3, pp. 165f.). Plutarch, in fact, bears especially impressive and vivid witness to the difference between ancient biography and ancient historiography:

> I do not write history, but lives. Neither are virtue and vice revealed always in a person's most famous deeds. Often an unimportant act, a brief statement, or even a joke, can reveal character traits better than battles with thousands of casualties or the greatest battle preparations or sieges of cities. Just as artists paint likenesses from faces and expressions around the eyes, where character reveals itself, and neglect the other parts of the body, it must be granted likewise to me, to explore the signs of the soul, so that I may fashion a portrait of each, leaving their great deeds and battles for others to describe. (*Alexander* 1.2–3; compare *Nicias* 1.1–2)[21]

Each person whom Plutarch portrays is brought into close proximity with the world inhabited by readers as well as with readers' experiences, so that they may themselves learn from the conduct and life lessons of these "heroes" – lessons both positive and negative (the latter especially in the paired lives of *Demetrius* and *Antony*). Plutarch's educational goals are founded on his conviction that moral fitness and probity derive from both personal predisposition *and* a conduct well instructed and guided by reason. This determines both the contents and the pattern of the biographies. In contrast to Suetonius (see above, Ch. 6.3.1, pp. 166f.), thematic categories are not pointed out as such, but are, in light of Plutarch's biographical approach and goal of ethical instruction, nevertheless inherent: (1) origin, personality traits, and education are the decisive points in childhood and youth; (2) once the subject reaches adulthood, Plutarch follows the development of a life with special attention to changes in conduct; it is here where the biographer exercises his greatest freedom in choosing his material; and (3) a life's summation and impact will be pursued through its last phase and the circumstances surrounding the subject's death (compare, for example, *Demetrius* 52f.).

Plutarch's ethical intent together with his philosophically stamped religiosity saved him, despite his adherence to traditional religion, from rejection and oblivion in later Christian times. His writings were especially popular in Byzantine times, and the thirteenth century produced the edition of his works that serves as the basis for the text we have today. Since their first translation (1559), his *Lives* have served as inspiration in Western Europe for dramatists like Shakespeare and Schiller, and, insofar as pedagogy aimed for moral education, they were likewise considered ideal for secondary (humanistic) education well into the twentieth century. Plutarch was thus effective long after his death in accordance with his own literary self-classification, not as an historian, but as a biographer with ethical aims. It was left to modern scholars of ancient history to find fault with the biographies written by Plutarch and others, when they (understandably enough) began to make use of them to supply the dearth of compelling historical data from other sources.

6.5 History in "Pocket-Size"

In the introduction to his history, *Livy* complained about the burden, with which the great mass of Roman history oppressed the historian (*Preface* 4; see above, Ch. 5.1, pp. 100f. and 104).[22] The longer Roman history continued past Livy's day and the greater the number of emperors who had reigned, and found their (frequently bad) end, the greater the mass and burden of Roman history grew that Livy had already considered too great. The more absolute and at the same time centralized bureaucratically the Roman empire became, the less real information about truly important decisions in governance and their justification reached the public. Rome's traditional historical writers, the senators, and their institution that was once so central to political decisions, the Senate, continually diminished in political importance. Only as a member of the emperor's advisory council could a senator still acquire knowledge about the government (see above, Ch. 6, pp. 121ff.; compare 6.1.3, pp. 143f.; Ch. 6.1.4, p. 155). Both of the developments mentioned here could have – in fact, they must have – pointed toward the same solution: to an abbreviated presentation. Tendencies toward popularization and a decline in interest in historical instruction could likewise have favored historical epitomes. An extreme form of this can be found already in the *chronicles* that were still written, or rather continued, and ultimately transformed into Christian works (see above, Ch. 5.2.4, pp. 119f.; below, Ch. 7.3.2, pp. 223ff.). Apart from this specialized genre, historical epitomes could be created in two ways: authors could compose new works, keeping them succinct, or they could abbreviate existing works.

6.5.1 From the epitome of Livy, the epitome of Trogus, and Florus to Lucius Ampelius

Two mutually complementary narratives of Roman history and non-Roman history that had been composed during the period of transition from the Republic to the Principate were subject to radical abbreviation. From the second century AD, Livy's *Roman History from the Foundation of the City* began to appear in increasingly abbreviated versions (*Epitomae*, *Periochae*: see above, Ch. 5.1, p. 100), and a certain *Justin* produced an outline of Pompeius Trogus' *Philippic History* (see above, Ch. 5.2.3, pp. 116f.). Classics of historiography were therefore also (or especially) targeted for abbreviation. This development favored the complete or partial loss of the fuller original versions of older works, and thus the gradual disappearance of more detailed presentations of the more distant past from the view of the advancing imperial age. On the other hand, the practice of abbreviation preserved at least some written tradition regarding early periods that, without easily accessible abbreviated versions, may have been lost completely because its narratives were too detailed, and thus perhaps seemed out of date. Ultimately, abbreviations later served as models and sources for subsequent outlines, and were thus often even further abbreviated and consequently coarsened in terms of content. Although we may be inclined to criticize the making of epitomes from fuller narratives as a failed intellectual enterprise, a careful consideration of all its aspects reveals that the practice does not deserve unilateral condemnation.

When abbreviating, whether by reworking a text or by composing afresh, abbreviators could travel diverse paths, especially when cutting down a text in the search for specific themes or composing a condensed general account. For example, in light of the fact that Rome became a universal empire through wars, one might limit one's narrative to this key topic, as did *Florus*, basing his work Livy. The Romans' pedantic observation of the will of the gods, especially as it related to political and military decisions and their consequences, could lead to the collection of prodigies, as, for example, in the work of *Julius Obsequens* (whom we will not discuss in detail), which excerpts a part of Livy's work – in fact, an already abbreviated version of Livy's work – for the years 190 or perhaps 249 BC to 11 BC. In the context of monarchy, an author could also summarize the history of the Roman empire by composing succinct biographies of the emperors (e.g., Sextus Aurelius Victor, *Caesares; Epitome de Caesaribus*). One could also, however, offer Roman history from its first origins to an author's present day in the shape of a slim volume (*Eutropius*). And, finally, mixed styles of abbreviation were also possible (*Festus*). Nor should we forget that historical outlines or selected passages on historical topics that focus exclusively on Roman history may have been disseminated in "handbooks" and textbooks with quite different puposes (*Ampelius*). We should now introduce some of these authors and works in chronological sequence. To these, we may add the work of *Juba* already in the Augustan period (see above, Ch. 5.2.1, p. 113). His example also demonstrates that the production of historical outlines was not a practice confined solely to authors writing in Latin.

Under the name *Lucius Annaeus Florus*, an *Epitome of Livy on All Rome's Wars over Seven Hundred Years* (*Epitomae de Tito Livio bellorum omnium annorum DCC*) has come down to us, which the author describes as a "short list" (*brevis tabella*; 1 *Preface* 3). Either Florus was at once a rhetorician, a poet, and an historian or we must distinguish two or three individuals who bore the same name. We know that at least the historian, as we surmise from his praise hailing Trajan as the rejuvenator of the Roman empire (1 *Preface* 8), lived under this emperor and perhaps still under his successor Hadrian as well. Although the work bases itself directly or indirectly on *Livy*, and consequently has a fixed historical endpoint, the author demonstrates a knowledge of other relevant authors, especially *Caesar* (1.45 = 3.10) and *Sallust* (1.36 = 3.1 and 2.12 = 4.1), whose moral outlook seems to have had a strong influence on Florus (e.g., 1.47.7ff. = 3.12.7ff.), and perhaps Tacitus.

Florus' epitome of Rome's wars survived in two manuscript traditions, a four-volume version and a two-volume version. Both offer the same content, which is merely divided differently. It is likely that the four-volume version corresponds with a conception of the history of the Roman people in terms of the four ages of an individual human life: childhood–youth–adulthood–old age (Book 1 *Preface* 5–8), a scheme that was first invented or applied, not by Florus, who only adopted it, but, at the latest, by the elder *Seneca* (*HRR* II p. 91, F. 1). On the other hand, Florus describes the wars of only the first three "phases of the life" of the Roman people extending to the Age of Augustus (250 + 250 + 200 years = 700 years: see below, p. 190). The fourth declining phase extended to his own day, or at least until the accession of Trajan, and was for Florus, as it had been also for *Tacitus*, an age negatively characterized by the "lethargy of the emperors" (*inertia Caesarum*), and thus provided scanty materials for reports on glorious wars (see above, Ch. 6.1.3, p. 142). Besides, his source Livy did not cover this phase of Roman history. As opposed to *Appian*, Florus includes in his epitome neither this period nor the rebirth of great conquests that Trajan initiated, and which, according to the scheme of "life phases" represented for Florus an unhoped-for "rejuvenation of Rome" (*reddita iuventus*) that would, to this extent, allow Rome to enter a fifth (if not again its first?) age (citation: Book 1 *Preface* 8; see above, Ch. 6.2.2, p. 162). A three-, as opposed to a fourfold, division of his work would therefore have been appropriate.

The logic of the two-volume version, on the other hand, consists in the type of war each book contains. The first book treats only foreign wars down to Carrhae in 53 BC (1.46 = 3.11) while the second above all treats Rome's domestic, i.e., civil, wars, beginning with Tiberius Gracchus (133 BC). This requires the acceptance of some chronological overlap between the two books, but has the advantage of offering a contrast in subject matter that is impossible with a division into four books. But the division into two books is also expressly connected to the scheme of life phases, inasmuch as the conclusion to the first book offers concise allusions to the third age of life, mature adulthood (1.47.1–3 = 3.12.1–3). This age of overseas conquests would have lasted two hundred years for the Romans, but it would have been divided into two halves. Its second half would have begun with the destruction of Carthage and Corinth (146 BC) as well as Numantia (133 BC) and the inheritance of Pergamum (also 133 BC), but, in addition to continuing conquests, it would have been a period of "domestic disasters, wretched and shameful" (§ 3).[23] A split thus runs through the third life phase of the Roman people. Rhetorically, it is represented through the unusual division of foreign from domestic wars. Because this literary principle corresponds to the actual distribution of material between the first and second book in the two-volume edition, we may conclude that this version represents Florus' original arrangement.

Florus' work ends with a majestic and daring flourish, drawing together various contemporary events (2.34 = 4.12.61ff.). Remorseful Parthians conclude a peace treaty with the people of Rome who are universally recognized as rulers of the world (20 BC). As a result, Augustus officially declares universal peace "in the seven hundredth year after the foundation of the city" (the doors of the temple of Janus are shut three times: in 29, 25, and 10 BC), and devotes himself to the service of peace through moral legislation (18 BC and AD 9). On account of his great achievements, he is declared *dictator perpetuus* ("dictator forever" – this is actually false; this was a title held by Julius Caesar from February 44 BC) and *pater patriae* ("father of the fatherland" in 2 BC), and he receives the title *Augustus* ("the divinely blessed one" in 27 BC). Hence, in short, the title of the work "Wars over Seven Hundred Years" (see above, p. 189). Those who demand precision in facts and dates from an epitome, will, in light of its immense inaccuracies, be disappointed by Florus' work. These inaccuracies may derive, on the one hand, from his methods in abbreviation, or possibly from following Livy only indirectly. On the other hand, as the two-book version of his work reveals more generally, and as the work's conclusion and, moreover, its rhetorically composed episodes packed with punches and full of antitheses (e.g., 2.30.29f. = 4.12.29f.) demonstrate in detail, the work's inaccuracies may have been part of Florus' plan.

From all this we may draw some conclusions about Florus' conception of Roman history. When, in the wake of literature on Rome's civil wars, he too in his second book reduces Roman history to the deeds and antagonisms of its politicians, he nevertheless strives to portray Roman conquests as fundamentally the accomplishment of the Roman people, who, although they may change according to their "life phase," are the subjects and agents of actions and events, and who (not quite as) consistently remain, as the object of Florus' narrative, the great constant factor of his work. He combines his praise of the greatness the Roman people won for Rome not only with the existential interplay of courage and fate (Book 1 *Preface* 2), but also with censure based on moral judgments. Florus' epitome thus became much more than a handy outline, and it exerted its influence in late antiquity on traditional adherents of classical religion and Christians alike.

In the second or third century AD, one *Lucius Ampelius* wrote under the title *Liber memorialis* a compendium of knowledge of what was likely then taught and examined in the schools. The historical part encompasses 41 of its fifty chapters with the result that other fields, astronomy (together with mythology) and geography (together with wonders of the world) receive short shrift. The *Liber memorialis* does not offer Roman history exclusively, but its main focus is on Rome. It is organized topically and according to groups of people, including such groupings as: "the seven world empires" (in chapter 10); "the most famous kings and generals of the Athenians" (in chapter 15); "men [actually only Romans of the Republic] who sacrificed themselves for the common good" (in chapter 20); "revolts" (in chapter 26 – actually only the four Roman disturbances and civil wars from Tiberius Gracchus in 133 to Livius Drusus in 91 BC, although in chapter 40 we find in addition "four civil wars" from Sulpicius to Octavian/Antony and Cleopatra); or "constitutional forms of government" (in chapter 50). Such general topics as the chapter on "revolts" are defined and discussed only in the simplest of conceptual terms. It is thus all the more astonishing that, after the three types of constitutions, monarchy, aristocracy, and democracy, we find mention and definition of the "mixed constitution," which was first identified by Polybius, and then popularized by Cicero as peculiarly and characteristically Roman, but which had, with the collapse of the Republic, long been obsolete. According to the topic of each rubric, details follow either chronologically or thematically. An historical continuum is, in all events, neither on offer nor even a goal, and the resulting bits of isolated knowledge not unlike what today's schools impart. Because the readership of historical narratives is more difficult to calculate, and because their readership was doubtless smaller, we can with more confidence draw conclusions about the knowledge and thinking of people in an epoch when historical instruction was located within the confines of a general handbook or primer, the contents and range of which offer good evidence of contemporary concerns. It is thus neither Tacitus nor Dio nor even Suetonius, but instead the bits and pieces of history in the *Liber memorialis* that represent the general extent of historical knowledge and historical awareness during the Roman empire.

6.5.2 The historical epitomes of the fourth century AD (Aurelius Victor, Eutropius, Festus)

The high tide of historical epitomes was the fourth century AD, the time of *transition from classical religion to Christianity*. This transition did not make itself readily apparent in the historical epitomes of the time, but did exert a subliminal influence. The composition of epitomes and their collection into compendiums that covered all Roman history evidently served, at a time of great uncertainty resulting from changes in both domestic and foreign affairs, to secure the Roman past, and with it cultural identity and continuity. To the extent that epitomes described a past that was traditional in its religious orientation, and did not attempt to transform that past into something Christian, or even hint at such an effort, but, on the contrary, described details of ancient forms of religious worship with sympathy and belief in their effectiveness, we must charcterize them as traditionally or classically religious (e.g., Aurelius Victor, *Caesares* 26.3–4 and 28.4ff.). For this reason, the failure of such works to mention Christianity indicates an indirect or concealed rejection of it (see below, Ch. 7, pp. 199f.). In light of this, when an epitome does mention Christians, not in the context of the "Constantinian Revolution," but instead in the context of the last classically religious emperor Julian's persecutions, and Julian is called "too zealous a persecutor (*nimius insectator*)" rather than simply censured as a "persecutor," then we discern an attitude that clearly does not identify with Christianity, and that, moreover, prefers to understand the dealings of the classically religious and Christians (both in the recent past and to some extent in the present too) as based on some foundation other than violence (*Eutropius* 10.16.3).

At the same time epitomes characteristically display a continuation of the senatorial point of view under the altered conditions of late antiquity (see above, Ch. 6.1, pp. 129f.). In this period, officers of high military rank and even soldiers themselves selected the occupants of the imperial throne from among their ranks. Senators, on the other hand, were excluded from military life altogether and served the state purely as civilian officials. It was therefore no longer possible to speak of an imperial regime's friendliness toward senators or the senate in terms of "freedom," however narrowly construed (see above, Ch. 6.1, pp. 127f.; Ch. 6.1.3, p. 143). Senators and civilian officials like *Aurelius Victor* and *Eutropius* were instead much more concerned to gain the favor of the reigning emperor in their rivalry with the military and their struggle against the military's disproportionate influence (whether real or imaginary) in the palace and in government. They also tried to win him over to civilian rule and literary culture, which the emperor was expected to cultivate as well (Aurelius Victor, *Caesares* 37.5ff. and 40.12ff.; see above, Ch. 6.1, pp. 129f.). With the exception of Aurelius Victor's *Caesares*, the abbreviated narratives that advocate such points of view appear rather simplistic. This reveals just how wide the gap was between the cultural and political aspirations of their lofty demand and the actual level of culture.

Late antique epitomes of the Roman imperial period that have come down to us as well as the *Historia Augusta* (see above, Ch. 6.3.3, pp. 171ff.) were likely based on a lost primary source whose existence was first postulated by Alexander Enmann in 1884, and which was accordingly dubbed the "*Enmannic History of the Emperors*" (and is more commonly known by its German title as the *Enmannsche Kaisergeschichte*). This work would have appeared shortly before or after AD 350, and narrated imperial history by way of short biographies, beginning with Augustus. Linguistic similarities as well as shared material, especially mistakes made in common, would seem to indicate a dependence on the same source. It is impossible, however, to establish a common tradition with final certainty when we consider the massive losses in the transmission of imperial historical writing (compare above, Ch. 6, p. 123; Ch. 6.1, pp. 128f.). Epitomes that survive from the fourth century made use also of epitomes from previous centuries like Florus' synopsis of Rome's wars, on which Eutropius based the first six books of his *Breviarium*, and epitomes from the late fourth century made use already of those that had been composed just a few years or decades earlier (see below, pp. 194f.).

Sextus Aurelius Victor was a high-ranking civilian official and a senator. In addition to other posts, he served as governor of the province of *Pannonia secunda* in AD 361 and, in 389, as prefect of the city of Rome. He must have published his *Book on the Emperors* (*Liber de Caesaribus*) shortly after 360. It was very soon, in all events still during the fourth century, joined together in a book with two works by an unknown hand that now likewise bear Aurelius Victor's name. The *Origin of the Roman People* (*Origo gentis Romanae*) explains, with the help of interwoven quotations from Vergil, the divine and human ancestry of the kings of Alba Longa to Romulus and Remus and then to the foundation of Rome. The book *On the Distinguished Men of the City of Rome* (*De viris illustribus urbis Romae*) contains 86 short biographies of personalities from Roman pre-history and Roman history, extending from the Alban king Proca as the grandfather of Romulus and Remus down to Antony and Cleopatra. The book thus covers Roman history from the foundation of Rome to the end of the Republic. The third work in this compilation, Aurelius Victor's *Caesares*, is devoted to Roman emperors. The first emperor whom Victor treats is Augustus. He thus follows in the tradition of *Tacitus*, and diverges from *Suetonius* (see above, Ch. 6.3.1, pp. 168f.). The last emperor he includes is Constantius II (who ruled from 337).

Together, these three works thus comprise at once a biographically based as well as a chronologically organized tour through all Roman history until the time of Aurelius Victor.

We find for the first time in Victor's *Caesares* the division of Roman imperial history into Julio-Claudian and Flavian dynasties, adoptive emperors, soldier emperors, and Dominate that remains customary to this day. In several biographies, especially in those portions closer to contemporary events, the report becomes more detailed and shifts to more historical narrative. Similar to *Florus* in his epitome, Victor, in the tradition of *Sallust*, pronounces moral judgments time and time again, and provides too his standards for appraisal (e.g., repeatedly in chapter 33). This moral appraisal is often clothed in a stylistically exacting garb that frequently shifts into general philosophizing or choice comparisons with an often truly distant past. He also combines this (most likely following Sallust) with his conception of the rise and fall of the Roman empire around an intermediary *turning point* that he identifies with the first of the soldier emperors (24.8ff.; see above, Ch. 4.5.1, pp. 91ff.; below, p. 195). Victor's imperial history was subsequently employed by the anonymous *Epitome de Caesaribus*, which abbreviated it still further, while bringing the history down to the death of Theodosius I in 395. Through *Jerome* the *Caesares* also entered into the chronographic tradition (see below, Ch. 7.3.2, p. 225).

Eutropius advanced to high command as a soldier, and participated in 363 in the emperor Julian's invasion of Persia, subsequently (from 364) served as the emperor Valens' *magister memoriae* ("personal adviser"), and later as pro-consul of Asia. At the emperor's request, and in a manner suited to the emperor's poor education, Eutropius composed in simple language a *Breviarium ab urbe condita* (*An Outline of the History of Rome from the Foundation of the City*). In ten short books (the Latin text occupies about 75 printed pages) he treats all Roman history to the death of the emperor Jovian in 364, the last emperor before the accession of the brothers Valentinian I and Valens. Contrary to customary practice, Eutropius hardly becomes any more detailed at all as he proceeds from early history to contemporary events. His work exhibits a distinct division into two parts. Books 1–6 treat primarily wars and battles, while Books 7–10 proceed biographically as well as anecdotally and are thus in accord with a trend noticeable in imperial accounts from the beginning of the first century AD (see above, Ch. 6, pp. 123f.; Ch. 6.3, p. 165). In this division of the material, Julius Caesar serves as a formal element in the transition between the two modes of presentation (6.17 – the end of the book).

As opposed to Caesar, whose regime was "ranged against traditional Roman freedom" and "almost a tyranny," Augustus' rule is praised as "supremely constitutional" and as the Roman state's most flourishing period. For this reason, Augustus is taken up in the course of Book 7, and his regime is in no way characterized as the dawn of a new era (6.25; 7.8–10).[24] It could not be the dawn of a new era because it is ultimately conceived of as the restoration of the freedom that was under threat from Caesar. Eutropius' characterization of Augustus' actions accords with the tenor of Augustus' self-representation in his *Res gestae* and also with the concluding assessment of him in the so-called "Last Judgement" of the deceased Augustus in Dio's version, but at the same time, Eutropius' characterization stands irreconcilably opposed to *Tacitus'* and the much later negative assessment of Augustus as the first Roman monarch laid out in the *Historia Augusta* (see above, Ch. 6.1.4, pp. 155f.; Ch. 6.1.3, pp. 140 and 149; Ch. 6.3.3, p. 172). On the other hand, because Eutropius makes his transition to a narrative mode aligning with a monarchical state of affairs already with Caesar (see above), he places the beginning of Rome's imperial period with Caesar as well, and the unavoidable conclusion we must draw from this is that, when monarchy continued to exist under Augustus, nothing had changed. The turning point toward corruption in Rome and the empire was for Eutropius, as it was for *Aurelius Victor*, the onset of the era of soldier emperors (9.1). When Eutropius employs a threat to liberty as the ideological basis for his criticism of Caesar, we must conclude that he anachronistically adopts the senatorial point of view from the early empire (see above, 6.1, pp. 127f.). The addressee, Valens, would no longer have been able to conceive of this as a rebuke directed toward him personally. On the other hand, the emperor could well have understood Eutropius' criticism of the first "soldier emperor" Maximinus Thrax (235–238), although he would hardly have shared Eutropius' opinion. It was after all the norm in his day to become emperor not from the ranks of the senatorial order and not primarily through the selection of the Senate and senators, but instead through the power of the "bayonet," and he himself became emperor from the ranks of the soldiers. Eutropius' fundamentally civilian orientation was thus remote from reality.

Despite the modesty of its contents and literary pretensions, the *Breviarium* enjoyed great success. It was used by the author of the *Epitome de Caesaribus* (see above, p. 194), by *Jerome* (see below, Ch. 7.3.2, p. 226) and by *Orosius* (see below, Ch. 7.3.3, p. 236). There was a contemporary translation into Greek, and another around AD 600. Among Latin historians, this was an honor otherwise accorded only to *Sallust*. And, finally, the *Breviarium* was continued in the eighth century and then again around 1000, and was from the early Middle Ages until the beginning of the high Middle Ages an important source of information about ancient Rome!

Rufius Festus (also known as *Sextus Rufus*) was a governor of Syria as well as Eutropius' successor in the offices of *magister memoriae* and proconsul of Asia. Like Eutropius and a few years after him, he too wrote at Valens' request a short history of Rome that likewise ended with Jovian. Festus' *Breviarium rerum gestarum populi Romani* (*Outline of the Accomplishments of the Roman People*) is based, among others, on the works of *Florus* and *Eutropius*. Festus' arrangement differs, however, from that of Eutropius, and, compared to Eutropius' already very short booklet, is even more severely abbreviated, weighing in at about a fifth its size. Of Festus' thirty chapters, chapters 1–14 offer a disjointed account of the Roman empire's growth to Festus' present. Chapters 15–30 begin with a new preface addressed to Valens, who is responsible for the eastern half of the empire, and they narrate chronologically the frequently unsuccessful battles of the Romans in the East until Jovian and his surrender of the city of Nisibis to the Persians (29). The instructive focus of this *Breviarium* in the East, as we may, in fact, surmise from closing remarks directed toward the reigning emperor Valens (30), served a real purpose: advertisement for Valens' military projects, which, after the experiences described by Festus, would appear both difficult and necessary, and whose success was exceedingly to be wished for. Festus' little work further influenced *Ammianus Marcellinus* as well as the Christian authors Jordanes and Isidore of Seville (sixth/seventh centuries). His work remains today an important source for the wars of Aurelian (270–275) and Diocletian (284–305) in the East and for the administrative division of the Roman empire in the middle of the fourth century.

Under the title *Origo Constantini Imperatoris*, the first of two parts of the so-called *Excerpta Valesiana* narrates chronologically from 305 the history of Constantine I and the persons around him. Its diction is succinct and the style like that of a chronicle. Because the work remarks on Contantine's Christianity only briefly (33) and because it mentions neither his laws and measures favoring Christians nor Galerius' edict of toleration for Christians, its author must have been an adherent of classical religion. This will not obviate the fact that parallels exist between the texts of the *Origo* and the universal history of the Christian author *Orosius* (7.28), inasmuch as Orosius' late antique sources include some composed by adherents of classical religion (see below, Ch. 7.3.3, p. 236). On the other hand, parallels with Orosius fail to help us in placing the *Origo* in an historical tradition. In all events, this little work could have been produced around the middle of the fourth century or perhaps also later.

6.6 *Exempla*-Literature and Historical Understanding

"Rome's moral values are embodied in concrete actions: historical moments thus render immortal such instances when spirit becomes flesh. This is the point of historical painting and of Roman historical reliefs," and with this in mind we may consider "the specific brief of Roman historical writing" (von Albrecht [Bibl. §1.3] p. 296): it must pay attention above all to individual deeds that are worthy of memory, either because we should imitate these deeds or because we should avoid them. The literary preservation of great deeds, in which, independent of narrative (or rather historical) context, readers might view the manifestation of moral values, led in turn to the creation of *exempla* that could serve educational purposes. And the compiling of these *exempla* ("standard-setting examples") in accordance with particular commonly prevalent moral regulations and values or according to the typical situations in which the conduct they illuminated would occur led to the development of a uniquely Roman literary genre, collections of moral *exempla*.

History offers in abundance examples for personal conduct that, in their various contexts, may serve either as moral paradigms or, on the contrary, as abominations to be shunned. One may thus exploit works of history in the same way as those of historical biography as quarries for moral *exempla*. Even history itself and its literary purpose can be redefined as, and transformed into, a mere collection of examples. What was the still coherent *mos maiorum* ("ancestral custom"), that is, an earlier society's real or hypothetical code of conduct, disintegrates into isolated *exempla maiorum* ("examples of our ancestors"). To extract examples from history and to rely on their immediately instructive effect can mean nothing else but the denial of any distinction between past and present as well as between diverse periods in the past. This attitude corresponded, to be sure, in large measure with the ancient classically religious conception of the course of history (see below, Ch. 8, p. 245). Nevertheless, erasing distinctions rooted in time renders appropriate evaluation of past events impossible. This holds true as well for the dismemberment of earlier occurrences into discrete examples of conduct, inasmuch as this destroys the continuity of events within the past, which is what allows history to unfold in the first place. The reduction of history to *exempla* thus represents the destruction of history. Precisely because of the momentary effects made possible with individual pregnant examples, a culture as deeply imbued as Roman and Greek culture was with rhetoric will, of course, always remain a culture of *exempla* (see above, Ch. 1.3.1, p. 20).

In Rome, although the basic conception of an *exemplum* is first and foremost bound up with moral content and moral purpose, examples of a practical and technical nature are also possible, and there existed in Rome (as well as among the Greeks) a literature of *exempla* of this sort, which was likewise extracted from history. Both types of *exempla* are connected by the idea that technical and practical procedures as well as conduct conforming to ethical norms can be learned in the same way. For the technical aspect, we need mention only Books 1–3 of the *Stratagems of War* (*Strategemata*) by Sextus Julius Frontinus (circa AD 30–104), whereas the fourth book, whose authorship remains disputed, provides, in all events, examples of a different sort, namely, in the moral conduct of a general.

Cornelius Nepos composed *exempla* early on (see above, Ch. 4.4, p. 82). In the latter part of the emperor Tiberius' reign, Valerius Maximus wrote *Nine Books of Memorable Deeds and Sayings* (*Factorum et dictorum memorabilium libri novem*). Valerius for the most part arranges his material thematically, and, further subdividing it according to whether the principal characters are Romans or non-Romans, he presents actions and conduct that illustrate each of his rubrics. Like Livy not long before him, Valerius places ancient and recent Roman values side by side (see above, Ch. 5.1, pp. 108f.). His *exempla* are intended to provide material for orators, because historical examples counted as fundamental evidence and were thus considered helpful for all contemporary situations (see above). Valerius' collection was quite successful, and was in late antiquity reworked into two abbreviated versions.

7

Roman History and Universal History between Classical Religion ("Paganism") and Christianity

Christianity itself first attracted widespread public notice from the time the first empire-wide persecution of Christians was ordered by Decius (AD 251). This was followed, however, by a more momentous development: the conversion of the emperor Constantine to Christianity, and, through him, the empire. Soon, suppression of adherents of classical or other ancestral religions ("pagans," to use the convenient, but derogatory, catchphrase of their adversaries) characterized relations between adherents of traditional religions and Christians. All these phenomena and processes unavoidably became central topics for an historiography that treated both events in the Roman empire and also the conduct of the emperor. And this historiography could not easily exclude a general indication of which side an historical writer or imperial biographer took. In this way, both a *decidedly Christian* as well as a not less *decidedly* and *traditionally* or *classically religious* historiography developed with Rome as its object – and we pass over in silence here other intra-Christian reasons for the development of a Christian historiography (see below, Ch. 7.3, pp. 216ff.). Of course, the suppression of traditional forms of worship from the middle of the fourth century could also lead to subliminal presentation of a classically religious position that would be expressed in terms that only the like-minded could recognize. They would, in other words, employ a "meta-language for those in the know" (Timpe [Bibl. § 7] Ch. 5)[1] that offered plausible deniability in case of necessity. At the very least, it was important to refrain from demonstrably

Roman Historiography: An Introduction to its Basic Aspects and Development,
First Edition. Andreas Mehl.
© 2014 Hans-Friedrich Mueller. Published 2014 by Blackwell Publishing Ltd.

anti-Christian adherence to traditional religion. The composers of historical epitomes made use of these options as did the author or the editor
of the *Historia Augusta* (see above, Ch. 6.5.2, pp. 191f.; Ch. 6.3.3,
p. 172). When Christians and Christianity fail to receive mention in these
works, it could, on the other hand, also imply that "pagan historiography
did not experience … Christianity … as an historiographical challenge"
(Timpe [Bibl. §7] Ch. 5), including (at least from our modern perspective) the implication that it underestimated the importance of Christianity's
past both for the present and for the future. We must also take into
account that contemporaries, whether adherents of traditional religion
or Christians, would not have had a partisan stake in literary as well as
in other struggles between traditionalists and Christians, because they, as
intellectuals, recognized the bias of the attitude on their own side or
because they were not irrevocably rooted in their ideology or belief and
were not immune from doubts. We should probably put Ammianus
Marcellinus in this category (see below, Ch. 7.2, pp. 215f.). In any case,
for a variety of reasons, it is not always easy to discern the battle lines
between Christians and adherents of traditional religion in the historical
writing of the mid- and late fourth century.

We find also a striking *discrepancy between East and West* in the Roman
empire, one that appears to result from more than mere vagary in textual
transmission. Although a fundamental debate over the right to practice
traditional forms of worship at the Altar of Victory in the senatorial
chamber was ignited in the Roman (city-)Senate, and the debate raged
among western adherents of traditional religion and Christians, especially
between the senator Quintus Aurelius Symmachus and Ambrosius, the
bishop of Milan, nevertheless we find little evidence from the Latin West
for historical accounts with a definite classically religious or at least somewhat pronounced anti-Christian bias, except perhaps for the fragments
of the *Annals* by *Virius Nicomachus Flavianus* (*HRR* II CCV / 151),
who in 394 was compelled to commit suicide because of his involvement
with the usurpation of Eugenius. Surviving fragments of this account
lack, alas, the power to offer clear testimony. In the Greek East, on the
other hand, works with a manifest classically religious bias were composed
until well into the period of Christian state religion in the early sixth
century. These works are well documented not only through references,
but also in lengthy excerpts and fragments, and, in one instance, in a
form that has survived for the most part complete (see below, Ch. 7.1,
pp. 204f., on Zosimus).

The Christian side is characterized especially by its numerous internal
disputes, partly doctrinal and partly over the organization of the church.

Because Christianity quickly acquired a role in the government after Constantine I (306–337), and became with Theodosius I (379–395) the official religion of the state, emperor as well as organs of the state's administration had no choice but to take a position in matters of Christian doctrine and the internal affairs of the church. They were also compelled to make decisions regarding the church and Christian groups, and to make decisions and to employ measures that included force, on the one hand, to promote and, on the other hand, to suppress. Among Christians, such measures would invariably be met with enthusiasm on one side and corresponding indignation on the other that in some cases led to bitter resistance and open rebellion against the emperor and the empire. These occurrences too left their various stamps on the historiography of the times, whether traditionally religious or Christian.

When we examine the impact of the new dispensation on the historiography of Rome, we must distinguish accounts of recently Christian emperors and empire from the extensive early history of Rome under the auspices of its ancestral religion. The former could be depicted and evaluated by both sides from their own points of view as history that had not yet been shaped fully. More remote ancient history had, however, long been thoroughly and extensively canonized in facts as well as in moral assessments (for early and high empire, see above, Ch. 6, p. 126). For early emperors, Christians felt obligated to provide additional material and to add their own judgments, only if, according to Christian tradition (or doctrine), an emperor had permitted the persecution of Christians. But even in these instances, not much changed. Christians considered emperors like Nero or Domitian persecutors of their religion and of their co-religionists, but, because these emperors had already been branded vicious tyrants by the earlier senatorial tradition, Christian assessment of these emperors could not do much more vis-à-vis the earlier classically religious tradition than apply highlights of their own to these pre-existing literary portraits. The general assessments of other emperors acquired a novel nuance, but nothing more: the tradition had been firmly established.

The negligible difference between the characterizations of emperors by the adherents of traditional religion as opposed to characterizations by Christians also demonstrates that Christianity, which upheld important new principles in ethics, at the same time adopted many *ancient* moral values, and that it had, in the process, changed little or nothing. In fact, despite the self-professed incompatibility its views had demonstrated with classical religion, the canon of Christian moral values absorbed classically religious values or even accommodated their values to them, especially with the entrance and incorporation of Christianity into the Roman state, and the pretension that it would from now on convert all Romans (in the wider imperial sense of that word) into Christians. Naturally, internal Christian opposition arose, but the main thread of development, even in Christian historiography and despite all efforts at differentiating themselves from adherents of traditional religion, saw Christians assimilating the ethical principles of their adversaries. For this reason, we cannot generally expect a Christian historiography whose assessments diverge in all respects from classically religious historiography or that is completely opposed to it, even in the portrayal of very recent history and contemporary events. Historical accounts and interpretations of the sort we find in the *Chronicle* of Sulpicius Severus (see below, Ch. 7.3.2, pp. 226ff.) thus represent rather astonishing exceptions.

We find other aspects of late antique historiography that, independent of the conflict between classical religion and Christianity, are typical. No matter what its perspective, senatorial historiography ceases to exist or has significantly changed its primary class-based purpose (see above, Ch. 6.1, pp. 129f.). Henceforth it demands the priority of civilian officials, especially senators, over the military or, according to its frequent formulation, over "barbarians" (see above, Ch. 6.5.2, p. 192; below, Ch. 7.2, p. 213). Furthermore, whether they composed in Latin or in Greek, earlier historians and biographers took it for granted that the Roman empire represented a unity from its northern to its southern and, above all, from its eastern to its western limits. Some Greek authors even went beyond this, stressing the great similarities between and equal worth of Greeks and Romans or justifying the political and military leadership of Romans together with their qualities (see above, Ch. 5.2.2, p. 115.; Ch. 6.2.2, pp. 162f.; Ch. 6.4.2, p. 185). From the fourth century, however, the eastern and western halves of the empire began to drift apart. This drift was occasioned by divergent doctrinal developments in the East and the West within Christianity, by a classically religious literary culture that remained active longer in the East than in the West, and, finally, after 395, by the division in the representation and government of the empire between two emperors and their functionaries, a state of affairs that soon led to rivalries between their two courts and administrations. This became manifest not only in contemporary politics, but likewise in people's access to information and their general awareness. Despite repeated calls for the unity of Rome, people began to narrow their focus to their own half of the empire, and this held true also for historians. As early as the fifth century, some historical writers of the East were writing contemporary *Byzantine* history. And, *Orosius*, a Christian who, on the basis of his historically informed theology, was a universalist, nonetheless confined the contemporary portions of his work, which he wrote in Latin, almost exclusively to events in the West (see below, Ch. 7.3.4, pp. 237f.; *History against the Pagans* 7.36–43).

7.1 Zosimus and his Predecessors: Classically Religious Historiography and Historical Interpretation in a Christian Age

Classically religious, but not yet anti-Christian, is how we may describe the coloring of the historiographical work by the prominent Athenian *Dexippus* (*FGrH* 100; circa 210–275). Dexippus served in his native city as a priest and archon. In his *Skythiká*, he described the incursions of various Germanic tribes from the North into the eastern half of the Roman empire between 238 and 274 as well as the defensive measures that were taken against them. (He himself led operations on behalf of Athens in 267.) He also condensed Arrian's *History of the Diadochi* (see above, Ch. 6.4.1, p. 182) under its original title, and, in at least 12 volumes, his *Chroniká* chronicled all history from primeval times until the death of Claudius II Gothicus in 270, dating everything as far as he could according to Oympiads, Attic archons, and Roman consuls.

Dexippus' universal chronicle was later continued with a decidedly classically religious and anti-Christian bias first by *Eunapius* of Sardis (*HGM* I 205, Blockley II, p. 2; circa 345–420). At the instigation of Oribasius, formerly the personal physician to Julian, the emperor who had returned to classical religion, Eunapius wrote after 386 a work manifestly directed against the Christians, his *Hypomnemata historiká* in 14 books. At a time when, from 392, Christianity was the only legal religion, Eunapius portrayed the events from 270 to 404, including even the persecutions of Christians by Diocletian and his co-emperors and subsequent political and religious revolution, that, beginning with Constantine I, first ushered in the toleration and promotion of Christianity, and then brought the suppression of classical religion. Fragments of his historical account reveal the thinking of literary and philosophical adherents of classical religion in the East around AD 400. Centuries later, the patriarch Photius, who excerpted many ancient Greek authors, understood Eunapius' history as an encomium of Julian, and, to this extent, also of classical religion.

Olympiodorus of Thebes (upper Egypt; *FHG* IV 57, Blockley II, p. 152; circa 370–425) also belongs to this category of late antique historical writing. In 412, he was an (East-) Roman ambassador to the Huns, and he described the events of the years 407–425 in 22 books, in other words, in great detail. Shaped primarily from a collection he made of documentary materials, his *Historikoí logoi* contained many personal reminiscences, and in this was similar to the Roman history of *Ammianus Marcellinus* written about a generation earlier (see below, Ch. 7.2, p. 209). Olympiodorus was, of course, not the first to respond to the issue of causality between the worship of Rome's state gods and the benefits that they conferred. This topic had some decades earlier led to virulent controversy in discussions about the Altar of Victory in the conference chamber of the Roman Senate. Olympiodorus was, however, likely the first historical writer to argue that the neglect of their – ancestral – gods had brought disaster on the Roman empire.

Around the turn of the fifth to sixth century, Zosimus, a former civil servant domiciled in Syrian territory, composed under the title *Historia nea* a Roman history from Augustus to the year 410, i.e., to the point immediately prior to the conquest of Rome by the Visigoths. This six-volume work has survived almost completely, although it was likely published in two editions, and there are, at the same time, some indications in the last book that it was left unfinished. With a reference to the Greek historian *Polybius* (1.1), Zosimus conducts an unstoppable forced march through Greek and Macedonian history from the time of the Persian wars (1.2–4), he abbreviates even more succinctly the history of Roman expansion, above all in the East, and the transition Romans made from republic to monarchy, and he includes a statement of his opinion of the latter (he accomplishes all this by 1.5), at which point he begins his actual historical account. He gathers the first three hundred years from Augustus to Diocletian in one book, and treats them in such a way that the first two centuries from Augustus to Didius Julianus (who died in 193) are crowded into just two chapters (1.6–7). For the third century, the account proceeds in two steps from Septimius Severus (from 193: 1.8–18) and then again in greater detail from Philip the Arab (from 244: 1.19–73, or perhaps the end of the book).[2] Books 2–5 (we leave aside Book 6 as incomplete) are devoted to the approximately one hundred years from 305 to 409, but the space devoted to the divisions of time within that span varies considerably.

Zosimus' work provides clear evidence that he must have studied rhetoric and law in his wider native territory. He demonstrates his literary education through his acquaintance with Greek historiography from Herodotus to *Eunapius* and *Olympiodorus* (see above, p. 203), with Greek rhetoric from Demosthenes to Libanius, as well as with Greek poetry and mythology. Zosimus is proud of the fact that the sad reality associated with obtaining an office did not apply to him. Unlike those who used personal connections or bribery, Zosimus instead built his official career on an intellectual and cultural foundation, which – according to contemporary attitudes – was what actually made him worthy of office, because only that foundation guaranteed good conduct in office (1.5.4). His education betrays an urban and upper middle-class background that may well also reveal his own origin. He devotes especially close attention in his work to urban affairs. Even though it is not ostentatious, Zosimus' legal training is also frequently on display in his *New History*. His simple diction may deceive, but allusions to earlier historians, rhythmic conclusions to sentences, archaizing names of peoples, official titles, etc., deriving from Greece's classical epoch, all demonstrate that he made full use of the arsenal provided by rhetorical training. In this last practice, he anticipates a characteristic of Byzantine historiography. On the other hand, he was not so steeped in rhetoric that he, like so many, if not most, ancient historians turned to inventing large numbers of speeches. On the contrary, this historian consciously joined the ranks of those who rejected the composition of set speeches in accordance with rhetorical principles (see above, Ch. 1.3.2, p. 29).

Because Latin remained the language for the official practice of law throughout the entire empire well into the age of Justinian's reign (527–565), Zosimus' study of jurisprudence provided acquaintance with this language and with it the capacity to read historical accounts in Latin as well. With such relatively few exceptions as *Eunapius* and *Olympiodorus* (see above, pp. 203f.), it is, however, not easy to discern on which older historical accounts Zosimus' *Historia nea* relies. For this reason, the extent to which Latin works numbered among his sources remains obscure. Specific characteristics of the Roman empire's – Latin – West are, in any event, not evident in Zosimus' account, and, although some of his descriptions of cities and other localities in the East rely on the author's personal knowledge (especially Constantinople 2.30ff.), we find no hints that Zosimus visited Italy or Rome.

In Zosimus' *New History*, some fundamental attitudes and views distinctly emerge, and it is possible that he composed his historical account for their sake. He begins the work with a reference to *Polybius*,[3] and he alludes to him again later elsewhere. This allusion offers Zosimus the means to depict a harsh contrast: whereas Greeks of the second century BC witnessed the rapid rise of Rome to universal dominion and power in the space of about fifty years, Zosimus paints a movement in the opposite direction as a mirror image: the likewise rapid destruction of the Roman empire by the Romans themselves (1.1.1 and 1.57.1). For both rise and fall, Zosimus offers the same ready explanation: both movements derive from the gods, the traditional, pre-Christian gods (1.1.2; 1.58.4; 4.59). The most recent of the authors mentioned above who were read by Zosimus (in addition to the historians *Eunapius* and *Olympiodorus*), i.e., the orator *Libanius*, would already allow us to conclude that Zosimus had acquired an education that was more strongly stamped by traditional religion than was at that time customary among Christians, but his argumentation about Rome's rise and fall demonstrates even more clearly that his religious attitude was completely classical and anti-Christian.

Like the classical religion of Romans and Greeks of the fourth century, Zosimus' religion is not oriented toward individual anthropomorphic gods, but instead conceivably includes all gods and abstract divinities – and to that extent perhaps even the Christian god too, but merely as one among many – and culminates in a general divine providence. Divine will manifests itself in the course of the stars, in signs of all sorts, and in oracles. These signs require proper observation (in general: 1.1.2; for examples: 1.57.2 and 58.1–3, among many others). Above all, however, the gods require fitting worship, that is, worship according to the rituals preserved and prescribed by antiquity. Under the two emperors Constantine I (306–337) and Theodosius I (379–395), the Roman empire, which had become Christian, first abandoned traditional cults (with the excuse or pretext that, in addition to other reasons, they simply cost too much), and then outlawed them altogether. These actions kindled divine wrath, which manifested itself in the rapid downfall of Rome (1.58.4; 4.59.3–4). For this very reason, Zosimus describes in detail Roman celebration of the secular games and along with them the traditional state cult, that in especially large measure guaranteed Rome's continued existence, and "without whose protection" since 313 "the state necessarily veered into the disaster that today envelops us all" (2.1–7; quote 2.7.2).[4]

Zosimus was firmly convinced that the manifest and exclusively negative consequences of the Roman empire's conversion to Christianity was associated with another defect. This shortcoming, however, he identified in the human realm, namely, the constitution of the Roman state since Augustus. Although even *Tacitus* and *Cassius Dio*, despite personal reservations and antipathy, believed that the Roman empire's size had made transition to monarchy necessary (see above, Ch. 6.1.3, pp. 140ff.; Ch. 6.1.4, pp. 155f.), Zosimus was convinced that imperial government, based as it was on the very slender foundation of just one person, was from its very inception condemned to break down, and that the

Romans had thus involuntarily procured excessive disadvantages (1.5.2–1.6.1). Although we may note that he offers no suggestion for another type of government for Rome and its empire, we must therefore consider him an opponent of monarchy as a matter of personal principle.

In the Roman empire of Zosimus' day, two potentially lethal conditions thus combine: monarchy and the neglect of the gods' worship that resulted from conversion to Christianity. Both are even causally connected with each other when Zosimus levels especially sharp criticism against the monarchs Constantine I and Theodosius I, whose religious and political interventions occasioned the subsequently rapid collapse of the Roman empire that had become a "home for barbarians" and whose former capital Rome would also serve as plunder for the barbarians (2.29ff.; 4.27ff.; βαρβάρων οἰκτήριον: 4.59.3; 5.36 through the end of the work). Even though we have no indication that Zosimus read the universal history of the Christian author *Orosius*, he advocates a point of view exactly opposite to the one we find in Orosius' historical theology where monarchy is the form of government ordained by God's will (see below, Ch. 7.3.3; p. 232). Zosimus is well aware, however, that the state of affairs before Constantine I could never be brought back, and even less so the one before Augustus. All that is left for him is the vague hope that Christian emperors might prove tolerant towards adherents of classical religion, that "it might be granted to each," as it was at that time in the West under rule of the emperor Honorius, "to administer his offices and serve in the military while maintaining his own religious beliefs," and thus to remain a subject on an equal footing (5.36.2–5, quote from § 4).[5] There could, however, be no hope of this in Zosimus' own lifetime and certainly none whatsoever after him in the reign of Justinian (527–565; see below, Ch. 7.3.4, p. 240). Ancient classically religious historiography thus came to an end in self-delusion, and possibly in complete despair.

7.2 Ammianus Marcellinus: Indifferent to Religion?

"I wrote this … as a former solder and as a Greek from the principate of Nerva until the downfall of Valens." In this *sphragis* (self-introduction) at the end of his historical work (31.16.9), Ammianus Marcellinus identifies an unusual aspect of his person. He wrote in Latin, but was Greek. This was true a little later also for the poet Claudius Claudianus, but was otherwise extremely uncommon. On the one hand, Ammianus deployed the Latin historiographical style of a *Sallust*, and even more the style of a *Tacitus*, and mixed it with elements of the administrative Latin of his day. On the other hand, he was unable, especially in his use of participles, to suppress Grecisms completely, and it was not at all unusual for him to reproduce quotations in Greek. He was, furthermore, not a senator or civil officer in the emperor's service, but instead had spent his entire career in the emperor's service as a soldier. In this respect, he differed even from *Eutropius*, who, after his military career, had then served the emperor in his civil administration (see above, Ch. 6.5.2, p. 194). Ammianus' social class was thus completely at odds with the norm for an author of Roman history. In his later years, after he had served in city office and was living as a large landowner, Ammianus made a literary defense of the interests of this class (14.7.1–2), but he failed to adopt the attitude of a traditional Roman senator, despite his many years in Rome and the social relations he enjoyed with the Roman nobility who remained consciously devoted to their traditions. Finally, his combination of "Greek" and "soldier" was unusual in an age when the Roman army was staffed increasingly with "barbarians," above all, Germans. And it is also possible that Ammianus had roots in neither of the two religious camps of his age (see below, pp. 215f.).

This historical writer's life did not follow a straight path. Ammianus was born around AD 330 in one of the Roman empire's largest and most magnificent cities, Antioch on the Orontes in northern Syria, and he grew up as the son of a wealthy family that had attained, we may assume, the rank of city councilors (*curiales*). Despite this background, he enlisted in the emperor's bodyguard as a young man. From 353, he served under Ursicinus, who was at that time supreme commander of the infantry in the praetorian prefecture of the Orient. Under his command and in his immediate entourage, Ammianus had a variety of experiences that would later become central to his historical work: treason trials in Antioch in 353/4; a stay at the imperial palace in Mediolanum (Milan) that was for a time threatened by intrigues directed against Ursicinus; suppression of the usurper Silvanus in Cologne in 355 and another stay there in 356/7, likely for the purpose of watching over Julian whom Constantius II had recently named a Caesar; a stay in Sirmium on the Save and then again in the East; the Persian invasion there; the Persian siege of the city of Amida in Armenia and its fall in 357/9; finally flight to Antioch; and, after Ursicinus' recall in 360, participation in the Persian campaign of the new emperor Julian in 363. From 363 to 380, Ammianus lived on inherited wealth in Antioch, visited Egypt, Greece and Thrace, and wrote. Later, he stayed at Rome, and maintained relations, though not especially close ones, with the classically religious circle of senators around the Symmachi and Nicomachi, and recited to public applause from his Roman history in progress (Libanius *Letters* 1063 Förster = 62 Fatouros-Krischer). Ammianus therefore wrote his Roman history in this period, and this is corroborated by the bits of hackneyed praise we find after Book 27 that are directed toward Theodosius I (279–395), including references to his father and sons.

The work is entitled *Res gestae* (literally "things done," but a common Latin idom for "history"), and treats in 31 books Roman history from the accession of Nerva in AD 96 to the catastrophic Roman defeat by the Goths in 378. We may surmise from the starting date that Ammianus saw his work as a continuation of Tacitus (see above, Ch. 6.1.3, pp. 138f.). As one who was Roman by choice, Ammianus in this way connected himself after some three hundred years to the last great historian of Rome to live in the city (see above, Ch. 6.1.3, p. 144). Books 1–13 of Ammianus' work, which are lost, treated the years 96–353. The remaining books reveal a gap at 24.7 and another gap of some three years at the beginning of Book 31, so, apart from these gaps, Books 14–31 handle the years 353–378. From this alone, we can tell that, like other historical writers, Ammianus also condensed the more distant past, and related recent history or current events in great detail (see above, Ch. 4.1, pp. 66ff.; Ch. 5.1, p. 101, etc.). In all events, two prefaces within the work (at 15.1 and 26.1) demonstrate that the entire work was divided (at a minimum) into three parts, and that the most recent past was divided into two parts in a peculiar way: Books 1–14 for the years 96–354; Books 15–25 for the years 354–364; and Books 26–31 for the years 364–378. Reckoning with books of approximately equal length, we find that it is not the most recent period (part three, with six books for 14 years), but instead the immediately preceding period (part two, with 11 books for ten years) that is recounted in greatest detail. This unusual expansion and division of the material corresponds, however, to the level of Ammianus' own participation in the relevant periods. Part one encompasses the period before Ammianus was born and before he became a soldier in the vicinity of the powerful. Part two encompasses his years with Ursicinus and Julian, including the events listed above, and part three the years after. With this thematic arrangement, Ammianus' historiography verges on memoirs, whose subject matter is, of course, more akin to the objects taken up by the historiography of one's own time than than that of a more distant past (see above, Ch. 4.2, pp. 69ff.; Ch. 4.3, p. 79). This accounts too for Ammianus' inclusive first-person plural style when relating events that he participated in himself as well as the fact that he reports only from the perspective of his own side when recounting battles he experienced. With regard to the latter, he does incidentally neglect to provide the obligatory objective description of the preparation for, and conduct of, a battle from the perspective of both sides, as was the practice already of Herodotus, the first Greek historian in the narrower sense of that term.

The statements we make here are valid only for the surviving portion of Ammianus' *Res gestae*, the portion that is identical with the section devoted to his own times. From his severe condensation of the material in comparison with other sources, we may conclude that he employed different criteria in his representation of earlier Roman history. The twofold division of recent events in Ammianus' account corresponds, we may assume, to a twofold division in Ammianus' access to information. Only for the years 354–364 does Ammianus' report derive mainly, if not almost completely, from his own experiences (15.1.1). To this we may add sources of the sort that would have been available for the following years 364–378 as well: documents in archives (16.12.70), among which we may reckon, for quite a few specific dates, official diaries; interrogation of witnesses (15.1.1); encomiums of the emperor (31.10.5); and more. The author's extended excursuses, to the extent that he did not rely on his own memory and education, would have required specific sources. These sources are partly identical with works that, and authors who, are not materially, but instead stylistically, relevant for Ammianus' manner of representation. In Latin: *Sallust* and *Tacitus, Florus, Cicero* (whom he cites 34 times!), *Valerius Maximus*, and *Aulus Gellius*. In Greek, above all, poets from *Homer* to the lyric poets, the astronomical poet *Aratus*, and the philosopher *Plato*. The fondness of a Greek for Plato *and* Cicero (likely uncommon in Ammianus' day) may stand for a self-conscious demonstration of the unity of ancient culture, both Greek and Latin.

In his account of recent events, topics include, as we would expect, foreign and domestic threats to the empire, domination of the army by foreigners, and "barbarians." Although these topics are indeed integrated into a narrative that proceeds chronologically, the annalistic basis of the work is violated in any number of ways, and retains significance only as an inherited and congenital vestige. As with all authors of the imperial history, biographical elements take center stage (see above, Ch. 6, p. 123; Ch. 6.3, p. 165). And this includes for Ammianus an obligatory concluding appraisal of an emperor after his death according to the categories of sex, outward appearance, and personal conduct and morality, which are further subdivided into virtues and vices. (For examples, see 14.11.27–34, concerning the Caesar Gallus; or 30.7–9, where

Valentinian I's appraisal is especially clearly and formally separated from the preceding account of events.) A differentiation of "good" from "bad" aspects occurs even in the appraisal of Julian, the emperor, who, from the very beginning, Ammianus esteemed a "god-like hero" (25.4.16ff.).[6] The general sequence of events and even the appraisal of deceased rulers tend to be interrupted by an exceedingly large number of examples represented as *exempla* of Roman moral tradition as well as by comparisons and by excursuses devoted to the most varied content, including even engineering and natural science. Promulgation of a comprehensive cultural education thus seems to be understood as one of the historian's primary aims, even though, from a modern perspective, this goal would have little to do either with history or historical understanding. A desire to achieve dramatic effects through a variety of means, including speeches, as, for example, those delivered by Julian, also played a role in determining Ammianus' arrangement of the material (25.3.15–20). Because of the great distances that lay between the various fields of action and because of the close connection of events to the regions where they took place, geography, in preference to chronology, represents the most important organizational category in arranging material, as it was sometimes for *Tacitus* too in relating provincial history, and was subsequently more generally for *Appian* as well in relating first the history of Roman expansion, and then again the civil wars (see above, Ch. 6.1.3, p. 146; Ch. 6.2.2, p. 163). Ammianus himself acknowledges and regrets that the coordination of events according to location necessitates jumping back and forth in time (29.3.1). But because he wants to write the history of both the emperors and the empire, he willingly accepts the resulting awkwardness. He fails, however, to satisfy completely the necessary criteria of an imperial history, because the detail of his account depends so heavily on the extent of his participation in events, and varies accordingly, with the result that details appropriate to memoirs overwhelm criteria for establishing the significance of events.

Ammianus comments on the duties of the historical writer at the beginning of both "internal" prefaces 15.1 and 26.1 as well as at the end of his work (33.16.9) when he introduces himself. When the historian maintains that he has offered his account in accordance with truth, he grounds his claim exclusively on not consciously omitting anything and on not lying. Truthful historical accounts are therefore, just like good government, exclusively a matter of morality, not of knowledge or of the mastery or application of whatever techniques and skills any given tasks require. Ammianus is for this reason miles away from the demands of a *Polybius* who insisted that historians should possess professional knowledge of political and military affairs. On the other hand, Ammianus is, to this extent, much closer to the average measure of ancient historical writers (see above, Ch. 1.3.2, pp. 28f.; Ch. 4.3, pp. 80f.). The lack of access to reliable information that afflicted historians with the advent of the imperial age was for Ammianus a problem not worth mentioning (see above, Ch. 6, pp. 123f.; Ch. 6.1.3, pp. 143f.; Ch. 6.1.4, p. 154). The great difference in this regard between the Republic and the monarchy is something Ammianus does not (or no longer) takes notice of, just as, in fact, the Republic no longer holds intrinsic worth for Ammianus (14.6.4–6).

Lack of information can generally be glossed over as well, because, according to Ammianus, the historian should not bother himself with details, but instead "must, as accords with the prescriptions of historiography, only run through the high points of events" (26.1.1; cf. 27.2.11).[7] Historiography's ancient linkage with grandeur, which demanded of the historical writer a "grand style" (*maiores stilos*: 31.16.9) and confined him in terms of content to great affairs, gains a new meaning here – and a rather convenient one at that – for the historical writer (see above, Ch. 1.3.1, p. 18). The question remains, however, which affairs are so insignificant that they may be omitted from the historical account. Ammianus includes a few examples with his general statement, but they do not cover everything that he himself leaves out. The circumstances that led to the condemnation of the elder Theodosius, the father of the future emperor, are not spelled out. Only informed and perceptive readers can surmise what they were from general insinuations (29.3.1–2). Ammianus does, however, offer an explanation for an omission like this. In the preface to the last part of his history, which treats current events, he mysteriously states that the author who chronicles current events "exposes himself to dangers that often lie next to truth" (*pericula ... veritati saepe contigua*: 26.1.1). After this, situations will arise, in which, for the sake of his own life, the historian will omit some details. This is another, much more life-threatening, exception to the prohibition against omitting events and actions, and one closely related to the silence of Roman senators under the tyrannical rule of Domitian, as observed by *Tacitus*. Ammianus, on the other hand, does not appear to have shared Tacitus' deep-seated shame for this depressing conduct (see above, Ch. 6.1.3, p. 143).

Ammianus is as little aware of a need for objectivity in the modern sense as other ancient historical writers (see above, Ch. 1.3.2, pp. 29ff.; Ch. 4.3, pp. 80f.). He can thus (and in this he is quite similar to Tacitus) equip one section of his history with an illustrious hero, the

Caesar and Augustus Julian. The prohibition against omissions and lies, however, results in the introduction of some unfavorable aspects of Julian's conduct in Ammianus' final appraisal of him as well as, on the other hand, the concession of some very few positive traits to Julian's sometime adversary, the emperor Constantius II (17.12ff.; 21.16.1–7; 25.4.16–21). The decisive comparative moment, in which Julian receives a negative, but Constantius a positive, assessment is when Ammianus describes what in late antiquity was taken for granted, the grandeur of the ruler's public comportment. In his conduct and maintenance of excessive ceremony as well as in the unapproachability of his person, Constantius is completely correct, and fulfills the obligations of the late antique Roman emperor. Julian, on the other hand, curries favor with the people, something that was advisable and customary in the early imperial period because it allowed the ruler to appear almost as a citizen and thus to display *civilitas*, but such conduct was for Ammianus long obsolete (21.16.1; 25.4.18).

The conflict-ridden relationship between high civil and military authorities is for *Aurelius Victor* as well as for Ammianus a fundamental phenomenon of his time, and, as such, a criterion for evaluating the quality of an imperial administration (see above, Ch. 6.5.2, p. 192). When the historical writer praises Constantius II as never having given preference to the military over civilians either in the distribution of offices or in the dispensation of rank or authority, this praise carries considerable weight precisely because it is accorded to the antipode of Ammianus' hero Julian. At the same time, this praise likely carries with it criticism of the very different conduct of the imperial brothers Valentinian I and Valens. As a former soldier with many years of service and as an unreservedly devoted supporter of his former commander Ursicinus, Ammianus places himself with this fundamental dissent on the opposing side, the side of civil society. We must leave the question open whether his family background or his later Roman associations manifest themselves here. In any case, Ammianus' view is all the more astonishing when he briefly addresses a contemporary issue related to this topic as if to brush it aside, the difficulties afflicting his commander Ursicinus, and attributes them not only, but indeed also, to the intrigues of civilians and their preferment by the highest authority (Books 14ff. *passim*).

Criticism of society represents for Ammianus an essential aim. It can be applied to phenomena that are of immediate importance to citizens and state such as court-pleaders who are indeed differentiated into four types, all of which are found to be harmful (30.4). Politically insignificant events and circumstances down to the level of goings-on in the taverns of Rome can, however, also give rise to social critique, as we find, for example, in the historian's first excursus concerning the social conditions of high and low society in the city of Rome (14.6; compare this to the second excursus on Rome in 28.4). The significance of such criticism lies not in the comparison of the present with some distant past and its reconstructed stern moral order. Instead, in the context of late antiquity's especially fully articulated class differences, the historian demands from society's leading individuals and families exemplary conduct that will serve as a model for common people, and he demands from state organs strict moral discipline. He decries the absence of morality in both state and society. Behind this critique stands the conviction that human beings are capable of both good and evil, that individual conduct determines the prosperity of the community, and that for this reason the conduct of persons in authority is especially important. As a result, the health and welfare of the Roman empire as a monarchy are ultimately dependent on the virtues and vices of the emperor. Politics is thus viewed exclusively as a function of morality, and because moral conduct can be guided through education, Ammianus offers so many pedagogically motivated *exempla* (see above, Ch. 1.3.1, p. 20; Ch. 4.5.1, p. 87; Ch. 5.1, pp. 108f.; Ch. 6.6, pp. 197f.; above, p. 211). As a moralist, Ammianus will have exerted an influence into modern times.

When the moral quality of a single man at the top determines the fate of the entire empire, one could imagine that a preference for some other form of government than monarchy might result, but we find in Ammianus neither trace of this nor more general constitutional discussions or analyses. On the contrary, the transition to monarchy represents for him a clever choice by a Rome that stood on the threshold of old age, an act that proved rich in blessings for city and empire down to his own day (14.6.4–6; for this comparison with the human life cycle, see above Ch. 6.5.1, p. 189). Ammianus combines his acceptance of monarchy as part of the natural order with his conception of moral conduct, and accordingly offers either approbation or censure of each emperor he appraises. At the same time, Ammianus' description and appraisal of an emperor's good and evil deeds as well as the ways in which he conducted himself serve to satisfy a psychological and moral hunger for knowledge. One could in this way, and only in this way, gain some insight into the inner life of the emperor who, in late antiquity, was removed from general observation: it is the "position of power itself," that "reveals the inner soul" (30.7.1: introduction to the appraisal of Valentinian I).[8] This idea is similar to the insights disclosed by *Tacitus* and *Suetonius* concerning the conduct of the emperor Tiberius, although not necessarily in combination, as they conceived it, with the concept of a change in conduct (see above, Ch. 6.1.3, pp. 146ff.; Ch. 6.3.1, p. 169).

Despite the importance of Tacitus for Ammianus, we must not overlook, however, that worldviews and the conception of human nature were very different in the fourth century from those of the early imperial period (and not just for Christians). Only on a superficial level does it appear that Ammianus accords the same great significance to the omens, dreams, and prophecies he records in such abundance (e.g., 23.1.7; 28.1.42). In recording these things, he follows the *annalistic* tradition that we find most clearly in *Livy*, but which we recognize in *Tacitus* too (see above, Ch. 5.1, pp. 107f.; Ch. 6.1.3, pp. 144f.; Ch. 6.5.1, p. 188). Ammianus also includes, however, religious and magical ideas and practices that were common in the fourth century. These are hardly the same thing. As opposed to the sober and regulated character of the Roman Republic's treatment of state prodigies, we find in late antiquity magic and the prophesying of individuals, of whose effectiveness all alike, including Christians, were convinced. The significance of prodigies thus remains uncertain in Ammianus. This leads to discussion of his religious position in general, which, in relation to an author of his period, is especially interesting.

Around the middle of the fourth century, the relationship between the Christian church and the emperor (or state) as well as the relationship between Christians and adherents of traditional religion represented the fundamental context in which events unfolded. Ammianus consequently addresses this topic in the greatest detail, and he takes it up in his own characteristic way. As a critic of morals, he finds fault with representatives on both sides. The classically religious emperor Julian is described as believing too much in omens, and as conducting too many sacrifices. The Roman bishop Damasus, on the other hand, is criticized for his sumptuous appearance in contradiction with the precepts of Christian humility as well as for his burning ambition (25.4.17; 27.3.12–15). We should not read this criticism of person and conduct of either the one or the other and certainly not both taken together as somehow constituting a demonstration of the author's negative attitude toward traditional religion or Christianity. The praise Valentinian I receives for his restraint and tolerance in religious affairs (30.9.5) could have been offered by a Christian who was disgusted by the intestine Christian conflicts of his day as well as by an adherent of classical religion who hoped for tolerance of his cause from the Christians who determined domestic politics. Ammianus' respect for the theology of the emperors' divinity is appropriate for his day, and, because this system was quickly and only superficially being adapted to the Christian system of belief, it can be interpreted as neither classically religious nor Christian. When the historian criticizes Constantius II's inclination toward Arianism as superstition as well as Julian's persecution of Christians (21.16.18; 25.4.20), we may view this together with the repeated praise for the elder and younger and infallibly orthodox Theodosius as the consequence of "Theodosius' formulation of doctrine" (Flach [Bibl. §1.3] p. 310). Precisely this does not allow us to draw a conclusion about Ammianus' own point of view. He proves himself a firm adherent of traditional religion (as were some senators of his day in the city of Rome) just as little as he proves himself a convinced Christian.

7.3 Christian Historiography

Christianity adopted two characteristics, among others, that are relevant here from *Judaism*, the religion that shaped it and from which it developed. In the first place, it is a religion of the book. This means that its doctrine is fixed in writing ("scripture"), and deemed binding in this form for its believers and its institution, the church. Secondly, the relationship between God and the people of Israel (i.e., the Jews), and subsequently between God and the Christians (or humankind more generally) manifests itself in individual and concrete actions on both sides, and all these actions stand at once in a chronological and causal relationship with one another. The great festivals of the Jews and Christians serve as important milestones of a religion that reveals itself in history. They commemorate unique and past events between God and whoever at the time were his human adherents or opponents. It follows from this that large portions of both Jewish as well as Christian doctrine preserved in scripture are of necessity historical in nature. Although they may not fulfill Greco-Roman historiographical criteria, those texts theology deems historical in fact occupy the greater part of the *Torah* (or *Old Testament*) just as they do the *New Testament*. In the case of the *Old Testament*, to name just a few examples here, we may mention the five *Books of Moses*, the two (or four) books of *Kings*, which include, in accordance with the modern conception of their content and form, the two books of *Chronicles*, and, in the case of the *New Testament*, the four *Gospels* and the *Acts of the Apostles*.

There are nevertheless important differences. Long stretches of the *Torah* as well as the *Old Testament* more generally dwell on the independent kingdom of Israel or Judah and the subsequent dependent principality of Judah under priestly rule. The *New Testament*, on the other hand, deals with "grand" political history only marginally because Christianity develops within a Judaism definitively no longer independent, in a province, and amid an ethnic group that is but one of many in the Roman empire, one that in general plays only a subordinate role, even if from time to time the group plays a determining role in events central to the Christian faith such as the trial and death of Jesus. The tradition that the *New Testament* describes focuses primarily on the life and works of the founder of the religion, Jesus Christ, and, to that extent, offers with its biographical orientation a parallel to the contemporary historiography of the early and high imperial periods. It also provides further accounts of Jesus' closest adherents and their works, and with them follows the movement's rapid growth first in Judaea and then soon in other places too within the Roman empire, forming a supraregional Christian community that at first remains within Judaism as another stream within it, but that splits off from it by the time of the catastrophe of Judaea and Jerusalem in AD 70 at the latest.

Hardly any contemporary historical accounts for the time after the activities of Jesus and his apostles were produced, and, to the extent that such accounts existed, Christians hardly took notice of them. The latter is true even for the *Acts of Apostles*, which, on the grounds that they were not necessary for the faith, were adopted into the canon of *New Testament* scriptures only at a very late date. The reason for this early Christian abstinence regarding historical appraisal of, and attention to, their own faith, followers, and organization lay in a central tenet of belief for early generations of Christians: the imminent end of the world together with the second coming of Christ and the Last Judgment. At least to the extent that historical reflection was not directed at core elements of their belief-system, the soon-expected end of all history seemed to render such reflection on the past superfluous. With the failure of the expected end of the world and its signs to arrive, Christian interest began to grow in the historical dimension of their faith that had, of course, in the meantime grown longer, and continued to do so.

The following *historical topics* were important for Christians: the life and works of outstanding Christians who could, and were supposed to, serve as inspiration for others; Jesus' successors and the development of their own community, in whose increase, despite setbacks at the hands of Jews and adherents of classical religion, they could, and hoped to, see confirmation of the truth of the Christian religion; and, ultimately, Christians wished to fill the ever-expanding temporal distance between the birth of the Christian religion and whatever its contemporary stage of development, which included the extent of the spread of Christianity as well as its role in those worldwide events that occurred after the earthly career of their savior and before final salvation and entrance into the kingdom of God. The strictly defined period between the creation of the world and the time of Jesus had already long ago received literary treatment within the Jewish historical tradition, which Christians considered the essential basis for the later period of salvation-history, and they consequently provided accounts of both periods in tandem. History did not consist for Christians of particular events. Instead, between the creation of the world and its destruction, world history was steered by the will of God along a goal-oriented course. Christian historical writers were therefore not required to collect empirical facts in hopes of eventually arriving at new insights on that basis. Their task was rather to confirm the course of history that God had for the most part already ordained. For Christians, history thus served to corroborate their faith. Much time would have to pass before Christian historiography could to some extent free itself from these shackles. We observe the effect of this in connection with current events, which require more painstaking original research than more remote history. In the fourth and fifth centuries, Christians, besides the specialized works of Eusebius, have nothing of their own to offer. Only in the sixth century does an author, *Procopius,* appear who is in possession of real personal stature (see below, Ch. 7.3.4; pp. 237ff.).

A variety of genres of Christian historiography developed out of the areas of special interest discussed above as well as from the peculiarities and limitations of those areas, and these genres developed under the influence of classically religious literary and historiographical culture. While not without contradictions, this influence was nevertheless effective, and, astonishingly, included the adoption of classically religious learning as a matter of course. We find *Acts of Martyrs* as the first product of Christian historiography. These are subsequently elaborated in *Lives* or *Legends of the Saints.* These texts document the miracles, and narrate the personal conduct of individual Christians who were persecuted. The lives of martyrs or saints stand in close proximity to the genre of ancient biography, but they quickly depart from what we may properly call "history," and we shall therefore not consider them in greater detail here (compare, however, below Ch. 7.3.2, p. 228). In *Histories of the Church,* the apostolic succession was drawn up first, and this was then continued. They also sketched the internal development of Christianity as well as its external relations within its wider social context and with particular emphasis on the state (see below, Ch. 7.3.1, pp. 219ff.). *Universal Chronicles* and *Universal Histories* described general political history from a Christian perspective, and comprehended indeed the entire world, at least in terms of their aims, because this was the only approach that accorded with the universal power of God and the claim of Christianity to universal truth (see below, Ch. 7.3.2, pp. 223ff.; Ch. 7.3.3, pp. 229ff.). To the extent that Christians identified with the Roman empire, they also acknowledged Rome's claim to world dominion, and additionally made use of that traditional claim for their own purposes: for Christians too world history and Roman history became one and the same. As a result, the historiography of Rome and its empire as well as its emperors were matters of interest for Christians too (see below, Ch. 7.3.3, pp. 230f.; Ch. 7.3.4, p. 240). Roman history also represented a special danger for Christian historiography: it ran the risk of losing its individual character when it joined the long tradition of Roman historical writing that flowed from Latin and Greek pens. On the other hand, the concept of Roman history as world history was precisely what made the incorporation of Christian universality within Roman history possible (see below, Ch. 7.3.3, pp. 230ff.).

Of the various genres of Christian historical writing that we described above in terms of content, one early work stands out: *Lucius Caelius Firmianus*, also known as *Lactantius*, composed *On the Deaths of the Persecutors* (*De mortibus persecutorum*) immediately after the persecutions of Christians by Diocletian, his fellow emperors, and their immediate successors came to an end (between 313 and 316). The theological meaning of these persecutions was naturally difficult for his contemporaries to understand, but Lactantius was able to transform them into a veritable triumph of Christianity, inasmuch as God punished the classically religious instigators of the persecutions with hideous deaths. – For many generations the Greek East would dominate the Latin West in the development of Christian theology and Christian literature more generally. This was the case in the development historiographical genres as well, and for this reason works composed originally in Greek were translated into Latin, adapted, and reworked (see below, Ch. 7.3.1, pp. 221f.; Ch. 7.3.2, pp. 225f.).

7.3.1 Church history (Eusebius and Rufinus)

Eusebius of Caesarea (circa 260/65–339/40) created the only genuinely Christian genre of ancient historiography, and was himself aware of this fact (*History of the Church* 1.1.5). Eusebius received a theological education in the tradition of Origen (circa 185/6–254), became Bishop of Maritime Caesarea (Palestine) after the conclusion of Diocletianic persecution of the Christians (303–311), and belonged to the emperor's inner circle during the reign of Constantine I (306–337), which was a decisive period in the development of Christianity. The Arian controversy became a concern for the emperor and the empire at the latest during the Council of Nicea in 325, and it remained so afterward. Eusebius worked actively on the side of reconciliation for the sake of the unity of church and empire. A so-called "theology of empire" may be traced back to Eusebius. This theology stipulated as necessary analogies: one God, one – Roman – empire, and, as its monarchical head, one emperor (cf., e.g., *Life of Constantine* 2.19). Some generations later *Orosius'* universal history incorporated this doctrine in its comprehensive theology of history (see below, Ch. 7.3.3, pp. 232 and 234). In three of his works, a *Chronicle* (see below, Ch. 7.3.2, pp. 224f.), an encomiastic *Life of Constantine*, and the *History of the Church*, Eusebius combined with his theological concerns elements drawn partly from universal history, partly from Roman history of the recent past, and partly from current events.

The central theme of the *Historia ekklesiastiké*, which brings events up to AD 323, is not (as we might surmise from the title) the general development of the church, but instead the apostolic succession, that is, the succession of bishops. This results from Eusebius' conviction that it is not the institution, but instead the *logos* (i.e., the content of Christ's teaching and that of his first successors) that constitutes the church. Because he focuses on this *logos*, Eusebius subjects a theme that is ahistorical by nature to historical considerations. The unavoidable difficulties that arose from putting this plan into practice were to some extent ameliorated by incorporating into the *History of the Church* additional topics that at the time were of interest to Christians: Christian teachers and authors, doctrinal deviants (heretics), fates met by Jews, especially their punishment, as well as the persecutions of Christians and martyrs. Persecutions and martyrdoms connect the history of Christians to the history of the Roman empire and thus to more general political history, thereby acquiring from the beginning more than merely marginal significance. As a consequence of Eusebius' "theology of empire," the Roman empire and the Roman emperor become central topics for Eusebius from the time of their first Christianization. But because his *Historia ekklesiastiké* concludes in the year 323, this consequence would not have its full effect until Eusebius' successors continued his work.

According to Eusebius' own words, his *History of the Church* supplies his *Chronicle* with material, and, vice versa, his *Chronicle* represents an abbreviated version of his *History of the Church* (*Historia ekklesiastiké* 1.1.6). Because he includes numerous documents, the latter is in some parts more a collection of materials than a narrative and interpretive history. Eusebius revised his work repeatedly, and it eventually extended to ten volumes. In some manuscripts, we find appended to the eighth volume an account of martyrs in Palestine during the persecutions of the Christians under Diocletian and his successors (303–311). A Syriac version, and from it an Armenian version, of Eusebius' *History of the Church* were produced, and Rufinus translated the work into Latin, and continued it (see below). In the fourth and fifth centuries AD, many church histories were produced in Greek-speaking areas as sequels to Eusebius' work.

Turranius (Tyrranius) Rufinus (born mid-fourth century) studied in Rome with Jerome, but later entered into a dispute with him over one of the major issues facing Christian intellectuals at that time (see below, Ch. 7.3.2, p. 225). After his studies, apart from a trip to Egypt, the birthplace of monastic orders, he stayed successively, always for an extended period, in Aquileia, his native city in northeast Italy, in Palestine, in Rome, and ultimately once again in Aquileia. He fled to Sicily in advance of the Goths who invaded Italy from what is now Slovenia, and died in Sicily in 410. Rufinus translated, and partially revised according to his own idiosyncratic standards, works written by Greek church fathers, especially by his model Origen and his circle as well as by two of the great Cappadocian fathers, Gregory of Nazianzus and Basil of Caesarea, and a *History of the Monks (Historia monachorum)*. Rufinus composed works of his own as well. In 402/403, at the time of the first great invasion of Visigoths into Italy, Rufinus translated the *History of the Church* by *Eusebius* at the request of the bishop of his native city, and continued it from 324 to the death of Theodosius I in 395. He divided the ten books of the original work into nine books, and added two books of his own. He abbreviated Eusebius' text by omitting documents. He also expanded it in places in order to glorify the asceticism that was practiced at the time above all by monks, and, as he did also in his translation of Origen, he altered theological statements that did not conform to his own thinking. In his own portion, Rufinus is concerned primarily with the controversies surrounding the view of Arianism or rather with providing an account of the significance of the controversy over Arianism, that occupied several decades of the fourth century, and often gave occasion to emperors to intervene directly in church affairs.

Many continuations of the *History of the Church* by *Eusebius* were produced in the Greek East of the empire. The jurist *Socrates* (circa AD 380–440) produced one for the period from 305 to 439 in seven books. In a logical continuation of his model, political history forms the framework of an account, into which Socrates introduces additional material from church history that he draws in part from the work of Rufinus. Although he was not a theologian, his attitude toward the doctrinal conflicts of Christians in the fourth and early fifth centuries was not neutral. Nevertheless, he was not personally involved in them. The nine books of the *History of the Church* by *Sozomen* (first half of the fifth century), who was likewise a jurist, are devoted to the years 324–439. These books, however, probably because the author died, remained incomplete. Sozomen follows the work of Socrates, and expands on it by including monasticism. Sozomen examined for himself sources that Socrates had cited according to Eusebius' work. The knowledge he gained by doing this allows Sozomen occasionally to correct his predecessor. In general, he makes an effort to align his work with the rules of historiography stylistically and by avoiding verbatim quotations. For general political history, both Socrates and Sozomen unambiguously employ such classically religious authors as *Eunapius* (see above, Ch. 7.1, pp. 203ff.). *Theodoret* (393–circa 466), bishop of the city of Cyrrhus in northern Syria, was a theologian who took an active part in the doctrinal controversies of his time, thereby embroiling himself in difficulties. Among his many writings, we find also a continuation of *Eusebius' History of the Church* for the years 325–428. He follows his model in reproducing numerous documents. His steadfast doctrinal orthodoxy conforms, however, to neither Eusebius nor his continuators Socrates and Sozomen.

The general historical basis of the church histories mentioned here has permitted them to serve in the modern study of ancient history as important sources for the history of the empire and the emperors of the fourth and early fifth centuries. This very fact, however, limits the independence of church history as an historiographical genre considerably. This manifests itself especially clearly inasmuch as the events of Christian history are not arranged historically and chronologically for their own sake, but are instead subordinated and organized according to a general political history that is accepted in advance as a narrative scheme. What is more, ecclesiastical historiography, by offering accounts as the sequel to various authors, adopted a long-standing practice of more general political historiography (see above, Ch. 4.1, pp. 66ff.; Ch. 5.2.1, pp. 111 and 113; Ch. 6.1.2, p. 135; Ch. 7.1, p. 203). The extensive work of church historians with sources actually better fulfills a demand made by some ancient historians (but met only in exceptional cases by them) than do quite a few earlier works of general historiography (see above, Ch. 1.3.2, pp. 28f.; Ch. 4.3, p. 80; Ch. 6.1.3, p. 148; Ch. 6.3.3, pp. 175ff.). *Sozomen*, by refraining from verbatim quotation in his effort to author a stylistically homogenous text, also points to another strand of conventional historiography: this is precisely how works of general political historiography were supposed to be composed, at least according to the literary and rhetorical rules that in the fourth and fifth centuries were still being taught and studied (compare above, Ch. 1.3.1, pp. 21f.; Ch. 1.3.2, p. 29; Ch. 7.1, p. 205). For this reason, ecclesiastical historiography, although in its beginnings it represented something completely new (because it demonstrated a departure from traditional historiography), did not develop further into a truly independent genre of historiography, but, on the contrary, was instead quite quickly led back onto the customary paths of ancient historiography. Here too the power of tradition was stronger than the drive to attempt the unknown and the daring to try the untested: Christians, whether laypersons or theologians, had been educated in a traditional literary and rhetorical culture that prescribed the adaptation and imitation of previous works – granted, in a personally modified style – as the greatest achievement of an educated and cultured person (see above, Ch. 1.1, p. 11; Ch. 1.3.1, pp. 18f.).

7.3.2 From classically religious chronography to Christian universal chronicle (Eusebius, Jerome, Sulpicius)

At the latest, Christians began writing chronicles in the period around AD 200 (Julius Africanus, circa 200; Hippolytus of Rome, died 235). Specifically Christian chronography goes, on the one hand, back to an effort to record the sequence of events to the present as they move forward from God's creation of the world and human beings, and toward their conclusion at the end of the world. This task required synchronizing the many events in which God manifested his relationship with the people of Israel (i.e., the Jews), the life and works of Jesus, the missionary activity of the apostles, as well as the origin and development of the Christian community with the history of other peoples and empires. Indeed, as Christians were well aware, the history of Israel and the Jews and, before the creation of Christian chronicles, the history of Christianity too were synchronized with, or connected to, universal chronology for individual events, but not at all for all events. On the other hand – and this was even more important than the mere documentation of the world's course and its connections – one could in this way, and only in this way, prove to the adherents of classical religion that Christianity by way of Judaism and the people of Israel (whose history Christians appropriated as a matter of course as belonging to their predecessors) was more ancient than all classically religious philosophy. In this regard, we must keep in mind that, according to prevailing modes of ancient thought, what was more ancient was automatically better than what was more recent (see above, Ch. 5.2.4, p. 120). With this, they took up a thread going back to the Jews of the Hellenistic age, and one that would be repeatedly woven into many arguments throughout the Roman imperial period (see above, Ch. 6.2.1, p. 159).

To the extent that pre-Christian (and traditionally religious) chronography had brought together at least two peoples or states and their dates and chronological schemes or had perhaps even combined all available dates and events for all peoples to construct a *universal chronicle*, the effort prepared the way for a Christian chronicle, inasmuch as universal chronicle was absolutely the only kind that would serve the purposes they had set for themselves (see above, Ch. 5.2.4, pp. 119f.; Ch. 7.3, pp. 218f.). Christians were happy to reap the rewards of such efforts, and it is for this reason that Christian chronography rests on the basis of a long pre-Christian tradition. For several generations, Christian and classically religious chronography existed side by side during the third century. It was thus possible for a late antique classically religious work of the genre to serve as the basis for Christian chronography in the early fourth century. In the *Universal Chronicle* of the neo-Platonic philosopher and scholar *Porphyry* (*FGrH* 260; AD 234–301/5) diverse chronological schemes were arranged in parallel. This provided Christian chronography with a framework, into which Biblical chronology could be inserted.

Eusebius, bishop of Caesarea (see above, Ch. 7.3.1, pp. 219f.), followed Porphyry. His two-volume work, which he revised himself, provides a chronicle down to AD 325. The first book tells the history of all peoples, and the second provides synchronized tables. In the columns of these tables, he lists empires and rulers as befit the various historical and chronological circumstances, and he adds enumerations of years for empires and administrations as well as assorted cultural, literary, and historical notices. The left-hand column represents the backbone for the whole: it provides years according to the birth of Abraham, because, as a Christian, Eusebius altered the basis of Porphyry's chronological system. He chose as his reference point the birth of Abraham, who was the progenitor of Israel, God's chosen people, and synchronized this date with the long familiar non-Christian chronology of the first great empire of the Assyrians. The forty-third year of their first king Ninus' administration corresponded in this scheme with the year of Abraham's birth (compare Ch. 5.2.4, pp. 119f.). Eusebius thus achieved a simultaneous beginning for universal political history, Israelite and Jewish history, and, by way of this history, the history of Christian salvation as well (see below, Ch. 7.3.3, pp. 231f. and 236). On this basis, it was easy to demonstrate that, among law-givers who were the most important instructors of civil discipline and moral conduct, Moses was clearly and significantly more ancient than Plato. This in turn demonstrated that Judeo-Christian teachings were superior to Greek philosophy. For the Christian era, Eusebius believed that his *Chronicle*, after a judicious selection of events, should also serve as the nucleus of his *History of the Church* (see above, Ch. 7.3.1, p. 220). The chronicle of the Roman empire and the chronicle of Christianity had become an interwoven unity, behind which lay his "theology of empire," just as it did his *History of the Church* (see above, Ch. 7.3.1, p. 220).

Eusebius' *Chronicle* of universal history was followed by many works of the same genre in Greek-speaking areas. In comparison with the history of salvation, general historical content came to occupy more and more space in these works. The 18 books of the *Chronographia* of *John (Ioannes) Malalas* are recognized by moderns as possessing some importance. *George Syncellus* ultimately combined in AD 800 the chronicles, or rather chronological systems, of Julius Africanus, Eusebius, and others. In a Latin translation, the influence of Eusebius' *Chronicle* also extended to the western Roman Empire and then later into the European Middle Ages.

The Latin adapter of Eusebius' *Chronicle* was *Jerome* (or *Eusebius Sophronius Hieronymus*, from before 350 to around 420) who early in life quit his chosen career in civil administration in favor of an ascetic life after the model of the monks. Even before his friend Rufinus, he traveled to the East, lived as a hermit in the desert of Chalcis (in Syria), was consecrated as a priest in Antioch, and learned Greek. Moreover, despite the then considerably anti-Semitic attitude of Christians and their clergy, he also learned Hebrew. In 382, he took part in the Council of Constantinople, after which he resided in Rome as Pope Damasus' secretary. When, after Damasus' death, he was passed over in the selection of a new pope, he left Rome in the company of several distinguished and rich widows, whom he had inspired to a life of asceticism. Finally, from 386, he founded three convents in and near Bethlehem as well as one monastery. He actively took part in Christian controversies about Pelagius, about John Chrysostom (the bishop of Constantinople), and about the teachings of the earlier church father Origen. His means were not always delicate, and his friendship with Rufinus was ruptured (see above, Ch. 7.3.1, p. 221; below, Ch. 7.3.3, p. 236). Jerome composed (often quickly and hurriedly) numerous theological compositions: commentaries on books of the Bible, defenses of the ascetic form of life, and overwhelmingly exegetical sermons and letters. Commissioned by Pope

Damasus, he revised existing Latin translations of the *New Testament*, and he undertook his own translation of the *Old Testament*. He combined the two into the still canonical Latin Bible (or *Vulgate*, the so-called *Biblia vulgata*). Some of Jerome's compositions are of more than theological interest. Based on Eusebius' *History of the Church*, these include the first *History of Christian Literature*, which covers more than 135 authors (*De viris illustribus*) as well as the biographies and obituaries of saints.

Jerome translated the *Chronicle* of *Eusebius* into Latin. More precisely, he translated, expanded, and extended to AD 378 the tables of the second volume in its second revised and improved edition. Jerome undertook this project while taking part in the Council of Constantinople in 382. He supplemented his exemplar with Roman material, including cultural, literary, and historical items from lists of magistrates, *Suetonius' De viris illustribus*, *Aurelius Victor*, *Eutropius*, and others (see above, Ch. 6.3.1, p. 166; Ch. 6.5.2, pp. 194f.). But his method was neither thorough nor consistent. For this reason, after he comes to the end of Suetonius' work, insertions of literary and historical notices simply cease. According to Jerome's own statements, his revised chronicle is divided into three parts: (1) from the first Assyrian king Ninus and the contemporary Biblical patriarch Abraham to the fall of Troy in what is purely a translation; (2) from Troy's destruction to the twentieth year of Constantine I (AD 325) as a translation with additions by Jerome from "Suetonius and other famous historians;" and (3) from 325 to 378 "completely my own work" (Jerome, *Preface to the Chronicle*, pp. 6–7, ed. Helm).[9] In the mass of its notices, it seems that Jerome's chronicle is an attempt to present history conceived in its comprehensive sense, that is, as politics *and* culture, in its shortest possible form. Cultural notes are ill suited for such a project because they lose much more meaning than do political notices when reduced to abbreviated bits of data. We view this most clearly when we read notices inserted by Jerome along the lines of "The poet / orator etc. A. becomes famous." Jerome himself revised his *Chronicle* many times. It became an important source in the Middle Ages for knowledge about the ancient world, and beyond this a model for subsequent chronicles.

The *Chronicle* that *Sulpicius Severus* (circa 363–400) composed belongs to the line of the Eusebian tradition only in a very restricted sense. Sulpicius, a native of Aquitania, was, like so many of his Gallic contemporaries, well-schooled in literature and a member of the nobility. He lived an ascetic life modeled after Martin (316/317–397), bishop of Caesarodunum Turonum (Tours), whose influence in Gaul was extraordinarily strong. Martin began life as a soldier adhering to tradi-tional religion, but he became a Christian monk and miracle-worker. Martin's person and his influence made a deep impression on the content of Sulpicius' writings. His *Chronicle* (*Chronica*) extends from the creation of the world to around AD 400, and makes use of Eusebius' notices, but also information from such non-Christian authors as Sallust and Tacitus, from whose works moreover Sulpicius took stylistic lessons. His *Chronicle* provides primarily Biblical and ecclesiastical history, but also from our perspective important testimony regarding contemporary events. Book 1 extends to the Babylonian captivity of the Jews (in *Jeremiah*), Book 2 from the same point (in *Daniel*) to the emergence and suppression of the Christian sect of Priscillianists. The division alone points to a conspicuous feature of this chronicle, that is more, and wants to be more, than a mere presentation of numbers and dates. Jesus Christ does not stand at the beginning of the second book, and thus does not mark in this way the beginning of a new age. He is mentioned only briefly in 2.27. The author then passes immediately to the persecutions of Christians under Nero. To the ninth persecution he appends his expec-tation for one remaining tenth persecution which he is convinced will mark the end of time with the appearance of the Antichrist (2.28–33). The *Chronicle* of *Eusebius* and of *Jerome* used traditionally religious authors to establish a definitive universal chronology as well as to mine their supply of earlier events and circumstances, among which Israelite, Jewish, and Christian history mattered, but did not determine the char-acter of their work. Sulpicius, on the other hand, pursued his own highly idiosyncratic Christian views that could only partially be derived from chronology.

Sulpicius' chronological notices demonstrate that the end of the world is near. In this respect, the author adheres to the expectant attitude of very early Christians. This would in the first instance have rendered the comprehension of history superfluous (see above, Ch. 7.3, p. 217), but in Sulpicius' peculiar view the expectation of end times represents a nec-essary and essential element of his historiographical account. When Hilarius, bishop of Limonum (Poitiers) from 356 to his death in 367/8, and above all Martin of Tours, issue warnings about the end of the world, it is possible that Sulpicius wants us to view them as the two witnesses of God who appear in *Apocalypse* 11. Sulpicius, however, is hardly a strict millenarian, as he does not refer to Christ's thousand-year kingdom of peace after his first victory over the Antichrist. On the other hand, his obvious interest in the grim events that take place after the establishment of the Antichrist's rule may well reflect contemporary threats to the

Roman empire and its inhabitants. The number and dates of Christian persecutions are significant in view of the outwardly tranquil and prosperous era that Christians enjoyed from the time of Constantine I and in relation to the expected appearance of the Antichrist because the martyrs are the witnesses of the future return of Christ. The time of tranquillity itself engendered strife among Christians, and this prevents them from offering the necessary testimony on behalf of God (2.35ff.). The tenth persecution, which Christians expected would occur at the hands of the resurrected first Christian persecutor Nero together with the Antichrist, would finally purge Christendom (2.28.1–3; 2.29.6). The unity of faith that Christians lost after the ninth persecution may remind us of the turning point in the moral conduct of (classically religious) Romans after the fall of Carthage, but, despite his knowledge of *Sallust* and *Tacitus*, we find in Sulpicius no allusion to this fundamental concept of Roman historiography (see above, Ch. 4.5.1, pp. 91ff.; Ch. 6.1.3, pp. 146f.). For Sulpicious a Biblical analogy with a completely different message is much more relevant: just as they did in the *Old Testament*, prophets rise up in the present to warn those in power.

The detailed description of the ecclesiastical controversies of the fourth century provided at the end of the work (2.35–51) is designed to portray, on the one hand, the "prophet" and ascetic Martin (who was not universally recognized as such by the church) in a positive light while, on the other, casting in a negative light the established clergy. Also tied up with this is Sulpicius' positive evaluation of Priscillianism in respect to its ascetic tendencies, a movement that was spreading quickly in Spain and southern Gaul, but which the church branded a deviation from true teaching (heresy). Martin of Tours is the person Sulpicius most frequently cites and mentions in the entire work, and his *Chronicle*, like all the other works of this author, thus proves itself a supplement to his *Vita Martini* (*Life of Martin*). His (universal) chronicle thus becomes a framework for an appreciation of a witness and a prophet of his own day, and by doing this it fails in its own generic purpose of providing an objective and sober report in brief compass. Sulpicius' idiosyncratic work leaves no traces on medieval chronicles. His theological premises, on the other hand – such as his high regard for asceticism, the ever-present need for prophets whose function it is to broadcast their warnings, the expectation of the Antichrist, and so much more – belong, of course, to the bedrock of late antique and medieval Christian faith. Again and again they stamped their vision of the course of human and world history onto a conception of history directed toward the future, and indeed, more precisely, toward the coming end of the world.

7.3.3 Orosius: universal history through the lens of theology

Paulus Orosius produced a synthesis of late antique Christian doctrines and concepts that had an effect on the interpretation of history. He applied this to universal history and to Roman history, which he conceived as the last phase of world history. Born in the late fourth century in Portugal or Spain, Orosius received rhetorical and theological training after the fashion of his age. By 414 at the latest he resided near *Augustine*, the already long-famous bishop of Hippo Regius (Annaba [Bône], Algeria). Augustine sent him to Jerome in Bethlehem in order to accuse the monk Pelagius (who was already under attack from Augustine) of false teaching (heresy) regarding original sin and the grace of God (see above, Ch. 7.3.2, p. 225). When Orosius in this controversy found himself counter-charged with false teaching, he composed a *Book in Self-Defense* (*Liber apologeticus*). We hear nothing more of his life after another sojourn with Augustine in 416/417.

Orosius lived in disturbed and dangerous times that left traces in his work. In the Christian controversies regarding Pelagianism, the adherents of Origen, and Priscillianism (which was particularly strong in his native land), Orosius actively worked as their opponent both in his speeches and in his writing (see above as well as *Commonitorium de errore Priscillianistarum et Origenistarum*). The distribution of the government in 395 between Thedosius I's two sons, together with the increasing dissonance between the two heads of the administrative divisions, had fatal consequences, especially for the weaker, western half of the empire, because it was exposed to much stronger Germanic invasions. These invasions no longer remained merely episodic, but led instead to the settlement of individual groups and tribes and to the establishment of kingdoms within the territory of the western half of the Roman empire and thus in Orosius' native land too. The number and importance of Germans within the Roman army and thus within the core of the Roman empire's power structure was increasing relentlessly, at least in the West. One of the Visigothic invasions of Italy culminated in 410 with the conquest and plundering of the city of Rome. Because, since the Celtic invasion of the fourth century BC, no one had witnessed victorious strangers within the walls of Rome, the city that had ruled the world, the event was, even beyond the misfortune it actually was, a shock and a scandal.

Orosius, who wrote in the wake of that catastrophe, composed an historical work entitled *Seven Books of History against the Pagans* (*Historiarum adversum paganos libri VII*) that defends Christians against adherents of classical religions, and is thus an apologetic work. According to his own testimony, Orosius wrote this first Christian universal history in the space of a year after his return to Augustine in 416 and at his request (1.*preface*.1ff.; 7.43.19f.; cf. 7.41.2). Orosius' relationship with *Augustine* clarifies the purpose of his work. Augustine composed Books 1–10 of his monumental *City of God* (*De civitate Dei*) between 412 and 416. In these volumes, the bishop of Hippo exposed every traditional and classical religion as a system of belief in demons that conferred no benefit whatsoever on human beings in the regulation of their affairs, but instead brought corruption to the very basis of human society. Books 11–12 of this same work were devoted to the proof that states and empires, because they are purely human institutions, come and go, and that true safety lies beyond them in the "City of God," whose earthly predecessor, Christianity, exists in a state of perpetual conflict with the "City of the World" (*civitas terrena*). This was the answer of a great intellect to the scandalous fact of Rome's conquest by Visigoths and to the resulting mental anguish that it elicited among Christians and the adherents of traditional religion alike. The devaluation of the state in general, however, and of Rome and its empire in particular that Augustine advocated in his *City of God* held little appeal for a general audience of any religious persuasion. On the one hand, Christians believed that the empire and its inhabitants (and thus themselves as well) stood under the special protection of God. On the other hand, adherents of classical religion advanced historical arguments that Rome's successes derived from the long adherence of the city-state and the empire to its ancestral religion in the past, and they connected current disasters and catastrophes to the transition to Christian worship and the concomitant neglect, and, indeed, prohibition, of traditional forms of religious worship (for the latter, compare Augustine *Letters* 136.2; *Retractationes* 2.43(70).1).

Orosius addresses himself to those who are not convinced by Augustine's method of proof. He employs a much more superficial strategy in his argument that not only leaves the traditional importance intact that Rome and its empire had for Christians and non-Christians alike, but even enhances it. Nevertheless, his method of proof begins from the same starting point as Augustine's: the conviction that the conquest of Rome by Visigoths was not a consequence of reverence for the unitary God and the neglect of ancestral gods. On this fundamental basis and in accord with his brief from Augustine, Orosius tells the history of humanity in general and of Rome in particular as a series of catastrophes, misfortune, and suffering occasioned partly by Nature and partly by human beings (1.*preface*.10). The Christian era was the first to bring about a

general improvement in human affairs, even allowing the Roman empire
to enjoy a rejuvenation. Again and again, Orosius invites his readers to
compare the grim events of classically religious epochs with the less grim
or even beneficial events of Christian times, and he offers comparisons
of his own that are unambiguous in their assessments as, for example,
this comparison central to the purpose of his work: the sack of Rome by
Gauls with its sack in Christian times by Visigoths. Orosius shifts from a
defense of Christians against adherents of traditional religion to an attack
on them, and he accomplishes this by turning their analysis of the quality
of the course of history on its head (1.*preface*.13–14; 2.19.3–16: the end
of the second book; 7.39.1–7.40.1). Some scholars have argued occasionally that Orosius differs from Augustine so fundamentally in his
approach that he could not possibly have written at his request. The
premise of this conclusion certainly hits the mark (see below, p. 235),
but we must not fail to recognize that in this instance two apparently
distinct paths begin from the same point and superficially lead to a likewise identical goal, namely, a defense against traditionally religious
arguments and keeping uncertain or even despondent Christians firm in
their faith. Because Orosius plays the less intellectually demanding role
in this undertaking, which is at once unified and divided in its approach
and means, his self-characterization as a humble and eager assistant to
Augustine, which he illustrates with the image of a dog serving his master,
is logically consistent (1.*preface*.2ff.).

   The structure and arrangement of material in the *History against the
Pagans* serve the author's strategy for his argument. Only with both
universal history and Roman history in combination can he prove what
he wishes to, and has to. In the first book, his work thus hurries, as a
universal history, through events from the creation of the world to the
foundation of Rome. He renders his narrative universal through a prefa-
tory geographical overview of the world that is unusual among works of
historiography (1.2.1–106), and this underscores the author's seriousness
of purpose in his task of writing universal history. The following books
are, in comparison, essentially, if not exclusively, Roman history or at
least history from a Roman point of view. Orosius takes the Greeks into
special account, inasmuch as he provides parallel accounts of Roman and
Greek history to the extent that it makes sense to do so, and he deals
with the sequence of four universal empires according to his peculiar
conception of it (see below, p. 235). In view of the expansion of Rome,
the extensive details of which fill most of Books 2–5, and in view of
Orosius' concentrated focus on the establishment of the Roman empire
at the end of Book 6 and at the beginning of Book 7, Roman history

(indeed finally) becomes universal history, just as it did of necessity for earlier authors too as a result of the course of its development (see above, Ch. 5.2, pp. 110f.).

Orosius' unambiguously positive assessment of Rome's establishment of its universal empire is, on the one hand, marked by the rule of Augustus, and, on the other, by God's taking on human form in the birth of Jesus (end of Book 6 through the beginning of Book 7; see below, pp. 234f.). Orosius likewise approves of the transition of Rome to monarchy that Augustus introduced, because he, like Eusebius before him, views monarchy as analogous to the sway of the unitary God and as an expression of God's will (see above, Ch. 7.3.1, p. 220). The seventh book – we must take note of the significance of this number to Jews and Christians as a symbol of completeness and perfection – is consequently the history of Rome and its monarchically ruled empire under a Christian and thus ultimately positive presage: first the history of a "pagan" empire, thanks to whose external security Christianity grows relentlessly, and then the history of the empire converted to Christianity, which is better able to survive dangerous circumstances than was "pagan" Rome. For this reason the seventh book does not end with the events of the year 410 and the sack of Rome by Visigoths, but instead Orosius continues his history to the year 417, in which year he concluded his work on the project. He is thus able to demonstrate that the events of 410 do not represent a permanent state of affairs, and that the empire had easily put this merely seeming catastrophe aside, and could now face the Germanic threat much better than it was able to just a few years before (7.43).

As befits the basis on which he chose to construct his argument, Orosius' history is for wide stretches the chronicle and portrayal of a series of catastrophes. To the extent that these are natural disasters, Orosius can for Roman history easily make use of classically religious literature, which connected these grim events that struck the community with the efforts made to expiate their – traditional – gods (compare especially *Livy* as well as *Obsequens,* who drew on him: see above, Ch. 5.1, pp. 107f. and Ch. 6.5.1, p. 188). The grimmest disasters, above all in terms of the greatest numbers of the dead, are, however, those that human beings impose on themselves collectively, including wars. Because ancient historiography, beginning with the Greek authors Herodotus and Thucydides, is extensively concerned with providing accounts of wars, Orosius is able in this regard to pull out all stops. His *History* is a universal history of wars and even more the atrocity of wars (5.1). Again and again, Orosius stresses the famines and epidemics that accompany wars, but above all he lets the numbers tell their tale. He takes figures for the numbers of those who fell, numbers that the ancient tradition had already taken delight in exaggerating, and rounds them up even further, and then he adds them up over longer periods of time, so that he arrives, for example, at a figure of 1,900,000 fallen Persians for the reigns of the great kings Cyrus, Darius, and Xerxes (see 2.11.8 for the figure that represents the sum of the numbers in 2.8.5 and 2.8.11 as well as 2.9.2). The gruesome murders committed among relatives, especially among brothers, that Orosius so often describes are increased in number by the collective addition of murders among "relatives" in civil wars, to which sum he also adds casualties resulting from frequent wars with and among usurpers under the auspices of the monarchical form of government in Rome. When Orosius caps off the Roman civil wars of the second and first centuries BC with a pointed account of a brother's murder, he establishes, as is well suited for events in pre-Christian times, a scenario of horror without compare (5.19ff. especially 5.19.13). On the other hand, not all wars can have been purely negative, because Rome's wars of conquest led, of course, to its universal empire, whose continued existence offers tremendous advantages that Orosius never tires of praising (e.g., 5.1.11ff.).

In his account of Roman history, Orosius combines the peculiar strategy of the work with his intellectual attitude as a proud citizen of the Roman empire. He is Roman by conviction and with pride. Although (in connection with the destruction of Carthage and Corinth) he is aware that Rome's attainment of power implied simultaneous misfortune for whatever states and peoples it faced, including his own native land, he nevertheless, considers it fortunate for all that the universal state under Rome's rule for the most part guarantees universal peace. Rome provides peace and security especially in times when parts of the empire face external threats, because one can escape to another part of the empire where one will continue to enjoy the same legal and social conditions: for "my country is everywhere, and my laws and my religion are everywhere," inasmuch as the worldwide legal unity of the Roman empire has been joined with the no less worldwide unity of Christianity, so that "I arrive among Christians and Romans as a Christian and a Roman." Payments of tribute, which were once upon a time the humiliating consequence of conquest by Rome as well as an enduring symbol of subjugation, had long since become the fair "price for peace" (5.1–3; quotation from 5.2.1 and 3 as well as 5.1.10).[10] The status of a Roman citizen is in Orosius' conception no longer tied to the city of Rome, but instead to the empire, which he equates with the Christian world. Orosius and every Roman

Christian like him thus becomes a Christian citizen of the world. For Orosius, this is likely the most important advance Rome has made on its path from the hut of Romulus to the Christian universal empire, and it is thus a central element of his argument against adherents of classical religion.

Universal peace as the highest good, which is paired with law, does not come into existence in some random way, but results instead, as does its maintenance, from the will of God and his work: indeed, Orosius' God intervenes again and again according to a fixed principle (*dispensatio, ordinatio*) in the world and its political development, inasmuch as he "replaces kingdoms and ordains the ages" (2.1 and 6.1; quote from 6.1.5).[11] Universal peace comes into existence over a long period of time through the sequence of four universal empires, the last of which, Rome, is the first truly to span the entire world. Orosius, although he is not the first Roman to do so, relies here on the old Near Eastern or Greek concept of a sequence of universal empires, which those who at various times adopt it always cast in different terms. Orosius formulates it as a progressively intensifying development that proceeds according to God's plan (2.1–2; 7.2).[12] Concretely and within the space of a short time Rome came to realize the fourth universal empire with the birth of Jesus and the simultaneous rule of Rome by Augustus (3.8.5–8 with foreshadowing of the end of Book 6/beginning of Book 7; more foreshadowing in 6.1.5–9; cf. especially 6.20–22 and 7.3): Although Orosius knew full well that the former adhered to traditional religion, neither Augustus nor the Christian Constantine I represent for Orosius personalities who act on their own, but they much rather act as instruments of God. Jesus and Augustus serve as the decisive turning point in world history's progress from evil toward the good. Because Orosius connects God's works in a fundamentally causal way to past and present political events, he establishes a theology of history. This theology rests on the conviction that "God is the master of all ages, kingdoms, and places" and that he ordains all things according to his will (6.1.5: see above, this page with note 11; quotation from 7.2.8).[13] Its basic tenet is, as it were, a political God who has, in the Roman empire under monarchical rule, forged his most important tool, a tool that he uses for his purposes.

How, after arriving at this apparently insuperable highpoint, can Orosius traverse the time from Augustus and Jesus to the present? He combines history with the doctrine of original sin to explain subsequent fluctuations in the affairs of the empire as well as the growth of Christianity, which, though steady, was frequently threatened by persecutions in which the Roman empire played a definite role. Original sin leads again and again to setbacks in general conditions which, from now on, are good (6.22.10–11: conclusion of Book 6; cf. 1.; 7.3.3). On the other hand, even an increase in the good is now possible as well, because it was the conversion of the emperor and the empire to Christianity that first allowed Christendom and the empire to become one. The good thus triumphs completely, and evil completely disappears – and we witness paradisiacal conditions before Paradise: "Death has been locked up, because this religion now prevails, and death will not exist at all, when this religion rules alone" (1.*preface*.14; cf. 1.*preface*.13ff.; 7.26ff., especially 7.28ff.).[14] Accordingly, the German threat of recent years must also pleasantly vanish, because their king "who was chosen by the Goths to destroy peace was raised up by God to strengthen peace," and the Germans in general behave as one of them stated to the emperor Honorius: "Enjoy peace with all and receive hostages from all! We fight among ourselves, and are destroyed at our own hands. We conquer on your behalf, which is an abiding gain for your empire, when we die fighting on both sides" (7.43, especially 4ff.; quotations from 10 and 14).[15] The most optimistic historical work of the ancient world ends with these words in a logical application of its theoretical principles. Only a Christian, not a "pagan," was able to conceive and compose such an argument. In light of the current political situation, Orosius may well have aimed to achieve the same thing as Augustine, but, with his paradise on Earth, he presented a profoundly different perspective.

In addition to his own personal experience, Orosius collected and made use of oral testimony from contemporaries for his account of the recent past and current events. The extensive geographical description of the world that Orosius provides before beginning his historical account (see above, p. 231) likely derives from a geographical handbook. For what is by far the largest portion of his work, Orosius consulted numerous and diverse sources in Latin. He follows the Christian chronography of *Jerome* – but not the chronicle of Sulpicius – and the church history of *Rufinus* (see above, Ch. 7.3.1, p. 221; Ch. 7.3.2, pp. 226ff.) as well as, of course, Biblical writings, partly for historical and partly for theological purposes. Orosius' thesis that everything became better in Christian times might go back to a Christian author like Arnobius of Sicca Veneria in North Africa. In his early fourth century defense (or apology) of Christians *Against the Pagans*, Arnobius had argued against any increase in the world's misery as a result of the spread of Christianity. Orosius could have transformed this denial of Christianity's negative influence into a rather stronger assertion of Christianity's postive effects (see above, p. 232). Orosius consciously draws on classically religious authors in large numbers because he can draw on them, as the best witnesses of the calamities of the pre-Christian era, to testify against the traditionally religious authors of his own times (see above, pp. 232f.). This includes such poets as the inescapable Homer (in Latin translation) as well as Vergil, who, as the most famous of great authors, is quoted without mention of his name, and Lucan, among others, and prose authors too, ranging from *Cicero* and *Sallust* (he draws only from the *Jugurtha* and the *Catiline*), to *Livy* and *Tacitus*, to *Justin's* epitome of *Trogus'* historical work, and to the authors of fourth-century abbreviations, especially *Eutropius*.[16] It remains doubtful, however, whether Orosius drew from older works directly or only through later intermediaries or even previous abbreviations of the material. We thus do not know from what source Orosius obtained Cato's date – as opposed to Varro's long-canonical date – for the foundation of Rome. Directly or indirectly, Orosius is, in any event, a witness at the end of the ancient world for much of what, like the majority of the *Histories* of *Tacitus*, exist for us neither in the original nor even in a reworked edition (see above, Ch. 6.1.3, pp. 138f.).

More important for judging his historical work as well as the types and aims of Orosius' argument is, however, his method: *how* he used the sources. Orosius had at his disposal the combined repertoire of the interpretive methods of rhetoric and theology. Unlike almost any other ancient historian, he searches the sources for very specific material that fit his conception. He continuously compares what comes before with what comes after, cause with effect. Biblical events are connected again and again with earthly events that are in the narrower sense historical. In this effort, he is served especially by interpretive strategies common in late antiquity and among early Christians: allegory and typology. The first king of the first universal empire, Ninus, and his contemporary (as established already by *Eusebius* and his successor *Jerome*), the Israelite patriarch Abraham, thus appear in a link central to Orosius' theology of history, as the commencement and convenant that connect Augustus, the first emperor of the fourth and therefore final universal empire, with the birth of Jesus under his rule as the completion and fulfillment (7.2.13–14; see above, Ch. 7.3.2, pp. 223f.). Because certain numbers have special meaning in the Judeo-Christian tradition, historical events and circumstances are aligned with them. Orosius provides a bold compilation for the number seven, which, he argues, has influenced all essential events involving the four universal empires, and thus the entire course of world history (7.2.9–15). In light of all this, we might well ask ourselves what Orosius is more likely to have been: a theologizing historical writer or an historicizing theologian?

We can find no trace of any influence that the *Historiae adversum paganos* may have had in the age of its author, but by the sixth century the work was frequently cited.[17] The work had an astonishingly strong impact on a Christian as well as on an Islamic ruler, who commissioned translations into respectively Old English (in the ninth century) and Arabic (in the tenth century in Spain). The work exerted its principal influence, however, on authors belonging to the clerical order, especially non-Romans, for whom its synthesis of *Romanitas* and *Christianitas* proved convenient. As examples, we may cite: *Venerable Bede* (672/3–735, England: *Chronica* and *Historia ecclesiastica*), *Paul the Deacon* (circa 720–799, Lombardy in North Italy: *Historia Romana*), *Freculphus* (first half of the ninth century, originally from southern Germany[?], resident in Lisieux in Normandy: *Chronica* to the death of Gregory the Great), and *Otto of Freising* (1111/15–1158, Freising, Germany: *Chronica sive Historia de duabus civitatibus*). Otto belonged to the high nobility of the House of Babenberg, and was the uncle of the emperor Frederick I Barbarossa. In his universal chronicle, Otto combined Augustine's doctrine of two states with Orosius' theology of history, especially his doctrine of the succession of four empires, and he applied the resulting amalgam to recent history. He makes the *imperium Christianum* of Charlemagne and the rule of the German kings and emperors who proceeded from him the fourth and final universal (or at least great) empire. This fourth empire continues to improve the reciprocal relations of spiritual with earthly power, and thus progressively realizes the City of God. Long after his own day, Orosius made possible and perhaps even brought into existence, the historical and theological foundation of the *Sacrum Imperium Romanum Teutonicorum* ("The Holy Roman Empire of the German Nation") whose validity would remain undisputed for centuries. Decisive impact of this sort, which we also see reflected in the astonishingly large number of surviving medieval manuscripts of the *Historiae adversum paganos*, was likely granted to no other Roman historian.

7.3.4 Procopius of Caesarea: the history of current events in transition from Rome to Byzantium

Priscus of Panium (Thrace) wrote a history of recent (or current) events corresponding approximately to the years 433–471. Just before and around the year 500, *Malchus* of Philadelphia did the same for the years 473–480 or perhaps for a much longer period beginning already with

Constantine I (*FHG* 4.69, 5.24, and 4.111). Both works bear titles that allude to, and contents that are concerned with, *Byzantium*. They well illustrate how, despite their continuing formal legal unity, the two halves of the empire were drifting apart. Neither author evinces especially close ties to Christianity. We cannot, therefore, especially in the case of Priscus, beyond doubt classify them under the rubric of "Christian historiography." The following work, however, presents a very different case. In the second part of the so-called *Excerpta Valesiana*, we find a Christian Latin chronicle-like history composed in the sixth century that was directed not only against the Goths, but also against Arians, whose doctrines the Goths adopted after their conversion, and it focused on Italy from 474 to 526, i.e., it focused especially on the reigns of the Germanic kings Odoacer (476–493) and Theodoric (to 526).

Procopius of Maritime Caesarea (Palestine) composed several historical works, in which he treated the re-conquest of Italy from the intervening reign of the Ostrogoths by Justinian (527–565), emperor of the eastern half of the still existent Roman empire, as well as other wars, some of which aimed at the re-conquest of additional parts of the empire and some of which were of a rather more defensive nature. He also wrote histories of current events within the empire. Procopius (490/507–after 553) was educated in the law, and subsequently occupied administrative posts in keeping with his training. At least a portion of the years of his historiographical activity (after 540) were spent in the capital and imperial seat of Constantinople. From 527 to 540 he was, however, actively engaged as an adviser (*consilarius*) to the general Belisarius. He accompanied him on various military campaigns in the Near East against the Persians, in North Africa against the Vandals, and in Italy against the Ostrogoths. From within Belisarius' inner circle, Procopius bore witness to the vicissitudes of Belisarius' career, which swung between extreme highs and lows, depending on the emperor's volatile favor or disfavor. All these things serve as the subjects of Procopius' historical writing, and they also by and large determine his point of view.

Procopius' *History of the Wars* (*Hyper tôn polemôn*) contains eight books. Books 1–7 are, like Appian's *Roman History*, organized by theaters of war (see above, Ch. 6.2.2, p. 164). Simultaneous events in the capital are inserted into the military accounts (e.g., 1.23–25: the Nika uprising in AD 532; 2.22f.: the epidemic in Constantinople in 542). Books 1–2 treat the Persians and the East, Books 3–4 the Vandals and North Africa, Books 5–7 the Ostrogoths and Italy. Book 8 (which is also counted as Book 4 of the Gothic wars) was written subsequently by Procopius in order to bring events in the various theaters up to date

(8.1.1–2): Chapters 1–16 treat affairs in the East, Chapter 17 North Africa, and Chapters 18–35 Italy until the final defeat of the Ostrogoths in AD 553. Procopius seeks with this change in strategy to solve the problem that faces every author who writes about recent events: while he conducts his research and writes, time continues its course, and he loses his connection to the present, which has meanwhile advanced into the future and away from the point that originally served as the goal of his account. In the main section of his account (Books 1–7), Procopius always introduces the wars with a short pre-history of the relevant conflicts. For example, for the Gothic wars, he goes back to AD 476, and includes the Visigoths (Book 5), and, after the conclusion of the war, Procopius proceeds further in the direction of the present, so that, in connection with North Africa, after the defeat of the Vandals in AD 533, he brings his report down to the year 548 (4.10–28). Central to Procopius' account, however, are the wars themselves with their military and political activities.

If this concentration on the history of wars leads to the suspicion that *Thucydides* serves here as a model, other indications demonstrate that this is indeed the case. Procopius' account of the "plague" (2.22f.) is astonishingly similar to Thucydides' description in his *History of the Peloponnesian War* (2.47ff.). Procopius at first, in Books 1–4, dates according to the year of the emperor's reign, but, in Books 5–8, he dates events according to the year of the war. Although we can derive the former method from the other "classic" among the Greek historians, *Herodotus*, with the latter method, he again imitates Thucydides. Procopius' numerous geographical, ethnographical, and mythological excursuses remind us most of Herodotus. Most reminiscent of Thucydides, however, is his technique of allowing others to express their own opinion through speeches and letters. Linguistically too, in diction, in phrases, and in formulas, Procopius repeatedly draws from Thucydides and Herodotus, although we find recognizable borrowings from other early historians as well, including, for example, Xenophon, Diodorus, and Arrian. If we examine Procopius' possible connections to authors writing only a generation before him, such as *Priscus* and *Malchus* (see above, pp. 237f.), who treated the periods immediately before those Procopius wrote about, and who, like Procopius, resemble earlier authors in language and style, we discover that these connections pale in comparison with Procopius' connections to older Greek historiography. Nevertheless, Procopius departs from his model *Thucydides*, who is more important to him than any other, to the extent that he has an ever-present hero, the general Belisarius, with whose first great victory at Daras in AD 530 he begins his account of recent events (1.13ff.). But Procopius was hardly alone in turning back to ancient models and to the glorious beginnings of Greek historiography. We find this same phenomenon in late antique and in Byzantine literature more generally. On the other hand, Procopius' *History of the Wars of Justinian* would also exert an influence beyond the ancient world, at least to the extent that Rome's adversaries were Germanic. Without Procopius' *Wars of the Vandals* and *Wars of the Goths*, the study of Germanic migrations could hardly have been established as an independent academic subject in nineteenth-century Germany.

Procopius' continuous stylistic dependence on classically religious authors results in his work's failure to borrow language from the Bible or to contain echoes of it. In this, his work is like that of the traditionally religious *Zosimus* (see above, Ch. 7.1, pp. 204f.), although, in the case of Zosimus, this is, of course, hardly surprising. On the other hand, his continuous forays into ancient historiographical works lead to the adoption of some concepts from classical religion, above all, their god of fate, Tyche. This sort of thing is, to be sure, anchored in secure Christian fashion in their unitary God (8.12.34; which, verbatim, is identical with *Anecdota* 4.44). Indeed, in spite of all his literary flirtation with traditional religion, Procopius is, and remains, a Christian within the framework that the customary faith of his day established, especially in regard to the unity of faith, emperor, and Christendom (see above, Ch. 7.3, pp. 218f.). From this point forward, the path leads to Byzantine historiography in both subject matter and its ideological basis, a place where we find Procopius too in terms of language and style.

Among Procopius' writings on contemporary domestic events, we find works devoted to the reigning emperor Justinian and his wife Theodora as well as to his great public buildings, above all the churches that Justinian erected in various places, which, beginning with the Hagia Sophia in Constantinople, express his ideology of empire and imperial rule. Procopius wrote *On Buildings* (*Perí ktismatôn*) late in his career in six books organized according to geography. The work is, we presume, an encomium of Justinian and his Caesaropapism, and one that Procopius composed, again we presume, at the request of the emperor (cf., e.g., 1.3.1). Criticism of the discrepancy between the conception of a Christian empire and Justinian's means of bringing it about and making it manifest or, more generally, criticism of the religious politics of this headstrong and high-handed emperor is perceptible only subliminally. According to the express desire of its author, we should classify this work, despite its choice of a topic found nowhere else in ancient literature, as *historical writing* (1.1.1ff.). Procopius did indeed recognize the tremendous political importance that can manifest itself in public buildings.

As a counterpoint to the *Buildings*, we find the *Anecdota* (also known as *The Secret History*), which acquired this title only later, because, not without reason, the work was intentionally published only long after the death its author (1.1ff.). It portrays not only Belisarius and his wife, but even more so Justinian and Theodora, viz., the emperor and empress, in extremely negative terms. The emperor is even demonized, which means, according to the theology current at the time, that he has been possessed by an evil spirit (demon), and works in collusion with the Antichrist. The textual transmission of this little work is obscure, likely as a result of its publication separately from Procopius' other historical accounts. It serves to reveal the atmosphere of the palace and its lethal effect on the development of otherwise upright persons as well as the process by which the decisions of high politics came about. It thus serves, as its author intended, as a supplement to his *History of the Wars of Justinian*. More generally, with its delayed publication and in combination with its content, the *Anecdota* reveal some phenomena specific to historians of recent history and current events under autocratic conditions. These phenomena include: the conflicted nature of praise for contemporary rulers and other leading personalities (something that was in Procopius immediately perceptible, although elsewhere this was not the case); the danger that existed for those who criticized present conditions or the persons putting their stamp on them; the desire, either immediately in secret or as soon as possible after the demise of the hated ruler, to tear him to pieces publicly – this latter phenomenon was, of course, already common in the early imperial period (see above, Ch. 6. pp. 125f.); and, to a certain extent, as a result of this, the insincerity that under such conditions the historian of current events or even the commentator on current affairs would adopt. And it is this insincerity that we are perhaps too quick to stigmatize as opportunism.

At the end of the ancient world stands the malicious criticism of a ruler in the *Anecdota* of Procopius. It does not, of course, question the basic premises of the prevailing monarchical constitution that had with the conversion of the emperor to Christianity become inviolable for Rome and for the empire. Beyond personal invective, it insists, moreover, on the "senatorial" point of view, demanding that the emperor exercise consideration for the privileges of rank, and, as a result of this, that he refrain from introducing any innovations into the social order. Procopius adopts an attitude that, while not in details, nonetheless in principle, is as ancient as the Roman empire itself and that always corresponds in its various articulations to the contemporary stage of the imperial system's development (see above, Ch. 6.1, pp. 127ff.; Ch. 6.1.3, pp. 140ff.; Ch. 6.5.2, pp. 192ff.). The criticism that Procopius directs toward the conduct of an individual emperor is, to be sure, not identical with the fundamental rejection of monarchy that we find in the *Historia Nea* of *Zosimus*, who just a generation earlier was the last unambiguous adherent of traditional religion among ancient historical writers (see above, Ch. 7.1, pp. 205ff.). Both their attitudes do, however, share at least some points of contact with each other. There was in particular on both sides of the divide between Christians and adherents of traditional religion still an object of common and positive interest, and even common effort and concern: Rome itself or the "idea of Rome," and, to put it in completely concrete terms, the special connection between the Roman state and the senatorial or civil elite who, in all events, had been educated in literary culture. Indeed, it was to this class, whether they wrote in Latin or Greek, that most historical writers belonged until the end of the ancient world.

8

Some Basic Principles of Ancient Historical Thought

Writing history did not mean simply *narrating* a story, and even simple narration did not imply that the author refrained from *interpretation*. In the narrative itself it was possible to insert quite a bit of interpretation. For this reason, ancient historiography, which was acutely aware of literary form, used the arrangement of material, i.e., composition, as a preferred means of historical interpretation (for example, in Livy, above, Ch. 5.1, pp. 104f.). Some ancient historians altered the course of historical events through the contraction or extension of time or even by reversing the sequence of actions and events in such a way that it would negate the absolute validity of a fundamental concept of historical causality based on chronology (*post quod, ergo propter quod:* "after this, therefore because of it;" see, for example, Sallust: above, Ch. 4.5.1, pp. 88f.). All of these interpretive interventions (manipulations in the worst case) did nothing, however, to alter the simple model to which ancient historiography remained forever bound: the causation of historical actions lay in *personal morality.* When this no longer sufficed or seemed to suffice, writers would seldom make use of technical or material causes in either a narrower or wider sense, but instead almost always looked to the gods or to fate or to chance. (Chance and fate could, of course, also be reckoned as gods in their own right, although they did not have to be.) Behind this practice stood their inability (it was for them perhaps impossible) to depart from the common intellectual perspectives of their time and to question the basic principles of historical thought and, consequently, to replace those concepts with others.

Roman Historiography: An Introduction to its Basic Aspects and Development, First Edition. Andreas Mehl.
© 2014 Hans-Friedrich Mueller. Published 2014 by Blackwell Publishing Ltd.

The historiographical explanations we take up in this chapter do not take much aim at the basic principles of Roman (and Greek) historiography: such concepts as patriotism, definite ethical, legal, or religious views or – what is especially important for Roman historiography – the attitude toward Rome as a city and as an empire and toward the emperors, to all of which we apply the label "worldview" or "ideology." We have already had something to say about these topics in our discussions of individual authors and in the introductory chapter to this book (see above, Ch. 1.2, pp. 12ff.; Ch. 1.3.1, pp. 18ff.). We wish instead to observe and discuss the basic abstract principles that lie behind each constituent element of ideology (or ideologeme). In other words, we must concern ourselves with those *principles* which the ancient world itself imagined and generally conceived of as determining the *course of history*. As a consequence, we will see that, in this regard, we can hardly perceive differences between Greek historical thought (especially before the era of Roman domination of the Mediterranean) and Roman historical thought. Nor is it necessary to work out these different points of view to the extent that most accounts of Roman history derive from the long period of Rome's "universal rule" in general and from Rome's imperial period in particular. It is much more important here to study the differences between Christian and classically religious historiography. We must realize from the start, however, that differences in worldviews, even diametrically opposed views, do not necessarily derive from different principles of thought.

During the age of the Greek or Athenian Enlightenment and without any moralizing pathos whatsoever, Thucydides excluded the possibility of fundamental changes in human conduct, thereby vouchsafing for the future the unrestricted validity of the instruction that he provided in his historical account (*Peloponnesian War* 1.22.4). This position had consequences even for Thucydides himself. When in his outline of Greek history from earliest times to the Persian Wars, the so-called "Archaeology," he described long-term changes, he understood them as purely quantitative, and he failed to derive from them any basic changes in the conduct of human beings or even changes to human nature (1.2–20). And when he detects changes in the conduct of Greeks within what is a relatively short span of time, the space of a few years of the Peloponnesian War, in extraordinary situations like the Athenian "plague" and the civil war on Corcyra (Corfu), he could only understand them as changes determined by the specific situation, and thus reversible, if the unusual circumstances disappeared, and consequently as changes that were not fundamental (2.47ff.; 3.70ff.). The basic principles that govern personal conduct, and these include among them moral principles as well, are thus for Thucydides without exception intrinsic to all human beings, and they are not subject to any historical changes whatsoever.

The constituent moral concepts according to which Greek and Roman historical writers evaluated personal conduct changed, of course, over time, but even in the wake of Christian conversion they did not change so much that anyone would ever find the application of presently prevailing (and thus unquestioned) ethical norms to the distant past as somehow problematic, let alone inappropriate. On the contrary, one assumed rather (no differently from Thucydides) that there existed a permanent equivalence between what was true once upon a time and what was the case today, and generally passed over this presumption in silence. From time to time, however, an author would explicitly assert that ancient and contemporary morality were identical. In classically religious times, one proceeded from the premise that the customs and codes handed down from the "good old days" retained their validity in any given present day. If one then detected differences in the present, these would be understood as deviations from a norm that had been established, justified, and rendered inviolable by its antiquity. These deviations consequently led in turn to a "world out of joint." The highest ethical task of someone interested in the past, and thus the historical writer in particular, was to inspire contemporaries and future generations to maintain forever, or return to, the codes of conduct established in earlier times. This encouraged, and even brought about, the idea that history was a collection of *exempla* and that the construction of historical accounts served to crystallize what should prevail in the present both positively through normative examples of actions and conduct and negatively through non-normative examples (see above, Ch. 1.3.1, p. 20; Ch. 6.6, pp. 197f.). It is worth noting that every attitude or action handed down as exemplary had at some point been raised up as an *exemplum*, thereby establishing a precedent for something new, but this view of the *exemplum* was an extremely rare exception vis-à-vis its conception as a predetermined norm, according to which – so it seemed – human affairs were irrevocably ordained.[1]

The unquestioned assumption that unchanging values – or, to put it in more modern terms, "anthropological constants" – determined the course of actions and affairs necessarily led to the result that ancient reconstructions of the past portrayed a "still picture that lacked the dimension of depth" (Timpe [Bibl. §3: Fabius] p. 967), because for Greeks as well as Romans the past was simply a template for the present and the present was merely repetition of the past. It seems, however, to contradict this picture that in the ancient world changes took place in the affairs of human beings – in government and politics as well as in the elementary spheres of life and lifestyle, in material civilization, and in the development of art and knowledge – and that changes of these sorts were often noticed. Even so, one did not view all the changes affecting human beings in a way that would have compelled the drawing of logical consequences from them regarding the morality of personal conduct. On the contrary, in order to guarantee a dependable social order, it was considered indispensable that codes of personal conduct would have to remain constant – especially when human beings inhabited a world whose circumstances had changed. The moral views of ancient historians feasted with monotonous uniformity over the course of many centuries on this fundamental conviction.

In the ancient world, however, one naturally had to recognize that in the course of time changes would occur in human conditions. The concept of gradual moral and material decadence was especially widespread, and may be traced – among the Greeks – back in the first instance to the archaic poet Hesiod's doctrine of the "world's four ages." As he describes it, humanity has descended by way of intermediary stages from a "golden age" to an "iron age" (*Works and Days* 106–200). Historical writers, however, especially Roman writers, were generally unwilling to take into account many small changes over short periods of time that could over a long stretch of time cumulatively have a significant impact. They were rather inclined, when they recognized a change as such, to describe it as a single fundamental volte-face that reversed a situation from what it was into its opposite. This idea was combined with another fundamental assumption that – at least in the sphere of morality – nothing became better, but everything grew worse, that change therefore tended toward decadence (see above), and that a drastic change was a catastrophe. A line of thought completely beholden to constancy – we could also call it stagnation – was therefore unable to discern gradual development as such, but instead perceived it as a standstill. This condition, when facts on the ground all too clearly contradicted the fiction of a steady state, would end in an eruption that – seemingly, and, again seemingly, quite suddenly – brought about a completely new situation.

Whereas we are inclined to perceive the results of evolution, they saw sudden drastic changes in social relations. (To put this in more modern terms, we could most readily express the idea with the word "revolution," were it not the case that, in light of the word's other basic connotations in the modern conception of revolution, we would thereby provoke misunderstandings.) Today we express this concept as the so-called *turning point* (see above, Ch. 3.2.2, pp. 56f.; Ch. 4.5.1, pp. 91ff.;

Ch. 6.1.1, pp. 131f.; Ch. 6.1.3, pp. 146f.). The fact that this concept was so often employed to describe changes in conditions may serve as the clearest indication of just how tied ancient thinkers were to the idea that things remained the same, and nevertheless suspected, even if they did not know or wish to know, that history never comes to a standstill.[2] Violating the logic inherent in the concept of a "turning point," some authors, and Sallust most clearly in this regard, arrayed several drastic changes in conditions one after the other (see above, Ch. 4.5.1, pp. 91f.). This could even pass over into a description of phased change, especially gradual deterioration of the sort that conspicuously characterizes Tacitus' portrait of Tiberius, but even so it remained obligated to the concept of a turning point (see above, Ch. 6.1.3, pp. 146f.). One therefore sensed, or even detected, how problematic it was to have a long standstill in development end in the sudden release of built-up tension. Nevertheless, pre-Christian and non-Christian historiography failed to depart from this conception of historical processes. Inasmuch as Orosius allowed that with Jesus and Augustus human affairs became fundamentally and durably better than they had ever been before, he too similarly interpreted history in terms of a turning point (see above, Ch. 7.3.3, pp. 234f.). New in all this was only that in this instance the volte-face led from a negative to a positive state of affairs. The idea that historical change results from a long period of stagnation that comes to an abrupt end in a sudden volte-face, which we call a "turning point," thus applies to a portion of early Christian historiography as well. The principle of thought is thus identical for authors like Sallust and Orosius. Christian historiography changed only the manner of its application, or, more precisely, its aim, but it did not succeed in replacing it with a different principle.

We may observe that in general two fundamentally different assumptions confront each other regarding the course of world history. One is non-linear, inasmuch as history is open-ended, and in no way at all aims at an "end of history." The other conception is linear, insofar as it presumes that history is indeed directed toward a pre-determined goal. Classically religious antiquity took the former view in its effort to preserve what was worthy of remembering. It did this intuitively in pre-Christian times, without thereby taking a position apropos the teleological alternative and without, in fact, being aware that an alternative even existed. For a goal-oriented conception of history, we turn to Christianity, which interpreted history as the course of world events from the fall of the first human beings from grace as the result of sin through well-defined intermediary starting and end-points en route to the end of the world and the paradise that would ensue as its final salvation, which could itself, according to some views, be anticipated to some extent already on Earth (see above, Ch. 7.3, pp. 217f.; Ch. 7.3.3, p. 235). The relationship between the past and present as well as between the present and the future is necessarily completely different, in fact, contradictory, in both views of history. In the non-linear conception, the difference between past and present, present and future, can be kept as small as one likes, and the good in its most well-articulated form may lie not in the present, but will likely instead be found somewhere in the past, and because in principle the possibility exists for past, present, and future to be similar, the good may even some day turn up – again. On the other hand, in the linear view of history, the difference not only between once upon a time and now, but also between now and some time in the future, must be as large as possible, inasmuch as the starting and end points of world events should differ significantly from each other, because this conception of history in fact acquires its dynamic force from the tension between them. And it is precisely this force that the non-linear view of history lacks. The way Christianity comes to terms with history, to the extent that it does not adopt classically religious elements, thus fundamentally contradicts classical religion's linking of past and present. Classical religion adheres to a static view, to constancy, and casts its gaze overwhelmingly toward the past, while Christianity, confiding in the future, adheres to the idea of progress. These views are mutually exclusive. At least this is how it seems.

If, however, we assign full credit for first conceiving of a teleological course of world history to the Christians, we do not grasp the full story of ancient historiography. Indeed, the idea that history moves toward a specific goal took root among adherents of classical religion too. We speak here of the idea of Rome. When, in the middle of the second century BC, the Greek historian Polybius adopts the idea that the politics of all states in the Mediterranean were "closely linked" just before his lifetime, i.e., around 220 BC, and that Rome in the little more than fifty ensuing years had evolved from supremacy in Italy to supremacy in the Mediterranean, becoming thereby a world empire, then he demonstrates with this thinking a conception of teleological development (the Greek words he uses for the idea of "close interweaving" συμπλέκεσθαι and συμπλοκή Polybius 1.3.3–4 and 1.4.11; cf. 1.1.1–3.6; 6.2.2–3). Rome as a universal empire is here *the* goal of world history, after which some further purpose can hardly reveal itself. Polybius, however, does not state this explicitly, inasmuch as he, like most other ancient historians, was not primarily teleological in his thinking, but instead thought more in terms of cyclical patterns in history's course of events. To this extent then, we must leave the question open whether for Polybius world history culminated in Rome and whether for him there was ever any completion at all in world history. In light of Polybius' enthusiasm for Rome's relentless path to world domination, a contemporary especially could easily have missed this uncertainty. But further expansion of Rome's universal empire and concrete experiences with it succeeded in any event in creating the appearance of its infinite expanse in both time and space (compare above, Ch. 5.2, pp. 110f.). And Augustan ideology made its own fully intentional contributions to this view of an "empire without end" (*imperium sine fine*: Vergil *Aeneid* 1.279).

A problem always arises when history is thought of as culminating, and thus reaching its ultimate goal, on Earth:[3] how do we take into account subsequent events, especially those of the sort that may or must lead us to conclude that the final endpoint we thought we had reached may once again slip away? We need merely to consider here how the ideology and the propaganda of the Roman emperors as well as the surviving portion of Roman historical writing that displayed unreserved loyalty toward the emperor (granted, it is a tiny portion) clung to the fiction that, once the empire was established, it was *for this very reason* established forever as an "empire without limits," and were never able to define another goal or purpose. To be sure, neither did that segment of historiography critical of the emperors (and which failed to see the culmination of history in the Roman empire of the Caesars) call on its readers to lift up their gaze toward "new shores," because this historiography too could discern no development beyond the realities of empire and imperial rule that its authors had experienced, and, to some extent, suffered under. Nevertheless, there was an exception, but the reach of its thought was rather limited, and it remained moreover without effect. For the late antique author Zosimus, an adherent of classical religion, who saw himself as the mirror image of Polybius, the breakdown of the Roman empire – as a consequence of its conversion from its ancestral religion to Christianity – was indeed an undesirable and terrible occurrence, but in principle no less possible an event than Rome's rise to universal rule (see above, Ch. 7.1, pp. 205f.). Rome's downfall could – but did not have to – result in a development that led to the rise of a new universal empire on a different ethnic and administrative basis. But this latter possibility lay beyond the interest or perhaps even the imagination of the "Roman" Zosimus.

Among their own "ideological" limitations, we find that Christians held two contradictory views regarding the Roman empire. One interpreted earthly history teleologically, while the other decidedly did not. To the extent that Rome's development, like all political history, appeared irrelevant to Christians for the final goal of achieving salvation, they had no need for Rome's eternity on Earth (Sulpicius Severus: see above, Ch. 7.3.2, pp. 226f.; Augustine: Ch. 7.3.3, pp. 230f.). In this view, the Roman empire did not represent the aim of history, neither as an anticipatory or temporary goal, and certainly not as its ultimate purpose, and the question (to the extent that anyone asked it at all) of what might come after Rome was an open one that required no definite answer. On the other hand, to the extent that Christians combined Rome as the final universal empire with the history of salvation after the birth of Jesus, Rome's universal empire had to exist until the end of the world, that is, until the arrival of the Antichrist. The Roman empire could thus, in principle (even though this is what looked increasingly likely in the situation confronting them around AD 400) *not* be replaced by another universal empire, for example, one dominated by Germanic peoples. On the contrary, these people were destined to strengthen Rome's universal rule and contribute to its continued existence (Orosius: see above, Ch. 7.3.3, p. 235). This peculiar application of the principle of teleological thinking – not the principle itself – forbade some new state of affairs from emerging after the Roman empire.

For a segment of Christians, just as it was for a segment of adherents of traditional religions, the accomplished purpose of Roman world rule was its permanent state, and for both the traditionally religious and Christians the very real tribulations of the Roman empire soon created problems of interpretation that were tackled in two ways, but the solution they offered was merely specious. When confronted with events and developments that did not fit the conceptual framework, one could either fail to see them or make them fit through reinterpretation. Imperial propaganda made use of both approaches as did those who composed encomiums of emperors (panegyric), taking as they did their subject matter and views from that propaganda. Orosius, the Christian enthusiast for Rome, made use of the second approach (see above). In addition to an attitude that expected no basic or fundamental changes to occur in political affairs or, if they did, that these changes would be for the worse, there existed both among adherents of classical religion and among Christians (for the latter only after they identified themselves with the Roman empire) an optimism for the future and for the course of Rome's political history. Neither view resulted from a fundamental division between Christians and adherents of classical religion, but instead basic attitudes, that indeed permitted, but did not compel, diametrically opposed assessments of Rome. The adherent of classical religion could choose between a goal-oriented and an open-ended course to historical events. This choice was not available to Christians, but, as the views of Augustine, on the one hand, and of Orosius, on the other, demonstrate, they were free to choose whether or not they made political history an element of their history of human salvation, and they were thus at least free to decide whether they interpreted political history as teleological or not.

The themes of this concluding chapter have been causality and some of the patterns for the course of history's events that were employed as basic principles for interpreting history. We have observed how ancient historical thought and by means of it the interpretation of concrete historical contexts were, and remained, tied to certain basic concepts of how history ran its course, and how, on this level, these ancient concepts were not replaced by new ones, even with the transition from the classically religious to the Christian era of antiquity. We must therefore proceed, at least for the centuries of Rome's "world rule," not from the idea that there was an evolution in ancient historical thinking, but instead from a permanent store of basic principles, that permitted diverse, even opposing, interpretations of history, and that were therefore employed by all, adherents of traditional religions and Christians alike. If we were to assume that a fundamental change took place in how the ancient world interpreted history, we would be deceived.

The historical writing of the ancient world and of Rome in particular – just as for historiography in general – was far more than, and completely different from, the accumulation of true or presumed facts and the more or less accurate recapitulation of documentary sources and literary models. As we established at the beginning of this book, historiography is truly the mirror that reflects the thought of the present through the application of the principles of interpretation upon a distant or nearer past. And the basic principles of Roman historiography, at least in that era of the ancient world, when Rome exercised its political dominance, proved astonishingly permanent.

Chronology: Select Dates in the Political History of Rome

after circa 270 BC	Rome is the dominant power in the Italian peninsula.
264–241	First Punic War (Rome–Carthage): Rome acquires Sicily and Sardinia in 238, which together in 227 become the first Roman provinces.
218–201	Second Punic War: Rome acquires Spain (two provinces) and becomes the dominant power in the western Mediterranean.
200–133	Rome makes repeated interventions militarily and diplomatically in Macedonia, Greece, and Asia Minor.
180	Prerequisites for a career in public office are established in law (*cursus honorum*).
149–146	Third Punic War: Carthage is destroyed.
148	*Macedonia* and, in 133, *Asia* become provinces.
133–30	Roman civil wars: 133–121: the Gracchi attempt reforms; 107–100: Marius is consul on six occasions; 91–88: war of the Italians against Rome; from 88: civil war of the Marians and Sullans; 82–79: Sulla is dictator; 77–62: extraordinary commands of Pompey (Syria becomes a province); 58–51: Caesar is governor of Gaul where he wages wars (Gaul becomes a province); 49–45: civil war between Caesarians and Pompeians (or the majority of the Senate); 44: Caesar, as dictator, is assassinated; 44–30: resumption of the civil wars (Egypt becomes a province); from 30: Caesar (Octavian) is sole ruler.

Roman Historiography: An Introduction to its Basic Aspects and Development, First Edition. Andreas Mehl.
© 2014 Hans-Friedrich Mueller. Published 2014 by Blackwell Publishing Ltd.

from 27   Establishment of the Principate (imperial rule) as a new system of government: Caesar (Octavian) receives the honorary name *Augustus* in 27 and through the exercise of the plenary powers of diverse offices is *princeps* until his death. Among others, additional provinces are established in the Alpine region as well as east and north of the Alps, but Germany between the Rhine and Elbe is lost through the defeat of Varus in AD 9.

AD 14   First transition of the position and power of the *princeps* to a successor (from Augustus to Tiberius), and thus the establishment of the Principate (imperial rule) on a permanent basis.

14–68   Julio-Claudian Dynasty: from 43: Romans advance into Britain (which becomes a province); 66–70: Jewish revolt and its suppression.

69–96   After the struggle for power of four emperors and claimants to the throne (69), the Flavian dynasty is established: from 82/90, two Germanic provinces are established along the Rhine.

96–192   So-called adoptive emperors: under Trajan (98–117), Dacia becomes a province; Marcus Aurelius (161–180) wages successful wars in the East against the Parthians, but in the North he wages defensive wars against invading Germanic peoples (Marcomanni and Quadi).

193–235   After the struggle for power of five emperors and claimants to the throne (193–197), the Severan dynasty is established: public life is militarized; on the other hand, in 212, citizenship is extended to all free inhabitants of the Roman empire.

227   Replacement of the Parthian Arsacids by the Persian Sassanids.

235–284   Era of soldier emperors with rapid change in emperors and numerous usurpers; in 250, the first empire-wide persecution of Christians; from 250, loss or abandonment of provinces (Germania, Dacia).

284–337   Reorganization of the Roman empire, especially under Diocletian (284–305) and Constantine I (306–337).

from 313   After the last great persecution (303–306/311), explicit toleration of Christians (311/313) is granted, and soon thereafter, under Constantine I, equality of rights with, and preference to, adherents of traditional Roman religion.

378	Threat from Germanic peoples; this becomes especially clear with the Roman defeat by Visigoths at Adrianople.
from 380/392	Under Theodosius I (379–395), Catholic Christianity becomes the only legal religion.
395	After the death of Theodosius I, there are two emperors with two administrations in Milan (later Ravenna) and Constantinople.
410	Visigoths sack the City of Rome; in the fifth century, territories outside Italy in the western half of the empire are lost to Franks and other Germanic peoples.
476	The western emperor is replaced by the Germanic Odoacer; from 493: Ostrogothic rule in Italy under Theodoric.
527–565	Justinian I is emperor, who, from his base in Constantinople, for a short time partially restores the Roman empire in the West.

Notes

Introduction: The Importance of Ancient Historiography and the Purpose of this Book

1 Chassignet's practice is peculiar insofar as authors are not consecutively numbered in the section of *AR* where their fragments appear on pages numbered with Arabic numerals, although these authors have been assigned ordinal numbers in the section of the work where (on pages numbered with Roman numerals) we find Chassignet's own accounts of the authors: e.g., Fabius Pictor = 1. Then again, the *Almanacs of the Priests (Annales pontificum)*, which are placed first, do not receive an ordinal number.

1 Ancient Literature and Roman Historiography

1 In the recent past and in the present too, some authors or works have enjoyed success in the literary world, despite the emphasis in the historical disciplines within the academy on exclusively scientific approaches (cf. "the *science* of history"). In 1902, Theodor Mommsen won the Nobel Prize for Literature for his *Römische Geschichte* (*Roman History*). Especially outside German-speaking areas, it is sometimes considered an admirable aim to write an historical work that not only adheres to academic and scientific standards, but also to aesthetic ones, including literary criteria.

2 These statements are not contradicted by the fact that the first (partly) surviving work of Latin literature, the epic *Odusia* of Livius Andronicus, is connected thematically with "Homer," and thus the beginning of Greek literature. The epics ascribed to Homer represented for Greeks of *all* epochs

Roman Historiography: An Introduction to its Basic Aspects and Development,
First Edition. Andreas Mehl.
© 2014 Hans-Friedrich Mueller. Published 2014 by Blackwell Publishing Ltd.

the fundamental basis par excellence of aesthetic and ethical education. "Homer" was thus a time-transcending phenomenon throughout antiquity. In general, early Latin epic adhered above all to the forms that Hellenistic Greek poetry, which was approximately contemporary, likewise observed in this genre.

3   Thucydides' practice of reporting a war according to the consecutive years of its duration (specifically, the Peloponnesian War from 431 BC) failed to gain acceptance, although there were a few exceptions such as Caesar's *Commentarii* (which, we hasten to add, should themselves not simply be classified as "historical writing" without further consideration; see below, Ch. 4.2.2, pp. 72ff.). Greek chronography limited itself to local histories, and became concerned with chronicling universal history only when confronted with Roman rule (for this latter development, see below, Ch. 5.2.4, p. 119).

4   Flach [Bibl. §1.3] touches on some Greek-language historians of the Roman imperial period, and treats only one of them in detail: Cassius Dio and his Roman history (pp. 260–271). Rüpke [Bibl. §1.4] reviews various imperial Greek historical writers in a very short chapter (pp. 163–169), but he does so without due attention to their place in the development of ancient literary forms and the genres of ancient historiographical literature. The present book with the methodology adopted here supplements the work of Klaus Meister [Bibl. §1.3] whose book on "Greek Historiography from its Beginnings to the End of Hellenism" appeared in 1990. The last historian whose work fits his theme is Diodorus (whom he treats on pp. 171ff.; this book treats him below, Ch. 5.2.1, pp. 110f.). Please note that Meister concludes his account with the end of *political* Hellenism. Hellenism as both a *cultural* and a *literary* phenomenon outlasted the absorption of Hellenistic states into the empires of the Romans and Parthians, and extended well into Rome's imperial period.

5   The visual arts were not represented by the Muses. According to ancient conceptions, the visual arts smacked too much of manual labor.

6   Historical works that may be characterized as "dramatic" or "tragic" (this especially) or "mimetic" and "sensation(al)" (both terms used by Meister [Bibl. §1.3] pp. 99f.) are often traced back by many scholars to the influence of the Greek author Duris of Samos (circa 330–280 BC; *FGrH* 76). But we find this sort of historiography already in the works of Greek historical writers of earlier periods, and we can ascertain this at any time in the work of Herodotus. We should thus view the Duris' achievement merely as the theoretical refinement of this sort of historical writing, from which his more general practice as an historiographer, at least to some extent, actually deviated (cf. Lendle [Bibl. §1.3] pp. 181–189, especially p. 187, and Meister [Bibl. §1.3], pp. 95–100, especially pp. 98ff.).

7   Instances of this threefold division begin with the young Cicero (*De inventione* 1.27) and an unknown contemporary (*Rhetorica ad Gaium Herennium*

1.12f.), and end in the seventh century AD with Isidore of Hispalis (today Seville; *Etymologiae* 1.44.5). Cf. Lausberg [Bibl. §1.4] pp. 165f. §290. The concepts of truthfulness held by Roman rhetoric – how could it be otherwise? – derive from Greek models. We content ourselves here, in reference to poetry and historical writing, with a single reference to Aristotle *Poetics* 9. For a simpler twofold division of *res gestae–fabulae fictae*, as we find in, for example, Cicero's *De finibus bonorum et malorum* (*On the Outer Limits of Good and Evil*) 5.51f., compare Ch. 3.2.2, p. 59, on Sempronius Asellio. On the other hand, we find the word *fabula* (without additional comment) in Cicero's *Letters to his Friends* 5.12 (on this, see Ch. 4.3, pp. 77ff.) deployed in reference to the account of his consulate, and the word thus acquires a definitively positive connotation.

8   This reproach runs explicitly and implicitly through the book of Flach [Bibl. §1.3]. Thucydides' objectivity has, by the way, not remained unassailed, and even Polybius was astonishingly dependent on biased sources.

2 The Formation and Establishment of Tradition in the Ruling Class of the Early and Middle Roman Republic

1   Another potential argument against the genuineness of the priestly annals for the first centuries of Rome in Scaevola's yearbooks would be the sack of Rome by Gauls in the early fourth century BC. On the other hand, the extent of the destruction and perhaps even the factuality of the event itself are part of the problematic tradition regarding archaic Rome, and they are thus themselves subject to doubts. These doubts derive from modern archaeology, but also from ancient historical writers (compare, for example, Livy *Ab urbe condita* 1.1.1–3 and 1.1.10).

3 Early Roman Historiography: Self-Justification and Memory in earlier Annalistic Writing

1   For explanations of how the fragmentary authors discussed in this chapter are cited, readers should refer in general to §1.2 of the Bibliography and the Introduction, pp. 5ff.

2   In her edition of the fragments of the Roman annalists, Chassignet (*AR*) separates "ancient annalistic writing" to Postumius Albinus and Acilius (*L'Annalistique Ancienne*: Volume I) from "middle annalistic writing" (*L'Annalistique Moyenne*: Volume II), which she begins with Lucius Cassius Hemina. Her separation of the material corresponds with subsections 3.1 and 3.2 of this book, but in both these sections, this book classifies the annalistic writing under discussion as "early annalistic writing," and does

not observe the distinction made by Chassignet. At the beginning of subsection 3.2.1, this book takes up Cato, to whose *Origines* Chassignet has devoted a separate volume: Chassignet [Bibl. §1.2: Cato].

3   A Greek inscription discovered in 1969 in eastern Sicily in what was once the Greek city of Tauromenium (modern: Taormina) also mentions the pre-history and foundation of Rome as themes taken up by Fabius' work. The inscription testifies to the likely presence of Fabius' historical account in the local library in the first half of the second century BC: *AR / FRH* Fabius Pictor F. 1.

4   Because many ancient historians clearly did not arrive at the endpoints they intended to reach in their historical accounts, and consequently left their works unfinished, we must often distinguish ideal from actual endpoints.

5   One must acknowledge, of course, that the passage in question has been added to Velleius' text by another hand.

4 The Historiography of Rome between the Fronts of the Civil Wars

1   More recently, some have occasionally held that these *libri lintei* were forgeries (see Rüpke [Bibl. §2]). On the other hand, that frags. 13–19 of Licinius always include the third element for any Roman name he mentions does not constitute proof: although *cognomina* were not at that time prevalent (frag. 19 reaches only 299 BC), Licinius could himself have subjoined a third name on the basis of his own conjectures or Livy, who serves as the source for frags. 13–19, could have taken the *cognomina* from the inscriptions of the consular lists (*Fasti consulares*) set up by order of Augustus and which, even for Romans of the archaic period, routinely supplied three-part names throughout (Attilio Degrassi, *Inscriptiones Italiae*, vol. 13, part 1, Rome, 1947).

2   Caesar *BG* 7.90.8: *huius anni rebus cognitis Romae dierum XX supplicatio redditur.*

3   Most scholars have considered Book 7 the conclusion to Caesar's share of the work, thus ending with the winter of 52/51, and attribute all of Book 8, including the letter at its beginning, to Hirtius. See, for example, Flach [Bibl. §1.3] pp. 104f. and von Albrecht [Bibl. §1.3] pp. 329f. and 343. The basis for this belief, however, was removed by Canfora [Bibl. §1.4] pp. 251f., who has convincingly unmasked the introductory letter at the beginning of Book 8 (even before the first chapter) as a later addition, if not outright forgery. The eye-catching first-person insertion of 8.48.10 thus takes on the role of signaling the continuation of Caesar's work by a new author (Hirtius), and it thereby announces a change in approach (summary reports), provides justification for it, and makes clear which parts of the *Commentarii de bello Gallico* no longer derive from Caesar's pen.

4 We must therefore reject the view that the excursuses of the *Gallic Wars* were later additions, with the exception, that is, of the report concerning fabulous animals that we find in 6.25–28 at the end of the excursus on Gauls and Germans.

5 The last sentence of Book 3 is absent in an important manuscript: "These things mark the beginning of the Alexandrian War."

6 Verus to Fronto, in the edition of the *Letters* edited by Michael P. J. van den Hout (Leipzig, 1988), pp. 108f., together with his commentary (Leiden, 1999), pp. 265–268. Cf. Fronto to Aurelius (actually a treatise under the title *Principia historiae*) pp. 202–214 (text) and pp. 462–487 (commentary).

7 That Cicero's vanity breaks through cannot be missed. On the other hand, we must be very careful not to interpret Cicero's general comments concerning historiography and historical writers as applying only to his estimation of himself.

8 To this extent, we must correct Geiger [Bibl. §4] who considers the development of political biography an "accidental byproduct" of the work of Cornelius Nepos.

9 Nepos *Epimonandas* 1.3: ... *exprimere imaginem consuetudinis atque vitae* ...

10 The adverb *carptim* derives from the verb *carpere* ("to pick [as in flowers], to select").

11 *Sallust Cat.* 4.2: ... *plebs senatui sicuti corpus animo oboedit* ... *populo supervacuanea est calliditas.*

12 This and the following evaluation of Thucydides as well as remarks on the collapse of moral standards and the concept of a turning point depend in part on Flach [Bibl. §1.3], pp. 109ff. and 114ff., but they also depart substantially from his analysis.

13 There is an argument (which one may reasonably refute) that the concept of moral collapse at a specific turning point for the worse is a further development of Greek political philosophy, but we do not have space to pursue it here. Compare Plato *Laws* 698b–c; Polybius 6.10f. and 57 as well as 31.25(32.11).3–4.

14 Of the three letters from Pollio among the collection of Cicero's *Letters to his Friends* 10.30-32, letter 32 gives the clearest idea of Pollio's style in his *Histories*.

15 Horace *Od.* 2.1.6–8: ... *periculosae plenum opus aleae* ... *incedis per ignes subpositos cineri doloso.*

5 Augustan Rome, Roman Empire, and other Peoples and Kingdoms

1 Syme [Bibl. §5] is almost alone in his view that Livy died *before* Augustus.

2 *HRR* does not collect these excerpts, but see the edition of Jal [Bibl. §1.1 under *Livy*].

3 Livy *Praef.* 9: *nec vitia nostra nec remedia pati possumus.*
4 Livy 43.13.2: *Ceterum et mihi vetustas res scribenti nescio quo pacto anticus fit animus, et quaedam religio tenet ... quae in meos annales referam.*
5 For Polybius, Posidonius, and Diodorus, one may compare the corresponding chapters of Lendle [Bibl. §1.3] and Meister [Bibl. §1.3], whose book concludes with Diodorus (on this, see above, Ch. 1.2, p. 13, with note 4 on p. 256).
6 Strabo F. 2 = *Geogr.* 1.1.22f.:
   ···τὸν μετασχόντα τῆς τε ἐγκυκλίου καὶ συνήθους ἀγωγῆς τοῖς ἐλευθέροις καὶ

   τοῖς φιλοσοφοῦσιν ... καὶ πολιτικὸν καὶ δημωφελὲς ... χρήσιμα ... εἰς τὴν ἠθικὴν

   καὶ πολιτικὴν φιλοσοφίαν ...
7 For Near Eastern and Greco-Roman conceptions of world empires and their sequence, see below, Ch. 7.3.3, pp. 234, with note 12 on p. 263.
8 Dionysius *Ant.* 1.8.2: ὅλον ... τὸν ἀρχαῖον βίον τῆς πόλεως.

6 Imperial History and the History of Emperors – Imperial History as the History of Emperors

1 One may get an impression of how vast these losses are from Schanz, Hosius & Krüger [Bibl. §1.4] II pp. 327–329 who cite eleven lost works that treated recent history from the reign of Augustus alone.
2 For contemporary and contrary assessments of Nero, compare, however, Flavius Josephus *Antiquitates Iudaicae* 20.154f., which was published during the reign of Domitian, i.e., before Tacitus' first work.
3 For this reason, the attempt of Flach's [Bibl. §1.4] pp. 161f. to make *a single* author responsible and, even more, to wish to identify him by name is futile.
4 On the other hand, early imperial historical writing will have viewed the adoptions within the Julio-Claudian clan not as a vestige of the Republic, but as a right to rule inherited within one's own family, and therefore as a manifestation of monarchical conduct.
5 *Contra* Dihle [Bibl. §1.3] p. 228, the *Agricola* for this very reason would not have struck the ancient (or at least the Roman) reader as unexpectedly odd.
6 Tacitus *Hist.* 1.1.3: ... *incorruptam fidem professis neque amore quisquam et sine odio dicendus est*: (authors, i.e. historians), who have proclaimed their own uncompromised credibility, must discuss each and every (ruler) without affection or hatred.
7 Tacitus *Hist.* 1.1.4: ... *rara temporum felicitate, ubi sentire quae velis et quae sentias dicere licet.*
8 Tacitus *Agricola* 2.3: *Memoriam quoque ipsam cum voce perdidissemus, si tam in nostra potestate esset oblivisci quam tacere.*
9 Many translations of the *Annals* fail to reproduce this adequately.

10   Tacitus *Ann.* 4.20.2–3: ... *an sit aliquid in nostris consiliis liceatque inter abruptam contumaciam et deforme obsequium pergere iter ambitione ac periculis vacuum.*

11   Tacitus *Hist.* 1.4.1: ... *ut non modo casus eventusque rerum, qui plerumque fortuiti sunt, sed ratio etiam causaeque noscantur.*

12   *Vita principum* is what we find as the self-described title in *Triginta Tyranni* 33.8. In the manuscript tradition, in *Codex Palatinus Latinus* 899 of the Vatican Library, written in the ninth century, and in which 57 biographies and groups of biographies are enumerated, we find the general title *Vitae diversorum principum et tyrannorum a Divo Hadriano usque ad Numerianum diversis compositi* (correct Latin would have been *compositae*). This title is surely based on the original title, but is, in its awkwardness, certainly not original. Also problematic is the naming of Hadrian as the first emperor of the collection. On this topic we will have more to say in what follows. – A tip as to citation: biographies and groups of biographies that appear in the collection with their own titles will be cited according to those titles without prefixing *Historia Augusta* to them. As a collection the *Historia Augusta* will be cited according to its standard abbreviation *HA*.

13   In addition to the few titles listed in §6 of the Bibliography, we may mention here also the meetings of the *Historia Augusta Colloquium* that took place in Bonn, Germany, and in Macerata, Italy, and their volumes of conference proceedings. When it comes to researching essential aspects of the *Historia Augusta*, effort and reward stand, alas, in stark disproportion to each other.

14   Straub [Bibl. §6] has taken an extreme position on this.

15   In the foreword to the German translation of the *HA* by E. Hohl and J. Straub [Bibl. §1.1], A. Rösger cites pregnant examples of this in regard to the textual transmission of the life of *Aurelian* (p. xli).

16   *HA Tacitus* 8.1: *ac ne qui me temere Graecorum alicui Latinorumve aestimaret credidisse* ...

17   A very late example for the literary cult of ancient authors, at least later than the *Historia Augusta*, is the historical work of Procopius of Caesarea. Compare below, Ch. 7.3.4, pp. 239f.

18   *HA Probus* 1.6: ... *polliceor* ... *res gestas, quas perire non patior. Probus* 2.7: ... *mihi quidem id animi fuit, ut non Sallustios, Livios, Tacitos, Trogos atque omnes disertissimos imitarer viros in vita principum et temporibus disserendis, sed Marium Maximum, Suetonium Tranquillum, Fabium Marcellinum, Gargilium Martialem, Iulium Capitolinum, Aelium Lampridium ceterosque, qui haec et talia non tam diserte quam vere memoriae tradiderunt.*

19   The interpretations of the *HA* presented in these last paragraphs diverge significantly from the consensus of the last few generations of scholarship on the *Historia Augusta*. Flach [Bibl. §1.3] pp. 271ff. offers a detailed summary of this consensus (accented, naturally, by his own point of view).

20   Curtius 6.2.1: ... *quem arma Persarum non fregerant, vitia vicerunt.*

21 Plutarch *Alexander* 1.2–3:
οὔτε γὰρ ἱστορίας γράφομεν, ἀλλὰ βίους, οὔτε ταῖς ἐπιφανεστάταις πράξεσι πάντως ἔνεστι δήλωσις ἀρετῆς ἢ κακίας, ἀλλὰ πρᾶγμα βραχὺ πολλάκις καὶ ῥῆμα καὶ παιδιά τις ἔμφασιν ἤθους ἐποίησε μᾶλλον ἢ μάχαι μυριόνεκροι καὶ παρατάξεις αἱ μέγισται καὶ πολιορκίαι πόλεων. ὥσπερ οὖν οἱ ζωγράφοι τὰς ὁμοιότητας ἀπὸ τοῦ προσώπου καὶ τῶν περὶ τὴν ὄψιν εἰδῶν οἷς ἐμφαίνεται τὸ ἦθος ἀναλαμβάνουσιν, ἐλάχιστα τῶν λοιπῶν μερῶν φροντίζοντες, οὕτως ἡμῖν δοτέον εἰς τὰ τῆς ψυχῆς σημεῖα μᾶλλον ἐνδύεσθαι, καὶ διὰ τούτων εἰδοποιεῖν τὸν ἑκάστου βίον, ἐάσαντας ἑτέροις τὰ μεγέθη καὶ τοὺς ἀγῶνας.

22 Flach [Bibl. §1.3] p. 137 (compare p. 140 n. 4), in his translation of the *Preface* was the first to make clear that Livy speaks here not of the Roman state, but of Roman history.

23 Florus 1.47.3 = 3.12.3: *Posteri centum (anni) ... domesticis cladibus miseri et erubescendi.*

24 Eutropius 6.25: *contra consuetudinem Romanae libertatis ... paene tyrannica.* 7.8.4: *civilissime.*

7 Roman History and Universal History between Classical Religion ("Paganism") and Christianity

1 The author of this book was able to make use of Dieter Timpe's book, cited above, while it was still in manuscript, and portions of Chapter 7 owe more to this book than the deliberately restrained method of citation employed in this book would indicate.

2 The end of Book 1 and the beginning of Book 2 are mutilated.

3 Πολυβίῳ is the first word of Zosimus' *Historia nea*.

4 Zosimus 2.7.2:
τούτου μὴ φυλαχθέντος ἔδει γ' ἀρ' εἰς τὴν νῦν συνέχουσαν ἡμᾶς ἐλθεῖν τὰ πράγματα δυσκληρίαν.

5 Zosimus 5.36.4:
...ἀποδοὺς ἑκάστῳ τῆς αὐτοῦ δόξης ἄρχειν τε καὶ στρατεύεσθαι.

6 Quotation comes from Ammianus 25.4.1. The introductory sentence of the appraisal begins *Vir profecto heroicis connumerandus ingeniis...*

7 Ammianus 26.1.1: *... praeceptis historiae ... discurrere per negotiorum celsitudinis assuetae.*

8 Ammianus 30.7.1: *... potestatis amplitudo ... nudare solita semper animorum interna.*

9 Jerome, *Preface to the Chronicle*, pp. 6–7, ed. Helm: *... quae de Tranquillo et ceteris inlustribus historicis curiosissime excerpsi. A Constanini supra dicto anno ... iterum totum meum est.*

10   Orosius 5.2.1 and 3: ... *ubique patria, ubique lex et religio mea est ... quia ad Christianos et Romanos Romanus et Christianus accedo.* 5.1.10: *tributum pretium pacis est.*

11   Orosius 6.1.5: ... *mutans regna et disponens tempora* ...

12   For the doctrine of successive universal empires in the work of the early Roman historian Aemilius Sura, see above, Ch. 3.1.2, p. 49. The customary derivation of this doctrine in Orosius's work from the *Historiae Philippicae* of Pompeius Trogus (compare Goetz [Bibl. §7] pp. 71ff.) is hardly certain in view of the arrangement of material in this work (see above, Ch. 5.2.3, pp. 116ff.). We also find a sequence of universal empires culminating in Rome (although there were actually *four* preceding powers: Assyrians–Medes–Persians–Macedonians) in the work of the Greek author Dionysius of Halicarnassus (*Romaïké Archaiologia* 1.2f.) who was approximately contemporary with Pompeius Trogus.

13   Orosius 7.2.8: ... *unum esse arbitrum saeculorum regnorum locorumque omnium deum.*

14   Orosius 1.*praef.*14: ... *illam (mortem) ... concludi, cum ista (vera religio) iam praevalet; illam penitus nullam futuram, cum haec sola regnabit.*

15   Orosius 7.43.10: ... *ad hoc electus a Gothis, ut pacem infringeret, ad hoc ordinatus a Deo, ut pacem confirmaret* (for the key word *ordinatus*, see above, pp. 234f.). §14: *tu cum omnibus pacem habe omniumque obsides accipe! Nos nobis confligimus, nobis perimus, tibi vincimus, immortali vero quaestu rei publicae tuae, si utrique pereamus.*

16   For details, see the extensive indices in the edition of Orosius by Zangemeister [Bibl. §1.1] pp. 681ff. and 684ff.

17   Compare the index in the edition of Zangemeister [Bibl. §1.1] pp. 701ff.

8 Some Basic Principles of Ancient Historical Thought

1   We find the quintessential exception to this conception in Tacitus' version of the inferences drawn by the emperor Claudius in the closing remarks of his speech to the Gauls (*Annals* 11.24.7). Compare above, Ch. 6.1.2, p. 134.

2   Rare exceptions are provided by *Livy* with the idea of long-term and slow-moving changes, both positive and negative, among the Romans and by *Claudius* who combined in a unique way the principle of unchanging conduct with a fundamental willingness to accept new forms of conduct (see above, Ch. 5.1, pp. 106f.; Ch. 6.1.2, pp. 134f.).

3   We can observe an example of this in quite recent times. F. Fukuyama hailed 1989 and the political changes that took place at the end of the 1980s in the Soviet Union and Europe as the "end of history." As we are now all-too-painfully aware, this diagnosis, as well as the discussions it sparked, were premature.

Select Bibliography

I General Bibliography

I.I Editions, Translations, and Commentaries for the Historiographical and Biographical Works Treated in this Book

Helpful Hints
- Ancient authors are arranged alphabetically according to their customary names in English. This name is printed in ***bold italic***.
- Dates refer to original publication, not the date of the latest reprint.
- Editions, translations, and commentaries that treat only a part or only individual books of larger works are included in the list below only selectively.
- For information on the publication of works that survive only in fragments, please refer to the introductory material provided for each author at the beginning of each relevant discussion in this book, to the standard collections of fragments listed in §1.2 of this bibliography, and to the guide to the citation of fragments in general on pp. 5–7 in the Introduction.
- The titles listed here correspond of necessity in the main with those listed by Flach [Bibl. §1.3] pp. 321ff. In his book, one will also find older titles.
- One may also conveniently consult:
  E. J. Kenney and W. V. Clausen, eds. *Latin Literature* (= *Cambridge History of Classical Literature*, vol. 2). Cambridge: 1982.

Roman Historiography: An Introduction to its Basic Aspects and Development,
First Edition. Andreas Mehl.
© 2014 Hans-Friedrich Mueller. Published 2014 by Blackwell Publishing Ltd.

P. E. Easterling, and B. M.W. Knox, eds. *Greek Literature* (= *Cambridge History of Classical Literature*, vol. 1). Cambridge: 1985.

S. Hornblower and A. Spawforth, eds. *The Oxford Classical Dictionary.* 3rd rev. edn. Oxford: 1998.

M. Landfester, H. Cancik, H. Schneider, et al., eds. *Brill's New Pauly: Encyclopedia of the Ancient World.* Leiden and Boston: 2006–.

M. Gagarin and E. Fantham, eds. *The Oxford Encyclopedia of Ancient Greece and Rome.* New York: 2010.

R. Bagnall, K. Brodersen, C. Champion, et al., eds. *The Encyclopedia of Ancient History* (in preparation).

Useful for those with some German:

R. Nickel. *Lexikon der antiken Literatur.* Düsseldorf: Zurich & Darmstadt: 1999.

O. Schütze, ed. *Metzler Lexikon antiker Autoren.* Stuttgart & Weimar: 1997.

– The list of authors and works employs the following abbreviations:

Txt = Edition of the text in its original language, generally with a critical apparatus that provides variant readings.

Tr = Translation (in English, French, German, or Italian), often with explanatory notes. Please note that most English translations will fall under the rubric **LCL** (see last item).

C = Commentary, linguistic and/or factual.

LCL = *Loeb Classical Library*, published by Harvard University Press (Cambridge, MA; and London). If an author's work is available in this series, **LCL** will be appended in bold at the end of the entry for easy reference. This crucial series offers bilingual editions of most (although by no means all) of the authors discussed in this book. The original Greek or Latin is printed on the left hand page with a facing translation into English on the right. Many volumes also include introductory essays, basic text-critical information, some explanatory notes, and basic bibliography. Publication details for individual authors and works are readily accessible on line: http://www.hup.harvard.edu/loeb/.

Ammianus Marcellinus: W. Seyfarth, L. Jacob-Karau, and I. Ulmann 1978 [Txt] – W. Seyfarth 1968–1978 [Txt, Tr-German] – P. de Jonge (Books 14–19) 1935–1982 [C] – **LCL**

Lucius *Ampelius*: V. Colonna 1980 [Txt] – M.-P. Arnaud-Lindet 1993 [Txt, Tr-French] – I. König 2010 [2009] [Txt, Tr-German, C]

Anonymus Valesianus: see *Excerpta* Valesiana.

Appian of Alexandria: P. Viereck, A. G. Roos, and E. Gabba 1905–1968 [Txt] – O. Veh 1987–1989 [Txt, Tr-German] – **LCL**

Arrian of Nicomedia: A. G. Roos & G. Wirth, 2nd edn, 1967–1968 [Txt] – G. Wirth & O. von Hinüber 1985 [Txt, Tr-German] – A. B. Bosworth (*Anabasis* Books 1–5) 1980–1995 [C] – (*Anabasis*) **LCL**

Augustine (Aurelius Augustinus): E. Hoffmann (*De civitate Dei*) 1899–1900 [Txt] – B. Dombart & A. Kalb 1928–1929 [Txt] – **LCL**

Aurelius: see *Victor*

Gaius Julius *Caesar*: W. Hering (*Bellum Gallicum*) 1987 [Txt] – A. Klotz (*Bellum Civile*), 2nd edn, 1950 [Txt] – A. Klotz (*Bellum Alexandrinum, Africum, Hispaniense*) 1927 [Txt] – M. Deissmann-Merten (*B. G.*) 1995 [Txt, Tr-German] – O. Schönberger (*B. C.*), 2nd edn, 1990 [Txt, Tr-German] – A. Bouvet & C. Richaud (B. Afr.) 1997 [Txt, Tr-French] – N. Diouron (*B. Hisp.*) 1999 [Txt, Tr-French] – L. Loreto (*B. Alex., Afr., Hisp.*) 2001 [Txt, Tr-Italian, C] – M. Rambaud (*B. G.* 2–5) 1965–1974 [C] – E. Siebenborn (*B. G.*) 1995 [C] – M. Rambaud (*B. C.* 1), 2nd edn, 1970 [C] – **LCL**

Marcus Tullius *Cicero* (see also, Bibl. §1.2): D. R. Shackleton Bailey (complete edition of the *Letters*) 1965–1980 [Txt, Tr-English] – H. Kasten (*Letters to Atticus* und *Letters to his Friends*) 1959 [Txt, Tr-German] – B. Kytzler (*Brutus*) 1990 [Txt, Tr-German] – R. Nickel (*On the Laws*) 1994 [Txt, Tr-German] – E. Courbaud & H. Bornecque (*On the Orator*) vol. 1: 4th edn, 1957; vol. 2: 3rd edn, 1959; vol. 3, 2nd edn, 1956 [Txt, Tr-French] – **LCL**

Quintus *Curtius* Rufus: K. Müller & H. Schönfeld 1954 [Txt, Tr-German] – H. Bardon, 2nd edn, 1961–1965 [Txt, Tr-French] – J. E. Atkinson (to Book 7.2) 1980–1984 [C] – **LCL**

Publius Herennius *Dexippus*: G. Martin 2006 [Txt, Tr-German, C]

Cassius *Dio*: U. Ph. Boissevain 1895–1931 [Txt] – O. Veh & G. Wirth 1985–1987 [Tr-German] – M. Reinhold (Books 49–52) 1988 [C] – J. W. Rich (Books 53–55.9) 1990 [C] – **LCL**

Dionysius of Halicarnassus: C. Jacoby 1885–1925 [Txt] – D. G. Battisti 1997 [Txt, Tr-Italian, C] – S. Pittia, et al. (vols. 14–20) 2002 [Txt, Tr-French] – **LCL**

Epitome de Caesaribus: see *Victor*

Eusebius of Caesarea: A. Cameron & S. G. Hall (*Constantine*) 1999 [Txt, Tr-English] – R. Helm (*Chronicle*) 1956 [Txt] – E. Schwartz (*Historia ekklesiastiké*: known as the *editio major* or augmented edition because it includes the Latin version of Turannius *Rufinus*, edited by Th. Mommsen) 1903–1909 [Txt] – E. Schwartz (*Hist. ekkl.*: known as the *editio minor* or smaller edition) 1914 – (*Ecclesiastical History*) **LCL**

Eutropius: C. Santini 1979 [Txt] – F. L. Müller 1995 [Txt, Tr-German] – H. W. Bird 1993 [Tr.-English]

Excerpta Valesiana: J. Moreau & V. Velkov 1968 [Txt] – I. König (only part 2) 1997 [Txt, Tr-German, C]

Rufius *Festus* (Sextus Rufius): M. P. Arnaud-Lindet 1994 [Txt, Tr-French] – J. W. Eadie 1967 [Txt, C]

Lucius Annaeus *Florus*: E. Malcovati, 2nd edn, 1972 [Txt] – P. Jal 1967/1968 [Txt, Tr-French] – E. Salomone Gaggero 1981 [Txt, Tr-Italian] – LCL

Granius Licinianus: N. Criniti 1981 [Txt] – B. Scardigli 1983 [Txt, Tr-Italian, C]

Herodian: C. Stavenhagen 1922 [Txt] – D. Roques 1990 [Txt, Tr-French] – F. L. Müller 1996 [Txt, Tr-German] – LCL

Historia Augusta = Scriptores Historiae Augustae: E. Hohl, Ch. Samberger, & W. Seyfarth 1971 [Txt] – J.-P. Callu (*Hadrian* to *Antoninus Pius*) & R. Turcan (*Macrinus* to *Elagabalus*) 1992–1993 (the series will be continued by various authors) [Txt, Tr-French] – E. Hohl & J. Straub 1976–1985 [Txt, Tr-German] – LCL

Jerome (Eusebius Hieronymus): A. Ceresa-Gastaldo (*De viris illustribus*) 1988 [Txt, C] – (*Chronicle*): see *Eusebius* of Caesarea – B. Jeanjean & B. Lauçon (continuation of the *Chronicle*) 2004 [Txt]

Flavius *Josephus*: B. Niese 1885–1895 [Txt] – H. Clementz & H. Kreissig (*Jewish War*), 6th edn, 1994 [Txt, Tr-German] – H. Clementz (*Jewish Antiquities*), 10th edn, 1990 [Txt, Tr-German] – G. Riciotti (*Jewish War*), 3rd edn, 1963 [C] – F. Siegert, et al. (*Life*) [Txt, Tr-German, C] – LCL

Justin (Marcus Justinus Justinianus; see also Pomponius *Trogus*): O. Seel (including *Prologi in Pompeium Trogum*) 1972 [Txt] – O. Seel 1971 [Tr-German] – J. C. Yardley & W. Heckel (Books 11–12) 1997 [Tr-English, C] – R. N. H. Boerma (Books 13–15.2) 1979 [C]

Lactantius (Lucius Caelius Firmianus), *De mortibus persecutorum*: J. Morau 1954 [Txt, Tr-French, C] – J. L. Creed 1984 [Txt, Tr-English]

Livy (Titus Livius): W. Weissenborn, 10th–12th edns, 1969–1982 [Txt] – R. M. Ogilvie et al. (Books 1–10 & 21–35) 1910–1974 [Txt] – T. A. Dorey (Books 21–25) 1971–1976 [Txt] – P. G. Walsh (Books 26–30) 1986–1989 [Txt] – J. Briscoe (Books 31–35 & 41–45) 1991 & 1986 [Txt] – J. Bayet et al. 1940–1991 [Txt, Tr-French] – H. J. Hillen & J. Feix 1991–2000 [Txt, Tr-German] – P. Jal (*Periochae* and Fragments) 1984 [Txt, Tr-French] – W. Weissenborn & M. Müller, 2nd–6th edns, 1880–1924 [C] – R. M. Ogilvie (Books 1–5) 1965 [C]

- S. P. Oakley (Books 6–10) 1997–2005 [C] – J. Briscoe (Books 31–37) 1973–1981 [C] – P. G. Walsh (Books 35–40) 1990–1999 [C] – **LCL**

Lucian of Samosata (*Pôs dei historian syngraphein / How to write history*): H. Homeyer 1965 [Txt, Tr-German, C] – **LCL**

Cornelius *Nepos*: P. K. Marshall 1977 [Txt] – P. Krafft & F. Oleff-Krafft 1993 [Txt, Tr-German] – G. Wirth 1994 [Txt, Tr-German, C] – **LCL**

Nicolaus of Damascus: B. Scardigli (*Life of Augustus*) 1983 [Txt, Tr-Italian, C] – M. Schüler & U. Staffhorst (*Aug.*) 1992, 1993, 1994 (in the series: *Jahresbericht des Bismarck-Gymnasiums Karlsruhe*) [Tr-German, C] – J. Malitz (*Aug.*) 2003 [Txt, Tr-German, C]

Origo Constantini Imperatoris: see *Excerpta* Valesiana

Origo gentis Romanae: see *Victor*

Paulus *Orosius*: C. Zangemeister 1882 (augmented edition) & 1889 (smaller edition) [Txt] – A. Lippold 1976 [Txt, Tr-Italian] – M.-P. Arnaud-Lindet 1990–1991 [Txt, Tr-French] – R. J. Deferrari 1964 [Tr-English] – A. Lippold 1985–1986 [Tr-German]

Plutarch of Chaeronea: *Biographies*: C. Lindskog, K. Ziegler, & H. Gärtner 1973–2000 [Txt] – R. Flacelière, E. Chambry, M. Juneaux 1961–1983 [Txt, Tr-French] – W. Wuhrmann 1954–1965 [Tr-German] – L. Amantini, C. Carena, & M. Manfredini (*Demetrius* and *Antonius*), Milan 1995 (more lives are planned for the series) [Txt, Tr-Italian, C] – *Moralia*: R. Flacelière et al. 1972–1996 [Txt, Tr-French] – (*Biographies* and *Moralia*) **LCL**

Polybius of Megalopolis: L. Dindorf & Th. Büttner-Wobst 1889–1905 [Txt] – H. Drexler 1961–1963 [Tr-German] – F. W. Walbank 1957–1979 [C] – **LCL**

Procopius of Caesarea: J. Haury & G. Wirth 1962–1964 [Txt] – O. Veh 1961–1977 [Txt, Tr-German] – **LCL**

Turannius (Tyrannius) *Rufinus*: see *Eusebius* of Caesarea (*Historia ekklesiastikê*)

Sallust (Publius Sallustius Crispus): A. Kurfess (*Catilina, Jugurtha*, lengthier fragments of the *Historiae*), 3rd edn, 1957 [Txt] – D. Reynolds (*Cat., Jug.*, select fragments of *Hist., Letters, Invectives*) 1991 [Txt] – B. Maurenbrecher (frags. of the *Hist.*) 1893 [Txt] – A. Lambert 1978 [Txt, Tr-German] – W. Eisenhut & J. Lindauer, 2nd edn, 1994 [Txt, Tr-German] – P. McGushin (frags. of the *Hist.*) 1992–1994 [Txt, Tr-English, C] – O. Leggewie (select frags. of the *Hist.*) 1975 [Tr-German] – K. Vretska (*Cat.*) 1976 [C] – P. McGushin (*Cat.*) 1977 [C] – E. Koestermann (*Jug.*) 1971 [C] – G. M. Paul (*Jug.*) 1984 [C] – R. Funari (frags. of the *Hist.*) 1996 [C] – **LCL**

Sextus Rufus: see Rufius *Festus*

Socrates Scholasticus: G. C. Hansen 1995 [Txt] – A. C. Zenos (*History of the Church* in: A Select Library of Nicene and post-Nicene Fathers of the Christian Church 2.2.1ff.) 1890 [Tr-English]

Sozomen: J. Bidez & G. C. Hansen, 2nd edn, 1995 [Txt] – C. D. Hartranft (A Select Library of Nicene and post-Nicene Fathers of the Christian Church 2.2.181ff.) 1890 [Tr-English] – G. Hansen 2004 [Txt, Tr-German]

Gaius ***Suetonius*** Tranquillus: M. Ihm (*Caesares*) 1908 [Txt] – G. Brugnoli (*De grammaticis et rhetoribus*) 1960 [Txt] – P. Grimal 1973 [Txt, Tr-French] – O. Wittstock 1993 [Txt, Tr-German] – H. Martinet 1997 [Txt, Tr-German] – A. Stahr & W. Krenkel (1985) [Tr-German] – R. A. Kaster (*De grammaticis et rhetoribus*) 1995 [Txt, Tr-English, C] – H. E. Butler, M. Cary, & G. B. Townsend (*Caesar*) 1982 [Txt, C] – J. M. Carter (*Augustus*) 1982 [Txt, C] – H. Lindsay (*Tiberius* & *Caligula*) 1995 & 1993 [Txt, C] – D. W. Hurley (*Caligula*) 1993 [Txt, C] – D. Wardle (*Caligula*) 1994 [C] – W. Kierdorf (*Claudius, Nero*) 1992 [C] – B. H. Warmington (*Nero*) 1977 [C] – K. R. Bradley (*Nero*) 1978 [C] – D. Shotter (*Galba, Otho, Vitellius*) 1993 [C] – H. Martinet (*Vespasian, Titus, Domitian*) 1991 [C] – F. Galli (*Domitian*) 1991 [C] – (*Caesars* & *Lives of Illustrious Men*) **LCL**

Sulpicius Severus: C. Halm 1866 [Txt] – P. Bihlmayer 1914 [Tr-German] – J. Fontaine (*Vita Sancti Martini*) 1967–1969 [Txt, Tr-French]

Publius Cornelius ***Tacitus***: E. Koestermann, 3rd edn, 1969–1971 [Txt] – M. Winterbottom & R. M. Ogilvie (*Agricola, Germania, Dialogus*) 1975 [Txt] – J. Delz (*Agr.*) 1983 [Txt] – A. Önnerfors (*Germ.*) 1983 [Txt] – H. Heubner (*Dial.*) 1983 [Txt] – H. Heubner (*Historiae*) 1978 [Txt] – K. Wellesley (*Hist.*) 1989 [Txt] – H. Heubner (*Annales*), 2nd edn, 1994 [Txt] – St. Borszák (*Ann.* 1–6) 1992 [Txt] – K. Wellesley (*Ann.* 11–16) 1986 [Txt] – A. Städele (*Agr., Germ.*) 1991 [Txt, Tr-German] – G. Perl (*Germ.*) 1990 [Txt, Tr-German] – H. W. Benario (*Germ.*) 1999 [Txt, Tr-English, C] – J. Rives (*Germ.*) [Txt, Tr-English, C] – H. Vretska (*Hist.*) 1984 [Txt, Tr-German] – W. Sontheimer (*Hist.*) 1959 [Tr-German] – M. Fuhrmann & E. Heller (*Ann.*) 3rd edn, 1997 [Txt, Tr-German] – A. Horneffer (*Ann.*) 1957 [Tr-German] – R. M. Ogilvie & I. Richmond (*Agr.*) 1967 [C] – A. A. Lund (*Agr.*) 1981 [C] – H. Heubner (*Agr.*) 1984 [C] – R. Much (*Germ.*), 3rd edn, 1967 [C] – A. A. Lund (*Germ.*) 1988 [C] – A. Michel (*Dial.*) 1962 [C] – R. Güngerich (*Dial.*) 1980 [C] – H. Heubner (*Hist.*) 1963–1982 [C] – G. E. F. Chilver (*Hist.* 1–2) 1979

[C] – K. Wellesley (*Hist.* 3) 1972 [Txt, C] – G. E. F. Chilver & G. B. Townsend (*Hist.* 4–5) 1985 [C] – E. Koestermann (*Ann.*) 1963–1968 [C] – F. R. D. Goodyear (*Ann.* 1–2) 1972–1981 [C] – R. H. Martin & A. J. Woodman (*Ann.* 3 & 4) 1996 & 1989 [C] – P. Wuillemier (*Ann.* 13) 1964 [C] – N. P. Miller (*Ann.* 15) 1973 [C] – **LCL**

Theodoret of Cyrrhus: L. Parmentier, 3rd edn, 1998 [Txt] – B. Jackson (A Select Library of Nicene and Post-Nicene Fathers of the Christian Church 2.3.33ff.) 1892 [Tr-English] – A. Seider 1926 [Tr-German, C]

Thucydides of Athens: H. S. Jones & J. E. Powell 1942 [Txt] – G. P. Landmann 1960 [Tr-German] – A. W. Gomme, A. Andrewes, & K. J. Dover 1956–1981 [C] – S. Hornblower 1991–2008 [C] – **LCL**

Pompeius **Trogus** (see also *Justin*): O. Seel (fragments) 1956 [Txt]

Valerius Maximus: J. Briscoe (including epitomes) 1998 [Txt] – R. Combès (Books 1–6) 1995–1997 [Txt, Tr-French] – U. Blank-Sangmeister (selections) 1991 [Txt, Tr-German] – D. Wardle (Book 1) 1998 [Tr.-English, C] – **LCL**

Marcus Terentius **Varro**: L. & A. Spengel (*Lingua Latina*) 1885 [Txt] – B. Cardauns (fragments of *Antiquitates rerum humanarum et divinarum*) 1976 [Txt, C] – M. Salvadore (*Fragments*) 1999/2004 [Txt, Tr-Italian] – (*On Agriculture* & *On the Latin Language*) **LCL**

Velleius Paterculus: K. Stegmann von Pritzwald, 2nd edn, 1933 [Txt] – W. S. Watt, 2nd edn, 1998 [Txt] – M. Giebel, 2nd edn, 1992 [Txt, Tr-German] – M. Elefante 1997 [Txt, C] – A. J. Woodman (2.41–93 & 2.94–131) 1983 & 1977 [Txt, C] – **LCL**

Sextus Aurelius **Victor**: F. Pichlmayr 1911 [Txt] – K. Gross-Albenausen, M. Fuhrmann (*Caesares*), 2nd edn, 2002 [Txt, Tr-German] – H. W. Bird (*Caesares*) 1994 [Tr-English, C] – M. Festy (*Epitomé*) 1999 [Txt, Tr-French, C] – M. Sehlmeyer (*Origo*) 2004 [Txt, Tr-German, C]

Zosimus: l. Mendelsohn 1887 [Txt] – F. Paschoud 1971–1989 [Txt, Tr-French] – J. J. Buchanan & H. T. Davis 1967 [Tr-English] – R. T. Ridley 1982 [Tr-English, C] – O. Veh & St. Rebenich 1990 [Tr-German, C]

1.2 Editions of Historiographical Works and Historical Epics in Greek and Latin that Survive only in Fragments

NB: For guidance in the use of collections of fragments, please consult the Introduction above, pp. 5–7.

Barchiesi, M. *Nevio epico*. Padua: 1962.

Beck, H. & Walters, U. *Die frühen römischen Historiker. I: Von Fabius Pictor bis Cn. Gellius. II: Von Coelius Antipater bis Pomponius Atticus.* Darmstadt: 2001–2004. (cited as *FRH*)

Blockley, R. C. *The Fragmentary Classicising Historians of the Later Roman Empire.* 2 vols. Liverpool: 1981–1983.

Chassignet, M. *Caton. Les origines (fragments). Texte établi, traduit et commenté.* Paris: 1986. (cited as *CC*)

Chassignet, M. *L'annalistique romaine. Tome I: Les annales des pontifes et l'annalistique anciennes (fragments). Texte et traduction. Tome II: L'annalistique moyenne (fragments) Texte et traduction. Tome III: L'analistique récente, l'autobiographie politique (fragments).* Paris: 1996–2004. (cited as *AR*)

Courtney, E. *The Fragmentary Latin Poets.* Oxford: 1993.

Dindorf, L. *Historici Graeci Minores.* 2 vols. Leipzig: 1870–1871. (cited as *HGM*)

Duff, T. *The Greek and Roman Historians.* Bristol: 2003.

Hermann, W. "Die Historien des Coelius Antipater. Fragmenta und Kommentar." Dissertation (Cologne): 1976.

Jacoby, F. *Die Fragmente der griechischen Historiker.* Berlin; later Leiden: 1923–1958. Additional volumes have been published since 1994 by various editors. (cited as *FGrH*)

Mommsen, Th. *Chronica Minora. Saec. IV, V, VI, VII.* Berlin: 1892–1898.

Müller, C. & Th. *Fragmenta Historicorum Graecorum.* 5 vols. Paris: 1849–1895. (cited as *FHG*)

Peter, H. *Historicorum Romanorum Reliquiae.* Paris: vol. 1: 2nd edn, 1914; vol. 2: 1906. Republished with bibliographical additions: Stuttgart: 1967 and 1993. (cited as *HRR*)

Santini, C. *I frammenti di L. Cassio Emina. Introduzione, testo, traduzione e commento.* Pisa: 1995.

Schönberger, O. *Marcus Porcius Cato. Vom Landbau. Fragmenta. Alle erhaltenen Schriften. Lateinisch-deutsch.* Munich: 1980.

Skutsch, O. *The Annals of Quintus Ennius.* Oxford: 1985 (rev. 1986).

Walt, S. *Der Historiker C. Licinius Macer. Einleitung, Fragmente, Kommentar.* Stuttgart & Leipzig: 1997.

1.3 Histories of Greek and Latin Literature, especially Historiography: Recent Surveys and Collections

Cameron, A., ed. *History as Text: The Writing of Ancient History.* Chapel Hill & London: 1989.

Dihle, A. Die griechische und lateinische Literatur der Kaiserzeit. Von Augustus bis Iustinian. Munich: 1989.

Flach, D. Römische Geschichtsschreibung. Darmstadt: 1998 (= 3rd printing of: Einführung in die römische Geschichtsschreibung. 1st edn, 1985; 2nd edn, 1992)

Erskine, A., ed. A Companion to Ancient History. Chichester, UK & Malden, MA: 2009.

Fuhrmann, M. Geschichte der römischen Literatur. Stuttgart: 1999.

Herzog, R. & Schmidt, P. L., eds. Handbuch der Literatur der Antike. Munich: 1989–.

Lendle, O. Einführung in die griechische Geschichtsschreibung. Von Hekataios bis Zosimos. Darmstadt: 1992.

Liddel, P. & Fear, A., eds. Historiae Mundi: Studies in Universal Historiography. London: 2010.

Marincola, J., ed. A Companion to Greek and Roman Historiography. Malden, MA: 2007.

Meister, K. Die griechische Geschichtsschreibnng. Von den Anfängen bis zum Ende des Hellenismus. Stuttgart: 1990.

Mellor, R., ed. The Historians of Ancient Rome. New York & London, 1998.

Musti, D. "Il pensiero storico romano." In: G. Cavallo, P. Fedeli, & A. Giardana, eds. Lo spazio letterario di Roma antica. Vol. 1. Rome: 1989. Pp. 177–240.

Sonnabend, H. Geschichte der antiken Biographie: von Isokrates bis zur Historia Augusta. Stuttgart: 2002.

von Albrecht, M. Geschichte der römischen Literatur: von Andronicus bis Boethius mit Berücksichtigung ihrer Bedeutung für die Neuzeit. Bern: 1992. (This work has been translated into English as: A History of Roman Literature: From Livius Andronicus to Boethius with special regard to its Influence on World Literature. Rev. by G. Schmeling and by the author. Leiden & New York: 1997.)

Woodman, A.J., & Kraus, C. S. Latin Historians. Oxford: 1997.

1.4 Ancient Historiography, especially Roman: its Basic Literary, Social, and Intellectual Contexts

Alonso-Núñez, J. M., ed. Geschichtsbild und Geschichtsdenken im Altertum. Darmstadt: 1991.

Balot, R. K., ed. A Companion to Greek and Roman Political Thought. Chichester, U.K. & Malden, MA: 2009.

Bardon, H. La littérature latine inconnú. 2 vols. Paris: 1952–1956.

Burde, P. *Untersuchungen zur antiken Universalgeschichtsschreibung.* Munich: 1974.

Canfora, L. *Studi di storia della storiografia romana.* Bari: 1993.

Dihle, A. *Die Entstehung der historischen Biographie.* Heidelberg: 1987.

Dominik, W. & Hall, J., eds. *A Companion to Roman Rhetoric.* Malden, MA: 2007.

Dorey, T. A., ed. *Latin Historians.* London: 1966.

Erren, M. *Einführung in die römische Kunstprosa.* Darmstadt: 1983.

Feeney, D. C. *Literature and Religion at Rome: Cultures, Contexts, and Beliefs.* New York: 1998.

Feldherr, A., ed. *The Cambridge Companion to the Roman Historians.* Cambridge: 2009.

Fornara, C. W. *The Nature of History in Greece and Rome.* Berkeley: 1987.

Fox, M. *Cicero's Philosophy of History.* Oxford: 2007.

Fuhrmann, M. *Die Antike Rhetorik.* 4th edn. Munich & Zurich: 1995.

Gentili, B. & Cerri, G., eds. *History and Biography in Ancient Thought.* Amsterdam: 1988.

Gill, G. & Wiseman, T. P., eds. *Lies and Fiction in the Ancient World.* Exeter: 1993.

Gunderson, E., ed. *The Cambridge Companion to Ancient Rhetoric.* Cambridge & New York: 2009.

Henderson, J. *Fighting for Rome: Poets, Caesars, History and Civil War.* Cambridge: 1998.

Kennedy, G. A. *Greek Rhetoric under Christian Emperors.* Princeton: 1983.

Kennedy, G. A. *The Art of Rhetoric in the Roman World: 300 B.C.–A. D. 300.* Princeton: 1972.

Kennedy, G. A. *The Art of Persuasion in Greece.* Princeton: 1963.

Klein, R., ed. *Das Staatsdenken der Römer.* 3rd edn. Darmstadt: 1980.

Lausberg, H. *Handbuch der literarischen Rhetorik: eine Grundlegung der Literaturwissenschaft.* 2 vols. 3rd edn. Stuttgart: 1990.

Malitz, J. "Das Interesse an der Geschichte. Die griechischen Historiker und ihr Publikum." In: *Purposes of History. Studies in Greek Historiography from the 4th to the 2nd Centuries B.C. = Studia Hellenistica,* 30. Leuven: 1990. Pp. 323–349.

Marincola, J. *Authority and Tradition in Ancient Historiography.* Cambridge and New York: 1997.

Marrou, H.-I. *A History of Education in Antiquity.* Trans. by G. Lamb. New York: 1956.

Mazzarino, S. *Il pensiero storico classico.* Bari: 1966.

Mehl, A. "*Imperium sine fine dedi* – die augusteische Vorstellung von der Grenzenlosigkeit des römischen Reiches." In: *Geographica Historica*, 7. Amsterdam: 1994. Pp. 431–464.

Meister, R. "Motive und Formen der römischen Geschichtsschreibung." *Das Altertum* 10 (1964): 13–26.

Misch, G. *Geschichte der Autobiographie.* Vol. 1 in 2 parts. Bern: 1949–1950.

Momigliano, A. *Studies in Ancient and Modern Historiography.* Middletown, CT: 1977.

Momigliano, A. *Studies in Historiography.* New York: 1966.

Mommsen, Th. *The History of Rome.* Trans. by W. P. Dickson. London: 1886.

Nicolai, R. *La storiografia nell'educazione antica.* Pisa: 1992.

Norden, E. *Die antike Kunstprosa vom 6. Jh. v. Chr. bis die Zeit der Renaissance.* 2 vols. 3rd edn. Leipzig: 1915. Reprint: 1983.

Pédech, P. *La methode historique de Polybe.* Paris: 1964.

Perl, G. "Geschichtsschreibung in der Zeit der römischen Republik und in der Kaiserzeit." *Klio* 66 (1984): 562–573.

Petzold, K.-E. "Kylos und Telos im Geschichtsdenken des Polybius (1977)." In: Petzold, K.-E. *Geschichtsdenken und Geschichtsschreibung. Kleine Schriften zur griechischen und römischen Geschichte.* Stuttgart: 1999. Pp. 48–85.

Pöschl, V., ed. *Römische Geschichtsschreibung.* Darmstadt: 1969.

Potter, D. S., ed. *A Companion to the Roman Empire.* Malden, MA: 2006.

Potter, D. S. *Literary Texts and the Roman Historian.* London, 1999.

Reichel, M., ed. *Antike Autobiographien: Werke, Epochen, Gattungen.* Köln: 2005.

Rosenberg, A. *Einleitung und Quellenkunde zur römischen Geschichte.* Berlin: 1921.

Rosenstein, N. & Morstein-Marx, R., eds. *A Companion to the Roman Republic.* Malden, MA, and Oxford: 2006.

Rousseau, Ph. & Raithel, J., eds. *A Companion to Late Antiquity.* Chichester, UK & Malden, MA: 2009.

Rüpke, J., ed. *A Companion to Roman Religion.* Malden, MA: 2007.

Rüpke, J. *Römische Geschichtschreibung: Zur Geschichte des geschichtlichen Bewusstseins und seiner Veröffentlichungsformen in der Antike.* Potsdam: 1997.

Schanz, M, Hosius, C., & Krüger, G. *Geschichte der römischen Literatur bis zum Gesetzgebungswerk des Kaisers Justinian.* Munich: vol. 1: 4th

edn, 1927; vol. 2, 4th edn, 1935; vol. 3: 3rd edn, 1922; vol. 4.1: 2nd
edn, 1914; vol. 4.2: 1920. (later reprints)

Strasburger, H. "Die Wesensbestimmung der Geschichte durch die
antike Geschichtsschreibung (1966)." In: Strasburger, H. *Studien zur
Alten Geschichte*. Ed. by W. Schmitthenner & R. Zoepffel, vol. 2.
Hildesheim & New York: 1980. Pp. 965–1016.

Vössing, K. *Untersuchungen zur römischen Schule – Bildung – Schulbildung
im Nordafrika der Kaiserzeit*. Aachen: 1991.

White, H. *Auch Klio dichtet, oder die Fiktion des Faktischen. Studien zur
Tropologie des historischen Diskurses*. Stuttgart: 1986.

Wiseman, T. P. *Historiography and Imagination. Eight Essays on Roman
Culture*. Exeter: 1994.

Wiseman, T. P. *Clio's Cosmetics*. Leicester: 1979.

Woodman, A. J. *Rhetoric in Classical Historiography*. London: 1988.

2 The Formation and Establishment of Tradition in the Ruling Class of the Early and Middle Roman Republic

Drews, R. "Pontiffs, Prodigies, and the Disappearance of the *Annales
Maximi*." *Classical Philology* 83 (1988): 289–299.

Flaig, E. "Die *Pompa Funebris*. Adlige Konkurrenz und annalistische
Erinnerung in der römischen Republik." In: O. G. Oexle, ed. *Memoria
als Kultur*. Göttingen: 1995. Pp. 115–148.

Flower, H. I. *Ancestor Masks and Aristocratic Power in Roman Culture*.
Oxford: 1996.

Frier, B. W. *Libri Annales Pontificum Maximorum:* The Origins of the
Annalistic Tradition. Rome: 1979.

Harris, W. V. *Ancient Literacy*. Cambridge: 1989.

Hölkeskamp, K.-J. "*Exempla* und *mos maiorum. Überlegungen zum kolle-
ktiven Gedächtnis der Nobilität*." In: H.-J. Gehrke & A. Möller, eds.
Soziale Kommunikation, Traditionsbildung und historisches Bewusstsein.
Tübingen: 1996. Pp. 301–338.

Mora, F. *Fasti e schemi chronologici. La riorganizzazione annalistica del
passato remoto romano*. Stuttgart: 1999.

Petzold, K.-E. "*Annales Maximi* und Annalen." In: Festschrift H.
Zimmermann. Sigmaringen: 1991. Pp. 3–16.

Rüpke, J. "*Fasti*. Quellen oder produkte römischer Geschichtsschreibung?"
Klio 77 (1995): 184–202.

Timpe, D. "Mündlichkeit und Schriftlichkeit als Basis der frührömischen
Überlieferung." In: J. von Ungern-Sternberg & H. Reinau, eds.

Vergangenheit in mündlicher Überlieferung. Stuttgart: 1988. pp. 266–288.

Timpe, D. "*Memoria* und Geschichtsschreibung bei den Römern." In: H.-J. Gehrke & A. Möller, eds. *Vergangenheit und Lebenswelt: Soziale Kommunikation, Traditionsbildung und historisches Bewusstsein.* Tübingen: 1996. Pp. 277–299.

Vansina, J. *Oral Tradition as History.* London: 1985.

von Ungern-Sternberg, J. "Überlegungen zur frühen frömischen Überlieferung im Lichte der Oral-Tradition-Forschung." In: J. von Ungern-Sternberg & H. Reinau, eds. *Vergangenheit in mündlicher Überlieferung.* Stuttgart: 1988. Pp. 237–265.

Wiseman, T. P. *Roman Drama and Roman History.* Exeter: 1998.

3 Early Roman Historiography: Self-Justification and Memory in Early Annalistic Writing

Alonso-Núñez, J. M. "Aemilius Sura." *Latomus* 48 (1989): 110–119.

Bömer, F. "Naevius und Fabius Pictor." *Symbolae Osloenses* 29 (1952): 34–53.

Bringmann, K. "Weltherrschaft und innere Krise Roms im Spiegel der Geschichtsschreibung des 2. und 1. Jh. v. Chr." *Antike und Abendland* 23 (1977): 28–49.

Bung, P. "Fabius Pictor, der erste römische Annalist. Untersuchungen über Aufbau, Stil und Inhalt seines Geschichtswerks anhand von Polybios I-II." Dissertation (Cologne): 1950.

Classen, C. J. "Zur Herkunft der Sage von Romulus und Remus." *Historia* 12 (1963): 447–457.

Effe, B. *Dichtung und Lehre. Zur Typologie des antiken Lehrgedichts.* Munich: 1977.

Forsythe, G. *The Historian L. Calpurnius Piso Frugi and the Roman Annalistic Tradition.* Lanham, MD: 1994.

Gutberlet, D. *Die erste Dekade des Livius als Quelle zur gracchischen und sullanischen Zeit.* Hildesheim: 1985.

Häusler, R. *Das historische Epos der Griechen und Römer bei Vergil. Studien zum historischen Epos der Antike. I: Von Homer bis Vergil.* Heidelberg: 1976.

Kienast, D. *Cato der Zensor.* Reprint with augmented bibliography. Darmstadt: 1979.

Kierdorf, W. "Catos *Origines* und die Anfänge der römischen Geschichtsschreibung." *Chiron* 10 (1980): 205–224.

Kierdorf, W. *Römische Geschichtsschreibung der republikanischen Zeit.* Heidelberg: 2003.

Mora, F. See above, §2.

Schetter, W. *Das römische Epos.* Wiesbaden: 1978.

Schmitt, T. *Hannibals Siegeszug. Historiographische und historische Studien vor allem zu Polybios und Livius.* Munich: 1991.

Scholz, U. "*Annales* und *Historia(e).*" *Hermes* 122 (1994): 64–79.

Timpe, D. "Fabius Pictor und die Anfänge der römischen Historiographie." In: *Aufstieg und Niedergang der römischen Welt.* Vol. 1.2. Berlin & New York: 1972. Pp. 928–969.

Verbrugghe, G. P. "L. Cincius Alimentus – his place in Roman Historiography." *Philologus* 126 (1982): 316–323.

von Ungern-Sternberg, J. "Die Wahrnehmung des Ständeskampfes in der römischen Geschichtsschreibung." In: Walter Eder, ed. *Staat und Staatlichkeit in der frühen römischen Republik.* Stuttgart: 1990. Pp. 92–102.

Wiseman, T. P. *Unwritten Rome.* Exeter: 2008.

Wiseman, T. P. *The Myths of Rome.* Exeter: 2005.

Wiseman, T. P. *Remus: A Roman Myth.* Cambridge & New York: 1995.

4 The Historiography of Rome between the Fronts of the Civil Wars

Adcock, F. E. *Caesar, as Man of Letters.* Cambridge: 1956.

Bosworth, A. B. "Asinius Pollio and Augustus." *Historia* 21 (1972): 441–475.

Bringmann. See above, §3.

Bringmann, K. "Geschichte und Psychologie bei Posidonios." In: Aspects de la philosophie hellénistique. Entretiens sur l'antiquité classique, Tome 32. Vandoeuvres-Genève: 1986. Pp. 29–66.

Büchner, K. *Sallust.* 2nd edn. Heidelberg: 1982.

Fleck, M. *Cicero als Historiker.* Stuttgart: 1993.

Franzoi, A. "Ancora sulla funzione dei prologhi nelle monografie di Sallustio." *Lexis. Poetica, retorica, e communicazione nella tradizione classica* 15 (1997): 189–196.

Fox, M. *Cicero's Philosophy of History.* Oxford: 2007.

Fuhrmann, M. "Erneuerung als Wiederherstellung des Alten. Zur Funktion antiquarischer Forschung im spätrepublikanischen Rom." In: R. Herzog & R. Koselleck, eds. *Epochenschwelle und Epochenbewusstsein.* Munich: 1987. Pp. 131–151.

Geiger, J. *Cornelius Nepos and Ancient Political Biography*. Stuttgart: 1985.

Griffin, M., ed. *A Companion to Julius Caesar*. Chichester, UK & Malden, MA: 2009.

Gutberlet, D. See above, §3.

Kierdorf, W. See above, §3.

La Penna, A. "Tendenze e arte del *Bellum civile* di Cesare." *Maia* 5 (1952): 191–233.

Leeman, A. D. "L'historiographie dans le *De oratore* de Cicéron." *Bulletin de l'Association G. Budé* 3 (1985): 280–288.

Lintott, A. W. *Cicero as Evidence: A Historian's Companion*. Oxford: 2008.

Mensching, E. *Caesars* Bellum Gallicum. *Eine Einführung*. Frankfurt: 1988.

Petzold, K.-E. "Cicero und Historie (1972)." In: Petzold, K.-E. Geschichtsdenken und Geschichtsschreibung. Kleine Schriften zur griechischen und römischen Geschichte. Stuttgart: 1999. Pp. 86–109.

Pöschl, V., ed. *Sallust*. Darmstadt: 1970.

Rambaud, M. *L'art de déformation historique dans les commentaires de César*. Paris: 1966.

Rasmussen, D., ed. *Caesar*. Darmstadt: 1980. (see especially pp. 116ff. for essays on Caesar's literary efforts)

Rawson, E. "L. Cornelius Sisenna and the early first century B.C." *Classical Quarterly* 29 (1979): 327–346.

Richter, W. *Caesar als Darsteller seiner Taten. Eine Einführung*. Heidelberg: 1977.

Riggsby, A. M. *Caesar in Gaul and Rome: War in Words*. Austin: 2006.

Rüpke, J. "Wer las Caesars *bella* als *commentarii*?" *Gymnasium* 99 (1992): 201–226.

Schütrumpf, E. "Die Depravierung Roms nach den Erfolgen des Imperiums bei Sallust, *Bellum Catilinae* Kap. 10 – philosophische Reminiszenzen." In: P. Kneissl & V. Losemann, eds. Imperium Romanum. Studien zu Geschichte und Rezeption. Festschrift für Karl Christ zum 75. Geburtstag. Stuttgart: 1998. Pp. 674–689.

Steidle, W. *Sallusts historische Monographien*. Wiesbaden: 1958.

Syme, R. *Sallust*. Berkeley: 1964.

Timpe, D. "Erwägungen zur jüngeren römischen Annalistik." *Antike und Abendland* 25 (1979): 97–119.

von Ungern-Sternberg. See above, §3.

Welch, K. & Powell, A., eds. *Julius Caesar as Artful Reporter: The War Commentaries as Political Instruments*. London: 1998.

Zancan, P. "Asinio Pollione: Dall'attività politica alla reflessione storiografica." In: *Aufstieg und Niedergang der römischen Welt*. vol. 2.30.2. New York & Berlin: 1982. Pp. 1265–1296.

Zecchini, G. *Cesare e il mos maiorum*. Stuttgart: 2001.

Zecchini, G. "Die staatstheoretische Debatte der caesarischen Zeit." In: W. Schuller, ed. *Politische Theorie und Praxis im Altertum*. Darmstadt: 1998. Pp. 149–165.

5 Augustan Rome, Roman Empire, and other Peoples and Kingdoms

Alonso-Núñez, J. M. "Die Weltgeschichte des Nikolaos von Damaskos." *Storia della Storiografia* 27 (1995): 3–15.

Burck, E. *Die Erzählkunst des Titus Livius*. Berlin & Zurich: 1964.

Burck, E., ed. *Wege zu Livius*. Darmstadt, 1977.

Burck, E. *Das Geschichtswerk des Titus Livius*. Heidelberg: 1992.

Chaplin, J. D. *Livy's Exemplary History*. Oxford: 2000.

Engels, J. *Augusteische Oikoumenegeographie und Universalhistorie im Werk Strabons von Amaseia*. Stuttgart: 1999.

Feeney, D. C. *Caesar's Calendar: Ancient Time and the Beginnings of History*. Berkeley: 2007.

Feldherr, A. *Spectacle and Society in Livy's History*. Berkeley: 1998.

Forsythe, G. *Livy and early Rome: A Study in Historical Method and Judgement*. Stuttgart: 1999.

Gabba, E. *Dionysius and the History of Archaic Rome*. Berkeley: 1991.

Jaeger, M. *Livy's Written Rome*. Ann Arbor, MI: 1997.

Lefèvre, E. & Olshausen, E., eds. *Livius. Werk und Rezeption. Festschrift für Erich Burck zum 80. Geburtstag*. Munich: 1983.

Martin, P. M. "L'oecuménisme dans la vision de Rome par l'historien Denys d'Halicarnasse." In: A. Barzanó, C. Bearzot, L. Prandi, & G. Zecchini, eds. *L'ecumenismo politico nella coscienza dell'occidente*. Rome: 1998. Pp. 295–306.

Mueller, H.-F. "The Extinction of the Potitii and the Sacred History of Augustan Rome." In: D. S. Levene and D. P. Nelis, eds. *Augustan Poetry and the Traditions of Ancient Historiography*. Leiden & New York: 2002. Pp. 313–329.

Pianezzola, E. *Traduzione e idologia. Livio interprete di Polibio*. Bologna: 1969.

Schmitt, T. See above, §3.

Seel, O. "Pompeius Trogus und das Problem der Universalgeschichte." In: *Aufstieg und Niedergang der römischen Welt.* Vol. 1.30.2 Berlin and New York: 1982. Pp. 1363–1423.

Seel, O. *Eine römische Weltgeschichte. Studien zum Text der Epitome des Justinus und zur Rhetorik des Pompeius Trogus.* Nürnberg: 1972.

Syme, R. "Livy and Augustus [1959]." In: R. Syme. *Roman Papers.* Vol. 1. Oxford: 1979. Pp. 400–454.

Toher, M. "Augustus and the Evolution of Roman Historiography." In: K. A. Raaflaub & M. Toher, eds. *Between Republic and Empire. Interpretations of Augustus and his Principate.* Berkeley: 1990. Pp. 139–154.

Urban, R. "*Historiae Philippicae* bei Pompeius Trogus. Versuch einer Deutung." *Historia* 31 (1982): 82–96.

Walsh, P. G. *Livy.* Oxford: 1974.

von Wickevoort-Crommelin, B. R. *Die Universalgeschichte des Pompeius Trogus.* Hagen: 1993.

Wirth, G. *Diodor und das Ende des Hellenismus. Mutmassungen zu einem fast unbekannten Historiker.* Vienna: 1993.

6 Imperial History and the History of Emperors – Imperial History as the History of Emperors

Alonso-Núñez, J. M. *Die politische und soziale Ideologie des Geschichtsscchreibers Florus.* Bonn: 1983.

Ameling, W. "Griechische Intellektuelle und das Imperium Romanum: das Beispiel des Cassius Dio." In: *Aufstieg und Niedergang der römischen Welt.* vol. 2.34.3. Berlin & New York: 1997. Pp. 2472–2496.

Anderson, R. L. *The Rise and Fall of Middle-Class Loyalty to the Roman Empire. A Social Study of Velleius Paterculus and Ammianus.* Ann Arbor, MI: 1984.

Arnaud-Lindet, M.-P. "'*Liber memorialis*' de L. Ampélius." In: *Aufstieg und Niedergang der römischen Welt.* vol. 2.34.3. Berlin & New York: 1997. Pp. 2301–2312.

Baldwin, B. *Suetonius.* Amsterdam: 1983.

Barnes, T. D. The Sources of the *Historia Augusta.* Brussels: 1978.

Baynham, E. *Alexander the Great: The Unique History of Quintus Curtius.* Ann Arbor, MI: 1998.

Bellemore, J. "Josephus, Pompey, and the Jews." *Historia* 48 (1999): 94–118.

Benario, H. W. "'*Ignotus*,' the 'Good Biographer.' In: *Aufstieg und Niedergang der römischen Welt*. Vol. 2.34.3. Berlin & New York: 1997. Pp. 2759–2772.

Bilde, P. Flavius Josephus between Jerusalem and Rome. His Life, his Works, and their Importance. Sheffield: 1988.

Bird, H. W. *Sextus Aurelius Victor: A Historiographical Study*. Liverpool: 1984.

Birley, A. R. "Marius Maximus: the Consular Biographer." In: *Aufstieg und Niedergang der römischen Welt*. Vol. 2.34.3. Berlin & New York: 1997. Pp. 2678–2757.

Bloomer, W. M. *Valerius Maximus and the Rhetoric of the New Nobility*. Chapel Hill: 1992.

Bödefeld, H. "Untersuchungen zur Alexandergeschichte des Q. Quintus Rufus." Dissertation (Düsseldorf): 1982.

Bonamente, G. Giuliano l'Apostata e il *Breviario* di Eutropio. Rome: 1986.

David, J.-M., eds. Valeurs et mémoire à Rome. Valère Maxime ou la vertu recomposée. Contributions recueillies et éditées. Paris: 1998. (with essays on Plutarch too)

De Blois, L. "The World a City: Cassius Dio's View of the Roman Empire." In: A. Barzanó, C. Bearzot, L. Prandi, & G. Zecchini, eds. *L'ecumenismo politico nella coscienza dell'occidente*. Rome: 1998. Pp. 359–370.

Den Boer, W. *Some Minor Roman Historians*. Leiden: 1972.

Dihle, A. See above, §1.4.

Dorey, T. A., ed. *Tacitus*. London: 1969.

Duff, T. *Plutarch's Lives: Exploring Virtue and Vice*. Oxford: 1999.

Fechner, D. *Untersuchungen zu Cassius Dios Sicht der römischen Republik*. Hildesheim: 1986.

Flach, D. *Tacitus in der Tradition der antiken Geschichtsschreibung*. Göttingen: 1973.

Flaig, E. *Den Kaiser herausfordern. Die Usurpation im römischen Reich*. Frankfurt am Main & New York: 1992.

Gentili & Cerri. See above, §1.4.

Goldmann, B. Einheitlichkeit und Eigenständigkeit der *Historia Romana* des Appian. Hildesheim: 1988.

Gowing, A. M. *Empire and Memory: the Representation of the Roman Republic in Imperial Culture*. Cambridge: 2005.

Hammond, N. G. L. *Three Historians of Alexander the Great: The So-Called Vulgata Authors: Diodorus, Justin, Curtius*. Cambridge: 1983.

Hartke, W. Römische Kinderkaiser. Eine Strukturanalyse römischen Denkens und Daseins. Berlin: 1951.

Havas, L. "Gibt es eine Konzeption der Weltgeschichtlichkeit bei Florus?" *Patavium. Rivista veneta di Scienze dell'Antichità e dell'Alto Medioevo* 10 (1997): 3–15.

Hershbell, J. P. "Plutarch's Concept of History: Philosophy from Examples." *Ancient Society* 28 (1997): 225–243.

Hose, M. Die Erneuerung der Vergangenheit. Die Historiker im Imperium Romanum von Florus bis Cassius Dio. Stuttgart & Leipzig: 1994.

Johne, K.-P. Kaiserbiographie und Senatsaristokratie. Untersuchungen zur Datierung und sozialen Herkunft der Historia Augusta. Berlin: 1976.

Jones, C. P. *Plutarch and Rome.* Oxford: 1971.

Klein, R., ed. *Prinzipat und Freiheit.* Darmstadt: 1969.

Kolb, F. Untersuchungen zur *Historia Augusta.* Bonn: 1987.

Kuntze, C. *Zur Darstellung des Kaisers Tiberius und seiner Zeit bei Velleius Paterculus.* Frankfurt am Main: 1985.

Luce, T. J. & Woodman, A. J., eds. *Tacitus and the Tacitean Tradition.* Princeton: 1993.

Manuwald, B. Cassius Dio und Augustus. Philologische Untersuchungen zu den Büchern 45–56 des Dionischen Geschichtswerkes. Wiesbaden: 1979.

Marasco, G. "Erodiano e la crisi dell'imperio." In: *Aufstieg und Niedergang der römischen Welt.* Vol. 2.34.4. Berlin & New York: 1998. Pp. 2837–2927.

Meissner, B. "Geschichtsbilder in der *Historia Augusta." Philologus* 137 (1993): 274–294.

Meissner, B. "Computergestützte Untersuchungen zur stilistischen Einheitlichkeit der *Historia Augusta.*" In: G. Bonamente & K. Rosen, eds. *Historiae Augustae Colloquium Bonnense.* Bari: 1997. Pp. 175–215.

Millar, F. *A Study of Cassius Dio.* Oxford: 1964.

Mossman, J. Plutarch and his Intellectual World. Essays on Plutarch. London: 1997.

Mueller, H.-F. *Roman Religion in Valerius Maximus.* London & New York: 2002.

Murphy, T. *Pliny the Elder's Natural History: the Empire in the Encyclopedia.* Oxford: 2004.

Pelling, C. B. R. *Plutarch and History. Eighteen Studies.* Swansea: 2002.

Peter, H. *Die Geschichtliche Litteratur über die römische Kaiserzeit bis Theodosius I und ihre Quellen.* Leipzig: 1897.

Pöschl, V., ed. *Tacitus.* 2nd edn. Darmstadt: 1986.

Pucci ben Zeev, M. Jewish Rights in the Roman World. The Greek and Roman Documents Quoted by Josephus Flavius. Tübingen: 1998.

Riedl, P. *Faktoren des historischen Prozesses: eine vergleichende Untersuchung zu Tacitus und Ammianus Marcellinus.* Tübingen: 2002.

Rogers, R. S. "The Case of Cremutius Cordus." *Transactions and Proceedings of the American Philological Association* 96 (1965): 351–359.

Schlumberger, J. Die Epitome de Caesaribus. Untersuchungen zur heidnischen Geschichtsschreibung des 4. Jh. n. Chr. Munich: 1974.

Schmitzer, U. *Velleius Paterculus und das Interesse an der Geschichte im Zeitalter des Tiberius.* Heidelberg: 2000.

Stadter, P. A., ed. *Plutarch and the Historical Tradition.* London & New York: 1992.

Stadter, P.A. *Arrian of Nicomedia.* Chapel Hill: 1980.

Stadter, P. A. & van der Stockt, L., eds. *Sage and Emperor. Plutarch, Greek Intellectuals, and Roman Power in the Time of Trajan (98–117 A.D.).* Leuven: 2002.

Steidle, W. *Sueton und die antike Biographie.* 2nd edn. Munich: 1963.

Straub, J. Heidnische Geschichtsapologetik in der christlichen Spätantike. Untersuchungen über Zeit und Tendenz der Historia Augusta. Bonn: 1963.

Swain, S. "Biography and Biographic in the Literature of the Roman Empire." In: M. J. Edwards & S. Swain, eds. Portraits. Biographical Representation in the Greek and Latin Literature of the Roman Empire. Oxford: 1997. Pp. 1–37.

Swain, S. Hellenism and Empire. Language, Classicism and Power in the Greek World, A.D. 50–250. Oxford: 1998.

Syme, R. *Tacitus.* Oxford: 1958.

Syme, R. *Historia Augusta Papers.* Oxford: 1983.

Timpe, D. "Geschichtsschreibung und Prinzipatsopposition." In: *Opposition et résistances à l'empire d'Auguste à Trajan. Entretiens sur l'Antiquité Classique* 33 (1988): 65–96.

Touloumakos, J. *Zum Geschichtsbewusstsein der Griechen in der Zeit der römischen Herrschaft.* Göttingen: 1971.

Urban, R. "Historische Untersuchungen zum Domitianbild des Tacitus." Dissertation (Munich): 1971.

Vielberg, M. *Untertanenpolitik. Zur Darstellung der Führungsschichten in der kaiserzeitlichen Geschichtsschreibung.* Munich: 1996.

Wallace-Hadrill, A. *Suetonius: The Scholar and his Caesars.* London: 1983.

Woodman, A. J., ed. *The Cambridge Companion to Tacitus.* Cambridge: 2009.

Woodman, A. J. *Tacitus Reviewed.* Oxford: 1998.

Zimmermann, M. *Kaiser und Ereignis. Studien zum Geschichtswerk Herodians.* Munich: 1999.

Zimmermann, M., ed. *Geschichtsschreibung und politischer Wandel im 3. Jh. n. Chr.* Stuttgart: 1999.

7 Roman History and Universal History between Classical Religion ("Paganism") and Christianity

Alonso-Núñez, J. M. "Die Auslegung der Geschichte bei Paulus Orosius: Die Abfolge der Weltreiche, die Idee der *Roma Aeterna* und die Goten." *Wiener Studien* 106 (1993): 197–213.

Anderson, R. L. See above, §6.

Barnes, T. D. *Ammianus Marcellinus and the Representation of Historical Reality.* Ithaca: 1998.

Bleckmann, B. "Bemerkungen zu den Annalen des Nicomachus Flavianus." *Historia* 44 (1995): 83–99.

Blockley, R. C. *Ammianus Marcellinus. A Study of His Historiography and Political Thought.* Brussels: 1975.

Brandt, A. *Moralische Werte in den Res gestae des Ammianus Marcellinus.* Göttingen: 1999.

Buck, D. F. "Did Sozomen use Eunapius' Histories?" *Museum Helveticum* 56 (1999): 15–25.

Cameron, A. *Procopius and the Sixth Century.* London: 1985.

Cameron, A. "Eusebius' *Vita Constantini* and the Construction of Constantine." In: M. J. Edwards & S. Swain, eds. *Portraits: Biographical Representation in the Greek and Latin Literature of the Roman Empire.* Oxford: 1997. Pp. 45–174.

Carolla, P. "Spunti tucididei nelle eipistole di Procopio." *Atene e Roma. Rassegna trimestrale dell'Associazione Italiana di Cultura Classica* 42 (1997): 157–176.

Croke, B. & Emmett, A. M. *History and Historians in Late Antiquity.* Sydney: 1983.

Demandt, A. *Zeitkritik und Geschichtsbild im Werk Ammians.* Bonn: 1965.

Den Boeft, J., et al., eds. Cognitio Gestorum. *The Historiographic Art of Ammianus Marcellinus.* Amsterdam: 1992.

Dormeyer, D. *The New Testament among the Writings of Antiquity.* Trans. by R. Kossov. Sheffield: 1998.

Drijvers, J. W. & Hunt, D., eds. *The Late Roman World and its Historian. Interpreting Ammianus Marcellinus.* London & New York: 1999.

Escribano, V. "Thryphè y cristianismo en Zósimo: la representación tiranica de Teodosio." *Athenaeum. Studi di Letteratura e Storia dell'Antichità* 86 (1998): 526–539.

Goetz, H. W. *Die Geschichtstheologie des Orosius.* Darmstadt: 1980.

Green, T. M. *Zosimus, Orosius and their Tradition. Comparative Studies in Pagan and Christian Historiography.* New York: 1974.

Hartke, W. See above, §6.

Herzog, R. "Orosius oder die Formulierung eines Fortschrittskonzepts aus der Erfahrung des Niedergangs." In: R. Koselleck et al., eds. *Niedergang. Studien zu einem geschichtlichen Thema.* Vol. 2. Stuttgart: 1980. pp. 79–102.

Kelly, G. *Ammianus Marcellinus. The Allusive Historian.* Cambridge & New York: 2008.

Leppin, H. *Von Constantin dem Grossen zu Theodosius II. Das christliche Kaisertum bei den Kirchenhistorikern Socrates, Sozomenus und Theodoret.* Göttingen: 1996.

Marasco, G., ed. *Greek and Roman Historiography in Late Antiquity: Fourth to Sixth Century AD.* Leiden & Boston: 2003.

Matthews, J. *The Roman Empire of Ammianus. With a New Introduction.* Rev. edn. Ann Arbor: 2007.

Momigliano, A. *The Conflict Between Paganism and Christianity in the Fourth Century.* Oxford: 1963.

Mueller, H.-F. "Orosius and the Spectacle of Roman Religious Defeat." In: C. M. Schroeder, ed. Cignifiliana: *Essays in Classics, Comparative Literature, and Philosophy presented to Professor Roy Arthur Swanson.* New York: 2005. Pp. 122–136.

Nellen, D. Viri literati. *Gebildetes Beamtentum und spätrömisches Reich im Westen zwischen 284 und 395 n. Chr.* Bochum: 1977.

Neri, V. Medius Princeps. *Storia e immagine di Constantino nella storiografia latina pagana.* Bologna: 1992.

Paschoud, F. Roma aeterna. *Études sur le patriotisme romain.* Rome: 1967.

Paschoud, F. "Zosime et Constantin. Nouvelles controverses." *Museum Helveticum* 54 (1997): 9–28.

Ratti, S. "Jérôme et Nicomaque Flavien: sur les sources de la *Chronique* pour les années 357–364." *Historia* 46 (1997): 479–508.

Riedl, P. See above, §6.

Rohrbacher, D. *The Historians of Late Antiquity*. London: 2002.

Rosen, K. *Ammianus Marcellinus*. Darmstadt: 1982.

Rosen, K. *Über heidnisches und christliches Geschichtsdenken in der Spätantike*. Eichstätt: 1982.

Schlumberger, J. See above, §6.

Seager, R. *Ammianus Marcellinus. Seven Studies in his Language and Thought*. Columbia: 1986.

Straub, J. See above, §6.

Timpe, D. "Was ist Kirchengeschichte? Zum Gattungscharakter der *Historia Ecclesiastica* des Eusebius." In: W. Dahlheim, W. Schuller, J. von Ungern-Sternberg, eds. *Festschrift Robert Werner. Zu seinem 65. Geburtstag*. Constance: 1989. Pp. 171–204.

Timpe, D. *Römische Geschichte und Heilsgeschichte*. Berlin: 2001.

van Andel, G. K. *The Christian Concept of History in the Chronicle of Sulpicius Severus*. Amsterdam: 1976.

Wallraff, M., ed. *Julius Africanus und die christliche Weltchronik: Julius Africanus und christliche Weltchronistik*. Berlin & New York: 2006.

Weber, S. *Die Chronik des Sulpicius Severus. Charakteristika und Intentionen*. Trier: 1997.

Index

Roman and Greek Historical Writers, Anonymous Historiographical Works, and Key Concepts

Roman Historiography: An Introduction to its Basic Aspects and Development, First Edition. Andreas Mehl.
© 2014 Hans-Friedrich Mueller. Published 2014 by Blackwell Publishing Ltd.